TAKING RISKS

SUNY series, Praxis: Theory in Action
Nancy A. Naples, editor

TAKING RISKS

Feminist Activism and Research in the Americas

EDITED BY
JULIE SHAYNE

FOREWORD BY
MARGARET RANDALL

SUNY PRESS

Cover: "Futuro," mural on Escuela N 20 Rawson, Prov. De Chubut, Argentina. 2003. An original mural by Nora Patrich. Courtesy of Nora Patrich.

Published by State University of New York Press, Albany

Printed in the United States of America

For information, contact State University of New York Press, Albany, NY
www.sunypress.edu

Production by Jenn Bennett
Marketing by Fran Keneston

Library of Congress Cataloging-in-Publication Data

Taking risks: feminist activism and research in the Americas / edited by Julie Shayne ; foreword by Margaret Randall.
pages cm. — (SUNY series, praxis: theory in action)
Includes bibliographical references and index.
ISBN 978-1-4384-5246-3 (paperback : alk. paper)
ISBN 978-1-4384-5245-6 (hardcover : alk. paper) 1. Feminism—History—North America. 2. Feminism—History—South America. 3. Social justice—History—North America. 4. Social justice—History—South America. I. Shayne, Julie D., 1966- editor of compilation.
HQ1150.T35 2013
305.42097—dc23

2013030255

10 9 8 7 6 5 4 3 2 1

In memory of my beloved father, Barry (1945–2001)

CONTENTS

ACKNOWLEDGMENTS

Editing this book was an incredibly all-consuming process, one which I could not have completed without the support and help of countless individuals. This book might not exist if Bruce Burgett (my then chair, now dean) had not asked me to organize a seminar about activist research in the Americas for the 2010 Imagining America conference. I thank the participants in that session for generating such a lively dialogue that, as a collective, I knew we had more to contribute than ninety minutes could provide; especially Marisela Fleites-Lear, Christina Marín, and Tamera Marko, all of whom contributed to this collection.

I also want to offer a special thank you to my spring 2012 "Interdisciplinary Inquiry" students for providing me such fresh ideas about activist scholarship, which I kept with me as I co-wrote the introduction and conclusion to this collection. Many people read early drafts of different chapters in this volume, and I would like to thank them all as well: Kari Lerum, Mahala Lettvin, Kristy Leissle, Carmen Rodríguez, Karen Rosenberg, Roberta Villalón, Erica Williams, and SUNY Press's anonymous reviewers. Thanks are also due Marisela Fleites-Lear and Jessica Monteiro Manfredi for double checking the Spanish and Portuguese, respectively.

Carmen Rodríguez is also owed a debt of my gratitude for putting me in touch with Argentine artist Nora Patrich, whose artwork has greatly enhanced this book. Needless to say, Nora also deserves my deep appreciation for sharing her art with me in exchange for only a fraction of the compensation her pieces are worth. I truly cannot offer enough gratitude to Margaret Randall for writing the foreword to *Taking Risks*. As I explain in this book's conclusion, I started reading

Margaret's books when I was an undergraduate women's studies student. Reading her books in a college classroom forever planted a seed that activism and scholarship should not be separated. Though I had to keep that seed dormant for much longer than I would have liked, I am beyond honored that Margaret's words are here to enrich this collection of activist scholarship.

In the course of writing or editing a book there always ends up being one person who becomes the sounding board for all of the unglamorous, behind-the-scenes issues. In the case of this book, Ron Krabill was my go-to man. Ron is one of my many overextended colleagues, yet he still made time to walk me through early logistical concerns and provided the guidance to move this book forward. Kristy Leissle, my coauthor of the introduction and conclusion, became my go-to woman in a different capacity. In short, I must thank Kristy for allowing me to treat her as a coeditor at times rather than a coauthor. She always responded to my requests for help that went way above and beyond the coauthoring job description for which she had originally signed on.

Mahala Lettvin was an undergraduate American studies student when I asked her to rework a paper she wrote for me into a chapter for this book. In typical Mahala fashion, her first instinct was to downplay her skill. But fortunately I was able to prevail upon her, and she ultimately produced a beautiful chapter for this collection. But my greatest appreciation goes to Mahala for eagerly agreeing to co-write the index for this book. I do not know another person as detailed-oriented as I am, and I have "happily" shared that job with her. Relatedly, I want to thank the Interdisciplinary Arts and Sciences "Initiatives to Develop Interdisciplinary Scholarship and Collaboration" (IDISCO) for providing the grant to fund Mahala's work on the index. I also want to acknowledge the University of Washington Bothell's Office of Research for funding Jessica's hard work on the section introductions.

Finally, thanks are due my family. My dad (Barry), mom (Lynda), and stepdad (Frank) who raised me to always speak my mind and chase my passions. Fortunately, following those passions landed my family and me back on the West Coast, ultimately providing the professional freedom to pursue this project. Appreciation and acknowledgment are also due to my daughter, Barrie, and son, Aaron, who had to spend more time in summer camp than perhaps they would have chosen, so I could finish this book during the precious few writing months my teaching load provided me. You two are awesome, and now you are entitled to say to me, with a tone of unwavering confidence: "You're welcome." To my beloved husband, Dave, whose everythingness becomes more unshakable as our tree-covered time together passes, I say to you, again, thank you.

FOREWORD

The Thing about Taking Risks

MARGARET RANDALL

I started college in the stifling 1950s. The nation was still grappling with McCarthyism. Classes at my hometown state university were traditional and mostly quite vacuous. I was soon bored and quit, spending the next several decades exploring the world. I went to New York City, where I met avant-garde artists and writers, made lists of books they mentioned or recommended, then hoped they would be willing to discuss them with me. I traveled to Mexico, then Cuba, and finally Nicaragua, learned about life outside the United States, took part in people's revolutions, raised four children, and honed my writing skills.

Along the way, the explosion of thought and action we call feminism's second wave entered my life. I was curious to know how the social change movements in those countries were affecting women's lives, and I became involved in a field that was new and burgeoning at the time: oral history. Without professional training, I had to find my own way. I made a great many mistakes, but I managed to draw on my natural empathy and developing political perceptions. I learned to listen, record, document, and give voice to many women whose stories would otherwise not have found their way into print.

I do not recommend this route. Universities are more interesting these days, and I've often felt inhibited by my lack of a formal education. I was fortunate to know early on that I was a writer and fortunate as well to have found myself in a number of places crucial to the shaping of twentieth-century history precisely at that history's moment of most intense change. Still, I believe there is a great deal to be said for seeking out creative thinkers in frontline places, and taking the risks inherent in doing things differently. If I start with this brief personal history, it is not to focus on myself but to say that I am well aware of the value offered by both scholarship and activism and how when each reinforces the other the whole becomes more than the sum of its parts.

The first thing that struck me about this collection is its title. I was delighted to read a book called *Taking Risks*. In my opinion, risk taking is one of the most important actions in which we can be involved. When I taught, again and again I urged my students to take risks. Many of them, products of this country's substandard public education system, couldn't really fathom what I was advocating. They wanted precise directions, familiar formulae. Risk taking is a subversive act in the most empowering sense of the term, and it flies directly in the face of our society's efforts to dull our wits and get us to conform.

In an academic environment that has not always been up to the demands of real discernment and analysis, scholarship and activism have long been seen as oppositional. The successful academic is not supposed to be an activist. Scholarship must be "scientific," impartial, and therefore safely removed from everyday life. We must not take sides when engaging with our subjects, much less become involved in joint projects that analyze the sources of their exploitation or may improve their lives. We are expected to distinguish ourselves in "acceptable" journals, not popular or movement publications. Woe to those who allow themselves to be drawn into real struggles. And, we are told, passion has no place in what we study or write about.

This sorry state of affairs has improved in recent years, though not nearly enough. If financial security is important (and for whom isn't it?), young academics must still favor the sort of scholarship and publishing that leads to job security. But change has come, to some institutions more easily and fully than to others. Women's studies, with its introduction of feminist thought and consequent analysis of power, has contributed greatly to this change. So have a range of ethnic and queer studies programs, and community-based projects.

Arizona's 2011 neofascist banning of books and criminal assault on Mexican-American studies gives us a vivid picture of the Right fighting back. The Tucson Unified School District understands that if students learn their own history it will be dangerous to official control. This sort of threat to learning has also taken place, over the past several years, in Texas, Alabama, and other states—where the history of slavery has been removed from school texts and references to the Middle Passage minimized.

In Latin America, university education has taken a different path. The 1918 University Reform, in Córdoba, Argentina, demanded three major changes: institutional autonomy; control of the university by a three-part body equally composed of faculty, alumni, and students; and that the education itself be geared to providing what the community needs. Not all Latin American universities still have these goals. Many have adopted the North American model. But others not only have remained true to this historic prescription; they are working to develop a second university reform, one that meets the demands of the twenty-first century. Uruguay's University of the Republic is one such institution. As a result, that country has opened four new university campuses in the interior of the country, each specializing in the cultural and production needs of the region. The tiny nation is the first in the world to have fully implemented the One Laptop per Child initiative in its public schools. Successful programs are lifting people out of poverty. And by 2016, 60 percent of Uruguay's energy will be sustainable. In every area, university students are taking risks, putting their creativity into the community, and changing the face of their nation. This is what taking risks is about.

The book you hold in your hands stands in vibrant opposition to the rewriting of history and stifling of diversity we see and feel around us. These writers' experiences, and their acknowledgment of the validity of those experiences, imbue these essays with great power and relevance. And, contrary to the dire warnings on the part of those who could not conceive of this particular sort of interdisciplinary work, the scholarship is no less rigorous and the impact even more profound.

Julie Shayne writes vibrantly of her own experience and that of other thinkers and teachers. And she has chosen a group of contributors who, together, offer an in-depth look at some of the ways scholarship can inform activism, and activism can provoke the questions that lead to deeper scholarship.

For example, Marisela Fleites-Lear describes the complexities of Cuban studies on the island and in the diaspora. A great merit of this volume is its refusal to pander to any one political line. Reading Fleites-Lear, we understand how biases on both sides of the divide only prevent scholars learning from each other and designing projects that benefit everyone.

In "Feminist Tensions: Race, Sex Work, and Women's Activism in Bahia," Erica Lorraine Williams asks: "What happens when we take our positionalities, social locations, and subjectivities seriously in the context of ethnographic research?" Her scholarly interest in the sexual economies of tourism in Salvador was sparked by her own visceral experience with other female friends on a beach in that city, and she answers the question from a perfectly balanced blend of research and experience.

In "Latina Battered Immigrants, Citizenship, and Inequalities: Reflections on Activist Research," Roberta Villalón explores the extreme vulnerability of immigrant women to interpersonal and structural violence. She documents the significant obstacles battered immigrant women encounter when they try to end their abusive relationships and become U.S. citizens. Some of the obstacles with which they must contend are embedded in the formalities of the immigration provisions themselves.

Shayne culls stories of feminist activism from among Chilean exiles, and in doing so she explores exile's rough terrain. In her moving first-person afterword, "Mother's Day," she documents her own struggle with being a mother while trying to meet the strict demands of academia. The book's other excellent contributions address such compelling issues as the femicide that continues to plague Ciudad Juárez, Mexico; the complex problems of immigration; the gendered face of trauma, and sex work. Carmen Rodríguez deals with writing as activism while recent college graduate Mahala Lettvin speaks from the other end; reading as activism via her analysis of gender and memory in South America. Shelly Grabe examines the role of women's land ownership in the activist efforts of the women's autonomous movement in Nicaragua. Robin Garcia asks: "Who owns the archive?" Tamara Marko's territory of exploration is the battered but exuberant city of Medellín, Colombia. Present throughout this volume is the question of who owns our stories and how we can make sure they remain in the hands of those who live them.

Coming from many different disciplines, the contributors to this book are rigorous in their methodologies while remaining open to the possibility that diverse situations sometimes demand new ways of compiling and assessing information. As Shayne writes, in her piece on Chilean exiles, "Despite the initial lack of support/disdain I received when beginning the exile project, *They Used to Call Us Witches* has received sociological and activist validation."

These authors not only take risks in their scholarship and in their activism, but they generously invite readers to ask questions with them, go down one road and then double back to explore another, doubt and analyze, and share conclusions. Shayne's and Kristy Leissle's final text, "Interdisciplinarity and Privilege," is at once open-ended and closes the collection in a way that calls on scholar activists to use their academic cultural capital in service of social movements. These authors break down barriers between scholarship and the arts. Methodology, literature, theater, film, archiving, and more figure prominently in these texts. Memory is featured, as it should be. These activist scholars use their own experience to inform their academic work and their academic skills to make of their experience something useful to the populations they study as well as to their readers. None of this would be possible had they not been willing to take risks. And the thing about taking risks is that it's the only way to tackle the immense tasks these difficult times require.

INTRODUCTION

Research, Risk, and Activism: Feminists' Stories of Social Justice

JULIE SHAYNE AND KRISTY LEISSLE

> If something compels you to try and change the world then you are an activist.
>
> —Amina Mama (2013)

> I realize I am a scholar activist not just because I believe in human agency and engaged scholarship but also because I believe in the future.
>
> —Jessica Gordon Nembhard (2008, 265)

When Julie Shayne's daughter, Barrie, reaches the sixth grade, her teachers will assign her a "passion project." Barrie was in fourth grade the first time she got to watch her upperclassmates' presentations about their passions. She would come home after the presentations and tell Julie about all of the cool things the other kids were passionate about—from inventing stuff, to gymnastics, to solar power, to cupcakes (Barrie's favorite). As of this writing, Barrie still has two years until she gets to do her own passion project, but she already knows that she wants to talk about dance.[1] Props to her wonderful teachers Kim Copeland and M Wellman for inspiring their kids to think about their homework two years in advance! If only college professors could do the same. It occurred to Julie recently, as editor of *Taking Risks*, that this book is her own passion project; indeed, she has wanted to edit/write/collaborate on some version of it for at least twenty years.

This collection is about social justice, feminism, and activist scholarship. Some of the contributors first met via email in preparation for an Imagining America seminar in Seattle, Washington, in September 2010. Julie designed the seminar to foster discussion about the tensions inherent in researching justice, resistance, and feminism in the Americas. Potential participants were asked to think about issues such as tensions between the researcher and the "subjects"; the researcher and her academic discipline; the researcher's insider and outsider positions; or competing interpretations of history. In response to her call for papers, Julie received a fascinating collection of essays. At the conference, seminar participants shared research agendas, with the dialogue additionally including discussions of some of the intellectual, political, and personal risks we take as activist scholars. This book is one product of that seminar.[2]

This introduction provides the conceptual background for understanding the case studies that follow. We begin with discussions of social justice/activist scholarship. Next, we look at the power of storytellers and their stories in documenting and archiving social justice movements and scholarship. We then consider how this collection of activist research and stories is an example of transnational feminist scholarship. Finally, we speak briefly to the risks of activist research.

Social Justice and Activist Scholarship

The contributors to this volume envision our collection in dialogue with activist scholarship and transnational feminist methodologies, using stories as the bridge between the two. In what follows we do not intend to provide an exhaustive history of either body of literature, but we highlight the key concepts that resonate with and thus provide a useful context for this collection.[3] Similarly, this book is not a "how-to" manual for conducting feminist social justice or activist research but rather a collection by scholar activists who do such work.[4]

What is social justice or activist scholarship? To begin, it is important to note that such scholarship falls under a variety of labels: feminist methods;[5] indigenous methodologies;[6] participatory action research or action research;[7] public scholarship;[8] community-based research;[9] engaged or critically engaged research,[10] and emancipatory, antiracist, or antioppressive research,[11] to name some of the most commonly used terms.[12] And, as is common with all things academic, there is overlap across labels. In this introduction and the chapters that follow, we use the terms "activist scholarship" and "social justice scholarship" interchangeably. The term "social justice scholarship" resonates with this collection's explicit grounding in a commitment to social justice. By this we mean justice in research, knowledge production, and pedagogy; most importantly, this includes a commitment to supporting the right of everyone to live a life absent of economic, political, social, and personal violence.[13] For the contributors to *Taking Risks*, the "social justice" in social justice scholarship refers to the factors that motivate us to research, along with the desired outcome to which we see ourselves contributing.[14]

Regardless of the preferred label, the commonality in activist scholarship lies in the starting point that methodology, activism, theoretical insights, and reflection are inseparable. This mixture of sentiments is often described as "praxis," a term attributed to educator and theorist Paulo Freire (Nagar and Swarr 2010, 6). Barndt defines praxis as "a cultivated awareness of one's condition and shared experiences: both reflecting and acting upon the world to enact social change; the dynamic interaction of active contemplation and reflective practice" (2011, 149). Similarly and succinctly, Nagar and Swarr define praxis as "the cycle of action, reflection, and action through which human beings work to transform their worlds" (2010, 6).[15] This volume is rooted in a praxis-informed perspective.

Though we see praxis as inherent to activist scholarship, social justice research is about more than praxis. Social justice or activist scholarship, and all of its other names, has different yet overlapping meanings to its practitioners. Julia Sudbury and Margo Okazawa-Rey, editors of *Activist Scholarship: Antiracism, Feminisms, and Social Change* (2009a), define activist scholarship as "the production of knowledge and pedagogical practices through active engagements with, and in the service of, progressive[16] social movements" ([b]3). We prefer their definition because it speaks to the broadness of scholarship: knowledge production (i.e., research) and pedagogy. Speaking more specifically to social justice research, we turn to Bickham Mendez and Potts and Brown. Bickham Mendez maintains that "[t]he aim of politically engaged research is to form an admittedly fragile and difficult coalition between 'grassroots,' 'local,' or 'experiential' knowledge and 'theoretical,' 'data-driven,' or 'scholarly' knowledge" (2008, 140). Similarly, Potts and Brown maintain that "[b]eing an anti-oppressive researcher means that there is political purpose and action to your research work. . . . Anti-oppressive research involves making explicit the political practices of creating knowledge. . . . It is about paying attention to, and shifting, how power relations work in and through the processes of doing research" (2005, 255).[17]

A host of common theorists and themes run through social justice and activist scholarship; Antonio Gramsci, Paulo Freire, Orlando

Fals-Borda, and Michel Foucault have proven quite influential. Gramsci's (1971)[18] theories of power, hegemony, and "organic intellectuals" (discussed below) help social justice scholars articulate the power of knowledge as communicated through cultural institutions, combined with the lack of access nonelite sectors have to advancing knowledge claims. Freire (1983) and Fals-Borda (1979; 1991) articulate ideas of popular education and research where the learners and educators, researchers and researched should ultimately be one and the same. Similarly, accessing, communicating, and teaching knowledge are forms of power from which popular classes are excluded if they are not active participants in those processes (see Rodríguez, this volume). Fals-Borda advanced these ideas in his articulation of participatory action research (PAR)[19] and notion of *vivencia* (discussed below). Finally, Foucault's views of truth and power are central to social justice scholarship. Foucault theorizes that "'truth' is linked in a circular relation with systems of power which produce and sustain it, and to effects of power which it induces and which extends it" (in Rabinow 1984, 74) or what he called "truth regimes."[20] Further, he argued that the "requisite characteristics of truth are courage in the face of danger, a duty to speak, risk in speaking, speaking to power, and a social or moral status from which to speak the truth" (Sanford 2008, 4). In other words, "truth" is a politically imbued social construct with the power to shape social norms. However, because of the constructed and thus malleable nature of truth, it can and must be challenged, and scholar activists can play a role in that process.

Social justice scholars draw on the aforementioned to offer critiques of positivism[21] and claims of objectivity. Such discussions are typically closely connected to conversations about the social construction of knowledge and subsequent designation of scholars as experts and popular classes as subaltern. Activist scholars speak to these processes to identify and critique the power with which knowledge and *some* knowledge makers are imbued, while others are excluded. Such critiques thus demand alternatives to the traditional academic arrangement of "expert" versus "lay person/nonexpert." Though all of the chapters in this volume do not explicitly engage these critiques, knowledge production is implicit in the following chapters via our prioritization of personal interviews, testimonies, literature, and other alternative forms of data. That is, we do not question the need for rigorous research to produce data, especially by activist scholars in support of social justice causes. Rather activist scholars move beyond standard and unquestioned data to the sources that are still marginalized. In the case of this collection, we turn to stories.

Reflexive researching, writing, and teaching practices are also themes which span the literature. Additionally, it is virtually inevitable to read something that speaks to the vulnerability of junior scholars who conduct this sort of research—the result of institutional norms that deem social justice scholarship as subjective, applied, atheoretical, and thus unscholarly. Related to this, much of the literature is dedicated to establishing the scholarly rigor with which the research is conducted. It is also common to read about a researcher's experiences of personal, professional, and pedagogical tensions and contradictions, including if/how we define ourselves as activists.[22] Not surprisingly, the literature discusses solidarity, alliances, and collaborations among scholars and grassroots activists. *Taking Risks* benefits from, builds on, and is illustrative of these earlier conversations. We now move on to the role of stories in advancing activist scholarship.

Story Listening, Archiving, and Telling

As noted, recent writing demonstrates the rigor of well-researched social justice scholarship; indeed, in some cases activist researchers argue that social justice scholarship is more "accurate" than that obtained through positivist and so-called objective models. Most recently the editors of and contributors to *Engaged Observer: Anthropology, Advocacy, and Activism* (2008) and *Engaging Contradictions: Theory, Politics, and Methods of Activist Scholarship* (2008) have written persuasively about the intellectual legitimacy of social justice scholarship. In the introduction to *Engaged Observer* Victoria Sanford argues,

> It is not uncommon within the academy for lived experience to be dismissed as unscientific or not relevant to real, objective scholarship. This is completely backward, because it is the academy that needs to be relevant to the reality of lived experience. Advocacy and activism do not diminish the validity of one's scholarly research. On the contrary, activist scholarship reminds us that all research is inherently political—even, and perhaps especially, that scholarship presented under the guise of "objectivity," which is really no more than a veiled defense of the status quo. (2008, 14)

This book adheres to the same argument: we access and thus share "lived experience" through the integration of stories. Similarly, social justice scholars remind us that traditional positivist formulations of research devalue certain types of knowledge. For example, Gaventa and Cornwall maintain that "dominant knowledge obscures or under-privileges other forms of knowing, and the voices of other knowers" (2008, 178), where "dominant knowledge" refers to that which is produced through positivist research. In our collection we too challenge that norm and privilege "other forms of knowing" by focusing on stories.

Part of the work of this collection is to elevate the storyteller and her stories. Additionally, it is about committing stories to the archives.[23] All of the contributors have their own archives in mind and different ways of documenting those stories—video, theater, social science texts, fiction, the classroom—but our commonality lies in the fact that even when we do not have direct access to the storytellers, stories are central (for example, see Marín, this volume). Stories and their tellers emerged as a theme in this project as many of us confronted academic barriers when we opted to prioritize storytellers as the main source of information in our research projects. In *Taking Risks* the storytellers—the activists—are intellectuals. As story listeners, we acknowledge the authority of activists, though academia typically doubts the "truth-quality of . . . testimonials" (Sanford 2008, 11). Though collectively we privilege the stories of activists, we are not closed to competing interpretations of similar experiences. Indeed, all rigorous scholarship, whether based on oral histories or census data, must be attentive to contradictory analyses. Similarly, like most practitioners of social justice scholarship, we are cognizant of the fact that privileging stories does not eliminate the power imbalances with which research and writing processes are imbued. That is, story listening does not inherently undermine "the hierarchy of knowledge producers" (Nagar and Swarr 2010, 8) where even the best-intentioned scholar activists still hold the power over a storyteller by the virtue of our power to edit and communicate the stories without the storyteller's presence to offer alternative analyses. (See Marko, this volume, for a discussion of how to subvert that power imbalance.)

Though some scholars acknowledge stories as a necessary entry point to intellectual inquiry, much of the theorizing revolves around turning to narratives to *explain* social or historical processes—for example, social movements and their organizational strategies.[24] Within that framework, also called "the narrative turn," stories and narratives (generally defined in this literature as one in the same) are used as "a method or means of studying social life" (Davis 2002b, 22). For example, Eric Selbin eloquently and insightfully asks how revolutionaries' stories are used to inspire future revolutionaries. He helps us understand the interplay of history and culture vis-à-vis storytelling in inspiring revolutions (2010). Much of this literature thus focuses our attention on the story as disembodied from the storytellers. In this collection, we see stories as a way to document social movements, rather than as something to be extrapolated by scholars to "explain" those movements. Latin American *testimonios* advance a similar approach, and *Taking Risks*' contributors collectively benefit from this pioneering activist scholarship (see, for example, Grabe, this volume).[25] Put another way, we see the storytellers as the experts or, in the Gramscian sense, as intellectuals.

Gramsci reminds us of the power of knowledge, particularly as communicated through schools, churches, and other institutions of culture, which serve as messengers of hegemony. That is, knowledge is "created" by and in the service of the elite, at the expense of the working class. According to Gramsci, "all men [sic] are intellectuals, one could therefore say: but not all men [sic] have in society the function of intellectuals. When one distinguishes between intellectuals and non-intellectuals, one is referring in reality only to the immediate social function on the professional category of the intellectuals" (1971, 9). Here, intellectuals are designated as such by the ruling class and thus serve as the architects and enforcers of hegemony.[26] Gramsci maintains, and we concur, that the "organic intellectuals" of the working class are not imbued with the social status that permits their intellectual skills to be considered *as* skills, let alone an indication of their analytical prowess.[27] In this book the activists and storytellers are indeed intellectuals, but their social status, particularly in contrast to "expert academics," does not codify them as such.[28] George Lipsitz offers a similar sentiment:

> Throughout our lives most of us have encountered serious people in all walks of life who lack the dignity of being taken seriously. Their acts of reflection, contemplation, and creation generally take place without any recognition or reward, in spaces quite unlike the Butler Library [at Columbia University]. They work with the tools available to them in the arenas to which they have access. Their names will never appear in newspapers, much less be chiseled into friezes on classic revival buildings. Yet they leave their mark on the world in other ways. They often mine unexpected and nontraditional archives. They generate fundamentally new imaginaries, fashioning ways of knowing and ways of being that are important to our understanding of the world in which we live as the great works of famous philosophers. (2008, 89)

This volume is, in part, about listening to and documenting the stories of such "serious people."

Colombian sociologist-activist Orlando Fals-Borda (1925–2008),[29] one of the founders of Participatory Action Research, articulates what he calls *vivencia*. He explains that "[t]hrough the actual experience of something, we [the researchers] intuitively apprehend its essence; we feel, enjoy and understand it as reality, and we thereby place our own being in a wider, more fulfilling context" (1991, 4).[30] Fals-Borda advanced this approach to research, which urged scholars to participate in the political actions they study. Fals-Borda believed this was necessary to most effectively understand the issue at hand while also supporting the activist movement being studied. In *Taking Risks* we depart slightly from that construct. That is, researchers must do more than "feel, enjoy and understand 'it'." Rather, we prioritize the activists, the Gramscian organic intellectuals, the storytellers that we meet in the course of our research, and activism as those who embody that *vivencia*. As activist scholars we turn to the storytellers for interpretations of social justice activism rather than our own experiences alongside them. Similarly, Potts and Brown advance a need to value Fals-Borda's concept of *vivencia*, which we reframe as stories:

> From an anti-oppressive perspective, knowledge does not exist in and of itself, isolated from people [read: stories]. Rather, it is produced through the interactions of people, and as all people are socially located (in their race, gender, ability, class identities, and so on) with biases, privileges, and differing power relations, so too is the creation of knowledge socially located, and socially constructed. Recognizing that knowledge is socially constructed means understanding that knowledge doesn't exist 'out there' but is embedded in people and the power relations between us. (2005, 261)

Implicit here is the need to value activists as intellectuals and their stories as a legitimate, if not primary, component of constructed knowledges.

As we know, one goal of social justice scholarship is to foster alliances with activists. From our perspective, to build lasting solidarity, scholars need to truly hear stories—what Potts and Brown call "political listening." That is, to listen "not for what we expect to hear or for what fits with what we already think, but for assumptions made both by ourselves as listeners and by speakers while attending to the dance of power" (2005, 272). Anthropologist Angel-Ajani Asale shares a similar sentiment: "Can we be engaged scholars or activist intellectuals if we do not know how to listen or if we seek or even demand knowledge that confirms what we already think we know? . . . [A]n anthropologist's job is supposedly based on the act of listening. Listening does not imply that the listener is an expert or an authority. I believe that there are valuable lessons to be learned if we open our ears to experiences that might not fit what we think we know" (2008, 87). "Political listening" can thus foster alliances, challenge subject/researcher power imbalances, and destabilize the rigidity and elite biases of positivist research.

Why do these stories and our attempts to document and share them matter to social justice scholars? Two key realities remind us of the importance of documenting and archiving stories: historical memory/national record and pedagogy. Shayne explains in her chapter in this collection that her book about Chilean exiles along with their feminist magazines have recently been added to the accessible holdings at the Documentation Center at the Museo de la Memoria y Los Derechos Humanos (Museum of Memory and Human Rights) in Santiago, Chile. Within a couple of weeks of learning this, one of Shayne's undergraduate students (Jessica Monteiro Manfredi, author of this volume's section introductions) sent her a link to a story about a pro-Pinochet film that was being both celebrated and protested in Chile.[31] The film was screened at an event sponsored by an organization of retired military officers and the September 11 Corporation. (The organization is named for the date of Pinochet's coup d'état; September 11, 1973.) The film has thus become part of the national Chilean archive "documenting" that nation's bloody past.[32] Needless to say, members of the Chilean and international community have challenged the "facts" and analysis upon which the film is built, as evidenced by the mass protests against the screening. In short, if films are circulated that tell an incomplete, misleading, and unsubstantiated story of the Pinochet dictatorship, human rights museums, memorials, and other archives which document the national tragedy must persist as well. Much of the story of the dictatorship can only be told by those who suffered and survived it, rather than those who orchestrated and violently perpetrated it. The reality is, even the most revolutionary soul is mortal and needs to be heard. If younger Chileans do not learn of their bloody past, at the risk of sounding cliché, history is well positioned to repeat itself.

In a similar vein, Tamera Marko discusses a video archive project in Medellín, Colombia, that documents women's contributions to rebuilding their city. These archives challenge the Medellín government's tourism narrative, which credits itself with the area's reconstruction. These video archives thus tell a more complete story, which represents the activism, agency, and dignity of the leading protagonists in the restoration project. Erica Williams explains how sex workers in Bahia, Brazil, articulate their needs and demands, often in direct contrast to what she (and others) call the "abolitionist" wing of the sex work movement. This wing is often blind to the wishes of the women they claim to "protect." In short, listening to and documenting the stories is a pressing issue if we are to guarantee a more complete and dignified collective and national record.

Teaching provides another urgent reminder of the need to collect, document, and validate stories. As Margaret Randall reminds us in her foreword, the U.S. educational system fails to teach our children about cultural and political histories, particularly those that expose the U.S.-supported human rights violations in the Americas and elsewhere in the global South.[33] As a result, our college students often come to the classroom with racist stereotypes of Latino/as and virtually no knowledge of our interlocking histories.[34] The task of catching up our students on the histories that U.S. K–12 schools have failed to teach them requires preserving the stories of those who experienced and shaped these histories. (See Lettvin, this volume, for a student's perspective on this challenge.) How can we expect our students to be engaged global citizens if they lack a critical understanding of a major part of their history? How can our students question and challenge contemporary U.S. policies if they have never learned of the human rights violations that have resulted from such policies? Paulo Freire reminds us that "[n]arratives of liberation are always tied to people's stories, and what stories we choose to tell, and the way in which we decide to tell them, form the provisional basis of what a critical pedagogy of the future might mean" (1993, xii). As social justice researchers, the onus falls upon us to locate, document, archive, and teach the "narratives of liberation" to which our university status affords us access.[35] We turn now to how the stories in this volume exemplify transnational feminist scholarship.

Activist Research and Stories as Transnational Feminist Scholarship

As stories of many different border crossings, framed by multi- and interdisciplinary research modes, the chapters in this collection make a contribution to the evolving field of transnational feminist studies. Regardless of whether authors identify their work explicitly with feminist approaches, we understand each story as a powerful illustration of the methodological priorities that transnational feminist theorists have brought into sharper focus for all researchers committed to social justice.

In their introduction to *Scattered Hegemonies* (1994), a volume that cultivated numerous discussions of transnational feminist methods, Inderpal Grewal and Caren Kaplan challenge texts that, though nominally feminist, demonstrate a "willing participation in modernity . . . that wittingly or unwittingly lead to the oppression and exploitation of many women" (2). Though hailed as a universal civilizational "goal" toward which we are all assumed to be working, the concept of modernity has been theorized from the privileged yet fictional position of the "European unitary subject" (7)—a subject generally conceived as white, male, heterosexual, educated, and able-bodied, who has citizenship in a developed, "Western" nation-state. The contributors to *Taking Risks* displace this subject, to foreground the lived experiences and critical practices of Others that modernist discourse has typically consigned to alterity: here, women across the Americas. We assert that these women's contributions as writers, artists, volunteers, researchers, activists, scholars, mothers, and laborers provide a fruitful starting point for understanding contemporary transnational political, economic, and cultural processes.

A key challenge of producing transnational feminist scholarship involves transgressing the binary divisions that structure modernist thought: male/female, white/nonwhite, heterosexual/homosexual, but also center/margin, global/local, and First World/Third World. Such skewed privileging is always antithetical to social justice, and the contributors to this collection blur these binary divisions. It is difficult, for example, to locate the position of Cuban-American researcher Marisela Fleites-Lear at either margin or center, "First" or "Third" World. Her personal investment in her research in both the United States and Cuba does not clearly align with either the privileges of the "global" or the marginalization of the "local," but is fraught with risk no matter what "side" people cast her on. Erica Williams's chapter on the sex trade in Bahia, Brazil, complicates scholarship that has cast sex work as a "last resort" for desperate women, revealing instead the "complex desires" and sometimes empowering life changes borne of this labor for workers she met. Williams further reveals Bahia as a dynamic site of "globalized" culture, rather than an unchanging "local" of fixed and repressive gender relations.

Transnational feminist methodologies involve another complicating binary transgression that is central to the stories in this collection: moving beyond the activist/academic divide (Alexander and Mohanty 2010; Grewal and Kaplan 1994). As Angela Davis reminds us, the "feminist critical impulse . . . involves a dual commitment . . . to use knowledge in a transformative way, and to use knowledge to remake the world so that it is better for its inhabitants" (2008, 20); that is, as feminist scholars we also must be advocates for justice.[36] But this remains a challenging subversion that can have significant and negative consequences for those who practice it. North American academia can be a "perilous" place to produce activist scholarship (Alexander and Mohanty 2010) and doing so remains a radical act—although, as contributor Roberta Villalón reminded us as we wrote this introduction, while blending activist and academic practices may yet be radical in the United States, it is common across Latin America.

As Julia Sudbury and Margo Okazawa-Rey point out so eloquently in *Activist Scholarship* (2009), the incursion of neoliberal hegemony into North American academia has shadowed its halls with a "culture of fear" (6), making it politic for some academicians to invalidate activist scholarship (for example, by denying tenure to candidates whose work is activist in nature), or claim that it compromises nation-state security. After criticizing the "war against terror" in 2001 at a conference in Canada, Sudbury returned to the United States to "electronic hate mail and death threats" (2). It is thus from personal experience that she poses the question, "Can scholars whose commitments are grounded in movements for social justice produce rigorous scholarly work that is true to their political commitments?" (2). In *Taking Risks*, we assert that it is possible. Indeed, it seems that Sudbury and Okazawa-Rey's most pressing question is rather, "What are the costs of not attempting it?" The answer is a heightened state of injustice, or at best maintenance of the status quo.

One of the strengths of this volume is that it is often difficult to distinguish scholar from activist in contributors' stories. Roberta Villalón, for example, is both researcher and volunteer at an organization that provides legal services for battered immigrant women in Texas. Villalón's own standing as an immigrant and her commitment to transnational feminist politics were important motives in her work, and her writing demonstrates constant, deliberate reflection on her position as an activist academic researcher. In Julie Shayne's chapter, the Chilean exiles of the *Aquelarre* collective in Vancouver struggle to classify the discourse of the feminist magazine they published, never really satisfied that it was activist or scholarly, and ultimately some accepting that it must have been both.

Transgressing the academic/activist binary changes the terms of who does the investigating and who or what is the object of that research. There is a great deal at stake in challenging this positivist tradition of maintaining a "strict separation between the knower and that which is conceptualized as knowable" (Brooks and Hess-Biber 2007, 12). Here, the insights of feminist standpoint theorists remain relevant to the stories in this collection (see Hesse-Biber and Nagy 2007; Naples 2003). As these pioneering feminist scholars have shown, "the situated locations of our bodies serve not as contaminants to building knowledge but instead as potential 'cognitive resources' that direct our attention to 'features . . . that we would otherwise overlook'" (Brooks and Hess-Biber, quoting Helen Longino, 2007, 14). Sandra Harding's notion of strong objectivity, which suggests taking the experiences of marginalized groups as a starting point for building knowledge (ibid, 10) and rejects the knower/known Cartesian separation, is a key methodological element for several of the contributors. Tamera Marko's chapter on video archiving the stories of *desplazadas* in Medellín, Colombia, and Shelly Grabe's work capturing the voices of *compañeras* in Nicaragua are compelling—and often poignant—illustrations of this methodology. There are also moments in this collection when the "knowers" are indistinguishable from research "subjects," and storytellers turn the analytical lens upon their personal experiences (especially Williams, Villalón, and Fleites-Lear), thus shifting the terrain of what is knowable by fusing researcher and research subject.

Indeed, we begin to see that what is "known" and who does that "knowing" are mutually constitutive. How could Erica Williams have understood the positive experiences of Bahian sex workers without examining her own gendered and raced positioning within Brazil? What personal and theoretical insights would she have lost without that (sometimes painful) self-reflexivity? Joyce McCarl Nielsen reminds us that "all researchers carry their particular worldviews, histories, and biographies with them into their research projects" (Brooks and Hess-Biber 2007, 13)—as we see in these stories, they also carry their passports. Each contributor shows how personal considerations of race, gender, and/or citizenship led to specific research experiences, even as her conceptual frames and self-knowledge were shaped by her inquiries and findings. This process of self-reflexivity similarly affects our contributors' students, colleagues, collaborators, and family members in several stories (see especially Rodríguez, Fleites-Lear, Marko, and Grabe).

Transnational feminist theorists have also brought a critical social justice lens to bear on analyses of the nation-state (for example, Caldwell et al. 2009; Grewal 2005; Kaplan, Alarcón, and Moallem 1999; Alexander and Mohanty 1997), and contributors to this collection highlight women's engagements with the nation-state across the Americas. In these pages, it becomes clear that the power and purview of nation-states are neither totalizing nor uncontestable. Richa Nagar and her colleagues (2002) have demonstrated the importance of looking beyond the nation-state in transnational feminist research, at bodies, individuals, households, communities, intra- or supranational regions, and global networks. When we focus our research lens on these scales and the relationships among them, we see that women's experiences at any one location are influenced by and shape actions at others. In this collection, Robin Garcia's chapter on community media, for example, shows that national politics in Venezuela faces constant pressure from community groups, whose demands are organized and broadcast on the radio. Without Garcia's focus on the community, we would lose this crucial insight into contemporary nation-state formation in Venezuela. Other contributors focus our attention on bodies (Williams), individuals (Villalón and Grabe), cities (Marko and Marín), or texts (Lettvin, Rodríguez, Fleites-Lear, and Shayne).

While the nation-state has often been a repressive force in women's lives across the Americas, related work on human rights discourses has shown that the state is not always antagonist and can also be an ally for some women. Nancy Naples (2002) has argued that activists working at the grassroots (local) level can profitably deploy human rights discourse to achieve progressive legal goals for marginalized women. As Dana Collins and her colleagues point out in "New Directions in Feminism and Human Rights" (2011), for example, Southern Mexican women activists "reshape human rights discourses in accordance with their own visions [and] lived experiences" (9). Their focus on specific women acting in a localized context, with or against a legal mechanism, emphasizes that women—of various races, nationalities, immigrant status, and sexual orientations—are also subjects and shapers of law. This methodological choice displaces the "European unitary subject" as the privileged figure that has been, philosophically and literally, the "human" of human rights. Working in this vein, Roberta Villalón (this volume) shows how Latina immigrant women in Texas who are survivors of intimate partner violence can benefit from even limited state protection and a special pathway to U.S. citizenship. Stories by Rodríguez and Shayne illustrate the transformations that occur in women's lives when they cross nation-state borders within the Americas and face the challenges and opportunities that come from immersion in a new national context.

As Richa Nagar and Amanda Swarr remind us in their introduction to *Critical Transnational Feminist Praxis* (2010), transnational feminism is not a "search for resolutions or closures" but an "inherently unstable praxis whose survival and evolution hinge on a continuous commitment to produce self-reflexive and dialogical critiques of its own practices" (9). The stories in this collection put forth transnational feminist scholarship as a mirror of the sometimes fragmented but also powerful and pragmatic attempts by women across the Americas to resist the hegemony of modernity. The contributors capture specific experiences of women struggling to enact social justice at this historical moment. These stories build up the historical archive to reflect the contributions of women and our intersecting identities—a project that is no less relevant now than it was when feminist scholars undertook to bring women's experiences into academic purview in the 1970s.

Unfortunately, though four decades have passed since the inception of feminist studies in North American academia, there are still academic and professional risks associated with advancing activist and transnational feminist scholarship. We turn now to a brief discussion of those risks.

Taking Risks

The chapters that follow document the challenges we confront as we make visible the stories of risk takers: activists and everyday citizens who inspire us to continue work that is not always personally or professionally advantageous, but that feels impossible to stop. We see our work as "passion driven scholarship."[37] This is not the first collection to make explicit our emotional connections to research. As Margo Okazawa-Rey has eloquently explained, "I am convinced, more than ever, of the need for a radically different relational practice alongside our analyses and political actions, a practice that emanates from our souls and energizes us" (2009, 221). David Domke proclaims: "Hope is a word that is almost entirely absent from the academic lexicon. Why? Because to talk of hope suggests that we might care, that we might be genuinely invested in the material that we research and teach about" (2008, 46). Perhaps most succinctly, using Gramsci's words, we practice an "optimism of the will" (cited in Leonard 1993, 156). The contributors to this volume are energized, hopeful, and optimistic about our research agendas, but we know we take risks in advancing them. At the time this project began only one of the contributors was tenured (Marisela Fleites-Lear) while the rest of us were a combination of students (graduate and undergraduate), postdocs, assistant professors, or off the tenure track entirely. As noted above, the literature on social justice scholarship is replete with examples of the challenges junior scholars and graduate students face when pursuing this sort of research and publishing agenda.[38] (Indeed, some of the contributors confronted barriers and "cautions" in the course of writing their chapters for this volume.)

We have all benefited from the work of senior scholars who are attentive to these barriers and opened doors for us. As Julia Sudbury and Margo Okazawa-Rey explain in the introduction to *Activist Scholarship,* "[b]y gathering together a group of academics, most of them in senior, tenured positions, who have dedicated their lifework to this endeavor, we wish to make activist scholarship possible as a viable mode of intellectual inquiry and pedagogical praxis (2009b, 3). Charles R. Hale, another senior scholar, notes in his introduction to *Engaging Contradictions* that graduate students and junior faculty are "regularly warned against putting scholarship in the service of struggles for social justice" (2008b, 2). Hale says elsewhere: "Welcome, come in, and please leave your politics at the door" (2008b, 1). The contributors to *Taking Risks* have decided not to leave our politics outside. All of this said, we wish not to inflate the risks that we take as academics. Our risks for the most part are professional. Some of us have risked physical danger in the course of our research, writing, and activism (Marko and Rodríguez) or permanent separation from family (Fleites-Lear), but for the most part our risk taking ultimately concerns career advancement, or a lack thereof. Certainly this is a real concern, but as scholars who are or are allies to activists who experience daily, unavoidable risks of a different sort, we hope not to convey a self-importance that our university positions, vulnerable or not, afford us.

Organization of the Book

The social locations of the contributors to this volume are varied and fluid. That is, we are a collection of scholars/activists/artists situated in the North (most of the time), writing about the South.[39] Some of us are motivated by our connections to our homelands (Argentina, Brazil, Chile, and Cuba) or adopted homelands (Colombia, Canada) and others by a deep sense of solidarity with the struggles to which we have gained access. The following chapters are meant to capture some of that fluidity.

The contributors in *Taking Risks* listen to stories in the forms that activists/intellectuals represent them: texts, performance, memorials, and activism. We open the book with a monument recognizing a 1955 massacre of Argentine civilians at the Plaza de Mayo. Artist Nora Patrich's brief description of the massacre and her memorial remind us of the importance to archive stories and teach history in the venues to which we have access. In part 1 we look at stories as represented through textual articulation. Chilean writer-activist Carmen Rodríguez begins the collection by speaking to the power of fiction as a form of activism. She explains how writing, particularly against revisionist histories, is an act of resistance.[40] Next, graduate student Mahala Lettvin looks at activist writing from the reader's perspective.[41] She uses the case of the Argentinian dirty war as documented through fictional texts and memorials to articulate reading as activism. Julie Shayne then looks at a feminist magazine produced by Latina exiles (including Carmen Rodríguez) in Vancouver, British Columbia. These feminists created the magazine to articulate and communicate the political and artistic accomplishments of Latinas in and outside of their homeland; the pages are thus replete with stories. In part 1's final chapter, Marisela Fleites-Lear talks about stories of literacy and literature through her analysis of underground libraries in Cuba and award-winning Cuban "desk drawer novels."

In part 2 we learn of performed stories. Tamera Marko opens this section with a discussion of a transnational, collaborative documentary project based in Medellín, Colombia, where women tell their stories of the reconstruction of their city. Next, Robin Garcia takes us to Venezuela to learn about community radio and television projects and the stories Venezuelan media activists are telling about their experiences with the Bolivarian Revolution. Christina Marín closes the section with a discussion of traumatic stories of femicide along the Juárez/U.S. border as articulated through three plays she has directed.

The third part addresses stories of grassroots activism. Erica Williams opens the section with a discussion of the conflicts in Bahia, Brazil, between sex workers and their advocates and abolitionist approaches to sex work. In a related discussion, Roberta Villalón's work in Texas conveys the challenges for Latina immigrant survivors of intimate partner violence and the restrictions often placed upon advocates working to further their rights. Finally, Shelly Grabe closes the section and examines the activist efforts of the women's autonomous movement in Nicaragua vis-à-vis the testimonies of two feminist leaders in the movement.

Julie Shayne and Kristy Leissle conclude these chapters with a brief discussion of interdisciplinary spaces, cultural capital, and social justice scholarship. *Taking Risks* closes with an afterword by Julie Shayne, where she speaks to the family-career divide and its risks, based on her own life-changing experience in the academy, an experience which ultimately provided her the space to pursue this passion project.[42]

Notes

We would like to thank Kari Lerum, Karen Rosenberg, Roberta Villalón, and Erica Williams for their extremely helpful feedback on an early version of this introduction. Additionally, Kristy would like to acknowledge Michelle McGowan in helping her think through the transnational feminism part of this chapter.

1. It is now a year since the first draft of this introduction was written. Barrie has since decided she wants to do her project on the basics of acting.
2. Interestingly, this is not the only book about social justice/activist scholarship to begin in a similar conference-type setting. See, for example, Nagar and Swarr (2010, 13–15); Sudbury and Okazawa-Rey (2009b, 8–9).
3. For the most part, we focus on scholarship produced in the past two decades.
4. We point the reader to the following texts for history, overview, examples, and/or suggestions for how to conduct feminist social justice scholarship: *Research as Resistance,* Brown and Strega, eds. (2005); *Just Methods*, Jaggar, ed. (2008); *Engaging Contradictions*, Hale, ed. (2008a); *Voices of Change,* Park et al., eds. (1993); *Nurtured by Knowledge*, Smith et al., eds. (1997); *The SAGE Handbook of Action Research,* Reason and Bradbury, eds. (2008); *Handbook of Feminist Research,* Hesse-Biber, ed. (2007); *Introduction to Action Research*, Greenwood and Levin, eds. (1998[a]); *Racing Research Researching Race,* Twine and Warren, eds. (2000). For good discussions of action research's roots in Latin America and the global South, see, Lykes and Mallona (2008); Nabudere (2008).
5. Hesse-Biber and Leavy (2007); Jaggar (2008); Nagar et al. (2002); Naples (2003); Sandoval (2000).
6. Brown and Strega, et al. (2005), Wilson (2008).
7. Fals-Borda (1979); Fals-Borda and Rahman, et al. (1991); Park et al. (1993); Smith et al. (1997); Barndt et al. (2011); Greenwood and Levin, et al. (1998a); Lykes and Mallona (2008).
8. Dempsey, et al. (2011); Downs, et al. (2006); Mitchell K., et al. (2008).
9. The Sociological Initiatives Foundation http://www.sifoundation.org/2007/03/what-is-community-based-research.
10. Hale, et al. (2008a); Sanford and Angel-Ajani, et al. (2008); Imagining America. http://imaginingamerica.org/about/our-mission.
11. Brown and Strega, et al. (2005); Twine and Warren, et al. (2000).
12. Greenwood and Levin use the term "Pragmatic Action Research" which we have not seen elsewhere in the literature (1998b, 11). Similarly, Dana-Ain Davis uses the term "pracademics," which she defines as "the bridging of theory and practice, in an effort to illustrate the meaning of being politically engaged" (2008, 229).
13. Peter Park and others describe their version of social justice scholarship, participatory research, similarly: "The explicit aim of participatory research is to bring about a more just society in which

no groups or classes of people suffer from the deprivation of life's essentials, such as food, clothing, shelter, and health, and in which all enjoy basic human freedoms and dignity" (1993, 2).

14. This is not to suggest that all of the contributors share an identical vision of social justice. Indeed, as editor of the collection, Shayne never explicitly asked the authors how they define the concept. Charles Hale, editor of *Engaging Contradictions: Theory, Politics, and Methods of Activist Scholarship* (2008a) offers a similarly general observation in his introduction: "By shared political sensibilities, I do not mean homogeneity, but rather a shared commitment to basic principles of social justice that is attentive to inequalities of race, gender, class and sexuality and aligned with struggles to confront and eliminate them" ([b]7).
15. Interestingly, and perhaps not surprisingly, both of these definitions come from books, like this one, which are also part of SUNY's Praxis: Theory in Action series, ed. Nancy Naples.
16. Roberta Villalón, contributor to this volume, notes that the term "progressive" does not always travel well internationally. Rather, it is more of a U.S.-bound term.
17. There are countless other definitions of social justice scholarship. Some others we appreciate include: "[A]ction research is neither a theory nor a particular set of methods. It is a way of orchestrating combined research and social change activities to pursue collectively desired outcomes" (Greenwood 2008, 330). Another useful one is: "The distinctive contribution of activist scholarship, rather, is to enact an alternative way of doing research that attempts to contribute to the social good and to modestly advance the frontiers of knowledge, while training a bright light of critical scrutiny on the inequities of university-based knowledge production and attempting to ameliorate these inequities through the research process itself" (Hale 2008b, 23).
18. Gramsci figures heavily into analyses and explanations of activist scholarship, particularly participatory action research (PAR). Similarly, Gramsci's ideas are typically paired with Paulo Freire. For example, see Barndt 2011; Hall 1993; Gaventa, 1993; Gaventa and Cornwall 2008.
19. Despite PAR's initial liberatory ideology and potential, it has since been criticized for being coopted by a host of oppressive institutions, including the World Bank. For example, see Potts and Brown (2005, 256, 281); Barndt (2011, 16, 141–42, note 79); Heaney (1993, 41–46); Gaventa and Cornwall (2008); Nagar and Swarr (2010, 8).
20. See also Weir 2008.

21. "Positivism is the belief that knowledge should be guided by facts, rather than by imagination, pure logic, or any other nonfactual source" (Applebaum and Chambliss 1997, 12).
22. A few of the many examples include Sudbury and Okazawa-Rey, et al., especially chapters 10 and 11 (2009a); Barndt (2011, 19). For discussions of the personal conflicts regarding scholars using the term "activist," see Chatterjee (2009, 134); Mitchell (2008). For reworkings of the term "activism" in the academic context, see Collins (2012, 16); Lykes and Mallona (2008, 117).
23. For a related discussion regarding the motivations behind writing and archives, see Morgan, 2006.
24. See, for example, Davis et al. (2002a); Maynes, Pierce, and Laslett (2008); Polletta (2006); Polletta et al. (2011); Selbin (2010); Smith and Schaffer (2004); Stone-Mediatore (2003).
25. See also Latina Feminist Group (2001) *Telling to Live: Latina Feminist Testimonios* (Durham, NC: Duke University Press).
26. See also Leonard 1993, 166.
27. For an interesting take on the "organic intellectual," see Morales 2001.
28. Bud Hall, in his introduction to *Voices of Change,* also speaks to the Gramscian notion of "organic intellectuals" as related to participatory research (1993, xviii); Glenn Omatsu offers a similar analysis in his discussion of community activists as his "mentors," whom he ultimately draws on when designing his courses (2009, 167–85).
29. http://www.guardian.co.uk/world/2008/aug/26/colombia.sociology (Accessed July 20, 2012).
30. The Viva Project (2011) also works from this point of departure, drawing on Susan Smith in *Nurtured by Knowledge* (1997).
31. See http://www.youtube.com/watch?v=G_vp8FPuF7g&feature=g-u-u and Bonnefoy (2012).
32. A disturbingly ironic component of the story is that the film was debuted in Santiago's *Teatro Caupolicán*. In 1983 this theater housed a massive demonstration of women and feminists against Pinochet. Estimates put the attendees at ten thousand women, and the event is credited by many as the first public act of women against Pinochet (Shayne 2004, 100–02).
33. We want to be clear that we believe there are a host of reasons why U.S.-educated K–12 students do not learn these histories, many of them entirely out of the control of the teachers, including teaching to standardized tests and, worse yet, having such topics literally deemed illegal as recently happened in Arizona (Lacey 2011).
34. See also Chatterjee 2009, 138; Warren 2008, 215.

35. For additional discussions of social justice pedagogy, see bell hooks, *Teaching to Transgress: Education as the Practice of Freedom* (1994), and *Teaching Critical Thinking: Practical Wisdom* (2010).
36. Even as we bridge or subvert the activist/academic divide, we face a contradictory challenge that M. Jacqui Alexander and Chandra Talpade Mohanty have emphasized in their recent work (2010): the possibility of reinscribing the notion that only those at "the top" produce valuable knowledge for enacting justice, relegating activists to "objects" of study or otherwise marginalizing their contributions as lesser to the theoretical work of academicians. Nagar and Swarr further caution us against "constructing the 'academic' as the 'global' and the 'activist' as the 'local'" (2010, 9), an analytical move that affirms the global/local binary even as it can celebrate the typically marginalized "local." In producing this volume, we acknowledge these contradictions and strive to move beyond them.
37. We borrow and then modify this term from JoAnn Miller (2011) who talks about some sociology as "purpose driven."
38. See, for example, Gaventa (1993, 31); Greenwood (2008, 319); Heaney (1993, 44–45); Nembhard (2008, 290).
39. Argentine Nora Patrich, the artist responsible for the art on the cover and in the book, divides her time between Vancouver, Canada and Buenos Aires.
40. Memoirs also have the power to write against dominant histories. Here we point the reader to *Something Fierce: Memoir of a Revolutionary Daughter* (2011), by Carmen Aguirre, daughter of Carmen Rodríguez.
41. Mahala began her chapter while an undergraduate student and writes it, in part, from that perspective.
42. See also Evans and Grant, eds. (2009).

References

Aguirre, Carmen. 2011. *Something Fierce: Memoir of a Revolutionary Daughter*. Vancouver, Canada: Douglas & McIntyre.

Alexander, M. Jacqui, and Chandra T. Mohanty. 1997. *Feminist Genealogies, Colonial Legacies, Democratic Futures*. NY: Routledge.

———. 2010. "Cartographies of Knowledge and Power: Transnational Feminism as Radical Praxis." In *Critical Transnational Feminist Praxis*, ed. Amanda Lock Swarr and Richa Nagar, 23–45. Albany: State University of New York Press.

Angel-Ajani, Asale. 2008. "Expert Witness: Notes toward Revisiting the Politics of Listening." In *Engaged Observer: Anthropology, Advocacy, and Activism*, ed., Victoria Sanford and Asale Angel-Ajani, 76–89. New Brunswick, NJ: Rutgers University Press.

Appelbaum, Richard P. and William J. Chambliss. 1997. *Sociology: a brief introduction*. New York: Longman.

Barndt, Deborah, ed. 2011. *¡Viva! Community Arts and Popular Education in the Americas*. Albany: State University of New York Press.

Bickham Mendez, Jennifer. 2008. "Globalizing Scholar Activism: Opportunities and Dilemmas through a Feminist Lens." In *Engaging Contradictions: Theory, Politics, and Methods of Activist Scholarship*, ed. Charles Hale, 136–163. Berkeley: University of California Press.

Bonnefoy, Pascale. 2012. "Hundreds Protest Screening of Pro-Pinochet Film in Chile." *The New York Times*, Sunday June 10, 2012. (Accessed July 24, 2012).

Brooks, Abigail, and Sharlene Nagy Hesse-Biber. 2007. "An Invitation to Feminist Research." In *Feminist Research Practice: A Primer*, eds., Sharlene Nagy Hesse-Biber and Patricia Lina Leavy, 1–24. Thousand Oaks, CA: Sage.

Brown, Leslie, and Susan Strega, eds. 2005. *Research as Resistance: Critical, Indigenous, and Anti-oppressive Approaches*. Toronto: Canadian Scholars' Press.

Caldwell, Kia Lilly, Renya K. Ramirez, Kathleen Coll, and Tracy Fisher, eds. 2009. *Gendered Citizenships: Transnational Perspectives on Knowledge Production, Political Activism, and Culture*. New York: Palgrave Macmillan.

Chatterjee, Piya. 2009. "Transforming Pedagogies: Imagining Intersectionalist/ Feminist/Antiracist Literacies." In *Activist Scholarship: Antiracism, Feminism, and Social Change*, ed., Julia Sudbury and Margo Okazawa-Rey, 131–148. Boulder, CO: Paradigm.

Collins, Dana, Sylvanna Falcón, Sharmila Lodhiad, and Molly Talcott. 2011. "New Directions in Feminism and Human Rights: An Introduction." In *New Directions in Feminism and Human Rights*, eds., Dana Collins, Sylvanna Falcón, Sharmila Lodhiad, and Molly Talcotte. New York: Routledge.

Collins, Patricia Hill. 2012. "Looking Back, Moving Ahead: Scholarship in Service of Social Justice," in *Gender & Society*. 26(1): 14–22.

———. 2012. *On Intellectual Activism*. Philadelphia: Temple University Press.

Davis, Angela. 2008. "A Vocabulary for Feminist Praxis: On War and Radical Critique." In *Feminism and War: Confronting US Imperialism*, ed., Robin L. Riley, Chandra Talpade Mohanty, and Minnie Bruce Pratt, 19–26. London: Zed Books.

Davis, Dana-Ain. 2008. "Knowledge in the Service of a Vision: Politically Engaged Anthropology." In *Engaged Observer: Anthropology, Advocacy, and Activism,* ed., Victoria Sanford and Asale Angel-Ajani, 228–238. New Brunswick, NJ: Rutgers University Press.

Davis, Joseph E., ed. 2002(a). *Stories of Change: Narratives and Social Movements*. Albany: State University of New York Press.

Davis, Joseph E. 2002(b). "Narrative and Social Movements: The Power of Stories." In *Stories of Change: Narratives and Social Movements*, ed., Joseph E. Davis, 3–29. Albany: State University of New York Press.

Dempsey, Sarah, Mohan Dutta, Lawrence R. Frey, H. L. Goodall, D. Soyini Madison, Jennifer Mercieca, Thomas Nakayama, with Katherine Miller. 2011. "What Is the Role of the Communication Discipline in Social Justice, Community Engagement, and Public Scholarship? A Visit to the *CM Café*." *Communication Monographs* 78(2): 256–271.

Domke, David. 2008. "The Something We Can Do." In *Practising Public Scholarship: Experiences and Possibilities Beyond the Academy*, ed., Katharyne Mitchell, 42–48. Malden, MA: Wiley-Blackwell.

Downs, Jim, ed. 2006. *Why We Write: The Politics and Practice of Writing for Social Change*. New York: Routledge.

Evans, Elrena, and Caroline Grant, eds. 2009. *Mama Phd: Women Write about Motherhood and Academic Life*. New Brunswick, NJ: Rutgers University Press.

Fals-Borda Orlando. 1979. "Investigating Reality in Order to Transform It: The Colombian Experience." *Dialectical Anthropology*, 4(1): 33–55.

———. 1991. "Some Basic Ingredients." In *Action and Knowledge: Breaking the Monopoly with Participatory Action-Research,* ed. Orlando Fals-Borda and Muhammad Anisur Rahman, 3–12. New York: Apex.

Fals-Borda, Orlando, and Muhammad Anisur Rahman, eds. 1991. *Action and Knowledge: Breaking the Monopoly with Participatory Action-Research*. New York: Apex.

Freire, Paulo. 1983. *Pedagogy of the Oppressed,* second edition. New York: Continuum.

———. 1993. "Foreword." In *Paulo Freire: A Critical Encounter,* eds., Peter McLaren and Peter Leonard, ix–xii. New York: Routledge.

Gaventa, John. 1993. "The Powerful, the Powerless, and the Experts: Knowledge Struggles in an Information Age." In *Voices of Change: Participatory Research in the United States and Canada*, eds., Peter Park, Mary Brydon-Miller, Bud Hall, and Ted Jackson, 21–40. Westport: Bergin and Garvey.

Gaventa, John, and Andrea Cornwall. 2008. "Power and Knowledge." In *The Sage Handbook of Action Research: Participative Inquiry and Practice,* second edition, eds., Peter Reason and Hilary Bradbury, 172–189. Los Angeles: Sage.

Gramsci, Antonio. 1971. *Prison Notebooks,* edited and translated Quintin Hoare and Geoffrey Nowel Smith. New York: International Publishers.

Greenwood, Davydd J. 2008. "Theoretical Research, Applied Research, and Action Research: The Deinstituionalization of Activist Research" In *Engaging Contradictions: Theory, Politics, and Methods of Activist Scholarship,* ed., Charles Hale, 319–340. Berkeley: University of California Press.

Greenwood, Davydd J., and Morten Levin, eds. 1998(a). *Introduction to Action Research: Social Research for Social Change.* Thousand Oaks, CA: Sage.

———.1998(b). "Introduction: Action Research, Diversity, and Democracy." In *Introduction to Action Research: Social Research for Social Change,* ed., Davydd J. Greenwood and Morten Levin, 3–13. Thousand Oaks, CA: Sage.

Grewal, Inderpal. 2005. *Transnational America: Feminisms, Diasporas, Neoliberalisms.* Durham, N.C.: Duke University Press.

Grewal, Inderpal, and Caren Kaplan. 1994. "Introduction: Transnational Feminist Practices and Questions of Postmodernity." In *Scattered Hegemonies: Postmodernity and Transnational Feminist Practices,* ed., Inderpal Grewal and Caren Kaplan, 1–33. Minneapolis: University of Minnesota Press.

———. 1994. *Scattered Hegemonies: Postmodernity and Transnational Feminist Practices.* Minneapolis: University of Minnesota Press.

Hale, Charles R., ed. 2008(a). *Engaging Contradictions: Theory, Politics, and Methods of Activist Scholarship.* Berkeley: University of California Press.

Hale, Charles R. 2008(b). "Introduction." In *Engaging Contradictions: Theory, Politics, and Methods of Activist Scholarship,* ed., Charles Hale, 1–28. Berkeley: University of California Press.

Hall, Bud. 1993. "Introduction." In *Voices of Change: Participatory Research in the United States and Canada,* ed. Peter Park, Mary Brydon-Miller, Budd Hall and Ted Jackson, xiii–xxii. Westport, CT: Bergin & Garvey.

Heaney, Thomas W. 1993. "If You Can't Beat 'Em, Join 'Em: The Professionalization of Participatory Research." In *Voices of Change: Participatory Research in the United States and Canada,* ed.,

Peter Park, Mary Brydon-Miller, Budd Hall, and Ted Jackson, 41–46. Westport, CT: Bergin & Garvey.

Hesse-Biber, Sharlene Nagy, ed. 2007. *Handbook of Feminist Research: Theory and Praxis*. Los Angeles: Sage.

Hesse-Biber, Sharlene Nagy, and Patricia Lina Leavy, eds. 2007. *Feminist Research Practice: A Primer*. Thousand Oaks, CA: Sage.

hooks, bell. 1994. *Teaching to Transgress: Education as the Practice of Freedom*. New York: Routledge.

———. 2010. *Teaching Critical Thinking: Practical Wisdom*. New York: Routledge.

Imagining America. "Our mission." http://imaginingamerica.org/about/our-mission/. (Accessed August 1, 2012).

Jaggar, Alison, ed. 2008. *Just Methods: An Interdisciplinary Feminist Reader*. Boulder, CO: Paradigm.

Kaplan, Caren, Norma Alarcón, and Minoo Moallem, eds. 1999. *Between Woman and Nation: Nationalisms, Transnational Feminisms, and the State*. Durham, NC: Duke University Press.

Lacey, Marc. 2011. "Rift in Arizona as Latino Class Is Found Illegal." *The New York Times*. January 7, 2011. (Accessed August 1, 2012).

Latina Feminist Group. 2001. *Telling to Live: Latina Feminist Testimonios*. Durham, NC: Duke University Press.

Leonard, Peter. 1993. "Critical Pedagogy and State Welfare: Intellectual Encounters with Freire and Gramsci, 1974–86." In *Paulo Freire: A Critical Encounter*, ed., Peter McLaren and Peter Leonard, 155–168. New York: Routledge.

Lipsitz, George. 2008. "Breaking the Chains and Steering the Ship: How Activism Can Help Change Teaching and Scholarship." In *Engaging Contradictions: Theory, Politics, and Methods of Activist Scholarship*, ed., Charles Hale, 88–111. Berkeley: University of California Press.

Lykes, M. Brinton, and Amelia Mallona. 2008. "Towards Transformational Liberation: Participatory and Action Research and Praxis." In *The Sage Handbook of Action Research: Participative Inquiry and Practice,* second edition, ed., Peter Reason and Hilary Bradbury, 107–120. Los Angeles: Sage.

Mama, Amina. 2013. "Plenary Speech: The Challenges Facing Feminist Researchers and Publishing." Sociologists for Women in Society winter meeting. Feb 7–10. Santa Ana Pueblo: New Mexico.

Massey, Doreen. 2008. "When Theory Meets Politics." In *Practising Public Scholarship: Experiences and Possibilities beyond the Academy*, ed. Katharyne Mitchell, 142–147. Malden, MA: Wiley-Blackwell.

Maynes, Mary Jo, Jennifer L. Pierce, and Barbara Laslett. 2008. *Telling Stories: The Use of Personal Narratives in the Social Sciences and History*. Ithaca: Cornell University Press.

Mayock, Ellen C., and Domnica Radulescu, eds. 2010. *Feminist Activism in Academia: Essays on Personal, Political, and Professional Change*. Jefferson, N.C.: McFarland & Co.

Miller, JoAnn. 2011. "Presidential Address: Social Justice Work: Purpose-Driven Social Science."*Social Problems* 58(1): 1–20.

Mitchell, Don. 2008. "Confessions of a Desk-Bound Radical." In *Practising Public Scholarship: Experiences and Possibilities beyond the Academy*, ed. Katharyne Mitchell, 99–105. Malden, MA: Wiley-Blackwell.

Mitchell, Katharyne, ed. 2008. *Practising Public Scholarship: Experiences and Possibilities beyond the Academy*. Malden, MA: Wiley-Blackwell.

Morales, Aurora Levin. 2001. "Certified Organic Intellectual." In *Telling to Live: Latina Feminist Testimonios,* ed., Latina Feminist Group, 27–32. Durham, NC: Duke University Press.

Morgan, Jennifer. 2006. "Why I Write." In *Why We Write: The Politics and Practice of Writing for Social Change,* ed. Jim Downs, 39–45. New York: Routledge.

Nabudere, Dani Wadada. 2008. "Research, Activism, and Knowledge Production." In *Engaging Contradictions: Theory, Politics, and Methods of Activist Scholarship*, ed. Charles Hale, 62–87. Berkeley: University of California Press.

Nagar, Richa, and Amanda Lock Swarr 2010. "Introduction: Theorizing Transnational Feminist Praxis." in *Critical Transnational Feminist Praxis*, eds., Amanda Lock Swarr and Richa Nagar, 1–20. Albany: State University of New York Press.

Nagar, Richa, Victoria Lawson, Linda McDowell, and Susan Hanson. 2002. "Locating Globalization: Feminist (Re)Readings of the Subjects and Spaces of Globalization." *Economic Geography*, 78(3): 257–284.

Naples, Nancy A. 2002. "The Challenges and Possibilities of Transnational Feminist Praxis." In *Women's Activism and Globalization: Linking Local Struggles and Transnational Politics*, eds., Nancy A. Naples and Manisha Desai, 263–277. New York: Routledge.

———. 2003. *Feminism and Method: Ethnography, Discourse Analysis, and Activist Research*. New York: Routledge.

Nembhard, Jessica Gordon. 2008. "Theorizing and Practicing Democratic Community Economics: Engaged Scholarship, Economic Justice, and the Academy." In *Engaging Contradictions: Theory, Politics, and Methods of Activist Scholarship*, ed. Charles Hale, 265–295. Berkeley: University of California Press.

Okazawa-Rey, Margo. 2009. "Solidarity with Palestinian Women: Notes from a Japanese Black U.S Feminist." In *Activist Scholarship: Antiracism, Feminism, and Social Change,* ed., Julia Sudbury and Margo Okazawa-Rey, 205–223. Boulder, CO: Paradigm.

Omatsu, Glenn. 2009. "Linking 'Book Knowledge' to 'Lived Experience': Incorporating Political Tours of Our Communities into Classrooms." In *Activist Scholarship: Antiracism, Feminism, and Social Change,* ed., Julia Sudbury and Margo Okazawa-Rey, 167–185. Boulder, CO: Paradigm.

Park, Peter. 1993. "What Is Participatory Research? A Theoretical and Methodological Perspective." In *Voices of Change: Participatory Research in the United States and Canada*, ed., Peter Park, Mary Brydon-Miller, Budd Hall, and Ted Jackson, 1–19. Westport, CT: Bergin and Garvey.

Park, Peter, Mary Brydon-Miller, Budd Hall and Ted Jackson, eds. 1993. *Voices of Change: Participatory Research in the United States and Canada*. Westport, CT: Bergin & Garvey.

Polletta, Francesca. 2006. *It Was Like a Fever: Storytelling in Protest and Politics*. Chicago: University of Chicago Press.

Polletta, Francesca, Pang Ching Bobby Chen, Beth Gharrity Gardner, and Alice Motes. 2011. "The Sociology of Storytelling." *Annual Review of Sociology*. 37: 109–130.

Potts, Karen, and Leslie Brown. 2005. "Becoming an Anti-Oppressive Researcher." In *Research as Resistance: Critical, Indigenous, and Anti-oppressive Approaches*, ed., Leslie Brown and Susan Strega, 255–286. Toronto: Canadian Scholars' Press.

Rabinow, Paul, ed. 1984. *Foucault Reader*. New York: Pantheon Books.

Reason, Peter, and Hilary Bradbury, eds. 2008. *The SAGE Handbook of Action Research: Participative Inquiry and Practice,* second edition. Los Angeles: Sage.

Sandoval, Chela. 2000. *Methodology of the Oppressed*. Minneapolis: University of Minnesota Press.

Sanford, Victoria. 2008. "Introduction." In *Engaged Observer: Anthropology, Advocacy, and Activism,* ed., Victoria Sanford and Asale Angel-Ajani, 1–15. New Brunswick, NJ: Rutgers University Press.

Sanford, Victoria, and Asale Angel-Ajani, eds. 2008. *Engaged Observer: Anthropology, Advocacy, and Activism*. New Brunswick, NJ: Rutgers University Press.

Selbin, Eric. 2010. *Revolution, Rebellion, Resistance: The Power of Story*. London: Zed Books.

Shayne, Julie. 2004. *The Revolution Question: Feminisms in El Salvador, Chile, and Cuba*. New Brunswick, NJ: Rutgers University Press.

Smith, Sidonie, and Kay Schaffer. 2004. *Human Rights and Narrated Lives: The Ethics of Recognition*. New York: Palgrave Macmillan.
Smith, Susan E., Dennis G. Willms, with Nancy A. Johnson, eds. 1997. *Nurtured by Knowledge: Learning to Do Participatory Action-Research*. NY: Apex.
The Sociological Initiatives Foundation. "What Is Community Based Research?" http://www.sifoundation.org/2007/03/what-is-community-based-research/ (accessed August 5, 2012).
Stone-Mediatore, Shari. 2003. *Reading across Borders: Storytelling and Knowledges of Resistance*. New York: Palgrave Macmillan.
Sudbury, Julia and Margo Okazawa-Rey, eds. 2009(a). *Activist Scholarship: Antiracism, Feminism, and Social Change*. Boulder, CO: Paradigm.
———. 2009(b). "Introduction: Activist Scholarship and the Neoliberal University after 9/11." In *Activist Scholarship: Antiracism, Feminism, and Social Change*, ed., Julia Sudbury and Margo Okazawa-Rey, 1–14. Boulder, CO: Paradigm.
Swarr, Amanda Lock, and Richa Nagar, eds. 2010. *Critical Transnational Feminist Praxis*. Albany: State University of New York Press.
Twine, France Winddance, and Jonathan W. Warren, eds. 2000. *Racing Research Researching Race: Methodological Dilemmas in Critical Race Studies*. NY: New York University Press.
Warren, Kay B. 2008. "Perils and Promises of Engaged Anthropology: Historical Transitions and Ethnographic Dilemmas." In *Engaged Observer: Anthropology, Advocacy, and Activism*, ed., Victoria Sanford and Asale Angel-Ajani, 213–227. New Brunswick, NJ: Rutgers University Press.
Weir, Lorna. 2008. "The Concept of Truth Regime." *Canadian Journal of Sociology*. 33(2): 367–389.
Wilson, Shawn. 2008. *Research Is Ceremony: Indigenous Research Methods*. Halifax & Winnipeg: Fernwood.
YouTube, 2012. http://www.youtube.com/watch?v=G_vp8FPuF7g&feature=g-u-u. Accessed July 23, 2012.

DEL CIELO LOS VIERON LLEGAR/ FROM THE SKY THEY SAW THEM COMING

Monument to Civilians Massacred at Plaza de Mayo

NORA PATRICH

Monument to Civilians Massacred at Plaza de Mayo recognizes a massacre at the Plaza de Mayo in Buenos Aires, Argentina. On 16 June 1955, navy planes dropped fifteen tons of explosives. Because the bombing predated DNA testing, bodies were completely unrecognizable, and people were too afraid to come forward and report their family member missing, the numbers killed is unknowable. However, official and unofficial estimates put the civilian casualties anywhere from 350 up into the thousands. This monument commemorates the victims and presently stands in the gardens of the government house, Casa Rosada, on the side of the Plaza de Mayo where most of the bombs were dropped.

The monument is full of symbolism. The heart of the monument is sixteen trunks, each seven and a half meters, placed in a circle. The trunks represent something that once was alive and is now dead. Just like the trees they come from; just like the people this monument remembers, once alive, now dead. They rise from the earth like reaching to the skies from where the bombs came.

On top there are bronze heads representing women, men, and children. I chose bronze because it is a warm metal. There are also three heads that represent horror and three arms with open hands, perhaps protecting, or reaching, or maybe imploring.

At the bottom there is a ribbon made of stainless steel that represents the airplanes. The ribbon encircles all six trunks and includes 350 names, the names of the people who were found. Originally it was the airplanes which left their mark on the human flesh; this time it is the people, with their names, that leave their mark on the metal.

It is a very totemic monument which also reminds me of my exile in Vancouver, Canada, because the First Nations people there carved totem poles. But it is also inspired by the poles used during the Independence Wars where there Spaniards would place decapitated heads of those that struggled to free our country.

Photo of *From the Sky They Saw Them Coming*, 7.5 meters (24.5 feet) tall.

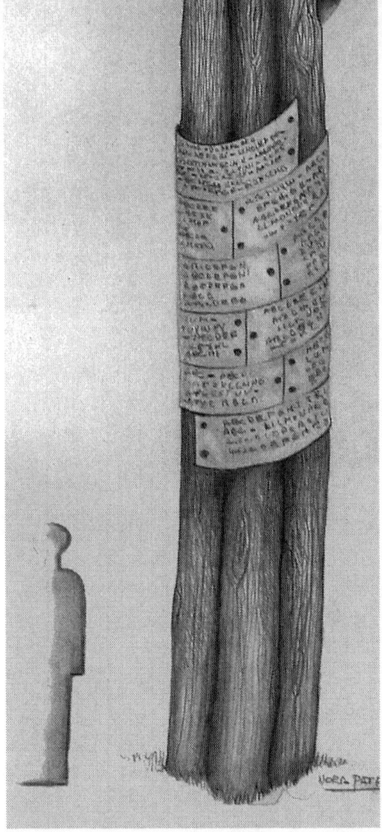

Study sketch of the monument.

PART 1

TEXTS, STORIES, AND ACTIVISM

INTRODUCTION TO PART 1

Texts, Stories, and Activism

JESSICA MONTEIRO MANFREDI

Stories, though originally an oral tradition, have been recorded in textual formats as a means to document "history." The privilege of writing history and the power that accompanies that position of authority typically belong to the elite. In much of the world, literacy remains the purview of the wealthy. Subsequently, those same elites control what is told in our children's textbooks. When a privileged minority usurps the authority to shape the historical narrative of the masses, the voices of those at the margins are usually oppressed, if not altogether silenced. The texts, stories, and activism in this section of *Taking Risks*, conveyed through the voices of feminist activists-writers-academics, defy this power structure by retelling and, most important, textually recording the outcomes of events that greatly shape history in the Americas. Ultimately, these chapters and the texts discussed within them give marginalized voices a medium to engage in the mainstream telling of our histories.

In Latin America, as elsewhere in the world, repressive governments have rewritten history as a mechanism to repress leftist movements. Though military regimes are largely a thing of Latin America's past, the intellectual damage they did still haunts us today. As a Brazilian, I have experienced this historical revisionism firsthand. While attending a prominent public high school in my home country, I believed I was part of an elite institution that exposed students to a politically progressive curriculum. Ironically, however, it was not until

I moved to the United States and enrolled in college that I had the opportunity to learn the stories of Brazilian antidomestic violence activist Maria da Penha, Las Madres de la Plaza de Mayo (Mothers of the Plaza de Mayo) in Argentina, Salvadoran and Nicaraguan women guerrillas, and a plethora of other notable Latin American women revolutionaries, their movements, and their remarkable achievements. Had it not been for the Latin American feminist activism imprinted in the pages of books like this one, scholarly articles, and magazines, I would still be unable to understand and embrace my Latina selfhood. As I turned the pages of the following chapters, I grasped their significance and power. These and similar stories do not merely educate, but they possess the ability to transform one's sense of history, place, and identity.

Much like the stories I presently read in some of my undergraduate courses, the activism narrated in this section enlightens us with alternative and moving perspectives on twentieth-century revolutionary struggles in the Americas.[1] From the election of president Salvador Allende, to the Argentine dirty war, to the Cuban Revolution and its effects, each chapter is intimately linked to turning points in Latin American history. One's placement within the context of these volatile events naturally differed according to where she lived, her political ties, and her levels of activist involvement, among countless other factors. As a by-product of these mass upheavals, the women activists we meet in the following chapters were physically, psychologically, ideologically, politically, and/or culturally displaced. Paradoxically, this displacement became one of the main driving forces behind the activism of the authors and subjects in this section.

Rodríguez and the Chilean exiles in Shayne's chapter were displaced after General Augusto Pinochet ousted Salvador Allende in a U.S.-backed coup d'état and installed a military dictatorship in 1973. The regime's repressive and draconian tactics designed to annihilate the opposition set in motion the Chilean diaspora. Rodríguez, like millions of other Chileans, fully supported and fought to see Chile flourish as a socialist country, and she was physically displaced in 1973 when she left her country out of fear of persecution. Her life in exile shaped one embodiment of her activism, her fictional writing, which is showcased in the first chapter of this book. Here, Rodríguez uses writing to preserve her memories, to grasp her "hyphenated existence as a Chilean-Canadian" through bilingual approaches, and, above all, to serve as an activist denouncing sexist manifestations and the injustices of the Chilean military coup. Rodríguez's chapter gracefully translates into words the challenges of exile. As an activist writer she uses her fiction as a way to contextualize and document the past and as a powerful tool to advance social justice and political change.

Shayne's "Chilean Exiles and Their Feminist Stories," in turn, recounts and analyzes the stories of feminist Latina exiles, mostly Chileans, who joined forces in Vancouver, Canada, to create the "transbordered feminist magazine" *Aquelarre*. Ironically, it was their displacement that made it possible for the magazine's founders to meet and craft this remarkable publication. Their efforts to textually record Latin American women's social, cultural, and political contributions and their ability to reach a transnational audience were extraordinary—especially given their limited resources. Mainstream displacement discourses tend to echo tragedy and victimization, but the creation of *Aquelarre* instead challenges this perspective: it empowered not only its authors living in exile but also women throughout Latin America. Hence *Aquelarre* was a bona fide example of activist writing as it defied a myriad of oppressive sociopolitical structures with global reach, all neatly packaged into one analytical, and artistically rich text.

Lettvin's chapter, alternatively, explores the absences in texts which are themselves the product of the physical, psychological, and political displacement and disappearance of tens of thousands during and after Argentina's dirty war. These are the stories of Argentines who, under General Videla's military regime, were permanently displaced in space and time. In Lettvin's chapter we read the texts produced by the survivors as they still attempt to fill the gaps between memory and identity. While acting as an "activist-reader," Lettvin asserts the connection between Argentines' displacement and her own as a U.S. citizen living in a culture of oblivion. Her chapter shows how the displacement of someone across the continent is linked to our own placement, privilege, and responsibility of reading and contextualizing marginalized voices. By acting as "activist-readers," we can assure that otherwise oppressed stories are not buried and forgotten for the sake of dominant discourses, but actively participate in the mainstream constructs of history.

Finally, Fleites-Lear's chapter addresses a two-fold ideological and political displacement: her own displacement as a Cuban who is not sternly anti-Castro living in the U.S., and the displacement of Cubans who became disillusioned with the outcome of the Revolution. Fleites-Lear thus reveals the Cuban underground systems of libraries, which were created by Cuban activists as a way to learn about alternative ideas and to nourish their love for texts. Fleites-Lear then shares the Cuban "desk drawer novels," or books written by Cuban writers who live on the island that are not a part of the official organizations dedicated to literature. These desk drawer novels and underground libraries arose, according to Fleites-Lear, from Cubans' determination "in writing their own history and telling their own stories." In so doing, Cuban writers and readers contest authoritative versions of their histories told by anti-Castro conservatives in the United States and their own ideologically rigid government. Whether through reading or writing forbidden texts, Cuban activists continue to forge a path through which their version of history cannot be ignored either on the island or abroad.

This section speaks to the intimate interconnections among history, displacement, activism, risk-taking, and the production and reading of texts. As mentioned, all of the following stories offer feminist windows into revolutionary struggles in the Americas. Though stories of displacement typically set the stage for calamity, the authors and activists in this section use displacement as a source of inspiration and empowerment. This empowerment occurs, in part, through writing, reading, and interpreting texts. Writing to assure these stories become permanent is in itself activism because it allows for feminist interpretations to make it into history books and human rights archives. Reading and interpreting these texts, conversely, helps students and others like myself who, once deprived of hearing these stories, now have the tools to understand their past, placement, and identity—leading us to navigate this world as conscious and critical activist-readers. Above all, this section expresses the power of textual stories as forms of empowerment, and as weapons to challenge formal versions of our history.

Note

1. As of this writing I am about to start my senior year in college.

1

WRITING AND ACTIVISM

CARMEN RODRÍGUEZ

Soccer, Power, and Words

When I was eight years old, I got my first explicit lesson on sexism and the hidden meanings of words.

My two older brothers—sixteen and nineteen—spearheaded a soccer team named after our street: Ferrari Fútbol Club. They used to practice right in front of our house, on Calle Ferrari, a slab of concrete plastered over a forty-five-degree gradient on Bellavista Hill in Valparaíso, the port in central Chile where we were living at the time.

They let me play with them—as second goalie at the lower end of the block—ensuring that the ball didn't keep rolling all the way down to Plaza Victoria—and, once in a while, as left winger. "You're much faster than all these guys put together," my brother Jorge would remark, as he briefed me in preparation for the scrimmage. "So, take advantage of your speed, and when you see an opening, just shoot!" he'd add, slapping my shoulder with his left hand and pointing to the improvised goal made up of two heaps of sweaters and coats with his right.

I would put my whole heart into my game—running up and down the hill, dribbling the ball the way my brothers had taught me, and shooting whenever I had a good chance. Quite a bit of the time I did score, which made me proud and my team happy. Clearly, then, I was an integral and valuable member of the Ferrari Football Club.

But it didn't take me long to realize that this assumption was nothing but a naive illusion of mine. When the opportunity to play a "real" game at Osmán Pérez Freire Stadium came up, I was not included on the team's roster.

"Tú eres mujercita" (You are a little woman), Jorge offered as an explanation.

"Yeah, you're too small," Nelson, the younger of the two continued, realizing how confused and upset I was.

"Then I can play when I get older?" I half-affirmed, half-asked.

My brothers looked at each other, clearly trying to find ways to soften the blow they were about to deliver.

"I'm afraid not," Jorge answered, shaking his head and staring at the ground.

"Women aren't allowed to play soccer—it's a very rough and difficult game. Only men can play, *y tú eres mujer* (and you are a woman)," Nelson concluded, looking at me with pitiful eyes.

I felt a surge of fury take hold of my gut and then rush out toward my hands and feet. I punched my brothers' chests and kicked their shins with all my might. I could hear their "ouches" and feel their hands trying to restrain me. But I couldn't stop. I don't know how long I kept at it. The next thing I knew, I was sitting on the curb, feeling defeated and exhausted. All I wanted to do was cry, but I didn't. I had understood perfectly well the meanings hidden within the word "*mujer*": weak, inept, incompetent, cowardly, spineless, incapable, pitiful, substandard, inferior—and I wanted to prove my brothers wrong, as at that moment they had come to embody all those who believed this to be true.

It took me years to understand the origins and history of sexism and other social injustices. As for the role of language in mirroring and perpetuating such injustices, eventually I was able to comprehend and articulate what my body had known for a long time: language is not only a sophisticated tool for reflection and communication, but also a weapon loaded with power.

Other Early Influences

I was born in 1948 in Valdivia, a city that the Spanish conqueror Pedro de Valdivia founded in 1552 on the banks of a wide, blue river in the south of Chile. Most of my young years were spent there and in Valparaíso, a strong-spirited and colorful[1] port on the central coast.

Both my parents were teachers, but my mother didn't get a chance to exercise her profession outside the home: she was too busy scraping and waxing floors, dusting, washing clothes by hand, ironing, cooking, knitting, and sewing. So, every afternoon she converted our dining room into a classroom and practiced her teaching with us, her children, and with our school and neighborhood friends. Right after lunch—the main meal of the day—the table was cleared of dishes and out came the books, notebooks, pencils, ink wells, fountain pens, and chalk. Yes, chalk. In addition to a big table, eight chairs, and a side board, our dining room sported an old free-standing blackboard that my mother had bought in a secondhand store. In that room, well in advance of entering first grade, I learned how to read and write.

Just like the rest of the family, I turned into an avid reader. My father nurtured our enthusiasm by ensuring that every month, right after payday, we all went to the bookstore to get a new supply of reading material. That's how I got hooked on the work of Jules Verne and Monteiro Lobato. These two writers taught me that a book can contain a whole world—people, places, and stories that I came to love as if they were part of my own life.

My mother enjoyed reciting poetry, and through her presentations at gatherings with family and friends I was introduced to the writings of Sor Juana Inés de la Cruz, Alfonsina Storni, Gabriela Mistral, and Juana de Ibarburú. For the longest time I didn't really understand the content of my mom's recitations, as my energies were focused on the mix of pride and embarrassment that overtook me on such occasions. But, as I grew older, I began to listen to the words behind her histrionic performances and had to conclude that, just as I had suspected all along, female preoccupations did go beyond the domestic domain and included anything and everything, from astronomy and social issues to existentialism and sexuality.

I also started to see my mother in a different light. How come she liked these particular authors? Wasn't she just a plain housewife and mother? Obviously not. I borrowed her books, and as I read Sor Juana, Storni, Mistral and Ibarburú, it became clear to me that those four women had dared to question and defy the machista society in which they had lived and had paid dearly for their honesty and courage.

Sor Juana Inés de la Cruz, who lived in seventeenth-century Mexico City, was forced to get rid of her scientific equipment, library, and writings and ended up sinking into hopelessness and penitence. Before turning forty, she committed to sacrificing her intellectual activity to purely religious duties. Four years later, she died while nursing her Carmelite sisters during a severe cholera epidemic.

In the first half of the 1900s, Alfonsina Storni, Juana de Ibarburú, and Gabriela Mistral, from Argentina, Uruguay, and Chile, respectively, fared much better than Sor Juana. They published profusely, their work was generally well received, and the calibre of Mistral's *oeuvre* was such that she obtained the Nobel Prize for Literature in 1945.

But still, they were subjected to derisive criticism by some of their male peers. Furthermore, Storni and Mistral endured isolation and even hostility in their personal lives: the former, because she had a child out of wedlock, and the latter, because she never married.

Our family's social gatherings also offered a venue for my father's engaging and skillful storytelling. From him, I learned about the power of personal narratives; the ever-changing nature of memories; the importance of telling a story "well"—describing places in rich detail; letting your characters speak in their own voices; using humor, no matter how serious the subject matter; creating suspense. But, perhaps most important, I also learned that he had grown up in abject poverty, even though his parents had worked incessantly at backbreaking jobs to provide for the family.

My grandfather was a miner, and my grandmother, a laundry woman. My dad was the oldest of thirteen children, but only four made it to adulthood. The other nine died as infants or as young children from preventable and curable conditions such as malnutrition, diarrhea, and pneumonia. My grandmother passed away of tuberculosis at age thirty-six, as did her two adult daughters at a similar age. My grandfather died of silicosis in his midforties, and my uncle Mario, of unknown causes in his early fifties. My dad made it to seventy-three.

But these tragedies did not hit me until much later, as my father always made sure to infuse his stories with adventure and humor, not to mention animated and colorful depictions of his native landscape, the Chilean northern coast. I could picture him vividly as a little boy, perched on a rock with a fishing line, feeling the bite and the pull of a humongous fish; falling in the ocean and swallowing buckets of salt water, but never letting go of the line; painstakingly climbing back on his rock, and finally winning the battle against the monster. At this point, believing that the story had come to an end, everybody would start to clap. But my dad would raise his right hand and arch his eyebrows. He was not finished. Following a suspenseful pause, he would continue: as it turned out, the creature he had pulled out of the sea and hurled over with all his might was not a fish; what now lay squirming on the beach was actually . . . a great big octopus! "Ah!" we would react in unison. He would pause again and finally deliver the closing scenes: killing the octopus by smashing its head with a rock, carrying it home wrapped around his shoulders, and offering it to his mother, who, delighted, had proceeded to cook a big stew that had fed the family for a whole week.

My father's stories were many, and they all involved taking chances. In his early years he had been close to drowning several times, had walked for hours carrying loads twice as big as him, had spent the night hidden in rat-infested sewage ducts, and had turned into a pickpocket and a thief. As the oldest child, he had taken it upon himself to risk his life over and over again so as to ensure that the family had enough food and clean water and so that he could bring home a few extra coins and building materials to repair the dilapidated shack in which they lived. In spite of all his efforts, though, most of his siblings had not made it, and his parents had also died young. But *he* had lived on, gone to school, and become a teacher. Not only that. He had been able to raise a healthy family of his own.

Many years later I would come to understand the subversive nature of my father's life. By all accounts, he should have died with the rest of them, the millions who over the centuries succumbed and continue to succumb to the wretched working and living conditions imposed by the conquerors, the imperialists, the mining companies, the land owners, the money-makers, the exploiters, the oppressors. He was meant to die, but he dared to live—the greatest risk of all.

Transformative Years

Between 1966 and 1970, I attended the Pedagógico—the Faculty of Philosophy and Education of the University of Chile in Santiago. This was the period leading up to the election of Salvador Allende, and the Pedagógico bustled with social and political activism. It didn't take me long to become involved in the literacy campaign sponsored by the Students' Federation in the shanty towns of Santiago. That's how I got to learn about and put into practice the philosophy and methodologies developed by educator Paulo Freire, who had been exiled from his native Brazil in 1964 and was now living in Chile.

The appalling poverty and sense of hopelessness that I witnessed in the marginalized communities where I worked led me to realize that Chilean society needed profound transformations. At the same time, the dignity, intelligence, and combative spirit of the people in the literacy groups I facilitated confirmed that the only way to achieve those transformations was through the development of a grassroots movement aimed at replacing capitalism and imperialism with a truly equitable society. So, by the time I graduated with a degree in English and obtained a teaching certificate, I had already joined millions of other Chileans who, like me, dreamed of and strove for a socialist country.

On September 4, 1970, Salvador Allende became the president of Chile. For the first time in history, a self-declared Marxist and socialist had been democratically elected as head of state. The program of the Unidad Popular (the Popular Unity coalition that he led), proposed a peaceful road to socialism, unlike the revolutionary war that took the Movimiento 26 de Julio and Fidel Castro to power in Cuba in 1959. Could it be done? Would Allende be capable of keeping a complex coalition of leftist parties together? Would the U.S. government, the multinationals, the Chilean landowners and capitalists, the political right and the military allow Chile to turn socialist?

Allende's election turned every corner of Chile into a breeding ground for social change. The U.S.-owned copper mines were nationalized. A land reform divided the estates of the traditional *latifundistas* and gave land to the impoverished countryside laborers. Factory workers took control of key industries. Shantytown dwellers and squatters built their own houses with the government's help. Reforms to the health and education systems allowed for more accessible services. An expanded literacy campaign resulted in thousands of adults learning to read and write. World and Chilean literature were massively produced by the state-owned publishing house Quimantú and sold at bargain prices. Theater companies, writers' workshops, musical ensembles, and artists' groups crafted new forms of popular culture everywhere.

Those who had never owned anything were taking a stab at controlling their own destiny, while the ones who had always owned everything and held a monopoly on power began to boycott and sabotage the new initiatives. Attempts to destabilize the country became blatant. The CIA provided expertise and millions of dollars to the government's opponents, including the national daily *El Mercurio* and the transportation industry. The United States imposed an economic embargo. Food distributors hoarded staples, creating a shortage and a black market. Landowners and industrialists left the country and took their money with them, leaving banks with insufficient funds. Allende's foes did everything they could to create chaos and force him to resign.

But, paradoxically, support for the Popular Unity grew, as demonstrated by the congressional elections of March 1973. It became evident, then, that the power mongers would not hesitate to strike with full force so as to turn the clock back and restore the economic and social order that was now under attack by Allende's reforms.

By April, rumors of a military coup were spreading like wildfire. In fact, there was an aborted coup in June. The transportation industry and some professional sectors went on an indefinite strike. The political right set about making inflammatory demands for military intervention. Allende attempted to appease them by appointing several generals to his cabinet. Industrial and countryside workers supportive of the government called for a state of alert as fascist paramilitary groups started to bomb bridges and power lines, and assault union and community leaders.

As the country became polarized, the Popular Unity coalition also began to show its internal differences. Some called for a strengthening of popular organizations. Others proposed further negotiations with Allende's opponents. A real revolution or a significant abandonment of the government's program appeared to be the two conflicting positions of the Left.

In the end, the military coup of September 11, 1973, found the majority of Chileans unprepared, and the horror that began that bright, spring morning went beyond anyone's imagination. These historical events changed my life forever. My family and I left Chile in December of 1973, and after eight months in California, we crossed the border into Canada on August 7, 1974.

Exile and Resistance

During my first years in Canada, all I wanted was to be back in Chile; not the Chile of the dictatorship, but the Chile of my childhood or the bustling Chile of the sixties and early seventies. I wanted to sit on my mom's lap and touch my father's hand. At times, the longing was so intense that I could literally leave Vancouver and transport myself to a Chilean Sunday afternoon at my parents', just in time for *onces*, tea time. I would help set the table, horse around with the kids, and pour the water into the gaping cups where Nescafé awaited.

There were many like me. We were the Chilean exiles, a wounded community that didn't only mourn the deaths of their murdered and disappeared *compañeros* and *compañeras*, but also the loss of their country and dreams of a better world.

We dedicated ourselves to convince the world that it was imperative to help the resistance movement in Chile. We were joined by many Canadians in founding committees, organizing *peñas*, forming singing groups, engaging in speaking tours, staging plays, starting radio programs, carrying out hunger strikes, boycotting Chilean goods, publishing newsletters, and liaising with unions, political parties, student organizations.

My involvement and commitment to the Resistance took a new, more direct form when I agreed to help provide logistical support to members who needed to go in and out of Chile. Thus, between 1979 and 1984, I lived in Bolivia and Argentina.

It took me quite a long time to get used to La Paz. When I began to have recurring dreams of waterfalls, aquamarine oceans, and gigantic trees, I realized how much I missed greenery and water. La Paz has virtually no vegetation and no bodies of water. At an altitude of thirty five hundred metres, the earth is brown and red, and the air is very dry and very thin.

I cried a lot. I cried when I got back from work because my feet and back hurt after having spent the whole day in high heels and a suit trying very hard to look like a respectable lady. I cried every time I figured I was putting my family at risk. I cried because I was tired. Very tired. Just leading a double life was exhausting enough, not to mention the amount of work that needed to be done after hours.

But I got used to it. I took pride in both, my paid job and my underground work. I made friends. I nearly forgot that there were no trees and water in La Paz. Life acquired a rhythm that felt quasinormal. But after three and a half years, it was time to move on and begin a new chapter in San Carlos de Bariloche in southern Argentina.

Bariloche is a beautiful mountain town on Lake Nahuelhuapi, at the foot of the Andes. People there are quite informal, so I could wear comfortable clothes to work and behave much more like myself. I loved having vegetation around me and being able to see the azure waters of the lake every day. Again, I made friends, and life continued to flow *almost* as if the family and I had been leading a "normal" life. But, we were not, and after one and a half years, it was deemed unsafe for us to stay on.

So we returned to Vancouver. The political scene in Chile was changing rapidly. In the early eighties, resistance to the dictatorship had grown, but so had the levels of repression. The more radical sectors of the movement had been targeted with particular viciousness, and Pinochet's forces had succeeded in eliminating some of our key leaders. By the mideighties, the more moderate segments of the opposition began to emerge as the conductors of a broad coalition determined to replace Pinochet's regime with some kind of democratic government. In a desperate move, Pinochet held a plebiscite in 1988, lost it, and had to call a presidential election. Patricio Aylwin, a Christian Democrat, was elected president of Chile.

Renewal

Between 1985 and 1987 I worked as a literacy instructor at the Native Education Centre. This was a very rich learning experience for me. Every day I discovered something new about the history of this country; about the values, beliefs and traditions of its many aboriginal peoples; about the hideous living conditions on reserves; about residential schools and the long-lasting effects of colonization; about the many faces of racism. But also, I learned about my students' love of life, sense of humor, persistence, and determination to grow and reach their goals. Above all, though, what I found most rewarding was to witness their ability to think critically, name the issues and challenges they were facing, reflect upon them, discuss them, understand them, make connections, draw conclusions, and articulate the individual and social actions necessary to bring about change.

My job at the Native Education Centre in Vancouver took me back to Santiago where, twenty years earlier, I had helped other groups of adults learn how to read and write. These were people who, just like the Chilean shanty-town dwellers, had been oppressed and marginalized, considered half-witted and ignorant. But there they were, proving to themselves and to the world that their lack of literacy skills had nothing to do with being stupid and everything to do with the workings of an unjust society.

This initial experience with aboriginal students was followed by many years of work with First Nations communities across the country. Most of these endeavors are documented in my educational publications.

When I wasn't working at my paid jobs, I was busy with the Aquelarre Collective, an organization composed of Latin American and Canadian women. The work was exhausting but utterly rewarding as every three months we had a very concrete product to make us proud: *Aquelarre Magazine*, a bilingual, feminist, and socialist publication, which served as a meeting place and a forum for Latin American women in Canada, Latin America, and around the world. In 1997, after nine years of labor, we had to stop production due to funding cuts. But the collective's legacy of twenty-one issues of *Aquelarre* remains in the collections of many libraries, in both print and digital versions. (See Julie Shayne's chapter, this volume.)

In the early nineties, I also began to teach prospective literacy instructors in the Adult Literacy Certificate Program of the Faculty of Education at Simon Fraser University. After ten years, the program was shut down, and I had to reinvent myself once again, this time as a sessional lecturer in the Latin American Studies Program of SFU, where I taught Latin American literature and cultural studies off and on until 2010. In 2009, I was also fortunate to be invited to serve as writer in residence and adjunct professor in the Department of French, Hispanic, and Italian Studies of the University of British Columbia.

Teaching Latin American literature and culture was both a challenge and an exhilarating enterprise. I had to stay abreast of what was happening in the Latin American scene. I had to design sound and interesting curricula. I had to make good use of an opportunity I never thought I would have when I first came to Canada: the opportunity to expose young people to the writers, poets, playwrights, musicians, thinkers, visual artists, dancers, actors, and filmmakers who make us Latin Americans proud.

I believe my students appreciated and were inspired by the works we perused together. How does one *not* enjoy a Pablo Neruda or an Alfonsina Storni poem, an Alicia Alonso performance in Revolutionary Cuba, an Antonio Carlos Jobim composition, a Cristina Peri Rossi or a Julio Cortázar short story, an Eduardo Galeano vignette, a song in the voice of Mercedes Sosa or Susana Baca, a novel by Gabriel García Márquez?

Along the years I had admired and enjoyed the work of these and myriad other Latin American cultural workers, and it gave me great pleasure to share that enjoyment with my students.

Bilingual Writing

Since the mid 1990s I have been a bilingual writer. A good part of the time, I complete my work in Spanish and then rewrite it in English. Some of the time, it happens the other way around. But most of the time, I write by traveling between the two languages.

This process has become an integral part of my work as, in many ways, it reflects the content of my writing—my own and my characters' journeys from Chile's volcano-studded south, its mystic Atacama Desert, and the jacaranda-lined streets of Santiago to the expansive beauty of the Canadian West Coast and bustling Commercial Drive in Vancouver. Back and forth I go, they go, mapping the everyday lives and emotional terrain of dual geographies.

It took me years to feel comfortable using both my mother tongue and my adopted tongue. I was afraid of making mistakes in English—still am—but I'm glad I took the risk, as bilingual writing has become a very pleasurable experience for me. I like the challenge. I love feeling the contrasting texture of the words in the two languages, hearing their divergent sounds, comparing meanings and rhythms, finding the terms and constructions that will mirror each other most fittingly.

Bilingual writing can turn into a long and involved endeavor. It entails creation and re-creation, fleshing out what is in the lines and in between the lines—the sounds and the silences. It often becomes tedious, but I keep at it. Why? Perhaps, because it's like giving birth to two distinct bodies that share one single soul; and, somehow, this act is symbolic of my own process of becoming bilingual and bicultural; it echoes, over and over again, my hyphenated existence as a Chilean-Canadian.

Writing and Activism

In 1989, the Chilean dictatorship was replaced by a lukewarm democracy. The neoliberal economic system and the 1980 constitution imposed by Pinochet were left intact, and the dictator himself remained as commander in chief of the armed forces and senator for life. It was a change; after seventeen years, Chileans had managed to get rid of the dictatorship; of course, this *was* a welcome change, but not the one I and many others had wanted. The socialist Chile we had fought for so fiercely had eluded us once again.

I turned to my writing. I collected the poetry, journal entries, and stories I had written through the years. I started to write again, and in the early nineties I decided to take a huge risk: to attempt to publish my work. I was fortunate. In 1992, Women's Press released my first book: *Guerra Prolongada/Protracted War*, a volume of poetry. A few years later, Arsenal Pulp Press put out the collection of short stories *and a body to remember with* and Editorial Los Andes, *De cuerpo entero*, its Spanish counterpart. And, most recently, Women's Press Literary published my novel *Retribution*.

So, at a critical point in my life, I decided to write and publish so as to keep my activist soul alive. I have continued to write because I love it. I love the challenge of transposing and translating the chaotic nature of life and the complex world of ideas and emotions into the linear, orderly world of language; of searching for the most effective ways to tell my stories and give shape to my feelings and thoughts; of crafting alluring narratives and engaging poems. For me, writing is a creative and pleasurable way of continuing my work as an activist; of uncovering, denouncing, resisting, celebrating, and hoping.

Selected Writings

I chose two poems, one short story, and excerpts from my novel to show the connection between my ideas and my writing.

The poems illustrate moments and states of mind at critical times in my life: "Idioma original"/"Original Language" was written shortly after the coup in Chile and "Sujeta"/"Subject," during my first year of exile in Vancouver.

The short story "In the Company of Words" exemplifies many of the concepts I present in my introductory essay: writing as a way of preserving our memories; the subtle and overt manifestations of sexism, as in the phrases *Girls*' School Number 20 and *Men*'s School Number 19, and the tragic result of a bungled abortion; exposing and denouncing such issues; the hidden meanings of words. I also chose it for its content: allusions to the Chilean military coup and to the difficulties of living as an exile in a new country.

My novel *Retribution* is the story of three generations of women connected not only by their familial ties, but also by the sociopolitical events that shape their lives. It spans seventy years in the life of the Martínez family, and it takes place in both Chile and Canada. The narrative unfolds as Tania, a thirty-seven-year-old Vancouver artist, struggles to understand the disturbing information contained in a letter she receives from a Chilean judge and sets out to re-examine the family stories she heard from her mother and grandmother through the years.

The two excerpts I selected from the first chapter of the novel introduce the main characters, the settings, the central conflict, and some of the issues and themes that the book addresses: art as means of understanding history and of giving shape to our aspirations and notions of a more equitable world. The excerpt I picked from chapter 3 narrates one of the characters' experiences as an activist and literacy instructor in the shantytowns of Santiago. This ministory within the larger story illustrates the direct correlation between language and activism—words as fundamental tools in the struggle for social justice and political change.

From *Guerra Prolongada/Protracted War*, a volume of bilingual poetry. Toronto: Women's Press, 1992.

IDIOMA ORIGINAL
Sollozos de máquina
voces
afuera
en el mundo
Yo mastico un cierto dolor
Entre mis piernas
pedazos de carne
con uñas mugrientas
pujan hacia arriba
fantasías antiguas
ya paridas
ya abortadas
Yo mastico un cierto dolor
Uñas mugrientas
negro
brillantes
rojo
Yo desangro efímeras imágenes
estertores en coro
Mi lengua

ORIGINAL LANGUAGE
Machine sobbing
voices
outside
in the world
I chew over a certain pain
Old fantasies
already born
already aborted
strain upwards
between my legs
like flesh
with filthy fingernails
I chew over a certain pain
Filthy nails
black
shiny nails
red
I bleed ephemeral images
death rattle in chorus
My tongue

inflada a la n potencia
revienta
un líquido espeso
ahoga el esfuerzo supremo
de articular
ar-ti-cu-lar
un sentido
Lo he olvidado todo
Mi arma está muerta
el futuro no existe

swollen to the nth degree
bursts
a thick fluid
drowns the supreme attempt
to articulate
ar-ti-cu-late
a meaning
I have forgotten all
My weapon is dead
the future does not exist

SUJETA
he creado un mundo para mí
cuatro pilchas viejas
unos cuantos libros
la mesa
música
un lugar ocupado por el orden
la armonía
el juego de colores y texturas
y el vino
blanco
seco
moviendo esta mano
resentida
ante la invasión autorizada de
hombre
niños
trabajo
cocina
necesarios enemigos
de esta parte mía
que goza el espacio
solitario
celular
que me he creado
aquí
dentro
esta noche fuera
dentro
mío
yo

SUBJECT
I've created a world for myself
some old clothes
a few books
the table
music
a place occupied by order
harmony
the play of colors and textures
and dry
white
wine
moving this bitter hand
before the authorized invasion of
man
children
a job
kitchen
necessary enemies
of this part of me
that rejoices in
solitary
cellular
space
of my own making
here
inside
this night outside
inside of me
this I

From *and a body to remember with*, a collection of short stories. Vancouver: Arsenal Pulp Press, 1997.

In the Company of Words

Hey Pilar Vallejo, remember when we used to run down Ferrari Street and the boats looked so small down there in the bay and were so goofy, pretending to be nuts, and then we hung around on the corner with our hands in our pockets and whistled *Madam Butterfly* arias after my brother took us to the Victoria to see the movie with Mario Lanza?

And remember School Number 20 on top of Bellavista Hill, those starched, white girls, ruffles and ribbons, shiny shoes and circles of Nugget shoe polish on our ankle socks, girls reciting *Piececitos de niño*, times tables, Arturo Prat's last words: *All aboard, boys*; and you raising your hand, saying, Miss Graciela, I think he was pushed, and Miss Graciela putting you in the corner for being a smartass and me making faces at you, throwing paper airplanes with messages inside?

And remember Mondays, when we were all spotless, even you and me, singing the national anthem at the top of our lungs in the playground of the *Girls'* School Number 20, listening to the boys across the street, the ones from the *Men*'s School Number 19, singing the national anthem at the top of their lungs but a little ahead or behind us? It was pandemonium, but finally we all finished together with Sanfuentes Street between us, *o el asilo contra la opresión*, oh shelter from oppression, oh shelter from oppression, oh shelter from oppression, da-da-da-da-da-da-da-da-da-da-da-dah, PA-PA-PUM.

If only they'd seen us, Pilar Vallejo, riding the scooter my Aunt Luca gave me, flying downhill, you in front and me in the back, stuck to you like a barnacle, watching the Vargas' house come upon us from under your arm and holding a high C so strong and clear, even Madame Butterfly would have been impressed. And you, swerving in the last fraction of a second, but we kept on flying, nothing to stop us now but the Blessed Virgin, oh my God, why didn't I listen to my mother, eyes closed and everything red, everything red, and you saying, did you see that, silly goose, we won and nothing happened . . . Yeah, nothing happened, except my broken arm, with no elbow or wrist, dangling from somewhere in between like the head of the kitchen mop, and that imbecile Gloria Bobadilla singing, *I'm telling your mo-om, I'm telling your mo-om.*

Oh, Pilar Vallejo, so many years have passed since that day I asked you about your mother, and you, blushing like a tomato, told me she was dead and that was that, and I wanted to know how did she die, what did she die of, and you said she was dead and that was that and then, insatiably curious and already quite the extortionist, I said that if you didn't tell me, I wouldn't play with you anymore or lend you my dolls, or the scooter, or anything else. But right away I regretted it and I hugged you because now you were crying and whispering, *From the abortion, from the abortion*, and I didn't understand a thing, but I comforted you anyway and made out as if I understood, and cried with you knowing I couldn't ask my mother or anyone because *from the abortion* reeked of secrecy and evil, and if Mama knew, it'd be goodbye to the invitations to Pilar Vallejo for tea and cookies, goodbye to going to the movies with Pilar Vallejo, goodbye to Pilar Vallejo, amen.

So many things have happened since then and sometimes, like now, stuck on the empty streets of this Vancouver suburb, stuck in this autoland, stuck missing Ferrari Street, with the neighbourhood kids playing soccer, hopscotch, and jump rope, stuck missing the Ideal Bakery and their pork buns at four in the afternoon, stuck in this interminable Vancouver lushness, I think about you, Pilar Vallejo, and wonder what's become of your life, if you went to high school, if you got married or lived in sin, if you had kids, if you ever left the hills of Valparaíso to roam like me.

I'm okay—more or less. Just think, Pilar Vallejo, I'm under another sky and another sun, far away from Valparaíso. My parents wait for the mailman in their house in Quilpué and look for my brother, who disappeared the eleventh of September, 1973. In Canada, I'm learning to speak again and trying somehow to make sense out of life here. I'm a janitor in a skyscraper in downtown Vancouver. From the thirty-second floor, I can see the boats in the bay—tiny, like the ones we used to see from Bellavista Hill, almost thirty years ago.

Who knows, one of these years when I come back, maybe we'll run into each other, strolling through Plaza Victoria. We could go see what Ferrari Street looks like now, and afterwards I'd buy you an ice cream at Bogarín's.

By the way, now I know the meaning of the word abortion.

Two excerpts from the first chapter and one excerpt from the third chapter of *Retribution, a novel.* Toronto, Women's Press Literary, 2011.

Chapter 1

Vancouver, Canada, March 2011

Tania

> Thirteen days ago, a letter from Chile arrived.
> White envelope.
> Registered.
> Official looking.
> Signed by Judge Arturo Leiva.
> A bomb concealed in a handful of circuitous sentences.

Judge Leiva writes that he would be extremely thankful if I were to approach the Chilean Consulate in Vancouver to arrange for a sample of my blood to be tested. He explains that a certain Marcelino Romero is on trial for allegedly having performed acts of torture and rape against women political prisoners at the "Londres 38" detention centre in Santiago, following the military coup of September 11, 1973. There is evidence to believe, he continues, that one of those women would have been Señora Sol Martínez. There is further evidence to presume that these unspeakable acts might have resulted in Señora Martínez becoming pregnant with Marcelino Romero's child.

Señora Sol Martínez is my mother.

Judge Leiva needs my DNA to determine whether Marcelino Romero is my father.

Until now, Miguel Rivera has been my father.

Miguel—curly fingers, hair shooting up to the sky, face of a naughty boy—principal violinist of Chile's Symphony. Miguel, one of the country's thousands of "disappeared."

I never met Miguel, but he has always been an integral part of my life. My mother and grandmother made sure that I grew to know him as thoroughly as the palms of my hands. My mom would tell me over and over again the story of how they came together when she was twelve and he, fourteen. My grandmother never tired of describing his humble demeanor and the magic of his violin playing.

But my grandma's accounts went much further back in time, to her life as a young woman in Santiago, when all she wanted was to become an elementary school teacher. She insisted on providing detailed explanations of the Chilean cultural and literary scene in those times and, at the drop of a hat, would begin reciting her favourite verses.

She was so passionate about poetry, that even her term of endearment for me came from one of her most cherished poems. Although my mami had countless names for me—"*mi gatita*—my kitty cat," "*mijita*—my little daughter," "*chiquitita*—little one," "*cosa más linda*—loveliest thing," "darling," "lovie," "precious," "*regalona*—cuddly one."—for my grandma, I was always "my queen." Morning, afternoon and night, rain or shine, whether I had behaved well or misbehaved, I would be my grandma's queen.

"My queen, go and do your homework right now."

"My queen, stop scratching your crotch and sit like a lady."

"My queen, you look beautiful in your organdy dress."

"My queen, come here so that I can braid your hair."

"My queen, how can you go out looking like *that*?"

When Queen Elizabeth appeared on TV, in her ludicrous hats and carting a little purse that up to this day I would like to open and peek at what's inside, I felt completely and utterly cheated. Why on earth would my grandma ever want to call me "my queen"?

One day I mentioned it to her. She burst out laughing and then explained that she didn't call me "my queen" because of Queen Elizabeth, but rather because of a Gabriela Mistral poem called "We Would All Be Queens." In that poem, Mistral talks about her childhood in the Elqui Valley and the friends that she used to play with, imagining that one day they would all have a life of gratification and joy, their dreams and hopes fulfilled forever; that they would all become queens. While brushing my hair, my grandma went on to tell me that when she was a girl, she also had wanted to have a prosperous and happy life, but destiny had decided to play havoc with her dreams.

"And as if that hadn't been enough, destiny also decided to mess up my daughter's life!" she added.

"That's my mami," I interjected.

"Yes my queen. That's your mami," she confirmed, as she set the brush down and picked up two colourful hair pins in the shape of butterflies from the top of her dresser. She put one between her teeth—the same way she would hold half a dozen pins when she was doing her sewing—carefully placed the other one on the left side of my head, took the second pin out of her mouth, positioned it on the other side, looked approvingly at me in the mirror, and then continued, as she rested her hands on my shoulders:

"So, when you were born, I decided to do everything in my power to help *you* become a queen; to make sure that you can realize your dreams and be a happy, happy person. That's why you're my queen, not because of Queen Elizabeth," she concluded, as she chuckled and then kissed the top of my head.

"Now go play!" she commanded, giving me a pat on the butt.

In addition to her recitations and explanations about poetry, my grandmother also offered vivid portraits of the beautiful trees to be found in Santiago's many parks. Not only that; she also drew and coloured them for me so that I could appreciate the particular shade of lilac of a jacaranda in bloom; the magnificent trunk and red, succulent flowers of a *ceiba*; the vibrant crimsons and golds of *liquidambars* in Autumn. But while I enjoyed her botanical descriptions and her poetry, I was far more interested in hearing about the pleats and cuffs of her chocolate brown school uniform, the cut and length of the home-made percale dresses she wore on Sunday and, most of all, about her engagement and marriage to my grandfather Andrés, a charming young man who, according to her, looked just like Clark Gable, a famous movie actor.

While my grandmother's memories of her youth intrigued me, the family's stories during the time they lived in a little house on Esmeralda Street in Valdivia enthralled me to the point of delusion. This was the place where my mom had become a rebellious teenager; where my uncle Andresito had fallen in love with his friend Carloncho; where my grandmother had witnessed her son's murder at the hands of the military.

As a child, I was immersed so deeply in those stories that I believed that I had been a witness to them all; that I had lived on Esmeralda Street with my grandma, my mom, and the rest of the characters that populated their past.

When I grew old enough to realize that these were nothing but borrowed memories, I felt completely betrayed and, for quite a while, stubbornly insisted that I had indeed attended the Valdivia Youth Orchestra's concerts; laughed at my grandfather's jokes as the family shared tea and apple *kuchen* at the kitchen table; celebrated Chile's third place in the 1962 World Cup at the town square; travelled to Santiago with my grandmother and met her shrewd and fashionable sister Amparo.

But, by the time I reached my teens, I lost interest in my mother's and grandmother's accounts and even resented not being Canadian-Canadian, born here, with a family history that didn't include military coups, concentration camps, resistance movements and relatives who had either been killed or made to disappear.

As for the letter from Judge Arturo Leiva, I've yet to decide whether I'll act on it or not.

The first few days following its delivery, I was both shocked and filled with insatiable curiosity. I carried the letter in my pocket at all times, fingered it, pulled it out, read it, put it back in my pocket once again. I couldn't eat, couldn't sleep. All I could do was think about the message enclosed in those oblique, yet clear words: there was a strong chance that Marcelino Romero and not Miguel was my father.

I knew that my mom had been abducted the day of the coup, but I didn't know when she had been taken to "Londres 38," the torture centre where Marcelino Romero operated. I spent hours researching calculators for childbirth due-dates, but basically they all offered the same information: conception and birth are approximately two hundred and sixty-six days apart. That meant that I would've been conceived on September 23. But, all calculators also cautioned that many births happen up to two weeks before or after the estimated due-date. The answers, then, didn't lie there.

I considered confronting my mother. A few times I took the letter out of my pocket and practiced in my mind the wording of the bomb I would drop on her. Once, I made it as far as her bed. But in the end, I decided that she doesn't deserve this bomb, particularly now that she's so close to the end. She lived a life fraught with hardships and has gained the right to die in peace.

My mami's dying of cancer of the bones, the same ailment that took my grandmother in 1998. It's not surprising, given that they shared so many things in life. Now I wonder if they also shared the knowledge that Marcelino Romero and not Miguel may be my biological father.

After the initial shock and curiosity brought on by Judge Leiva's letter, I entered a state of supreme wrath. How could anyone even begin to suggest that a repugnant torturer and rapist might be my father? When I felt as if I was about to explode, I would get in my car and go for long drives on the freeway. There, hidden in the insular protection of my vehicle and tempered by the noise of the traffic, I'd scream and scream until I had no voice left.

Now, I have arrived at a place of exhaustion and exasperating indecision. I don't know what I'll do about Judge Leiva's request. One minute I believe that I will not be able to go on living until I know the truth, but the next I convince myself that Miguel and only Miguel is my father. A few days ago I went as far as picking up the phone and dialing the Chilean Consulate's number, only to hang up before anybody could answer the call.

Until I muster the courage to make a decision, I will rely on my art to help me pull through these disturbing times.

Yesterday I began working on an exhibition based on my family's history. Every surface of my studio is covered with the sketches, drawings and paintings I have produced along the years. I have also been going through my notebooks and our photo albums; gathering the various objects that my grandma and mom brought with them to Canada; my mother's tapestries, my grandmother's pottery pieces and watercolours.

But, as I sit here, surrounded by a disarray of memories, keepsakes, images and words, I wonder if I will ever be able to do justice to the stories that took my family through its many journeys. I don't know if I'll manage to convey the ordinary yet unique ups and downs of my mami's and grandma's daily existence before the Pinochet coup. If I'll have the courage to portray the horror that followed. If I'll dare trace and bring out the underlying forces that shaped my mother's and grandmothers' lives.

Most daunting of all though, is the unavoidable challenge of having to delve deep inside myself. If I really want to understand my family's history, I will have to do my best to understand myself as well. After all, a good part of who I am is a result of that history and conversely, a good part of that history was shaped by my passage through this world.

Art will be my compass, my lens, my tool.
Art as memory.
Art as healing.
Art as creation and beauty.
Art as truth.

Chapter 3: Chile, March 1, 1967–September 10, 1973 SOL

In March of 1967 I began to study Social Work at the University of Chile. Miguel had moved to Santiago two years earlier, as he had been awarded a full scholarship to pursue his violin studies. We were euphoric. After an eternity of communicating by mail and seeing each other only during the holidays, we would be living in the same town again, this time in the capital city of the country.

On my first day of classes, we had agreed to meet for lunch. I was running late, so I bolted into the cafeteria trying to figure out how I would find Miguel in the midst of the hustle and bustle of that hub of student activity. I was met by absolute silence and stillness instead. Everybody had turned into statues—dozens of spoons were suspended halfway between bowls and mouths, while all eyes were fixed on one single point: a tall, long-haired boy wearing John Lennon glasses. It was Raúl, President of the Student Federation, standing on top of a table.

I was drawn immediately to his convincing and calm words, the clear ring of his voice, not at all strident, but still full of emotion. Much of what he said that day I had already heard from Miguel, Miss Blanca, Gloria, my brother, my father: we lived in an unjust world, where the rich exploited the poor, where many people starved to death while others indulged in luxury; we were part of a society in dire need of change. Also, the images of Miguel's home and family were still imprinted in my mind. Certainly, these were issues I knew about, but Raúl's speech brought them into focus for me. He was a natural leader: clear, humble, patient, disciplined, and with a vocabulary that could persuade even tables and chairs.

After he finished his speech and jumped off the table, Raúl was surrounded by students wanting to talk to him. I waited patiently and finally made my way to the front of the small crowd.

"I want to do something," I said. "What can I do?" I asked him.

He smiled and invited me to go talk to him at the Student Union's office that afternoon. That's how, encouraged by Raúl, I got to *La Esperanza*, a shanty town in the south end of Santiago.

I had never seen such poverty in my whole life: shacks made of tin and cardboard, where an entire family spent the night huddled together on the dirt floor, covered with a few sheets of newspaper; thirty year old women as wrinkled as raisins and with no teeth in their mouths; men made of skin and bones, their eyes popping with the anger and shame they carried inside for not being able to provide for their families; a dirty pot filled with dirty water on top of a feeble bonfire, going by the name of "soup"; children with bellies like barrels and legs like pins; children splashing around in the stench of an open sewer; children dying, the way the children of the poor die, with no fuss, no melodrama, simply dying in their mothers' arms.

There I met Señora Guillermina. Her youngest baby, "Blondie," the blue-eyed one, the one that looked so much like her aunt Filomena and had won her daddy's heart, Manuelita was her actual name, had died just a little while ago. She had also been her older brothers' pride—they had loved to take her around the neighbourhood inside a wooden box that the gentleman from *La Tranquera* grocery store had given them and to which they had added a set of wheels they had found in the dump. But the baby girl had decided to become an angel just before turning seven months and, most likely, she was now flying around, who knows where, dressed as a butterfly or disguised as a cicada while she sang songs to the sun.

Señora Guillermina, her old man, Don Arnulfo, and their five children had come to Santiago from Potrero Chico Grande, inland from Curicó. They had come to the capital city looking for a better life—they had been migrant countryside workers and had grown tired of the constant comings and goings and the instability of that kind of life. Besides, some friends had told them that for sure in Santiago Don Arnulfo would find a job in construction and Señora Guillermina could work as a laundry woman. Also, the kids could finally start going to school. But, it was already three months since they had arrived and nothing had turned up. If it hadn't been for the neighbours, who had helped them to set up the shack, the children who panhandled on the main street and came back with a few coins, plus the good-hearted ladies who shared their tea and bread with them, Señora Guillermina wouldn't have known what to do. Even her own milk had dried up and now that she thought about it, perhaps her baby had died because the only thing she had been giving her in the last few weeks was warm tea, quite weak, but with a little bit of burned sugar to take away the bitter taste.

Señora Guillermina's grief streamed down her face when she talked about her baby, or when she whispered in my ear that her children went to bed hungry every night and her old man had walked all day but hadn't been able to get one bit of work. Her cheeks would be flooded with tears, but she didn't make any noise at all. It was as if at that moment her voice had left her body and joined the world of the dead.

For the longest time I didn't know what to do, other than contribute to the situation with the noisy evidence of my own anxiety. Whatever I was learning in the Department of Social Work, if anything at all, I'd forget completely when I went to *La Esperanza* and all I could think of was to show up with a dozen *hayuyas*, a piece of *chanco* cheese, a few slices of ham, a bag of pinto beans, some potatoes, a couple of onions. At the beginning I would spend the bit of money my mom sent me for the bus and other minor expenses; a few weeks later I began to dig into my food allowance until finally, I had to stop because by May fifteenth I had nearly exhausted my monthly stipend.

That evening I decided to go to the cafeteria before taking the bus back home to my grandma's and aunt Amparo's place. I was looking for Miguel, but above all, I was looking for an answer to my dilemma. I felt completely powerless in the face of what I witnessed during my visits to *La Esperanza* and I couldn't get Señora Guillermina and her family off my mind. Everything seemed completely absurd compared to that crude reality. What was the sense in enjoying one of Bach's fugues, understanding the psycho-social experiments of Wilhelm Reich, Karl Marx's analysis of the capitalist system or Simon de Beauvoir's feminist proposals if at the same time there were so many people starving to death?

Raúl and Miguel were having a coffee and right away they knew that something was wrong. Miguel comforted me with hugs and kisses, while Raúl guided me with his words:

"Sol, it doesn't make sense to go hungry yourself so that you can play tricks with the stomachs of Señora Guillermina's children once in a while," he said, while taking my hand. "First, you have to take care of yourself, okay? Your own health is important. Second, you're not solving anything. That situation is the result of years and years of injustices," he added.

"But what can I do, then!?" I cried out in desperations.

"Why don't you become involved in the literacy campaign—that would be a good contribution, something that could lead to many other changes . . ." he offered.

"Yeah . . . But I wouldn't know where to start, what to do" I responded hesitantly.

"Sol, you won't be doing it alone—the Federation is already holding workshops in many shanty towns around Santiago. I'll let the people in charge know that you are interested and they'll help you set the program up in *La Esperanza*," he concluded, as he got up and put his coat on.

"Okay . . . Sure . . ." I replied, wondering how it would all work, questioning in my mind the importance of learning how to read and write when you didn't have enough food to eat, a place to live, a job . . . But I decided to give it a shot.

Pastor, an arts and literature student, was in charge of the literacy campaign in the South end of Santiago. The following week, he took me on the back of his motorcycle to *La Esperanza*. This time, I was empty-handed and, on our way there, I explained my discomfort to Pastor. In response, when we arrived at Señora Guillermina's shack, my new friend took paper and pencil crayons out of his bag and produced a series of pictures for the kids: toothless cows with a daisy behind their ears, traveling ants wearing wide-brimmed hats while they carried leather suitcases in their tiny hands, zigzagging polka-dotted caterpillars with lumpy shoes on their feet. The children couldn't stop laughing and then had great fun drawing their own creations with Pastor's materials.

Señora Guillermina and Don Arnulfo told us that neither one had ever gone to school, but along the way she had learned to read a few things here and there, and Don Arnulfo was good with numbers, though not at all with letters. When we explained about the literacy campaign promoted by the Student Federation in shanty towns around Santiago, they took an immediate interest. The kids were sent out to pass the word around and a while later we were a group of more than twenty people sitting on pieces of cardboard and newspaper around a bonfire.

At the beginning, you could only hear the crackling of the fire and the children's giggles. Then, Señora Guillermina began to tell the odyssey of the family's journey to Santiago, their hope for a better life, the tragedy of their baby Manuelita, the desperation of not having work, food, or a decent house to live in. Everybody nodded, their hands extended towards the fire, their mouths closed tight, their eyes, downcast. But, little by little, other stories, other preoccupations began to emerge and rise over the filigree of smoke, first in whispers, then like a chorus of common understandings and coincidences. From that circle of voices, we got the first word that would serve as a starting point for our educational work: *casa*—"house."

On Saturday mornings, Pastor and I would arrive in *La Esperanza* at around ten o'clock. During the winter months, we used Señora

Guillermina's place as our meeting place, but as soon as the weather improved, we held our learning circles outdoors. The kids would help us to pitch a few poles and we'd build an improvised awning with a couple of old sheets I brought from home. There we'd settle and would start to read and talk with whoever wanted to take part.

Pastor made a compilation of Latin American and Spanish poetry and one afternoon, at the Federation of Students' office, I spent a few hours cutting the stencils and mimeographing fifteen copies of the booklet we named "Word Masons." That's how, for the first time in their lives, the dwellers of *La Esperanza* had the opportunity to read or hear the words of Gabriela Mistral, Pablo Neruda, Alfonsina Storni, Federico García Lorca, Antonio Machado and Juana de Ibarburú.

A few weeks later, some of the participants began to bring their own poems. With downcast eyes they'd hand us a shaky sheet of paper and ask us to read it to the group. The words buzzed between the columns of dust, while everybody widened their eyes and half-opened their mouths as if yearning to be nourished by those words, caravans of bandy-legged little spiders, carriers of so many emotions. Several years later, when the Allende government created the Quimantú Publishing House, some of those poems made it into an anthology of popular poetry with an introduction by Pablo Neruda.

Conclusion

I came to understand the connection between language and activism many years ago through my work in adult literacy and also through my readings. From Paulo Freire and the popular education movement I learned that language is not a neutral tool for communication, but rather a loaded weapon; that the oppressors have used it since time immemorial to keep large sectors of the population subdued and to explain and justify their actions; that the oppressed can and do use it as a tool for liberation: to name the world, reflect upon it, narrate their stories, give shape to their memories, express their ideas, and articulate the actions *they* can take so as to build a more equitable society.

All over the planet and through the centuries, the oppressors have done everything in their power to stop the voices of those who expose their opprobrious practices and put forth divergent views. They have monopolized the media and used it to conceal or distort the facts, misinform the public, and outright lie. They have used overt and covert censorship. When these kinds of methods have not been sufficient—like during the Chilean dictatorship—they haven't hesitated to resort to unmitigated repression: imprisonment, torture, and murder, not to mention the burning of thousands of books in public places.

However, the voices of dissent have never stopped. The oppressed and—to echo Paulo Freire's words—those of us who have suffered and fought at their side, have always managed to assert our views, tell our stories, sing our victories, and lament our losses. Everywhere and at all times, we have used our words to protest, remember, bear witness, denounce, provoke, and propose.

For me, writing and activism, then, go hand in hand. To write is to use the tool, the weapon called language in pursuit of justice so that horror can turn into beauty, shame into dignity, and deceit into truth.

Notes

I would like to thank Arsenal Pulp Press for allowing me to reprint selections from *and a body to remember with* (1997) and Women's Press Literary for allowing me to reprint selections from *Guerra Prolongada/Protracted War* (1992) and *Retribution* (2011).

1. Given that Carmen Rodríguez lives and works in Canada, she uses Canadian English expressions and spelling in her writing. However, for consistency, her chapter has been rendered in U.S. English.

References

Flores, Angel, and Kate. 1984. *Poesía Feminista del Mundo Hispánico*. Ciudad de México: Siglo Veintiuno Editores.

Freire, Paulo. 1972. *Pedagogy of the Oppressed*. New York: Herder and Herder.

———. *Education for Critical Consciousness*. 1974. New York: Seabury.

Mistral, Gabriela. 1955. *Antología*. Santiago: Empresa Editora Zig-Zag.

Rodríguez, Carmen. 1992. *Guerra Prolongada/Protracted War*. Toronto: Women's Press.

———. *and a body to remember with*. 1997. Vancouver: Arsenal Pulp Press.

———. *Retribution*. 2011. Toronto: Women's Press Literary.

Romero, María, editor. *Poesía Universal (Grandes Poemas)*. 1957. Santiago: Empresa Editora Zig-Zag.

Seminar on Feminism and Culture in Latin America. 1990. *Women, Culture, and Politics in Latin America*. Berkeley: University of California Press.

Storni, Alfonsina. 1977. *Antología poética*. Buenos Aires: Editorial Losada.

2

ABSENCE IN MEMORIES

Reading Stories of Survival in Argentina

MAHALA LETTVIN

I first learned of the U.S.-supported human rights violations occurring in the 1970s and 1980s in Latin America duing my time as an undergraduate student at the University of Washington Bothell. As I researched the atrocities, I attempted to understand how these shocking events had been withheld from my public school education. Although requirements for course work placed a heavy demand on my time, I made every effort to dedicate my research projects and "free" time to reading testimonies of survivors. These testimonies occurred throughout scholarly articles to demonstrate an author's argument, or alternatively in anthologies, poetry books, novels, short stories, art, sculptures, and political and social groups. Reading testimonies would elicit emotional connections between my own identity and the extremely troublesome subject matter I encountered. Through these testimonials I was forced to place myself within these historical events, asking questions related to my own ignorance, the public school education I received, and the culture of oblivion I had grown comfortable in. I dedicated my personal and academic ventures to learning about the events that had been withheld from my understanding. I was accepted to the Summer Institute in the Arts and Humanities where students pursued individual research projects through a lens of Borderlands. One afternoon, I was sipping coffee with a friend as we commiserated about our struggles to keep up with readings, the density of the subject matter, and our shared anxieties surrounding the impending due date for our research papers. She asked, "So has this summer influenced your plans for grad school at all?" Like all previous encounters with this question, I avoided answering, delicately maneuvering the conversation to focus instead on her plans, "I haven't really decided yet, what about you?" She explained that although she loved engaging in classroom discussions, she did not want to go to graduate school because she perceived a disconnect between academia and the real world. She went on to say that instead of *just* reading and writing, she wants to be an active part of the change that scholars only write about. Her response was, I believe, a typical notion surrounding academia, an idea that has indeed influenced my perception on the importance of the various research projects I have embarked upon. My friend's response forced me to think about why my education mattered—why my GPA mattered, why I battled with childcare in order to attend classes, why over the past twelve years I had struggled to obtain a degree that hypothetically should have taken four. More importantly, it forced me to consider what consequences reading had on actively doing something—in essence how reading becomes activism.

Shortly after this conversation with my friend, Professor Julie Shayne asked me to contribute this chapter to her book using research I had conducted with her in the year prior; she asked me to frame the chapter through the lens of "reading as activism." I was confronted with the issues that were previously brought up in a casual conversation and asked to respond in a way that mattered: a way that situated my position as a reader as somehow important, as somehow not at all disconnected from the real world. After all, the research I conducted dealt specifically with memories of women survivors of the dirty war in Argentina, a traumatic reality for tens of thousands of Argentines in the 1970s and 80s. This chapter engages with the crucial ways in which memories act as a tool of resistance and thus how reading stories of survival is indeed very much connected to the real world.

Introduction

The dirty war (1976–1983) was a period of institutionalized violence led by General Jorge Videla. Systematic exclusionary methods were imposed on the left wing opposition, or "subversives" as the government classified them. Ridding the nation of subversives would, in the government's eyes, cleanse the country of the "Marxist cancer" that threatened the status quo and deconstructed the power dynamics that perpetuated inequality. The Process of National Reorganization, as it was called, terrorized the country into submission under the guise of disarming violent left-wing guerrillas. In reality, those that the government targeted included any civilian with real or suspected ties to the leftist movements: clergy; human rights activists; lawyers; political party organizers; union activists; professors, students, educators, and the books they wrote and read; generally anyone who merely sympathized with or was perceived to have somehow provided aid to the leftist political movements. In fact "subversive thought," meaning simply an inclination that there was a relation to leftist ideology (Dworkin 1986, xiii), was evidence enough for the military to target these civilians. The state-sanctioned violence caused an estimated thirty thousand *desaparecidos* (disappearances). In addition, the systematic kidnapping of children—either those children whose parents were detained or those born in detainment centers—resulted in an estimated five hundred children being raised by individuals who contributed to the death of the children's biological parents. Clandestine detention centers emerged to torture, intimidate, and eventually disappear those suspected of anti-government ideology. In combination with the extreme restrictions placed on citizens of Argentina, the methods implemented during the dirty war sought to physically exclude subversives from the country, while intimidating the rest of the nation into silence. Merely participating in society created suspicion; therefore, silence became a necessary means for survival. The climate of terror prevented voices from being heard; therefore, stories were not written or told, or, if they were it was at great risk. The pages that follow contain stories of surviving the dirty war in Argentina. When looking to the memories, the silences mandated by the dictatorship are ultimately represented via absences. That is, what we do not read is as illustrative of the violence and repression as that which is explicitly articulated. These absences function in a variety of contexts with wide-ranging purposes. We will see literary absence in the short stories of author Alicia Partnoy, as well as spatial and metaphorical absences in a few of Argentina's memorial projects. Reading these memories highlights the fact that absences function not just as residual silence due to widespread censorship but also as ways to allow claims to identities that were long excluded from society.

I begin by providing the analytical framework through which I understand and examine the memory productions discussed throughout this chapter. Specifically, I outline the intersections of theoretical concepts on memory and identity and the ways absence can be included in these concepts. I then examine memories in Argentine author Alicia Partnoy's collection of short stories, *The Little School: Tales of Disappearance and Survival* (1986/1998).[1] Here, the gendered nature of absences in memory is highlighted as women were systematically abused and tortured both because of and through their sexual anatomy. These discussions are meant to frame absence both as an expected characteristic of women (submissive, silent, invisible) and as a tool of communication (using absence or silence as resistance). *The Little School* narrates absence in both these ways. I then examine theories that link memory to historical truths and national identities. Memory projects construct absence for purposes of either perpetuating exclusion or alternatively as a way of continuing and encouraging collective memory processes. I analyze Argentina's state-sponsored memory park, Parque de la Memoria; a grassroots memorial site, Club Atlético; and an organization influencing museum culture, Memoria Abierta. Through the readings of these stories, in the form of written texts and memory sites, I attempt to locate and highlight the multiple forms and functions of absences within memories of the dirty war.

When studying the repressive regime and the subsequent attempts for democratic reconciliations, theorists tend to focus discussions on collective memory or the ways in which individual memories define a shared history, collective identity, and signification for the present (e.g., Huyssen 1995; Jelin 2002/2003; Olick and Robbins 1998). This research analyzes a small selection of memories that emerged after the dirty war, including both written stories and the stories told by memory projects. These memories are performances of identities; identities that were excluded during and after the repression. Stuart Hall's (1990) theory surrounding diaspora and cultural identities provides insight into understanding the complexities of intersecting memories and identities. Hall describes identity processes as a positioning within narratives of the past, rather than an achievement fixed in time and space: "Far from being eternally fixed in some essentialised past, [identities] are subject to the continuous 'play' of history, culture and power. Far from being grounded in a mere 'recovery' of the past, which is waiting to be found, and which when found, will secure our sense of ourselves into eternity, identities are the names we give to the different ways we are positioned by, and position ourselves within, the narratives of the past" (225). In other words, identity is an ever-changing process of positioning ourselves, and being positioned by others. Identities are not static, fixed arrivals at some understanding of ourselves. Rather, they are influenced by changes in time, location, interpretations, and social actors who contribute to forming a collective memory and identity. Memories—through storytelling, textual recounts, parks, museums, and other representation—are essentially performances of identity, serving as claims of our own positions within our own narratives or narratives of others. As described by Ron Eyerman (2004), "memory provides individuals and collectives with a cognitive map, helping orient who they are, why they are here, and where they are going. Memory in other words is central to individual and collective identity" (161). In the case of Argentina, claims to identity become a negotiation with state powers seeking to exclude subversive identities. The authoritarian rule targeted subversives and robbed them of their identities through systematic physical and psychological torture. Further, despite Argentina's attempts to reconcile with the past through the new democracy's pleas for forgiveness, identities remain absent, buried in the ruins of institutionalized violence perpetuated by a culture of oblivion.

Understanding memories as claims to identity necessitates "absence" as an analytical tool. Although much has been written about the way absence functions in music, speech, discourse, and so on,[2] absence in the case of remembering Argentina's dirty war is particularly telling, not only of the violent censorship imposed on a nation but also of the way absence can represent the unrepresentable and thus serve as intentional resistance to the imposed silence. In Argentina's case, where identities were violently excluded, identity processes depend on locating and representing this absence. These absences are both a tool of resistance and a tool of repression. I take each up in turn. Throughout this chapter, memories are analyzed with an eye toward the absence constructed within, with particular attention to the ways in which this absence either encourages or further excludes identity processes.

The Little School, by Alicia Partnoy

Memories often materialize in textual recounts of trauma. In this section the literary styles in *The Little School: Tales of Disappearance and Survival* (1986/1998) by Argentine author Alicia Partnoy are analyzed. The book is a collection of twenty short stories documenting Partnoy's imprisonment in the Little School, one of Argentina's 250 detainment centers. Partnoy has also published collections of poetry, *Little Low Flying/Volando bajito* (2005) and *Revenge of the Apple/Venganza de la manzana* (1992). Partnoy is also editor of the anthology of literature and testimonials from Latin American women exiles entitled *You Can't Drown the Fire: Latin American Women Writing in Exile* (1988). From 2003 through 2008 she was coeditor of *Chicana/Latina Studies: The Journal of Mujeres Activas en Letras y Cambio Social.* She is now faculty at Loyola Marymount University in Los Angeles (Agosín 2005). In addition, Partnoy provided testimony to the Argentine Commission for the Investigation of Disappearances and indeed took great risks to aid in the prosecution of military torturers. Clearly, despite the government's best efforts, Partnoy was not silenced, and in fact she has done much to assure her voice is heard. She chose to make her personal stories public and suffered (the real or imagined) threat of censorship and punishment after government-imposed silence. Recall that Argentina's authoritarian government defined subversives using broad language to include those individuals thought to have even the smallest inclination of antigovernment thought. These inclinations could, and often did, lead to torture and disappearance. This fear, especially when combined with experiences of detention and torture, left residual anxieties in much of the population. Self-imposed silence was used as a tool for survival. However, Partnoy published her short stories just three years after the official end of the dirty war, risking her own life to share her story and, by extension, her fellow prisoners' stories. Before analyzing the absence within her stories, it is crucial to understand the way women, like Partnoy, were treated in prison.

Women's experiences during the dirty war were particularly brutal. The military government in Argentina attempted to eradicate the so-called threat of Marxism. In order to do so effectively, those who were captured were tortured, threatened, and otherwise manipulated into providing information on political organizations, names of other subversives, and addresses of political party leaders. That is, torture was used as a tool to derive any information that would lead to the arrest and disappearance of more subversives in order to reorganize the nation. If prisoners refused to share information, they were subjected to unrelenting torture to break them into speaking. As Chilean anthropologist Ximena Bunster (1993) explains, women were targeted for their public involvement in antigovernment demonstrations or because of their mere (actual or suspected) relation to male subversives. Based on her research in Argentina, Chile, and Uruguay, Bunster provides a disturbingly detailed account of torture directed toward women. Arguing that a woman's torture was more excruciating because methods were systematically directed toward her sexual identity and anatomy, Bunster details the extreme torture inflicted to manipulate and break a woman by way of "playing" upon her role as a selfless mother and thus her expected sympathy for others. Torture began upon arrest, where often women were humiliated and detained in front of their young children and other family members. Transported, blindfolded, and registered at one of the many detainment camps, women were then physically and psychologically tortured. In addition to the inhumane living conditions inside detainment centers, women suffered the military torturer's attempt to break them through forcing detainees to witness the rape of pregnant prisoners, delivering information that the captive's family and friends had been killed (whether true or not), threatening disappearance/murder (in many cases, following through with the threat), torturing the captives' children or other family members, directing electric prods toward her genitalia, raping her, and imposing other heinous forms of torture.

Argentina's state-solicited National Commission on the Disappearance of Persons (CONAPED), a group that collected testimonies of survivors and family members, published an "official" version of truth (examined in greater detail below) which speaks to the torture systematically directed toward women. Carlos Alberto Campero's (file No. 1806)[3] testimony exemplifies the play upon motherhood/womanhood:

> My mother was taken to the shop and, threatening her life, [the military] beat her in a way that should not even be used on wild animals. In the shop we had a ventilator fan . . . and [they] used it to give her electric shocks. . . . [W]hile they were committing this savagery, another one of them was hitting her with a belt until her body was bleeding and her face disfigured. After some considerable time they decided to take us all with them, except for the six-month old Viviana, who was left behind with Griselda, my thirteen-year old sister. (Comisíon 1984, 18)

Campero highlights not only the physical torture, but also the psychological torture of a mother knowing her children are witnessing this savagery. Being a female prisoner during these times magnified the marginalization of women because the physical torture methods were directed against her sexual anatomy, and the psychological torture played upon her prescribed role as selfless mother and caretaker. The systematic torture directed toward suspected subversives was an extension of patriarchal society which heightened the masculine military as the supreme dominant force over others (Jelin 2002/2003). The authoritarian governments exerted their power through silencing the "others," rendering them invisible, breaking their physical bodies, and denying them self-identification. Memories of these brutal tortures and attempts of exclusion often emerge through absences. I turn now to the literary absence as articulated in the works of Alicia Partnoy.

The symbolic and poetic absences that Partnoy narrates throughout her stories emerge as representations of her own identity processes, as well as a collective identity of a nation. Absences inherent in her stories demand that readers position themselves in Partnoy's narratives. In analyzing her stories, I note two elements of absence. The first is Partnoy's use of "narrating the other" (Jelin 2002/2003)[4] in order to represent those who can no longer represent themselves (the thirty thousand disappeared, many of whom were detained with Partnoy in the Little School). Through this literary style, absence emerges as an omission of personal details and a focus on others' experiences. The second element of absence is the lack of details in her stories, especially apparent when compared with the aforementioned detailed accounts of torture provided by Bunster (1993). One can assume that Partnoy experienced torture similar to Bunster's description; however, those details are absent from her stories, even when it would seem somehow appropriate or strategic to write of the torture endured. As opposed to "narrating the other," this absence is all encompassing, and rather than providing details of others' experiences, this absence fails to provide any detail at all. Absences throughout Partnoy's work represent identity as a process based on collective significations.

As mentioned previously, women and men had different experiences during war. Similarly, there are also certain cultural and social norms that influence the way memories are narrated. Here, I rely on Jelin's (2002/2003) theory regarding engendered memories:

> In the case of memories of repression, moreover, many women narrate their memories in the context of their more traditional gender role, that of caregiver and nurturer, of "living for others." This is linked to the definition of an identity centered on tending to and caring for others, generally within the frame of family relations. The ambiguity of the position, between that of active agent and that of passive companion and caretaker, may show up then in a displacement of their own identity, prompting them to "narrate the other." (83)

As we know, torturers played upon women's assigned concern for others, by torturing the prisoner's children, families, friends, and fellow activists. This play upon a woman's motherhood and womanhood was used as a specific torture mechanism and can be translated into the way in which women remember as well. Women tend to focus narratives on the experience of others, "negating or silencing testimony about her own life experiences" (Jelin 2002/2003, 83). Below, I borrow from Jelin's concept of "narrating the other" to show the ways in which Partnoy narrates the traumatic absence of the disappeared.

In *The Little School*, narrating the other presents a challenge because prisoners were punished severely for attempting any mode of communication. The prisoners were blindfolded, and little if any human contact was permitted, save the physical torture. Because of this imposed silence, there is minimal dialogue when Partnoy narrates her experience in the Little School. Despite this silence, the reader is able to understand the bonds between prisoners: the loyalty, friendship, and love that persisted in an environment that sought to destroy any trace of compassion. Narrating the other, then, is arguably more laborious because of the lack of dialogue. In other words, if Partnoy herself did not live through the experiences of others, and further if she was unable to witness their experiences, what mechanisms allow her to pay tribute to their memory? Partnoy's decision to focus on others' memories through narrating the other allows for collective memory, hers and others'.

Throughout these short stories, readers may find it difficult to differentiate between narrators. For example, the story "Graciela: Around the Table" chronicles the infamous treatment of pregnant prisoners, ranging from electric prods to the abdomen, to "allowing" exercise by walking around the table while blindfolded. If it was not for the title of the story, the reader would remain uncertain about who is narrating the story, as the voice throughout these stories seems to transition and flow as if it were one. The story does mention the narrator by name, through the voice of the husband, who is being tortured. Upon realizing his wife is witnessing his torture, he whispers "'be strong, Graciela. Take heart. Do it for Adrianita . . . for the baby'" (55). This is an indication that Graciela is the narrator. Graciela (through Partnoy's writing) ends the story by talking to her child, "Don't forgive them, my child. Don't forgive this table, either" (56). The ability of Partnoy to fragment her own experience with those of Graciela is remarkable. The transition of voices, the narrating of the other, is not immediately apparent, also illustrated in the story titled "Nativity." It begins: "'Sir, when's the doctor coming?' The labor pains and contractions are almost constant, very close together. This child wants to get out. What will they do to me after it's born? They've said they'll transfer me to a regular prison where I'll be able to take care of the baby. I'm scared" (119).

Again, there is no indication that the narrator has changed; the passage merely introduces the reader to the scene of birth in captivity, without explaining the context or the change in narrator. As the story continues, the birth of the child is nearing but is interrupted by the military guards complaining about headaches, relationships with their superiors, and not being able to find a doctor to assist with the prisoner in labor. The narrator reclaims the story after the guard's disrupting conversation, "He's pushing . . . Don't take him away . . . If only I could keep my baby inside . . . Ugh . . . Now I have to push, if I don't it hurts more. If we could survive, my child, if we survive . . ." (121). Immediately after this plea to her child, the narrator's voice changes, although, again, it is not immediately apparent. Upon a closer reading, it seems Partnoy is narrating the final passage: "A new cry makes its way through the shadows fighting above the trailer. Graciela has just given birth. A prisoner child has been born. While the killers' hands welcome him into the world, the shadow of life leaves the scene, half a winner, half a loser; on her shoulders she wears a poncho of injustice. Who knows how many children are born every day at the Little School?" (121). The above words could be that of any prisoner at the Little School. The transitions from one voice to another would otherwise exist to fragment narratives, but in Partnoy's poetic and flowing language, the voices unify, becoming one. The above passage not only ends the story, but contains the final words in the collection of stories. However, the words indicate anything but finality. Partnoy strategically placed this story at the end for two reasons: first, the voices were changed numerous times throughout the story which gave it an all-encompassing inclusion of stories from everyone involved, and second, the story ends with a question about life and the impossibility of arriving at any fixed conclusion or official version of events. Graciela's fate is never revealed through the stories; she gave birth in captivity, and the story with a question.[5] Indeed, in doing so, Partnoy narrates in the voice she intended, to the "generation of Argentines lost in an attempt to bring social change and justice" (18). Partnoy indicates she wrote these stories in order to represent the thousands of Argentines lost, and it is clear that she succeeds in doing so through absence: omitting personalized stories and detailed torture scenes, and instead highlighting the narratives of others. The poetic transition between these different experiences becomes one, narrating a collective memory and the spaces for additional memories and identities to emerge.

Absence emerges not only in narrating the other, but also in the absence created by Partnoy's intentional omission of details and fragmented style surrounding her own experience. This absence demands that readers posit their own interpretations to fill in the gaps of what is not being written. Jelin (2002/2003) discusses the many different forms of forgetting, where definitive forgetting defines the erasure of the past and evasive forgetting avoids recalling potentially upsetting memories (18–19). This evasive forgetting is present in Partnoy's short stories, but rather than avoiding upsetting memories, Partnoy highlights them by relying on the absence of words to describe them.

The chapter entitled "Toothbrush" describes a scene where the prisoners at the Little School are given orders to brush their teeth. They are each given a toothbrush, which seems absurd because moments before "he [the military torturer, Vaca] entered the room again and put a gun in my mouth" (81). After describing the process of lining up to brush their teeth, the story ends, "Today at noon, they took away the brushes. A while ago, Vaca entered our room and pointed a gun at my temple. I felt the cold of the metal. 'It's loaded,' he said. 'Are you scared?'" (82). The chapter ends abruptly, leaving the reader with an image of impending death. Immediately following this unsettling ending, the next story, "Bread," begins describing, in spectacular detail, the portions of bread allotted to prisoners, the ways in which the narrator savors the little balls of bread she creates, the taste, and the unspoken sharing rituals between prisoners. The story "Toothbrush" is never revisited. Partnoy never describes what happened after Vaca pointed the gun and threatened her. She never describes a feeling of relief, nor the fear during the incident. She presents the experience as fact and abruptly, without transition, maneuvers the readers' attention to bread. Partnoy intentionally leaves out the details of the incident surrounding Vaca's threats to allow her personal narrative to become collective. The absence that is narrated into this story demands that readers ask questions: What happened to Vaca? Did he shoot another prisoner? Why didn't he shoot Partnoy? Why wasn't this story revisited? Did something else happen that was too painful to recall? All these questions, and more, are necessary for allowing collective identity within Partnoy's stories. Partnoy's work embodies many elements of collective memory. Absence is written both to function as representation for the unrepresentable and to give voice to the disappeared Thus, through these literary absences, Partnoy's stories provide a collective memory and encourage ongoing identity process.

Through what Partnoy writes, but mainly through what she does not write, I was forced to locate myself within these narratives. Where do I fit in to this story? What role did my privilege of *not* living through any comparable experience contribute to how I interpreted and read it? Maybe the absences represented experiences and memories that I simply could not and will not have; the memories intended for only Partnoy or only those who lived through it. The first time I finished reading *The Little School* I knew I was not done. Though this desire to keep reading does not alone indicate that I am an activist, I do know that reading her stories made it impossible for me to stop learning about these atrocities, often perpetuated in my name. Partnoy's story contained many different forms of absence, those literary absences described above, and also for me personally, the absence of my previous knowledge was highlighted as I confronted my own position in these events. I turn now to a different sort of reading of memories by discussing the stories in memorial projects put forth by both the State and a few grassroots organizations.

Representations of Memory

Though women deserve credit for much of the memory projects in Argentina,[6] in this section I move away from a gendered analysis and focus on memorials and national projects. Memorials are visual and physical texts, and through the narratives put forth by these projects, we are able to read the stories being told. In this section I discuss three prominent memory projects in Argentina and the absences inherent in them. These absences serve either as a perpetuation of systematic exclusion or alternatively, as a platform for self-representations. I begin by looking at the state-organized Parque de la Memoria, to show how the "ownership of memory" (Jelin 2002/2003) can perpetuate exclusion. I then address two grassroots projects, Club Atlético and Memoria Abierta, both of which intentionally construct absence not to further exclude identities, but rather to encourage and highlight identity as ongoing processes.

Attempts to memorialize the past are often exemplary of the powers of the state. In Argentina, the state dictated an official story and encouraged collective efforts to come to terms with the past in order to secure a more peaceful future. President Raul Alfonisín was democratically elected in 1983 and established the National Commission on the Disappeared (CONAPED), which published fifty thousand pages of investigation into the human rights violations during the dirty war. The report was published in a book, titled *Nunca Más* (in English, *Never Again*) and translated into five different languages which sold over five hundred thousand copies by 2008 (Crenzel n.d., 1). Ernesto Sábato led the commission and wrote in the prologue to the publication: "It is with sadness and sorrow that we have carried out the mission entrusted to us by the constitutional President of the Republic. It has been an extremely arduous task, for we had to piece together a shadowy jigsaw, years after the events had taken place, when all the clues had been deliberately destroyed, all documentary evidence burned, and buildings demolished" (Comisíon 1984, 5). Here Sábato indicates that the fragments of testimonials relied upon in their investigation are nowhere near able to portray a complete narrative of the past. The deliberate destruction of evidence, fear instilled in a people, and forced silences prevented testimony from being offered. This contributes to the culture of oblivion that makes reading stories all the more important: to combat the forgetting that seeks to silence and negate stories, memories, and identities.

Historian Thomas Wright (2007) points out that the governments' efforts in creating truth reports limited history to include only "the most egregious crimes: murder and disappearance. This approach . . . implicitly suggested that indiscriminate detentions, torture, rape, and forced exile were unimportant" (35). Dominating, institutionalized narratives of the past essentially determined what was important and what was not, but in doing so encouraged an ongoing dialogue about what happened. When I first learned of the truth report in Argentina, I perceived a closure in my research. I figured that since the government acknowledged the past and provided a space for testimonies to be heard, the labors of current memory work were less important than if this report was not published. As shown throughout the discussions below, however, despite state attempts to provide official stories and monuments of truth, these attempts often exemplify power dynamics and thus perpetuate the exclusion experienced during the dirty war.

Parque de la Memoria

In 1998, proposals to build a memory park in Buenos Aires were approved, and by 2001, the Parque de la Memoria was complete. The three years between the initial acceptance of the proposal and the actual construction of the park were spent entertaining international competitions, with over 650 sculptors from all geographic areas submitting their work (Dolf-Bonekämper 2002, 6). However, the Parque de la Memoria does not represent the past as intended because absence is not purposefully and meaningfully constructed. Instead, its absence functions as a tool of furthering repression and excluding identities, as explained below.

The Parque de la Memoria, though not constructed on land directly associated with the dirty war, is located right next to the Río de la Plata. The river's proximity is perhaps the only connection to the past the park seeks to memorialize. Dworkin (1986), in introducing CONAPED's investigations into the disappearances, describes the significance of the river and bodies of water in general: "Disposing of the bodies presented a tactical problem. First they were buried in mass unmarked pits, but later a more efficient final solution was discovered. The disappeared were loaded into planes with an open door, flown over the sea and then thrown out. Most of them were first drugged or killed, but some were alive and conscious when they left the plane" (Dworkin 1986, xvii). For many then, the park's direct proximity to the *Río de la Plata* represents a burial ground for bodies that have not been recovered or accounted for. This relation is important, as the government at the time denied any responsibility or knowledge of the whereabouts of the tens of thousands of disappeared. Therefore, to have a park close to the river that was funded by the new Argentine democracy was significant for many of those wishing to have a physical location to mourn the loss of their loved ones. But this attempt to commemorate the past and the victims of the dirty war seems superficial at best, as the river's proximity is the only significance in the location of the park, and indeed the only significance of the park as a whole. The absence inherent in this lack of meaning can be best explained under the term “ownership of memory.” This ownership is an extension of patriarchal society and further prevents self-representations. This ownership is best described by Jelin (2002/2003):

> Practices of commemoration and the attempts to establish memory sites always involve political struggles. The principal adversaries in these conflicts are, on the one hand, the social forces that demand markers of memory and, on the other, those who seek to erase these markers on the basis of rendering a narrative of the past that minimizes or eliminates the meaning of what the others wish to remember. There are also confrontations over the “appropriate” forms or means of remembering, as well as over which actors have legitimacy to act, that is who has the (symbolic) “truth” or the power to decide the contents of the memory to be conveyed. These conflicts can be discussed under the label of the issue of the “ownership” of memory. (43)

The Argentine state attempted to own memories by dictating what memories were represented, thereby determining which memories were authentic, true, and important. The memorial that claimed to signify the suffering of the nation’s recent past instead provided a master narrative, disallowing diverse stories, identities, and memories to exist in conversation with the state’s story in the park.

In addition, the park solicited international artists to contribute to the structures and aesthetics of the memorial. Despite this strategy increasing awareness about Argentina’s bloody past, the decision to compensate international artists also disallowed Argentina’s own citizens who suffered through the dirty war to contribute their memories and identities. The lack of symbolism in the location along with the solicited international contributions, seems to indicate more of an aesthetic and politically calculated project rather than a genuine attempt to memorialize the past. Indeed, the park truly highlights the ownership of memory, not only through the State’s power in creating the memorial, but also through the memories themselves being taken from survivors and given instead to international artists.

National monuments and state-sponsored memory projects have been discussed by many scholars. Particularly with regards to the ownership of memory, these projects often discredit the diverse stories, experiences, and identities by dictating an official story of what actually happened. The construction of Argentina’s park is part of a larger global trend attempting to fix memories in the past. Scholars have debated about the many issues inherent in state-sponsored monuments. Andreas Huyssen (1995) discusses some of these controversies:

> The museum emerged as the paradigmatic institution that collects, salvages and preserves that which has fallen to the ravages of modernization. But in doing so, it inevitably will construct the past in light of the discourses of the present and in terms of present-day interest. Fundamentally dialectical, the museum serves both as burial chamber of the past—with all that entails in terms of decay, erosion, forgetting-and as a site of possible resurrections, however mediated and contaminated, in the eyes of the beholder. No matter how much the museum, consciously or unconsciously, produces and affirms the symbolic order, there is always a surplus of meaning that exceeds set ideological boundaries, opening space for reflection and counter-hegemonic memory. (15)

Huyssen points to the larger complexities of memorial sites; in other words the ownership of memory. In creating memorials and museums, there will always be stories not told or the surplus of meaning that simply cannot be represented by memorial projects. However, the state made minimal efforts to combat these difficulties. The park contains open fields scattered with winning proposals of architecture allegedly representing the disappeared. The absence exists both in space and meaning and therefore perpetuates the exclusion experienced by tens of thousands of Argentines.

This type of absence—the absence which fails to incorporate the multilayered truths and diverse stories from events in the past—silences memories that contradict the official story or master narrative of the past. In addition, the location of the park creates no link between Argentina's past and the sculpted representations which might exist if it was, for example, built on the grounds of a former concentration camp or other such site of pertinent memory. There is no visual representation as to the park's purpose. In fact, the Parque de la Memoria made the Project for Public Space's (an online blogging community that focuses on public spaces and their attractions) "Hall of Shame." In his summary of why the park fails, Brian Davis (2012) explains that he nominated it for the Hall of Shame for various reasons: the pathways in the park lead to nothing; there is no space for viewing the breathtaking beauty of the Rio de la Plata; the sculptures are of great size and only recognizable as "self-important" art; it is uninviting; nobody visits; there is a lack of plants, and what plants do exist are simplistic and contained (as Davis eloquently suggests, a good metaphor for the park itself); and there are no participatory elements or activities hosted there. Davis goes on to write that the architecture "seems to be an exercise in hilarity. Surely some silly architect decided to see what expensive and asinine design they could convince someone to build" (2012). Clearly, the space encourages no thought about Argentina's past; Davis himself makes no mention of the intention of the park to serve as a memorial, which he surely would have had he known. The park serves merely as superficial reparation to the Argentine people, but lacks significance both in community involvement and in choice of location. Absences emerge in aesthetical and metaphorical failures. In a way, being constructed so close to the symbolic Rio de la Plata burial ground suits the Parque de la Memoria well, as it too is a burial ground for memory.

Club Atlético

Even in the instances of failed memorials such as the Parque de la Memoria, dominating truths and ideological reparations offered by the state, at the very least encourage conversations about the past and identities (as seen by the truth commissions and the dialogue encouraged by its production). Grassroots movements that incorporate counter-narratives within their structures seem to represent memory in fragmented, contradictory, multilayered truths through the use of absence. Club Atlético, is an unofficial memorial that distinguishes itself from the Parque de la Memoria in many ways. The absence constructed in Club Atlético, rather than excluding stories, allows the space for these stories to be told thereby encouraging identity processes to take place.

Club Atlético was a former concentration camp in Buenos Aires, Argentina, that held up to two hundred people at a time. It was used mainly for the interrogation of prisoners, and it is estimated that approximately fifteen hundred Argentines were detained here. In July 1996, close to five hundred members of human rights organizations and sympathizers gathered at the location and constructed a large papier mâché tree with faces of victims as a public reminder and tribute to those lost. That same night, a firebomb was placed at the memorial. The tree and all those it sought to honor disappeared yet again (Jelin and Kaufman 2000). One year later, in August 1997, human rights organizations again united to build representation of the past (Jelin and Kaufman 2000). The space chosen and the continued obstacles to prevent these memories represent the constant negotiations inherent in processes of identity, memory, and history projects.

Today, the Club has been transformed into an unofficial memorial. Located under a highway overpass, the grassroots construction of this memorial, although lacking in visibility, is illustrative of memorials that seek to encourage dialogue and present contradicting truths. The use of a former detention center provides the building site a direct link to the atrocities of Argentina's past. Gates-Madsen describes the memorial: "The highway support that rises out of the dig is covered with figures that appear to be climbing out of ruins. Other support columns that extend along the street have been covered with graffiti, including poems and drawings that depict faces or bodies in various poses of torment or resistance. . . . Yet despite the fact that the site is aesthetically unattractive, or perhaps precisely because of it, the Club Atlético remains a powerful space for memory" (Gates-Madsen 2011, 163). The site remains an unofficial memorial site for those that disappeared. The memorial introduces and maintains continued conversations about the past through the constructed absence within that further encourages gatherings, rituals, and opportunities to educate citizens. Dolf Bonkämper (2002) describes the ceremonial structure as "a large human figure, outlined on an embankment by metal tubes that can be filled with oil and set on fire to shine light far into the neighborhood" (6).

When comparing the relatively small and unknown Club Atlético to the institutionalized, dominant, and marketed truth contained in the Parque de la Memoria, it is clear that the grassroots origin of the Club Atlético discourages one all-encompassing, static identity. When speaking of museums and memorial projects, Huyssen (1995) refers to the space required to encourage these crucial narratives:

> What needs to be captured and theorized today is precisely the ways in which museum and exhibition culture. . . . can offer multiple narratives of meaning at a time when the metanarratives of modernity, including those inscribed into the universal survey museum itself, have lost their persuasiveness, when more people are eager to hear and see other stories, to hear and see the stories of others, when identities are shaped in multiply layered and never-ceasing negotiations between self and other, rather than being fixed and taken for granted in the framework of family and faith, race and nation. (34)

Indeed, this grassroots memorial inspires and represents memory, truth, and history by acknowledging the fact that there are no fixed histories or unquestionable truths. It serves as a mediator for identity in all forms: personal, national, historical, political, and cultural. Unlike the state-sponsored park, this memorial does not destroy meaning or silence the voices of survivors. Nor does it attempt to own memory or dictate what is important and what is not. Although sponsored by the city in the excavation process, the Club Atlético remains a memorial constructed by the people who wish to remember alternate histories and experiences. As Jelin and Kaufman (2000) point out:

> When the aim [of a memorial or monument] is opposed and blocked by other social forces, the subjectivity and the will of those women and men who are struggling for the monument or memorial come out into the public view, renewing their strength to continue struggling. There is no pause, no rest, because it has not been "deposited" anywhere—it has to remain in the minds and hearts of the people. In a way, the need to turn unique, personal and nontransferable feelings into public and collective meanings is left open and active. (98)

The Club succeeds in representing Argentina's past, paying tribute to the tens of thousands of victims that suffered, but also represents the continued struggle for visibility. The absence constructed within amplifies voices of those otherwise silenced. The Club Atlético represents an urgent need to fight an ongoing political battle in claiming the right for self-representations.

Memoria Abierta

As we have already seen in this chapter, there are varying contexts and purposes of Argentina's memorial projects. In 1999, Memoria Abierta responded to the country's outcry for a museum and memorial. The organization consists of five human rights organizations: Permanent Assembly for Human Rights (APDH), the Center for Social and Legal Studies (CELS), the Argentine Historical and Social Memory Foundation, Mothers of the Plaza de Mayo-Founding Line, and the Peace and Justice Service (SERPAJ) (Asociación 2005–2011). These groups collaborate to advance a collective memory about the state terror that ensued during the dirty war in Argentina. Although Memoria Abierta is not linked to any direct site of conscience, it works with the International Coalition of Sites of Conscience as well as the International Network for Peace to effectively represent former sites of traumatic memories. Memoria Abierta obtains documents, oral archives, and produces educational material. The absence that is explicitly mentioned in the organization's mission statement (in the form of not being able to provide answers to questions) assures that memories and identities previously excluded are made visible and part of a national story.

Memoria Abierta has four main components: Documentary Heritage Program (currently over twenty-five thousand written records have been collected from the dirty war); the Photographic Archive (photographs of human rights organizations documenting the abuses); the Oral Archive (filmed testimonies which include over one thousand hours of footage); and the Topography of Memory (public urban spaces to be used for representing the past, including a map of all former concentration camps and sites of abuse) (Asociación 2005–2011). The organizations also participate in proposals for Argentina's Museum of Memory and in the Coalition of Historic Site Museums of Conscience. Members of Memoria Abierta host events, seminars, and conferences on various issues vital to keeping memory alive.

Memoria Abierta continuously finds ways to work with the state to secure support and provide resources to Argentina's citizens. It publishes educational resources for teachers, a "collection of audiovisual testimonies of witnesses of each period of history, accompanied by newspaper articles, recording of radio broadcasts, photographs, flyers, and other materials" (Guembe 2008, 66). This collection, "On Memory: Testimonies, Texts, and other resources about State-led Terrorism in Argentina," was made available to school teachers, free of charge. The team that produced this resource included historians, educational consultants, specialists, the human rights groups that make up Memoria Abierta, and the Buenos Aires secretary of education (Guembe 2008). Needless to say, Memoria Abierta is dedicated to the education of a new generation of Argentines.

Memoria Abierta, in advancing its mission to educate future generations, communicates and teaches through its website, providing a wealth of resources regarding its work, links to other websites, and access to the information the organization has compiled. Additionally, there is a map of all clandestine detention centers, photographs of objects they have collected representing the dirty war (old clothing, letters, etc.), a catalog of films, archives of oral and written testimonies, and a list of all museums and memory sites in Argentina (Asociación 2005–2011).

Clearly, Memoria Abierta's collective efforts have produced a wealth of accessible information on Argentina's past. Success of this organization is largely attributed to the fact that the organization admits that there are still unanswered questions. In admitting there are no universal truths or correct answers to their complex questions, the organization assures that the past continues to emerge in diverse stories. There are still questions on how to present the material remnants and evidence of Argentina's bloody past, questions that will open "the debate about issues that are still not addressed in public spheres" (Guembe 2008, 67). Maria Guembe (2008) also highlights the obstacle of telling multiple stories as one: "The question is how to tell the story. How can we tell it in such a way that our contribution will not be a unilateral narrative; in such a way that each visitor can find answers, but above all formulate questions that will encourage him or her to participate in a collective debate?" (71).

Telling a singular narrative is obviously not Memoria Abierta's goal. The information it provides needs to be interpreted by others, and in order to transmit a collective knowledge it "need[s] to highlight the connection between the individual and group experience and the fact that many diverse groups were affected by it" (Guembe 2008, 67). In this way, Guembe states, individuals are given the possibility to connect "their own history with the history of many others" (68). The efforts of the organization highlight that history does not belong to one person; it belongs not only to those who were affected, but it belongs to everyone.

Indeed, Memoria Abierta fulfills its mission through underscoring the absence of any one, all-encompassing national memory. The absence of answers allows the space for conflicting, intermingling, and contradicting truths and versions of the past. By focusing on the individual as collective, the organization gives hope in restoring sites like Parque de la Memoria with new meanings that successfully represent the nation's past. With the work of human rights groups, like those working with Memoria Abierta, memories can be represented in ways that do not further exclude stories that do not fit within the official story dictated by those in power. Through the absence of answers to questions posed on how to represent the past, Argentines and others will continue to be able to locate themselves within the multilayered histories and truths.

Concluding Thoughts and Reflections: Memory Labor and Activism

Throughout the dirty war in Argentina, the military government attempted to silence a population into submission. Through threats, torture, imprisonment, disappearances, and censorship, remembering became a subversive act, an act of great risk. And although democracy has now returned to Argentina, the exclusion of memories and identities continues through the ownership of memory, as shown in the state's memorial projects. The idea that remembering and acknowledging the past will prevent further atrocities in the future assumes that all stories have been told, that one truth has been narrated, that somehow this master narrative will act as grounds for forgiveness and movement toward a hopeful, peaceful future. This ownership of memory essentially asks individuals to view their identities as fixed in time and space, rather than a constant set of negotiations and positionalities (Hall 1990). With thirty thousand citizens disappeared and hundreds of thousands of more suffering the repression and loss experienced through violence, coming to terms with the past through one authentic, state-dictated truth is not achievable, nor should it be. There are many stories that have yet to be heard and many that will never be heard. But the absences that are constructed into memories allow the acknowledgment of this fact. The belief of one national truth, or one official story, perpetuates the exclusion suffered by Argentines. However, these dominating memories can be ruptured. These ruptures occur through the absences narrated and constructed through memories. These absences acknowledge the impossibility of arriving at a universal truth or uniform national memory and instead encourage a range of histories for all citizens who (directly or indirectly) suffered at the hands of the state. Constructing, writing, and narrating these absences allow for the wounds of repression to keep bleeding,[7] allow for the past to continue influencing the present, and encourage identities and memories, both individual and collective, to emerge as unfixed processes rather than achievements in coming to terms with the past.

Engaging in this research and reading memories of survivors has changed the way I interpret the world around me and influenced the ways I interact with everyone in my life, including my two small children. Although I did not realize it at the time, throughout the course of this research, I have been confronting my friend's criticism about the disconnect between academia and the real world, mentioned earlier in this chapter. In a binder, I have hundreds of scholarly articles, media printouts, photocopies of book chapters, and pages and pages of notes. On the front of this binder, I collected and pasted photographs that I encountered in this research process. Particularly moving to me were the photographs of the mothers and their babies, before they were kidnapped and taken away from their children; photographs of the babies that were stolen when they were born in detainment centers, often raised by the military torturers responsible for their parents' deaths. These photographs served as reminders of why this research mattered to me, why I was not only interested in learning as much as I could, but also very emotionally connected to these events.

One day, in the midst of impending deadlines, midterm examinations, and an overwhelming amount of reading, laundry, dishes, and bedtime stories to complete, my daughter, Hadassah (Haddie), then just four years old, asked me, "Mom, what is all this paperwork? Why do you have this photograph of a mommy and a cute little baby? Is that me and you—or you and Malachi?" Malachi, my son, two and a half years old at the time, was standing close by, and both children looked to me in anticipation. As they waited for my response, I remembered the pain I felt, the embarrassment, the ignorance that was so apparent when I first learned of these atrocities at twenty-seven years old. I remembered feeling angry, first at everyone else—the public school system and anyone that played any role whatsoever in raising and educating me. And then, perhaps more realistically, I felt angry at myself for not being more informed, for not actively seeking out knowledge about these events when it now seemed so apparent, when it now flooded my news stream, my e-mail, and my thoughts. And I remembered the anger I felt, that has continued to this day, and will continue until the day I can no longer remember.

I looked at my children, and I felt an overwhelming sense of security, knowing they were safe, healthy, and most importantly they were with their mother. I simply could not *not* tell them of these events.

"Once upon a time," I began, "in Argentina there were very mean people who wanted lots of money, and they wanted to tell everyone what to do." As my children listened to me, unusually interested and patient, I explained, as best I could, that the mean people arrested people with different beliefs. And when they arrested them, they were even meaner to them, beating them up, and not letting them eat any food. And so mean," I continued, choosing my words carefully, "that the women that gave birth had their babies taken away from them."

"That's not nice! All mommies love their babies! Where did they get their milk?" My daughter blurted out in a fit of four-year-old rage against the injustices we were both struggling to articulate. Upon explaining a bit more of the history, showing my children where Argentina was on their annoying talking globe, and assuring them that they were safe, my children helped me to understand the importance of reading and learning, inspired me to keep researching, and provided validation to my decision to inform them of such events. Malachi furrowed his brows, crossed his arms, and exclaimed, "I don't like those mean people *at all*! I want to help all babies! We can drive the train there right now and help those babies!"

Haddie agreed, "Those mean people need to be put in jail forever and ever, and I would say to them, 'That behavior is not allowed! You are mean to those babies and everyone who loves them! You will stay in here for the rest of your life and think about what you've done!" And my children, agreeing on what absolutely had to be done, ran into their room and returned moments later—toy handcuffs and a train whistle in hand, and of course their superhero capes tied around their necks—ready to take the train to Argentina to save the babies. Despite their lack of understanding about the time that had passed, or the impossibility of completing this task, my children's perception of injustice was and is very real. Hearing stories of trauma demands that we take action. And though my children and I cannot take the train to Argentina, nor can we handcuff those mean people, we can be informed, and we can plot what we *can* do. This story is not meant to make light of the human rights abuses occurring in Argentina. Nor is it meant to be parenting advice to readers of this chapter. Rather, I believe that this story illustrates how reading (and writing and researching) serves as a vital tool to inspire an activist conscious, to enact justice, to change our perceptions about the world around us and our role in that world.

So, in response to my friend who voiced her concern over the disconnect between academia and the real world, writing this chapter helped me to articulate a response to her concern. Who is to say academia is not part of "the real world?" The stories I read and memories I researched were sadly based on a very traumatic reality, a reality that I only learned about because of my privileged access to academia. Certainly I do not believe that reading and re-reading *The Little School* and the stories in the memorials I have described automatically brings the torturers to justice. I can say, however, that not reading, not identifying the absences, and not scrutinizing the memorials and our positions within them, allows the torturers to continue to operate with an impunity that suggests their actions were completely acceptable and justified. It is not coincidental that books, professors, and students are always targets of military violence. The historical record is replete with images of piles of books being burned and destroyed, images which speak to the power of reading. I know that the reading I have done to learn about the dirty war has permanently changed me and the way I choose to operate in the world, from the way I raise my children to the career I intend to pursue. I also know I have no intention to stop reading these stories from the (sur)real world.

Notes

This research was made possible through the generosity of the University of Washington Bothell Undegraduate Research Award. I would also like to thank my mentor, Professor Julie Shayne, for her encouragement, guidance, expertise, and patience throughout this research. And I thank my parents, Denise and David Lettvin, and my siblings, Moishe, Hosanna, and Avram Lettvin, for listening to me and providing encouragement and inspiration in my academic pursuits. Thanks also to my children, Haddie Josephine and Malachi Jericho Hunt, for being both energetic and accommodating and for being alive.

1. All of the texts I examined have been translated into English.
2. See, for example, Maria-Luisa Achino Loeb, ed. *Silence: The Currency of Power* (New York: Berghahn Books, 2006); Patrick Fuery, *The Theory of Absence: Subjectivity, Signification, and Desire* (Westport, CT: Greenwood, 1995); Helene Carol Weldt-Basson, *Subversive Silences: Nonverbal Expression and Implicit Narrative Strategies in the Work of Latin American Women Writers* (Cranbury, NJ: Associated University Presses, 2009).
3. The work of CONAPED was translated into several different languages. Here, I am relying on the translation provided by Writers and Scholars International Ltd.
4. The word "other" in the context of "narrating the other" refers to a person besides oneself. It should not be confused with the sociological definition meaning the denial of self-representation.
5. It should be noted that although the stories do not indicate the fate of Graciela and her baby, or any prisoner for that matter, Partnoy writes in her introduction, "This past summer I met Adriana, the daughter of Graciela and Raul. When her grandparents visited the authorities to request information about their children, this girl, then four years old, furiously pounded the table and demanded, 'Sir, give me back my parents and my little brother!'" (Partnoy, 18). Partnoy's introduction seems to present the facts on which her stories are based. Despite her taking the opportunity to provide this context, note that she still relies on narrating the other, through the voice of Adriana, to indicate the disappearance of Graciela and Raul.
6. Many human rights organizations including the Mothers and the Grandmothers of the Plaza de Mayo, took active roles in remembering. The cultural productions resulting from women's organizations are detailed on the Abuelas De Plaza De Mayo website, http://www.abuelas.org as well as previous scholarship. See for example, Arditti, Rita *Searching for life: The Grandmothers of the Plaza de Mayo and the Disappeared Children of Argentina* (Los Angeles: University of California Press, 1999).
7. "Bleeding the wounds" was a phrase that commonly emerged throughout my research. I first encountered this saying from an interview with Argentine author Alicia Kozameh who wrote *Steps*

under Water in 1987. In an online interview, she speaks of her intention in fragmenting the novel, "I feel the need to jump from one thing to another; probably in order not to be invaded by an emotional state that would not even allow me to express myself in writing. I think that the origin of the fragmented literature has to do with a determined capacity or incapacity to dwell on a topic without bleeding the wound (quoted in Portela 2009, 94).

References

Agosín, Marjorie. 2005. "Partnoy, Alicia." In *The Oxford Encyclopedia of Latinos and Latina in the United States*, ed., Suzanne Oboler and Deena J. Gonzáez. Oxford: Oxford University Press. Retrieved from: http://www.oxfordreference.com.offcampus.lib.washington.edu/view/10.1093/acref/9780195156003.001.0001/acref-9780195156003-e-708?rskey=0d3rv2&result=709&q=.

Agosín, Marjorie, and Emma Sepúlveda. 2001. *Amigas: Letters of Friendship and Exile*. Trans. Bridget M. Morgan. Austin: University of Texas Press.

Asociación Civil Memoria Abierta. 2005–2011. Memoria Abierta. Retrieved from http://www.memoriaabierta.org.

Avelar, Idelber. 1999. "Restitution and mourning in Latin American Postdictatorship." *Boundary* 26 (3): 201–224.

Brennan, James. 2005. "Argentina's Dirty Warriors." In *Encyclopedia of Genocide and Crimes Against Humanity*. (Vol. 1), ed., Dinah L. Shelton, 65–67. Detroit: Macmillan reference USA.

Bunster, Ximena. 1993. "Surviving Beyond Fear." In *Surviving Beyond Fear: Women Children & Human Rights in Latin America,* ed. Marjorie Agosín 98–125. Fredonia, NY: White Pine.

Comisión Nacional sobre la Desaparición de Personas. 1984. *Nunca Más*. (Writers and Scholars International Ltd., Trans.). Argentina: Editorial Universitaria de Buenos Aires.

Cosgrove, Serena. 2010. *Leadership from the Margins: Women and Civil Society Organizations in Argentina, Chile, and El Salvador*. New Brunswick, NJ: Rutgers University Press.

Crenzel, Emilio. n.d.. "Between the Voices of State and the Human Rights Movement: *Never Again* and the Memories of the Disappeared in Argentina." *National Council of Scientific Research* (CONICET) University of Buenos Aires.

Davis, Brian. 2012. "Project for Public Spaces. Hall of Shame Nominee Parque de la Memoria Buenos Aires, Argentina." Retrieved from www.pps.org/great_public_spaces/one?public_place_id=896.

Dolff-Bonekämper, Gabi. 2002. "Sites of Hurtful Memory." In *Getty Conservation Institute. Newsletter* 17.2 Summer.

Dworkin, Ronald. 1986. "Introduction." In *Nunca Más,* Comisíon Nacional Sobre la Desaparición de Personas (1984). (Writers and Scholars International Ltd. Trans.). Argentina: Editorial Universitaria de Buenos Aires.

Eyerman, Ron. 2004. "The Past in the Present: Culture and the Transmission of Memory." *Acta Sociologica.* 47 (2): 159–169.

Gates-Madsen, Nancy. 2011. "Marketing and Sacred Space: The Parque de la Memoria in Buenos Aires." In *Accounting for Violence: Marketing Memory in Latin America,* ed., Ksenija Bilbija and Leign Payne, 151–178. Durham, NC: Duke University Press.

Gomez-Barris, Macarena. 2010. "Witness Citizenship: The Place of Villa Grimaldi in Chilean Memory." *Sociological Form* 25 (1): 27–46.

Guembe, Maria L. 2008. "Challenges on the Road to Memory." *The Public Historian* 30 (1): 63–71.

Hall, Stuart. 1990. "Cultural Identity and Diaspora." In *Identity: Community, Culture, Difference,* ed., Jonathan Rutherford, 223–237. London: Lawrence and Wisher.

Huyssen, Andreas. 1995. *Twilight Memories: Marking Time in a Culture of Amnesia.* New York: Routledge.

Jelin, Elizabeth. 2003. *State Repression and the Labors of Memory.* Trans. Judy Rein and Marcial Godoy-Anativia. Minneapolis: University of Minnesota Press. (Original work published 2002).

Jelin, Elizabeth, and Susana Kaufman. 2000. "Layers of memory: Twenty years after in Argentina." In *The Politics of War Memory and Commemoration,* ed. T.G. Ashplant, Graham Dawson, and Michael Roper, 89–110. New York: Routledge.

Kaiser, Susana M. 2011. "Grandmothers of the Plaza de Mayo (Argentina)." In *Encyclopedia of Social Movement Media,* ed., John D. H. Downing, 216–217. Thousand Oaks, CA: Sage.

Klawans, Stuart. 2004, April 26. "Chronicle of a Disappearance." *The Nation,* 278.

Kozameh, Alicia. 1996. *Steps under Water.* Trans. David E. Davis. Los Angeles: University of California Press. (Original work published 1987).

Mandelbaum, Juan (Director) and Roxana Salamone, Lucia Mandelbaum, Francisoco Garcia Faure (Producers). 2008. *Our Disappeared* [Motion picture]. Watertown, MA: Geovison, Inc.

Marini, Margaret M. 1990. "Sex and Gender: What Do We Know?" *Sociological Forum* 5 (1): 95–120.

Méndez, Juan E. 2005. "Argentina." In *Encyclopedia of Genocide and Crimes Against Humanity*. (Vol. 1), ed., Dinah L. Shelton, 63–65. Detroit: Macmillan.

Olick, Jeffrey, and Joyce Robbins. 1998. "Social Memory Studies: From 'Collective Memory' to the Historical Sociology of Mnemonic Practices." *Annual Review of Sociology* 24: 105–140.

Paolantonio, Mario. 1997. "After the 'Dirty War': Reading the limits of national reconciliation." *Alternatives: Global, Local, Political* 22 (4), 433–465.

Partnoy, Alicia. 1998. *The Little School: Tales of Disappearance and Survival*. Trans. Alicia Partnoy, Lois Athley, and Sandra Braunstein. San Francisco, CA: Midnight Editions. (Original work published 1986).

Portela, M. E. 2009. *Displaced Memories: The Poetics of Trauma in Argentine Women's Writing*. Cranbury, NJ: Associated University.

Romero, Simon. 2012 "Do Argentines Need Therapy? Pull Up a Couch." *The New York Times*. August 18. Retrieved from http://www.nytimes.com/2012/08/19/world/americas/do-argentines-need-therapy-pull-up-a-couch.html?pagewanted=all.

Sanders, Peter (Director). 2007. *The Disappeared* [Motion picture]. New York: Eight Twelve Productions.

Selbin, Eric. 2010. *Revolution, Rebellion, Resistance: The Power of Story*. New York: Palgrave Macmillan.

Shayne, Julie. 2004. *The Revolution Question: Feminisms in El Salvador, Chile, and Cuba*. New Brunswick, NJ: Rutgers Univesity Press.

———. 2009. *They Used to Call Us Witches: Chilean Exiles, Culture, and Feminism*. Lanham, MD: Lexington Books.

Sutton, Barbara. 2010. *Bodies in Crisis: Culture, Violence, and Women's Resistance in Neoliberal Argentina*. New Brunswick, NJ: Rutgers University Press.

Wright, Thomas C. 2007. *State Terrorism in Latin America: Chile, Argentina, and International Human Rights*. Lanham, MD: Rowman & Littlefield.

3

CHILEAN EXILES AND THEIR FEMINIST STORIES

JULIE SHAYNE

On September 11, 1973, Chilean army general Augusto Pinochet, with the help of the United States government, orchestrated a coup d'état against democratically elected Marxist Salvador Allende. Under the guise of a "state of war" and an around-the-clock curfew, the military launched a reign of terror against leftist activists and sympathizers, government officials, intellectuals, union leaders, and the poor. They used mass arrests, beatings, torture, summary executions, and military sweeps of shantytowns to terrorize the population into submission. The military took control of the media and broadcast calls demanding that specified individuals immediately turn themselves in to the new authorities. Santiago's two major soccer stadiums were converted into mass jails, torture centers, and death chambers filled with prisoners, while the hospitals overflowed with the wounded, and the morgues with dead bodies. General Pinochet stayed in power until 1990. He was finally forced out by the presidential election he was required to call after losing the 1988 plebiscite he devised, ironically, in an attempt to remain in power. The 1993 Rettig report has confirmed that 2,279 people who disappeared during the dictatorship were subsequently murdered for political reasons (1993a, b). Steven Stern (2004) suggests that the numbers of detained, disappeared, and/or murdered are substantially higher. According to Stern, based on a conservative methodology, a reasonable estimate for deaths and disappearances at the hands of state agents and those in their employ is 3,500–4,500, with political detentions between 150,000 and 200,000, and torture estimates surpassing 100,000.

Exile was also an infamous tactic of the dictatorship. By the middle of 1978 nearly thirty thousand Chileans went into exile in Western Europe alone, and by the end of the decade an estimated two hundred thousand Chileans had fled their country for political reasons. By the end of the dictatorship approximately 1 million Chileans (of a population of 10 million) fled their country. At least two hundred thousand left because they were blacklisted and politically forced from the country, while the others fled because the economic situation under the dictatorship made life unlivable. Canada was one of the approximately 140 countries where Chileans fled (Wright 1995, 198; Wright and Oñate 1998; 2007). This chapter is about the Chilean women exiles and their supporters who organized as feminists in Vancouver, Canada, at the end of the Pinochet dictatorship. Here I discuss the transbordered feminist magazine *Aquelarre* created by Latina feminists in Vancouver. Latina exile feminists organized and articulated their politics and culture from within the diaspora, a space by definition lacking in clearly defined borders. They circulated the magazine all over the world, predominantly in the Americas, inadvertently contributing to the inherent fluidity between diaspora and homeland. Their magazine embodied the circumvention of borders.

In retrospect this project started while I was doing my field work for my dissertation/first book, *The Revolution Question: Feminisms in El Salvador, Chile, and Cuba* (Rutgers 2004). I interviewed Chilean women in Chile who had either been active with Allende and/or in the feminist and anti-Pinochet movements. Nearly all of them spoke of living in exile and the unique and somewhat indescribable trauma it produced. While living in Chile I met many people not connected to my research who had also lived in exile, or at least outside of the country during the dictatorship. The Chilean national television station even had a program about the Chilean diaspora which focused on Chileans living in different parts of the world, and while in Chile I saw episodes about Chileans in Hong Kong and Australia. Needless to say, there was no discussion as to why Chileans left in the first place, but a transnational diaspora is so much a part of the collective Chilean reality, a TV program actually focuses on it.[1] However, exile was not part of my research about revolution and feminism, so I filed away the curiosity in my dissertating and then book writing, tenure-seeking, cluttered brain.

Once I sent the edited proofs of my manuscript off to my editor I started formal research for my second book. (At the time I was a tenure-track professor at a private Research-One university. I had a joint appointment in sociology and women's studies with a tenure home in a fairly traditional, predominantly quantitative sociology department.) I immediately returned to my interest in exile. I knew there were hundreds of thousands of exiles around the world, including in Canada. I had colleagues in Vancouver, British Columbia, contacted them, and learned that there was a sizeable Chilean community there and thus began my search for their stories. Part of what is expected of an assistant professor to be eligible for tenure is a significant publication record and a well-launched second research project; this varies according to the university and department, of course. I had the first, a book, and I was on to the second.

I secured very small grants (not much was needed), got my Institutional Review Board approval, found my contacts, went into the field, and started my interviews. I did not know what I was looking for, but I knew I was interested in the stories of Chilean women exiles, and not long after I started the research I knew I was interested in their protest movement against Pinochet and their feminist activism. I was touched by their resilience and personally saddened by their stories of separation from their families, usually their mothers, and thus their children's alienation from their grandparents. At the time I was living at the opposite corner of the United States from my own family and daughter's grandparents, which was painful enough, and there was no violence or political loss involved. After my first summer of field work I went back to school and presented my work to a department colloquium. I knew it was a work-in-progress, particularly in the theoretical and conceptual sense, but I was so interested in and moved by the stories that I was eager to dig into whatever literature seemed to make sense. Unfortunately, my enthusiasm for the topic and confidence that the stories of exile, resistance, and feminism were there to be told was not enough to demonstrate to my colleagues that my second project was indeed underway. I was told: "This may be interesting, but telling stories is not sociology." I was mortified; I was about to go up for a major pretenure review that determined whether I was even eligible for tenure, and apparently story listening was not a good way to start.

I decided to include this chapter in this collection because it is the result of my eagerness to hear stories. The more stories I heard, the more committed I became to making sure the stories were entered into growing historical archives of Latin American women's activism. In the course of writing the book from which this chapter originally appeared (Shayne 2009) I took myself off of the tenure track to move back to the West Coast, specifically Seattle. (See the afterword to this volume: "Mother's Day.") Once I made that extremely liberating decision my audience became a combination of academic reviewers and the activists whose stories I was telling rather than tenure reviewers that needed to be convinced that these stories were indeed sociology. That added a bit of pressure in some ways but was intellectually empowering as well. In what follows I seek to tell the story of the Chilean and other Latina exile feminists and their supporters in Vancouver, BC. In this chapter I will begin by discussing my methodology. Next, I provide a brief overview of the transnational Chilean solidarity movement. From there I discuss exile feminism in Vancouver, Canada, as manifest in the grassroots magazine *Aquelarre*. I then speak briefly on the significance of organizing outside of borders and conclude with a note on stories, scholarship, and activism.

Locating Stories

Canada was home to one of the largest and most politically active exile communities in the diaspora. I focus on Vancouver because it was often the first choice of Chileans who went to Canada due in part to its agreeable climate, not much different from the south of Chile (Gilbert and Lee 1986, 143). Vancouver also lends itself to a study of this sort particularly given my interest in both culture and gender. First, Vancouver was one of only a handful of cities where Chileans set up and owned their own housing cooperative. Additionally, to the best of my knowledge, Vancouver is the only city we know of where women organized a feminist collective and magazine published primarily after the dictatorship.[2] Given the lack of documentation and plethora of solidarity movements in the Chilean diaspora, this study could have been done in practically any major city in the world.[3] Understanding the Vancouver case serves as another building block in the future synthesis of the greater Chilean exile experience.

Data for this study was collected in four specific ways: (1) one-on-one interviews and focus group discussions; (2) content analysis of primary documents from the solidarity and feminist movements and media coverage of the events; (3) minimal participant observation with a Vancouver-based email group composed of Latinos/as and Latin Americanist activists and scholars; and (4) secondary sources. I conducted the fieldwork in Vancouver and Victoria, British Columbia, in June 2004 and 2005. I located the informants via a snowball sample. In total I spoke with twenty-five women, all Chilean save one, and one Canadian man who ranged in age from twenty-seven to seventy-one, with the majority in their fifties at the time of our interview. Class status was fairly heterogeneous: on one side of the spectrum was a woman whose family's economic situation propelled her to begin working at the age of seven, while at the other end were those who came from several generations of the privileged, professional classes. However, social class is somewhat hard to determine when talking about exile since it often changes dramatically, generally dropping, when one is forced to relocate to a new country. Of the Chilean women I interviewed, only four are married to the same men with whom they left Chile. Most have long since divorced (at least once) with only two of them remarrying and staying married. Two married after they arrived in Canada, and only one of those marriages lasted. Of the six that were children at the time of exile, four are currently married, one divorced and not remarried, and one, the youngest of the entire sample, never married. Only one of the Chilean women who left as an adult has never married. Of the two Canadians, both are currently married. The woman was divorced once and remarried a Chilean. We never explicitly discussed sexuality or sexual orientation.[4]

Some of the Chilean women are literary, visual, and/or dramatic artists in the formal sense, others are self-taught, and still others have no artistic inclinations whatsoever. One of the Canadians is a folk-music festival organizer and historian, and the other a part-time fiction writer. Many of the women left Chile as a direct result of threats to their lives for their involvement in a variety of political projects. Other women left as young children (or, in one case, in utero) when their parents' lives were being threatened, while others followed their partners. Nearly the entire sample remains politically active in some capacity, be it through their course of study, their cultural productions, and/or their paid and voluntary involvement in progressive organizations. Interviews and focus group discussions lasted between two and four hours, in a place chosen by the interviewees, and all but one were in English. All of the interviewees were given the transcripts to read, and in some cases edited the transcribed version of their interviews before I used any of their quotes.

The Chilean Solidarity Movement

As we know, approximately 1 million Chileans fled their country by the end of the dictatorship. They went to as many as 140 different countries (Wright and Oñate 1998, 91; 2007) including Algeria, Angola, Argentina, Australia, Bangladesh, Brazil, the Cape Verde Islands, Colombia, Costa Rica, Cuba, East Germany, England, France, Greenland, Holland, Israel, Italy, Japan, Kenya, Mexico, Mozambique, the Netherlands, Nicaragua, Peru, Scotland, the former Soviet Union, Spain, Sweden, the United States, Uruguay, Venezuela, West Germany, and of course Canada. The diversity of host cities and countries certainly led to a variety of experiences, however, according to Wright and Oñate: "[T]he effects of exile were fundamentally similar whether one was in Costa Rica or Sweden, Mozambique or Canada, the USSR or the United States" (1998, 94; 2007, 36). It is hard to know the exact numbers per country for a variety of reasons: most statistics collected only counted official refugees; many Chileans remained uncounted, and people moved around a lot. For example, many Chileans started in Argentina but were forced to leave once the coup happened in that country while others tried to resettle elsewhere in Latin America but found the economic conditions insufficient to guarantee stability (Sznajder and Roniger 2007, 22).

For a great majority of these Chileans, exile became permanent. It is estimated that currently 1 million Chileans still live abroad. The country is divided into thirteen regions, each numbered, and Chileans abroad, many of whom were/are exiles are said to make up "Region XIV." Chileans in region 14 remain active in politics in their homeland with varying degrees of efficacy (Arriaza 2005, 291). The current political clout of Chileans abroad is arguably tied to their political efficacy during the dictatorship. Postexile has also become a permanent part of the Chilean political and social landscape. Nearly everyone was touched by exile, even those who never left. Virtually everyone knew someone who left, including their own family members. Some eventually returned to Chile, while others did not.

One of the primary goals of the dictatorship was to destroy leftist parties and their irrefutable influence on Chilean politics. The junta's main tactic was to remove all of the leaders from the country, either by murdering or disappearing them or by forcing them into exile. In other words, a great majority of the exiles were politically active and networked leftists. Once they arrived in their destinations, party militants reconstituted their parties. Within months of leaving Chile, exiles replicated the Chilean Left in dozens of countries around the world. Over time the role of the parties in exile shifted. While the parties inside of Chile (the "interior") put some of their differences aside, many in exile became more fractured and eventually demobilized. Many activists left their parties and joined organizations autonomous from the political parties because the dogmatic methods adhered to in Chile made little sense in exile. Some of the women I interviewed laughed as they recalled the "documents from the interior" and never-ending splits in the parties. The men's persistent ideological bickering, which, among other things, ultimately wasted a lot of time women did not have, compounded by a sense of masculine political arrogance combined to further alienate women from party politics. These practices are quite entrenched inside Latin America, and many of these same trends were apparent in exile as well.

The degree of coordination among exiles with their *compañeras* and *compañeros* in Chile was quite remarkable especially given the absence of the Internet, combined with the politically dangerous terrain in which Chileans in the interior organized. The two primary goals of the solidarity movement, regardless of the city or country in exile, were to provide material and political support to the anti-Pinochet movement in the interior. The money from even the smallest of fundraising events was sent back to Chile to support the movement there. One woman exiled in Montreal recalls, "I worked in the solidarity movement for Chile. We made 500 *empanadas* every Saturday to collect money and . . . to send it to the women in Chile" (quoted in Wright and Oñate 1998, 150). Salvador Allende worked for a revolution "*a la Chilena* with '*empanadas* and red wine.'" Exiles took this declaration to heart and transformed *empanadas* into a universal symbol of exile and resistance. Cooking and selling *empanadas* were tasks that typically fell to women exiles. Indeed, in the words of Margaret Power, some women had "*empanada* fatigue" by the end of the dictatorship (personal communication, 2008)! As one exile recalled, "I don't plan to ever make another [*empanada*] in my life" (quoted in Wright and Oñate 2007, 39). I met many women in Vancouver who conveyed that exact sentiment. Certainly selling *empanadas* did not generate the same amount of funds that the Soviet Communist Party was able to channel to the Communist Party in Chile, but from the perspective of the activists in exile and the interior, it was equally integral to their movement.

International solidarity was also important. It came from all parts of the world, and was manifest in many different ways. Chilean exiles received material support from a range of donors, including individual union members from around the world and Eastern Bloc governments. Regardless of the dollar amount this outpouring of solidarity translated into political support in the diaspora that Chileans tapped as a resource to pressure the Pinochet dictatorship. The political support also created a momentum necessary to keep the movement flourishing, particularly in the face of much political infighting. And finally, international solidarity was even delivered in the form of guerrilla combat training inside of Chile as an armed movement hoped to assassinate Pinochet. Regardless of the varied political and ideological battles present in all of these sorts of relationships, the exiles benefited tremendously from international solidarity and were never oblivious to its presence and significance.

Chilean women exiles played a major role in the solidarity movement. They contributed in all capacities, from leadership, to returning to Chile to fight with the underground movement, to baking *empanadas* to sell for fundraisers. (I discuss this in great deal in chapter 5 of my book *They Used to Call Us Witches*, 2009.) Once Pinochet was finally ousted from power women started shifting their focus from inside of their home country to feminism in their adopted homeland and the Americas more broadly. Women took their organizational skills, resources, and networks acquired through the solidarity movement and transitioned into a feminist movement. Not coincidentally, a similar process was happening within Latin America: Revolutions and wars were coming to an end, and women who participated in them were also starting to take on feminist causes en masse (Shayne 2004). By the time Chilean women (and other Latinas and internationals) began organizing as feminists in the diaspora, in this case, Vancouver, Canada, they had been living outside of their home borders for so long transnational citizenship was far more familiar than one bounded by the physical borders that marked either Chile or Canada.

Exile Feminists in Vancouver Organize without Borders

Once feminists started organizing in Vancouver they had significant cultural and political accomplishments of which to boast as did their colleagues in Latin America. Similarly, by the time they began organizing as feminists they were so firmly rooted in Vancouver that they expected to remain there rather than return to Chile as they had originally intended. So, in part as a way to share their accomplishments with Latinas who stayed in their home countries, Canadians, and other internationals in their new country of residence, they began the bilingual (Spanish and English) magazine *Aquelarre: A Magazine for Latin American Women/Revista de la Mujer Latinoamericana. Aquelarre* means "illegal gathering of witches."

The first issue came out in July 1989, just before Pinochet officially relinquished power. The following words appear on the first page of the first issue:

> Rebelliousness, resistance, and creativity have taken many forms in the history of the Latin American continent, but the beginning has always been a meeting, a gathering. Co-operation and organization are needed in order to do things. And as people meet and gather they start to create unions, musical groups, shanty-town organizations, publications, soup

> kitchens. People get together and remember, they speak, resist and struggle to change the world. They get together and make history, even if their names don't appear in books.
>
> We are women from here and there, Latin American women. We are all present: those of us who never left, those who left and continue to be "Latinas" in far-away lands, those who left and then returned, and also those who, having been born in other parts of the world, share our love for Latin America.
>
> We bring our voices, our pain, our banners, our ointments, our needles and brushes, our cooking pots, our handfuls of soil, our potions, our instruments, our brooms. We have come along different roads, but we are going in the same direction: we share a vision of a future where there is room for life, LIFE in capital letters.
>
> We also share an increasing confidence in our capabilities as women and the conviction that together we can find new ways to advance and reach our destinations. We have power, we are witches. We will sweep away the fears and the hurdles and we will search our memories. We will recover the magical and silent work of the past and share our present efforts. We will start showing, speaking, discussing, fantasizing and inventing together. That's what brings us together in this magazine, which is one more space among the many that women have taken over. Let us all share it. We are all invited. Let us begin the AQUELARRE. (*Aquelarre* 1989[a], 2)

These opening words alert the reader that the contributors and themes included in the magazine share the border of the Americas—from the top of the Northern hemisphere and bottom of the Southern and the more than thirty countries in between.

The *Aquelarre* collective lasted for nearly ten years and produced twenty-one issues (sixteen individual magazines; some are double issues), two thousand copies of each issue. Each issue used a variety of creative means to accomplish the goals implicit in the above statement. That is, the magazine strove to document the typically overlooked social, cultural, and political contributions of Latin American women. The collective also sought to create a space for the development and cultivation of feminist ideas and interpretations of a plethora of sociopolitical issues from human rights, to art, to globalization. The magazine is a remarkable accomplishment given the collective's limited resources and unlimited ambitions. Here I will discuss the development of the magazine, including logistical and thematic concerns. I conclude by analyzing some of the more illustrative issues which best capture the goals the collective was attempting to achieve.

Aquelarre 's History

In the course of this research I was fortunate to speak with five of the *Aquelarre* collective's original members. The collective was made up of about twelve core women and fifteen volunteers, both men and women. However, numbers varied from issue to issue. A good number of the members were Chilean exiles, while others were from elsewhere in Latin America, including Argentina, Colombia, Mexico, and a handful from Canada.[5] In other words, most of the founders and core members were living outside of their original borders. I spoke to five of the founding members as well as some volunteers about the magazine's origins. There was some implicit agreement that the idea for a magazine was in the air, in part as a result of conversations and brainstorming sessions at a regional feminist conference that had recently occurred, but there were different interpretations regarding the prime catalyst for the magazine. I suspect that these differences are the result of what each woman remembers as the moment most important to her decision to commit herself to the magazine.

The members of *Aquelarre* did not hold formal titles beyond "member of the collective and the editorial board." However, Carmen Rodríguez[6] informally took on the role of a coordinator and head of the editorial committee. For Carmen the magazine is in part the result of an art exhibit in Vancouver in 1987 organized by the Canadian feminist organization Women in Focus. Three Chilean artists—Damiela Eltit, Lotty Rosenfeld, and Nelly Richard—came to Vancouver as curators of an exhibition by a total of thirteen Chilean artists. Diamela Eltit stayed with Carmen and was quite impressed with the work of the women in the solidarity movement. She suggested that the exiled Chileans create a magazine to share their accomplishments with other women, in and outside of Canada. Carmen then traveled to Chile (for the first time in fourteen years) and, among other things, did a bit of research about potential themes and stories for the magazine. Upon her return she and about nine other women from Chile, Argentina, Colombia, Canada, and the United States had their first brainstorming session. Carmen recalls it this way:

> We all talked about what we would like to see in a magazine. And from that very first session . . . the bilingual aspect came up; that it was important to be bilingual because we wanted

> to reach people here [Canada] as well as Central and Latin America. But not only because we wanted to reach people in Latin America but because it was a statement of who we are and where we come from. And we wanted it to be a political magazine, a feminist magazine. We wanted to cover all kinds of issues, political things to social things, to arts. Everything. We wanted it to look beautiful, and we wanted to write it collectively.

The final product definitely suggests that the collective met all of these goals.

Irene Policzer, another founding member, identifies a different catalyst for the magazine, also implicitly tied to art. Irene recalls receiving a call from a Chilean exile friend of hers who was working on her degree in photography. She explains:

> One day [she called me] and said: "I am desperate! I need to have [at least] twenty-five . . . photographs of Latin American women! Can you help me?!" So she came here [Vancouver] and we organized a tour. . . . Gena . . . had a particular style of taking the picture; she would ask the woman how she would like to appear in the picture . . . [and] everybody chose something that would define her. . . . She asked me to go with her partly to introduce her to the different women but also to do the talking to keep the women sort of away from the camera. . . . So my job was that; . . . not distracting exactly but [something like that]. . . . [S]o those conversations happened [and] a lot of them [were] about the conference and . . . what had happened there. . . . It was some time . . . after the conference . . . [a]nd Gena had come with me to the conference . . . so she was aware of all those issues also, so it was kind of a natural [flow of events].

After the seeds were planted as a result of some conference attendees wanting to keep their voices out there, the Women in Focus exhibit, and Gena's photography project, a group of women met at Irene's for a brainstorming session. They decided to have an event at La Quena Coffee House to announce the idea and gather support and volunteers for the project. (La Quena was a *peña* style café started by Chileans and Canadians.) One woman, Magaly Varas, recalls seeing an announcement for the event. She attended with great enthusiasm, feeling as though the project spoke to her personally and politically. Magaly explains at our focus group meeting:

> I heard about [the magazine] . . . and I was typist, a secretary at that time. . . . I met you [Carmen][7] at La Quena and I met Margarita [another founder] for the first time . . . I told them . . . "I am not a writer but . . . I want to join this project." . . . I was not involved in politics [at the time but] I have . . . always [been] involved with the Latin American community. For thirty years, I have never stopped doing that. So I wanted to do something with women, and that project was the perfect one for me.

Magaly stayed with the magazine for ten years, from the beginning until the end. She eventually became the only paid staff member for the collective.

The women were very committed to a certain vision of *Aquelarre*; they wanted a cultural text that spoke to and reflected a diverse group of Latin American women. According to a grant application they submitted to the Canada Council:

> We want to provide a concrete space for Latin American women living in Canada, Canadian women and Latin American women living in Latin America to carry out a cultural dialogue. We want to hear from and reach those women who, like many of us, have left Latin America and now live in some part of Canada. We want to show the cultural expressions of their experiences. At the same time, we want to hear from and reach those women who, like us, are from Latin America but, unlike us, never left their country of origin. We want to know in what ways our artistic expressions are still alike and how they have grown different. And finally, we want to hear from and reach Canadian women who have an interest in Latin American culture. . . . When women create their own spaces to express their cultural experiences or to take action, the results are quite distinct. AQUELARRE Magazine intends to provide such a space for these innovative artistic expressions. (*Aquelarre* Latin American Women's Cultural Society 1988b, 3, 9)

The women immediately started to organize furiously and not always harmoniously in order to create the magazine that the collective envisioned.

Organizational Efforts

Cecilia Tagle was involved from the beginning. She shared a schedule of meetings with me (*Aquelarre* Latin American Women's Cultural Society, 1988a). According to the schedule the women met as often as every day but typically once every four days. The chronology starts with a meeting on April 13, 1988 and goes all the way until February 1989. It includes planning meetings, editorial meetings, fundraising *peñas* at La Quena, scheduled mailings, and so on. In other words, it appears that from the beginning the women thought of everything. A grant proposal dated September 15, 1988 also reflects the organizational savvy of the collective. The application was submitted to the Exploration Program of the Canada Council and in it the collective requested $14,600Can to cover limited staff support and office supplies over a one-year period. According to the proposal it was one of many requests for support, some logistical, like office space, others for funding. The collective approached a cross-section of groups—local, national, and transnational—including the Chilean Community Association of B.C., the Vancouver Status of Women (who eventually provided office space), Oxfam Canada, B.C., Women's Tour to Nicaragua, and El Salvador Information Office. According to the inside cover of the first issue their requests were successful: "Aquelarre is partially funded by the Explorations Program of the Canada Council. We also gratefully acknowledge the assistance of OXFAM-Canada, Vancouver Status of Women, Kinesis, *La Quena* Coffee House, Co-op Radio, and many others" (*Aquelarre* 1989a, i).

In our focus group discussion, Carmen and Magaly recalled with pride and amazement how hard they all worked in the ten years they dedicated to the magazine:

> Carmen: You know, when I look back . . . I have no idea how . . . we did this; it was so much work!
> Magaly: And when we had a deadline to publish, remember? We were [working] until three, four, five o'clock in the morning!
> Carmen: [At] the office, or at somebody's house, my house, remember?
> Magaly: . . . The first issue took us about nine months to publish. . . . And after that we had to write the final report, the budget, everything, so it was . . .
> Carmen: It was exhausting, but it was great . . . And it was such constant hard work; it was so all encompassing.
> Magaly: And [by the end] we did not have any energy left.
> Carmen: Yeah, we were drained.
> Magaly: It was exhausting. . . . And in the meantime everybody had different jobs.
> Carmen: Yeah, I worked full time.
> Julie: And you were all mothers, are mothers.
> Magaly: Oh yeah, single mothers.

One aspect of the magazine which was particularly time consuming was fundraising. Each issue cost $5,000Can to print and required its own source of funding, which meant the collective had to research different funding sources, write grant proposals, and eventually write reports to funders after an issue was completed. Additionally, the collective did grassroots fundraising, like silent auctions, garage sales, and *peñas* in an ongoing way. Not only was the fundraising a constant job, but graphics and layout were exceedingly time consuming as well. For the most part the magazine predated simple desk-top publishing computer programs; the women literally had to cut and paste articles and do the layouts by hand. Their graphics were surprisingly sophisticated given the technological limitations. Indeed, at least initially, they did not even have a fax machine; rather they had to use one at one of the members' husband's office.

Attending meetings and making decisions about content and so forth was also time consuming. In retrospect, some women felt they should have trusted one another more, which would have minimized the amount of time spent in meetings, but at the time everyone felt a need to be invested in all decisions, which led to very lengthy and often heated discussion. Cecilia Tagle explains:

> We would discuss for each issue the theme, the pictures, and I guess we were so collective that we were all involved in *all* of the discussions, even [regarding] the color part, even in the little picture. And that was exhausting for many of us. We should have . . . delegated more and trust[ed] that the other [committees] were doing their parts, in the sense that the values and the objectives were present. . . . I think I should have been more patient, but . . . I am *proud* of that magazine; what we did was incredible, and the first year, all the work that we did, it was very, very good . . . a lot of creativity. Incredible; it was excellent!

On top of the fundraising, brainstorming sessions, meetings, bickering, writing, translating, and page layouts, members of the collective spent time finding other artists, writers, poets, and activists to interview and experts in given fields to also contribute to the magazine. In short, the women of the *Aquelarre* collective worked tirelessly for ten years and produced a professional-grade magazine with very limited resources.

How was this relatively small group of women able to produce sixteen magazines, all of which were thematically, graphically, and culturally rich, in their so-called spare time? In addition to political commitments to feminism the members of the collective brought together a variety of skills and experiences. According to the Canada Council grant:

> We are a group of Latin American and Canadian women determined to publish a bilingual (English-Spanish) cultural magazine by and for women. Although we come from different parts of the Americas, we have many things in common: . . .
>
> —Many of us practice some kind of cultural expression: writing, music, pottery, photography, drawing and painting, weaving, jewelry making, etc. Others have experience in publishing and printing.
>
> —We are established members of the Latin American, women's and/or cultural communities of Vancouver. We all have a history of involvement with other organizations that have successfully carried out and continue to carry out projects related to culture and/or women's issues. This has resulted in tremendous community support for AQUELARRE Magazine in terms of concrete donations, voluntary work, subscriptions, attendance to fund-raising events, free publicity and others. (Aquelarre Latin American Women's Cultural Society, 1988b)

The qualifications the women described here illuminate patterns parallel to the development of feminism in Latin America. That is, all of the women involved in the collective had real political (and in this case cultural) tools already at their disposal, many of which were acquired by participating in other social movements, namely, the solidarity movement. Similarly, the women also had networks from which to work, also resulting from their earlier political work. In other words, prior political involvement positioned the members of the collective to more successfully advance their ambitious project. The sociopolitical context of the Chilean diaspora in Vancouver is certainly different than that of revolutionary movements inside of Latin America. However, a commonality exists across borders with respect to women participating in leftist social movements and eventually taking their acquired skills and networks to organize feminist projects in the aftermath of leftist ones. By the time the women started *Aquelarre* (late 1987) many already had over ten years of political experience in Vancouver, so despite the tremendous workload, the transition from one social movement to another was relatively seamless.

The Audience

Who read *Aquelarre*? The issue of audience was tricky for the *Aquelarre* collective as it often is for feminists; striking a balance between "accessible" and "sophisticated" proved challenging. Some members of the collective were more satisfied with the group's ability to achieve this balance than were others. Some felt that despite the group's stated intention of producing a magazine relevant to a diverse cross-section of women, it ultimately ended up being elitist and exclusive. Others, however, felt the collective had concrete strategies to make the magazine appealing to more than just intellectuals. One way they attempted to do this was to interview activists and other women who were not writers but whose stories made sense to include. Similarly, while some women felt the magazine only valued so-called high art, others felt just the opposite and were quite proud of their ability to create an inclusive publication. Some felt the magazine truly represented the women's space they hoped to create, while others felt the magazine only spoke to the converted.

One way to get a sense of the magazine's readership is to look at the distribution strategy of the collective and the letters received. Additionally, during my focus group discussions and one-on-one interviews, I spoke to several members of the collective about this topic. In response to The Canada Council grant application's question: "How will the proposed work be presented to the public?" the collective wrote:

> AQUELARRE Magazine will be distributed to bookstores, Latin American groups, women's organizations and individuals, primarily throughout Canada but also in the United States and Latin America. Several bookstores and groups have already committed their assistance with distribution. . . . At the same time, a mailing list of hundreds of prospective subscribers has been compiled. These people will be re-contacted in order to consolidate their subscriptions. (Aquelarre Latin American Women's Cultural Society, 1988b, 5)

According to the letters to the editors *Aquelarre*'s strategy was successful. In the front of the first fourteen issues, after a short introduction to the issue's central topic, was a section the editors called "todas las voces, todas/all the voices." There were anywhere from four to ten notes included from all over the world. In reviewing the letters from every single issue I found readers in the following countries/states/cities: Argentina (Bariloche, Mendoza, and Paraná); Canada (Fredericton, Montreal, Nelson, Ontario, Ottawa, Rexdale, Salt Spring Island, Saskatchewan, Telegraph Creek, Toronto, Vancouver, Vernon, and Victoria); Chile (Santiago); Colombia (Bogotá); the Dominican Republic (Santo Domingo); Ecuador (Quito); France (Lyon); Germany (Berlin); the Netherlands (Leeuwarden); Nicaragua (Matagalpa); Paraguay

(Asunción); Peru (Lima); the United States (California, Massachusetts, and Oregon), and Uruguay (Montevideo). It is not clear how many readers there were per country, especially outside of Canada, but clearly this list suggests a transnational readership. It is also safe to assume that much of the international distribution was the result of other exiles living in those countries.

Despite this international interest in the magazine some in the collective remained unhappy with what they felt was a limited audience. The issue of accessibility, as I noted, was tricky and another point which caused much friction within the collective. I spoke to Irene Policzer and Cecilia Tagle, both together and separately, at great length about the magazine. They were pleased with *Aquelarre*, at least initially, but eventually left the collective in large part because they felt the audience was too limited and did not reflect the original intentions of the collective. (Recall both Irene and Cecilia were involved from the very beginning.) Irene explains:

> At the beginning we [had] . . . this dream, this idea, this vision, and at the beginning it . . . seemed [we all had] . . . the same vision but as we started to work, no, it was not the same vision. Really there were two very distinct visions, [with respect to] what content? What is the philosophy? And so I wanted something accessible . . . more easy to understand, more chatty, more gossipy. I did not know about popular education at that time; had I known [about] it I would have said: "Yes! This is what I want!" . . . [S]omething that had to do with women's everyday lives; cooking, recipes, or whatever. . . . [Issues] . . . that women talk about or are interested in and within that, yes, [you] have content a bit more than just cooking recipes, but not [in] . . . such a blatant [way]. . . . It [ended up being] . . . a magazine [that] pitched to the convinced. So that was the kind of tension that started to arise I think within the group not too long after [we started], the first year.

Irene continues, speaking more directly to the issue of language:

> Probably it is a magazine that looks much more attractive to . . . the academic community rather than to . . . the community in general because it has a lot of very innovative things, and has a lot of courage . . . and [shows] . . . a lot of resourcefulness to [accomplish]. . . . The language probably sounds very familiar and maybe even a bit naïve to academics because it is not really [a] very sophisticated language; it is a pretentious

> language [but] it is not sophisticated language, I think. It is an interesting phenomenon to study, I think, but for the community that we wanted to target, I do not think we reached them.

Irene is very educated. She and her husband are both architects and her son is a professor. She is concerned about the language being alienating to women less educated and familiar with academic rhetoric than she is. Irene hoped to create a magazine that reached women who were not as familiar with feminist and cultural discourse as she and most of the founders were.

Magaly Varas and Carmen Rodríguez, also involved from the beginning, felt the collective was quite effective in striking a balance between accessible and exclusive. They believe the collective achieved this balance by including a diversity of types of articles—fiction, interviews, political analysis, and so on. Carmen, herself a writer, explains:

> I had this idea . . . that we could apply for some grants to have . . . writing workshops because we really wanted . . . a variety of voices; we did not just want writers, right? . . . The way that we got around that was with the interviews. . . . [T]hat was another debate that we would have; the level [of] the audience. . . . [T]here were people that would complain because there were articles, sometimes they were too elevated, right? And we said: "That is ok. There is one of those but there is also one that is like a conversation . . . and there is another one that is a story, and there is another one that it is a [political] analysis["] . . . so that was the whole idea. . . . So we tried to incorporate everybody's voice but really incorporating voices of people that were not, that did not have experience writing, [was extremely challenging].

These different perspectives were more than just theoretical debates and thus led to lengthy and heated meetings. Indeed, certain themes addressed in the magazine offer concrete examples of the opposing positions.

The issue on violence against women (16/17) was quite illustrative of this tension. For example, Irene Policzer felt quite certain that the way the collective chose to articulate this important topic ultimately alienated the women who really needed to read it; that is, the sufferers and survivors of violence. However, Carmen Rodríguez and Magaly Varas felt that issue was one of the more appreciated ones because it was useful to social workers and the like. Irene explains one perspective:

> When we were producing [*Aquelarre*] one of the problems we had was "who would buy it?" It was very difficult to sell, so it survived based on the grants. [Y]ou should see the amount of issues that were . . . not distributed . . . because it was very difficult to distribute. . . . It looks intimidating; . . . even the issue of violence, looking at it now, if I did something today about [violence] that is not the way I would [do it]. The woman subjected to violence probably is not going to buy a magazine [that] says: "Violence against women" . . . on the cover; it has to . . . be in [a] more subdued way, [on the] inside but not so open. . . . [A woman might think:] "If I buy that . . . I am going to be seen as one of them. If my husband sees it . . . on my night table or something, what is he going to think?" . . . So there is a way of talking about violence . . . and I think we did not do it right because we did not know; we did not know enough about the issue of violence at that time. . . . [The magazine was] not high-brow proper; [it] is not an intellectual magazine . . . but it tries to appear as something [that is].

From Irene's perspective the presentation of the magazine had such an intellectual feel to it that the practical gains an issue on violence could have provided to abused women were undermined by the alienation they experienced when seeing the magazine.

Once again, Carmen and Magaly had virtually opposite opinions about this issue. I asked both of them in our focus group discussion what they thought women not involved with *Aquelarre* felt about the magazine. They felt it was very well received; specifically, this same issue Irene felt was useless:

> Julie: What do you think that women not involved with the magazine thought about it?
>
> Carmen: They loved it. For example, the magazine about violence against women was used all throughout British Columbia by women's groups, by social workers, we went to workshops, [to Magaly] remember?
>
> Magaly: And also I remember [we went to] . . . a Council of Women Counselors at Vancouver Family Services; Family Services of Vancouver . . . got quite a few [copies] of that issue.
>
> Carmen: And the thing is, if people were not involved in the collective, they were involved in some way because we featured their stories, or their art, or their work, or because they volunteered to do whatever [we needed].
>
> Magaly: We had tons of volunteers.

In other words, Carmen and Magaly feel the magazine was well read and appreciated because they got concrete feedback from women's advocacy groups to that effect. Additionally, the collective's commitment to featuring women of the community and what felt to them like an outpouring of volunteer support suggests the magazine involved and spoke to women beyond just the collective. Certainly any activist project that demanded this much intense, unpaid work, one where the goals of advocacy, education, and expression were at once tied together while also competing with one another, is likely to be fraught with tension. Additionally, the members of the collective all had their own personalities and personal issues, which led to conflicts at the superficial level and ultimately translated into friction within the magazine. The tensions resulted in some members of the collective leaving rather than the entire project imploding. They did eventually stop producing magazines, but at least from the perspective of Carmen and Magaly, two of the women who stayed with it until the end, for no other reason than that they were exhausted and ran out of money.

Format

What did the magazine look like? What sort of articles did the editors include? What were some of the repeating themes? For the most part, *Aquelarre* was a very professional-looking publication, particularly given the limited budget and lack of access to computer graphic programs. Most of the covers were very colorful, and all text, including the dates of publication, was written in both Spanish and English. Nearly all of the covers include some sort of original art, including photography, paintings, drawings, and the like. Some have collages that appear to be made by the editors where things were literally cut and paste and organized thematically.

Despite the covers which looked relatively professional, there are a several inconsistencies which hint at the grassroots nature of the magazine. For example, some issues are identified by months while others by seasons. Some issues are solo (e.g., 2) while others are combined (7/8). Additionally, some issues have the English first and others the Spanish, and some have a price listed on the cover while others do not. There are also inconsistencies regarding use of capitalized and lower case letters, in both Spanish and English. Similarly, any given issue used multiple fonts.[8] Interestingly, the price actually varied sometimes as low as $3.50Can or as high as $5.00. The back of most issues bears the English and Spanish version of the following quote: "*Aquelarre* means 'illegal gathering of witches'. They used to call us witches. What do they call us now? Arpilleristas, weavers, union leaders, women in exile, political prisoners, mothers of the disappeared, artists . . ."[9] and what appears to be indigenous art portraying women in a circle. The magazine's standard graphics also speak to the theme of witchcraft. Most articles are concluded with what appears to be a small pot of "witches' brew," and the inside cover, which includes information about the collective and publishing details, typically includes a picture of a witch riding a fountain pen rather than a broom.

The content of each magazine is also somewhat standardized. After the table of contents, most issues begin with a page called "se abre el aquelarre/getting started."[10] This page includes an overview of the issue's theme. Typically, the next section is "todas las voces todas/all the voices," which includes the letters the collective has received presumably since the last issue. Most issues also have a "crítica/reviews" section. Reviews are generally of books and films. Additionally, most issues contain a list of resources and organizations often under the heading "otros aquelarres/other aquelarres." The majority of the issues also have a section called "noticias/news," and the stories are from Latin America and Canada. The editors also include cartoons in most issues, presumably to lend a bit of comic relief to often very serious subjects. For example, in the issue about immigrant women there are a few cartoons which depict some women immigrants' embarrassing moments upon arriving in Canada. The cartoons also convey the grassroots nature of the magazine since they are all handwritten.

Other sections include: "vamos al grano/getting to the point," the nonfiction articles; "palabra de mujer/woman's word," the fiction and poetry; "quehaceres/women do this," stories about women's cultural and/or political activism; "manos a la obra/hands on" typically first-person narratives or interviews; and "así somos/as we are," writings about identity. All issues include advertisements, most for political organizations, including bookstores and groups doing solidarity work in Latin America. Though most are local, some ads reflect a national and international audience. And while some are very small establishments, for example, La Quena Coffee House which advertised in multiple issues, there are also some big name advertisers, like Ms. Magazine.

Each issue (save 1 and 6) is organized topically. The common threads to all of the magazines are women, feminism, and strength. It would take an entire book to discuss each issue individually. Rather, I want to offer a sense of what topics were important to the collective as reflected through the themes upon which they focused. In analyzing the different issues I have found that there are four overarching themes into which the different issues fit: identity politics, cultural production, human rights, and sociopolitical issues. The following four issues fit into the category identity politics: *immigrant women* (3); *Latin America & the Caribbean Feminism* (7/8); *First Nations Women of the Americas: 500 Years of Resistance* (10/11), and *Ethnic and Cultural Diversity* (12/13). Three issues fit into the category cultural production: *Women and Art* (4); *Latin American Women Writers* (9), and *The Cultural Work of Latin American Women in Canada* (15). Three others fit under the rubric human rights: Human Rights and the Rights of Women (2)[11]; *Violence Against Women: What Is to Be Done?* (16/17), and *When History Hurts* (18). The remaining four issues fit into the category sociopolitical issues: *Literacy* (5); *Globalization of the Economy or of Poverty?* (14); Labor/Globalization (19);[12] and *Popular Education: from and with women* (20/21). Without even looking at the details of each magazine one can see the potential for overlap. Indeed, poverty (issue 14) can be considered a form of violence (issue 16/17). Each issue is replete with examples of *Aquelarre*'s vision of feminist inspired justice, but I have chosen only two issues to discuss in some detail: the inaugural issue (1) and the issue on feminism (7/8).

The Inaugural Issue

The editors of *Aquelarre* in part saw their tasks as documenting and inspiring the creative works of Latin American women; particularly those labors dedicated to social justice. From the collective's perspective social justice projects took many forms—from poetry to cartoons to feminist conferences. The first issue of *Aquelarre* was in July/August/September 1989, and it introduces the reader to the collective's vision of the interconnection between cultural production, women's voices, and political empowerment vis-à-vis a space of one's own. In this issue the collective begins the "quehaceres/women do this" section with an article entitled "Historias de Viajes Inesperados/I Wasn't Born Here," which centers on a theatrical piece written, performed, and about Latin American women living in Victoria, British Columbia. For the article, *Aquelarre* interviews director Lina de Guevara (a Chilean exile) and some of the other actresses who collectively wrote about their own experiences as Latinas in Victoria. *Aquelarre* asked the women: "What changes have you gone through since the beginning of the play?" Yolanda, a Chilean who has been in Canada since 1975 explained: "I now have more confidence in myself. I was coming out of a hole. I was really depressed; I couldn't speak. My teeth chattered. Then I decided to learn how to drive. Now I think I could even pilot an airplane" (quoted in Aquelarre 1989b, 6). Yolanda's words capture much of what *Aquelarre* was about: women's cultural production as an embodiment of strength and resistance. Toward the end of the interview Lina explains her vision for the type of theater she does: "I want our theatre to be healing. This is the reason the play has had such a good reception. I think people feel that the play brings a message that heals wounds. We [Latina exiles and immigrants] have all experienced feeling attacked and injured from every side. Even though the play touches upon some very sad and tragic subjects, the outcome always shows that we are not alone" (quoted in Aquelarre 1989b, 7). Here we see the women using cultural production politically while simultaneously nursing the emotional wounds caused by exile. *Aquelarre* very much supported that approach as evidenced by the articles, stories, and images that filled their pages.

The *Aquelarre* project was fueled by passion. Indeed, the collective could not have survived so long, and done so much tedious and time-consuming work, for no pay, if the satisfaction of the product was not worth something in and of itself. One article in the first issue which really captures the contributors' passion appears in the "así somos/as we are" section. It is a story about a Salvadoran refugee in Vancouver known as "La Abuela" (the grandmother). Included in this section is a poem written by La Abuela called "Yo Quiero/I Would Like":

> I would like to be a messenger
> of love, work and well being.
> Let us struggle against war
> and love all that is life. . . .
> I would like our cry of protest
> to be heard in every corner of the world.
> We renounce war
> because we want to live. . . .
> I would like them [the warmongers] to abandon
> their ambition and resentment
> because in the third war
> there will be no winner. (Villacorta 1989, 12)

This poem speaks to the explicit political convictions of the collective in its use of terms like "warmonger." (La Abuela uses the same term earlier in the poem.) The editors' choice to include the poem alerts the readers that the magazine is about much more than Latinas in Canada; it is about global social issues that are in part responsible for forcing the women from their homelands in the first place.

The final example from this first issue which speaks to their vision of documenting and supporting the varied efforts of Latinas toward social justice appears in the "crítica/reviews" section. It is a brief review of a book entitled *La Mujer Proletaria* written by Chilean Cecilia Salinas. The reviewer writes: "Researcher Cecilia Salinas takes on the difficult task of tracking down and following the until now invisible story of women's involvement in the Chilean working-class movement between 1880–1920. She satisfies a long overdue and ever urgent need, raising many questions and issues" (in *Aquelarre* 1989c, 28). Once again we see the collective's support and celebration of the work of Chilean women intellectuals in their task of documenting and disseminating the political history of women. Similarly, reviewing a book by a Chilean author which was only published in Chile speaks to the collective's desire to stay linked with Latinas in the interior. The penultimate section of the magazine, "otros aquelarres/other aquelarres" also speaks to their connections with Latinas and feminism inside of Latin America. It includes a brief notice about the upcoming regional feminist *Encuentro* in Argentina, including contact information for more details. In other words, *Aquelarre* was one link in the border-crossing, transcontinental feminist movement which was flourishing in this post-dictatorship era.

The Feminism Issue

Aquelarre's issue 7/8 is *América Latina & el Caribe Feminismo/Latin America and the Caribbean Feminism*, and it came out spring/summer 1991. The "se abre el aquelarre/getting started" section of this issue is quite telling. The editors titled it "Una Semana en la Vida Feminista/A Week in the Life of a Feminist." It is a cut-and-pasted graphic of a detailed to-do list, handwritten, and meant to look like a page from a spiral-type notebook. The list conveys the full-time nature of a feminist's jobs and inserts humor apparently as a way to diffuse the stress brought on by the workload. A few choice entries include:

> Monday
> 8:00—Take the kids to school and go to work
> 10:15—Emergency union meeting
> 12:00—Call the printer/organize meeting for Wed/check vegetable prices for festival end of week/schedule for volunteers/call teachers about Juanito's progress
> 5:00—make supper
> 7:00—editorial meeting. Café Roma
> 8:30—collective meeting—discuss graphics policy
> 10:00—pick up kids, put them to bed

10:30—write and translate intro to poets' article
1:00—bed/no dreams—how are we going to pay the printer?

Then skipping down to the weekend:

Saturday
6:00 [am]—load the truck/sell food all day at the festival/ handout *Aquelarre* leaflets—other brujas [witches] are starting production of the magazine

Sunday
same as Saturday
midnight—take down the stand/load the truck, count the money
2 am—Manuel wants to . . .
I have a headache . . . (Aquelarre 1991b, 2)

This section is telling for a variety of reasons. First, it very much concurs with the stories the women told me over and over regarding how busy they were with paid, domestic, and feminist labor. It hints of course at an inability to keep one's intimate relationships a priority in the face of the stress of the "week in the life of a feminist." The list also very much reflects the actual schedule of meetings that one of the women shared with me and the collective's propensity toward making all decisions cooperatively rather than delegating things and thus minimizing everyone's workload. And finally, the format of this "getting started" section is in contrast to most of the other issues that tried to lay out a clear agenda and rationale for the topic at hand. The "getting started" section tells the reader about the feminist workload rather than the content of the magazine to follow.

The predominant approach to feminism in this issue is that the feminist ideologies and projects are about much more than middle-class white women; they include positions of race, nation, ethnicity, class status, age, sexuality, and so forth. The editors attempt to present feminism as an inclusive rather than exclusive project. They do this in part by including articles and interviews with a variety of different women who talk about feminism from their own social positions and challenge the hegemony of heterosexual, white, middle-class women in many feminist organizations. The issue starts with an overview of feminism in Latin America and the Caribbean based on reports from the fifth *Encuentro* in Argentina. The article is at once celebratory and cautious, ambitious and realistic. The article implies that feminism is about political economy and democracy as much as it is about women.

The reader gets the sense that feminism in the region is on the verge of something; assessing the new postdictatorship political context and attempting to insert a gendered analysis into it. Much the same was happening in the diaspora. The solidarity movement had ended years prior, and this magazine helped Chileans and other Latinas sort out their leftist pasts with their feminist futures.

Another entry that captures the ideological breadth of feminism is aptly called "¿Qué es el Feminismo? What is Feminism?" by Macarena Bernabei. It starts out:

> Hi! I'm Macarena. I'm 12 years old and in Grade 7. I'm going to tell you about how I came to interview feminist women.
>
> One day I heard that a lot of ladies, more precisely feminist women, were going to come here. So I asked my Mom why they were coming. She told me I should go and ask them.
>
> Curious as I am, I took some sheets of paper, a pen and I began to ask questions.
>
> The more questions I asked, the more I enjoyed it. . . . I managed to do 50, from all sorts of different countries.
>
> I took my work to school to show others. But everyone, even the teachers, treated me very badly. Maybe they were just jealous. But fortunately I didn't let that upset me, since in this way I had the satisfaction of meeting people from other countries, to learn about their customs, how they respond to different problems and above all else to know what feminism is in their countries. (Bernabei 1991, 14)

The article then goes on to include quotes from feminists from Argentina, Ecuador, Guatemala, Germany, Basque Country, Spain, Uruguay, Peru, and Paraguay. Macarena concludes her part of the article, as a highly sophisticated, passionate twelve-year old: "Well, I learned from doing these interviews that it is very nice of you to have come to defend us from men who think badly of women, for men to not be such machos in front of women and that you defend us a little so that the men don't think they own the whole world. . . . Thank you for everything" (Bernabei 1991, 17). Here *Aquelarre* is simultaneously tackling accessibility and diversity. It attempts to show that if one wants to know about feminism, all one has to do is ask like twelve-year old Macarena did. For the "brujas" of *Aquelarre*, feminism is not meant to be exclusive and alienating but rather accessible and empowering as evidenced by Macarena's response to her whole process.

That said, the *Aquelarre* collective was not naïve to the fact that feminism, particularly at this historical moment (early 1990s), has a history of being very closed to certain groups of women, namely, women of color and lesbians. In the article "Hacia el Desarrollo de un Feminismo Incluyente/Towards the Development of an Inclusive Feminism" author Noga Gayle confronts the issue of feminist racism head on, invoking African American feminist thinkers like bell hooks, Patricia Hill Collins, Audre Lorde, and Angela Davis to support her arguments. The author writes: "If the goal of feminism is transformation towards social justice for all women, then there must be a better understanding of the diversity of women's experience and concerns. The factors of class and race in feminist analysis must be given centrality. All women's experiences should be regarded as equally valuable. So far, this has not been the case" (Gayle 1991, 25). The article speaks to the feminisms in the Americas—Canada, the United States, Latin America, and the Caribbean—and articulates the way racism crosses borders, is ideologically similar across nations, but operationalized differently, particularly within feminist communities. The language is powerful and forces the reader to confront topics that, particularly at this time, were extremely underacknowledged. *Aquelarre* unequivocally established that for them, race and racism are feminist issues.

In a further attempt to present feminism as an inclusive project *Aquelarre* also addresses the taboo issue of homosexuality, a topic which was conspicuously overlooked by feminists in Latin America for a prolonged period. (See Alvarez et al., 2003; Sternbach et al., 1992). The magazine includes two separate pieces. One is a first-person testimony, "Me Llamo Erika y Soy Lesbiana/My Name Is Erika and I Am a Lesbian"; the other is a more academic piece entitled "El Continuum Lesbiano/The Lesbian Continuum." Both pieces attempt to break the silence about sexuality which in many cases is imbued with homophobia. In Erika's testimony she boldly shares:

> We love like you do in your heterosexual relationships; we give flowers as gifts, we pamper each other, we make love with the same intensity as you; long kisses, impassioned embraces. And yes, we touch each other's vaginas, our breasts. We play with our tongues until we get tired. We dance together. Tell me, what do you know when you can barely handle this subject? Why are you silent? Why do you feel uncomfortable? Go ahead and tell me, ask me questions, even though they may be stupid. I don't want any more silences; I want to come out, liberate myself from that other self which I have carried for a long time because I was afraid of you. I don't blame you. (Espinoza 1991, 42)

Aquelarre's decision to include this essay as well as the other one about lesbianism speaks to its commitment to break silences and document women's lived experiences, even the painful aspects which reflect tensions, conflicts, and prejudices among each other. *Aquelarre* was committed to creating and maintaining a feminist dialogue across the Americas, and this issue was a clear example of that goal.

Feminists and the Absence of Borders

Chilean women exiles began functioning without borders as soon as they left their homeland during the Pinochet dictatorship. None of the women wanted to leave their beloved Chile, but none of them felt safe staying. As soon as they got out they found other exiles, fellow leftists, and started organizing internationally, across borders, to denounce and dethrone the dictatorship. At the time, the borders they were the most focused upon, Chile's, were the ones they were forbidden from living within. Early on in their exile Chilean women (and men) became accustomed to living in a transbordered reality, or, perhaps more accurately, a borderless one. Just as their colleagues in Latin America were beginning to put their feminist movements in high gear, so too were Chileans and other Latinas in the diaspora. They joined forces to produce a magazine that spoke not just across borders but across hemispheres as well. Transnational feminist activism helps us to see the arbitrary nature of borders; it helps us see that the elimination, circumvention, and transgression of borders—voluntarily or not—contribute to a vibrant political culture which should be considered central to an ideal vision of globalization based on human connections and cultural exchange.

Conclusions: Feminist Stories and Archives as Activism

Rethinking this chapter in the context of this book, two and half years after the original book was published, has been a gratifying process. Despite the initial lack of support/disdain I received when beginning the exile project, *They Used to Call Us Witches* has received sociological and activist validation. I was greatly honored in March 2011 to win the Pacific Sociological Association's Distinguished Scholarship Award for the book. Indeed, my peers concluded that the feminist stories, when looked at with a sociological imagination, ultimately are sociology.

I have also worked with some of the founders of *Aquelarre* to gain their permission for a digitization project involving the University of

Washington and University of British Columbia Libraries. The journal run is now hosted in electronic form by the University of Washington Libraries and is available worldwide at http://uwashington.worldcat.org/oclc/20661625. And finally, *They Used to Call Us Witches* has been added to the accessible holdings at the Documentation Center at the Museo de la Memoria y Los Derechos Humanos (Museum of Memory and Human Rights) in Santiago, Chile.

I am also very pleased to have collaborated with Carmen Rodríguez, one of *Aquelarre*'s founders, in this collection. Carmen and I have stayed in touch ever since I began my research in 2004. She was my first real contact, and without her *They Used to Call Us Witches* never would have come to fruition. Since publishing the book, we have spoken on a panel together, sent each other pictures of our children and (her!) grandchildren, and celebrated each other's accomplishments. After finishing Carmen's award-winning novel *Retribution* (Women's Press Literary, 2011) I kept thinking about the power of fiction to document history and thus asked her to write about that process for this collection. Fortunately, she agreed, further solidifying the activist-scholar relationships that *Taking Risks* hopes to support. (See chapter 1.)

I very frequently say that women, gender, and sexuality studies is about growing the archives to adequately reflect history. I have always envisioned my role in that as teaching. Needless to say, I have had whimsical visions of my research and books contributing to that goal but honestly, I never really envisioned how that would happen. The gratification and honor that comes from contributing to and being displayed in material, worldwide archives, far exceeds any rigid scholarly stamp of approval for which I would have been forced to comprise these feminist stories.

Notes

I would like to thank Rowman & Littlefield Publishing Group for allowing me to use excerpts from *They Used to Call Us Witches: Chilean Exiles, Culture, and Feminism* (Lexington, 2009) in this chapter.

1. I do not know if the program is still on the air.
2. Historian Thomas Wright shared this information with me based on his and Rody Oñate's extensive research on the Chilean diaspora (personal communication 2006).
3. As of this writing, only a few books about Chilean exiles and/or the solidarity movement exist in English (Eastmond 1997; Kay 1987; Wright and Oñate 1998).

4. Demographic data refers to time of the interview.
5. One of the Canadian women was born in the United States but left for Canada during the Vietnam War, so her now exhusband would not be drafted.
6. See Carmen's chapter in this collection about writing fiction as a form of activism.
7. In reviewing this chapter for me Carmen clarified that it was the first time she and Magaly had met in many years; they had lost touch, but they were best friends between 1975 and 1978.
8. I thank my former graduate student Ej Juarez for pointing the font issue out to me.
9. The title of my book *They Used to Call Us Witches: Chilean Exiles, Culture, and Feminism* comes from this quote.
10. All section headings are lowercase.
11. This issue does not have a specific name.
12. This issue does not have a specific name.

References

Alvarez, Sonia E., Elisabeth Jay Friedman, Erika Beckman, Maylei Blackwell, Norma Stoltz Chinchilla, Nathalie Lebon, Marysa Navarro, and Marcela Ríos Tobar. 2003. "Encountering Latin American and Caribbean Feminisms." *Signs: Journal of Women in Culture and Society* 28 (2): 537–579.

Aquelarre Latin American Women's Cultural Society. 1988(a). "Mtgs [sic] Chronology—Aquelarre," by Cecilia Tagle. April 13.

———. 1988(b). Initial grant application to Exploration Program of the Canada Council. Ottawa, Ontario. September 15.

———. 1989(a). *Aquelarre: A Magazine for Latin American Women/ Revista de la Mujer Latinoamericana*. Julio Agosto Septiembre/ July August September. Issue 1.

———. 1989(b). "Historias de Viajes Inesperados/I Wasn't Born Here." *Aquelarre: A Magazine for Latin American Women/Revista de la Mujer Latinoamericana*. Julio Agosto Septiembre/July August September. Issue 1.

———. 1989(c). "crítica/reviews." *Aquelarre: A Magazine for Latin American Women/Revista de la Mujer Latinoamericana*. Julio Agosto Septiembre/July August September. Issue 1.

———. 1991(a). *Aquelarre: A Magazine for Latin American Women/ Revista de la Mujer Latinoamericana*. "América Latina & el Caribe Feminismo/Latin American & the Caribbean Feminism." Primavera/Verano/Spring/Summer. Issue 7/8.

———. 1991(b). "Una Semana en la Vida Feminista/A Week in the Life of a Feminist." *Aquelarre: A Magazine for Latin American Women/ Revista de la Mujer Latinoamericana.* "América Latina & el Caribe Feminismo/Latin American & the Caribbean Feminism." Primavera/ Verano/Spring/Summer. Issue 7/8.

Arriaza, Bernardo T. 2005. "The Chileans." In *The Peoples of Las Vegas: One City, Many Faces*, ed. Jerry L. Simich and Thomas C. Wright, 4–7. Las Vegas: University of Nevada Press.

Bernabei, Macarena. 1991. "¿Qué es el Feminismo? What is Feminism?" *Aquelarre: A Magazine for Latin American Women/Revista de la Mujer Latinoamericana.* "América Latina & el Caribe Feminismo/ Latin American & the Caribbean Feminism." Primavera/Verano/ Spring/Summer. Issue 7/8.

Eastmond, Marita. 1997. *The Dilemmas of Exile: Chilean Refugees in the U.S.A.* Göteborg, Sweden: ACTA Universitatis Gothoburgensis.

Espinoza, Erika. 1991. "Me Llamo Erika y Soy Lesbiana/My Name is Erika and I am a Lesbian." *Aquelarre: A Magazine for Latin American Women/Revista de la Mujer Latinoamericana.* "América Latina & el Caribe Feminismo/Latin American & the Caribbean Feminism." Primavera/Verano/Spring/Summer. Issue 7/8.

Gayle, Noga. 1991. "Desarrollo de un Feminismo Incluyente/Towards the Development of an Inclusive Feminism." *Aquelarre: A Magazine for Latin American Women/Revista de la Mujer Latinoamericana.* "América Latina & el Caribe Feminismo/Latin American & the Caribbean Feminism." Primavera/Verano/Spring/Summer. Issue 7/8.

Kay, Diana. 1987. *Chileans in Exile: Private Struggles, Public Lives.* Wolfeboro, NH: Longwood Academic.

Policzer, Irene. 2004. Founding member of *Aquelarre* collective; supporter of the Chilean solidarity movement, interview by author, tape recording, Vancouver, Canada.

Rettig Guissen, Raúl, Jaime Castillo Velasco, José Luis Cea Egaña, Mónica Kiménez de la Jara, Ricardo Martin Díaz, Laura Novoa Vásquez, Gonzalo Vial Correa, and José Zalaquett Daher. 1993(a). *Report of the Chilean National Commission on Truth and Reconciliation, Vol. 1.* Notre Dame, IN: Center for Civil and Human Rights, Notre Dame Law School.

———. 1993(b). *Report of the Chilean National Commission on Truth and Reconciliation, Vol. 2.* Notre Dame, IN: Center for Civil and Human Rights, Notre Dame Law School.

Rodríguez, Carmen. 2004. Writer and educator, interview by author, tape recording, Vancouver, Canada.

Rodríguez, Carmen, Magaly Varas, Isabel López, and Ana María

Quiroz. 2005. Focus group discussion with the author, tape recording, Vancouver, Canada.

Shayne, Julie. 2004. *The Revolution Question: Feminisms in El Salvador, Chile, and Cuba*. New Brunswick, NJ: Rutgers University Press.

———. 2009. *They Used to Call Us Witches: Chilean Exiles, Culture, and Feminism*. Lanham, MD: Lexington Books.

Stern, Steve J. 2004. *Remembering Pinochet's Chile: On the Eve of London 1998*. Durham, NC: Duke University Press.

Sternbach, Nancy Saporta, Marysa Navarro-Aranguren, Patricia Chuchryk, and Sonia E. Alvarez. 1992. "Feminisms in Latin America: From Bogota to San Bernardo." In *The Making of Social Movements in Latin America: Identity, Strategy, and Democracy*, ed. Arturo Escobar and Sonia E. Alvarez, 207–239. Boulder, CO: Westview.

Sznajder, Mario, and Luis Roniger. 2007. "Political Exile in Latin America." *Latin American Perspectives* 155 34 (4): 7–30.

———. 2009. *The Politics of Exile in Latin America*. New York: Cambridge University Press.

Tagle, Cecilia. 2004. Former member of the Women's Sector of the Chilean Solidarity Movement and early member of the Chilean Housing Cooperative. Vancouver, Canada.

Tagle, Cecilia, and Irene Policzer. 2005. Focus group discussion with the author, tape recording, Vancouver, Canada.

Villacorta, María Luisa. 1989. "*La Abuela*." *Aquelarre: A Magazine for Latin American Women/Revista de la Mujer Latinoamericana*. Julio Agosto Septiembre/July August September. Issue 1.

Wright, Thomas. 1995. "Legacy of Dictatorship: Works on the Chilean Diaspora." *Latin American Research Review* 30 (3): 198–209.

Wright, Thomas, and Rody Oñate. 1998. *Flight from Chile: Voices of Exile*. Albuquerque: University of New Mexico Press.

———. 2007. "Chilean Political Exile." *Latin American Perspectives* 155, 34(4): 31–49.

4

NAVIGATING THE CUBAN IDEOLOGICAL DIVIDE

Research on the Independent Libraries Movement

MARISELA FLEITES-LEAR

Distrust of the Left and Right on Both Sides of the Strait of Florida

"I know about you, and you can't participate in our panel." As she aggressively tapped my shoulder with her right hand, these were the words used by the head of the women's studies Cuban delegation to the Latin American Studies Association (LASA) Congress in Washington D.C., 1995. I had submitted an individual paper entitled "Women, Family, and the Cuban Revolution: A Personal and Sociopolitical Analysis," and after the panel I was initially assigned to was canceled, the LASA organizers (unbeknownst to me) included my presentation in the panel devoted to Cuban women's issues organized by the Cuban delegation. It was a logical decision by LASA given the nature of my paper, but the Cuban delegation protested. When LASA organizers told them that the panel had to accept my presentation, the Cuban delegates said: "Yes, but she cannot sit with us at the panel table. She has to wait until we are done." And so it was, to the amazement of the audience, that I had to sit with the audience while they read their entire papers. When I stood up to present, in the five minutes they left to me, the Cuban participants stepped down from the panel table and sat amongst the public to distance themselves from me. In the end, the critical content of my paper was not very different from what the Cuban delegates had presented.[1] But the fact that I am a Cuban-born academic living in the United States, vocal in both my support and my criticism related to Cuba's policies toward women and elsewhere, was not acceptable. The Cuban delegates, regardless of the content of my paper, had to make a stand to be able to return to Cuba without "contamination" from a "black sheep."

I use this example to introduce the difficulties faced by Cuban and Cuban-American academics when doing research about Cuba, both inside and outside the island.[2] Trying to find a balance between academic honesty, freedom of expression, political commitment, and activism in the field of Cuban studies has been a difficult tightrope to walk, to say the least. Perceived by leftist friends and activists in the United States as a "token Cuban," a "child of the Revolution" who is not fiercely anti-Castro, I have tried to offer a more balanced view of Cuban reality than the one put forward by both the Cuban-American right-wing community and the uncritical supporters of the Cuban Revolution in both Cuba and the United States. My attempt has proven very difficult given the readiness of the Right to dismiss anything positive about the Revolution and the defensive position of the Left vis-à-vis any criticism of that process. Similarly, doing research within Cuba has been very challenging, given the mistrust of all Cuban-American academics/activists (or for that matter, the limits imposed on all Cuban academics). To gain access to some archives in Cuba I have had to use a third party and even twist the truth about my own identity. Even trying to arrange humanitarian donations to Cuban institutions via the U.S.-Cuba sister city relationship I helped established has been very difficult given that mistrust.[3] For Cuban scholars living outside the island, a layer of complication is added when we have relatives living in Cuba, as most do: there is always the fear of being denied an entry visa by the Cuban authorities to visit our families compounded by the risk of endangering our Cuban relatives on the island in any way. That the personal is political is probably truer in Cuba than anywhere else.

This chapter focuses on the recent organization of independent libraries around the island and my attempts at learning more about it given the aforementioned difficulties. Since the independent libraries movement presents itself as an alternative to the official state-sponsored libraries, it has been persecuted and condemned by the Cuban government. For the same reason, it receives the support of anti-Castro organizations outside of the island and the U.S. Interest Section Office. Due to the lack of diplomatic relations between the United States and Cuba, the United States does not have an embassy on the island but rather a sort of U.S. *consulate* housed as part of the Embassy of Switzerland in Havana. The support from the U.S. Interest Section thus taints the movement, allows the government to brand its members as mercenaries, and leads to further persecution. In this case, my attempts at contacting the organizers in the United States, not as a volunteer or as someone trying to join the Friends of Cuban Libraries organization in New York, but as an academic interested in researching it have been met with silence. On the other end, any visit to one of these libraries in Cuba implies risking having my visa to visit my relatives revoked.[4] Given these difficulties, I owe much of the fieldwork for my current research to Dimas Cecilio Castellanos who lives in Cuba.[5] Castellanos, a participant in the alternative political online journal *Desdecuba.com* with his excellent blog entitled *El blog de Dimas*, was a professor of Marxist philosophy at the University of Havana and a specialist in academic informatics at the Agrarian University until his expulsion in 1989. He also holds a masters degree in biblical and theological studies from the San Carlos Institute in Havana. He is a Cuban independent journalist, a member of the editorial board of the digital journal *Consenso*, a founder and ex-member of the Cuban Corriente Socialista dissident group and one of the editors of the Latin American in Focus Series 2013 volume on Cuba (Henken, Celaya, and Castellanos 2013).

Drawing on the readings of documents put forward both by the movement in Cuba and by the Friends of Cuban Libraries in New York, an analysis of the novels that have received the prize Franz Kafka Novelas de Gaveta (Desk Drawer Novels) sponsored and facilitated by the Independent Cuban Libraries Project, and interviews with patrons of the libraries in Cuba, my goal here is to examine the objectives of the movement, its connections with other organizations, and the potential impact inside the island. I propose to examine the independent library movement against the framework of the complex educational policies developed within the Revolution; a movement which I argue is an inevitable consequence of these same policies. The dynamic of the existence of these libraries might be seen as a sort of cross between "*Cría cuervos y te sacarán los ojos,*" and "*Saturno devorando a sus hijos*" ("Raise crows and they will peck your eyes out" and "Saturn Devouring His Children"). In other words, the libraries might be seen as a result of the existence of a highly educated population (thanks to the efforts of the revolutionary process to emphasize education and reading), while at the same time, this unexpected and unwanted offspring of the revolutionary parents is opposing the state tutelage, so the same government who encourages people to read and to be educated feels the need to devour these unwanted newborns.

The Proyecto de Bibliotecas Independientes: Origin and Characteristics

The first national library of Cuba was independently founded in 1901 by a group of intellectuals who had spent years in exile (mostly in Paris, Spain, and New York) and who had formed the Organizing Junta of the National Library and Museum of the Island of Cuba (Pérez-Matos 2010, 218). It had as the most important antecedent the library of the Sociedad Económica de Amigos del País (Economic Society of Friends of the Country), founded in 1793, the first public library on the island, which, by 1900 had around 41,487 volumes. The first director of the National Library of Cuba was Domingo Figarola Caneda, who also spent many years in exile, and met the group of intellectuals who nominated him for the position while in Paris. The island was under the occupation of the United States; hence the first National Library was legalized by the U.S. government in Cuba under military decree no. 234 on October 18, 1901. The first books were the personal collection of Figarola Caneda, consisting of around three thousand volumes (Biblioteca Nacional, 2007). It is interesting to note that the first director was not a librarian, but an encyclopedic intellectual who had studied medicine, worked as a journalist, translator, and bibliographer and was a noted bibliophile (Silva Crespo, 2006). From 1901 on, particularly from 1933 until 1959, there was "a widespread creation of information institutions, the appearance of specialized journals, meetings and events, and establishment of library science studies in Cuba" (Pérez Matos and Fernández Molina 2010, 223).

In 1959 the Reforma Integral de la Enseñanza (Comprehensive Education Reform) was declared in Cuba, followed by the 1961 Campaña de alfabetización (Literacy Campaign), and the approval in June of 1961 of the Nationalization of Education Law that eliminated private education in Cuba. As part of the reforms, the development of the national adult education program was very important, as well as the establishment of mandatory education for children up to ninth grade. All of this led to an unprecedented growth in the number of readers on the island, whose thirst for books was satisfied by the growing national production of books. The law establishing the National Press of Cuba in March 1959 was one of the first measures of the Revolution. Another significant event was the creation of the National Writers Union in 1962—whose first director was the internationally renowned novelist Alejo Carpentier. In 1967 The Cuban Book Institute foundation consolidated the book publishing system in Cuba. Additionally, there was a concerted effort to develop a national library system (which includes municipal and provincial libraries as well as school and university libraries). According to Rhonda Neugebauer, as of 2002 there were four hundred public libraries and six thousand school libraries in Cuba (including university libraries). Before the Revolution, there were only thirty-two public libraries in the whole country and very few school libraries, especially in small towns and the countryside. The enthusiasm for books in Cuba is particularly evident in the annual international book fairs. Even from 1990 through 2013, amidst an extremely dire economic situation, people continued to line up to buy books with the same intensity they form lines in the mornings to buy bread.

The economic crisis of the 1990s led to a huge decline in the publication of books in Cuba and to the increase in the price of those sold. During the VIII International Book Fair in 1998, President Fidel Castro explained the difficulties of satisfying the demands of a very literate public while declaring that there were no prohibited books in Cuba. The economic crisis also impacted the conditions of the libraries around the country, limiting their ability to enrich their holdings and physically maintain the buildings and their inventories. It is in this context that the Project of Independent Libraries appeared in 1998, as part of a growing number of institutions in an incipient alternative civil society on the island.

It is not the first time in Cuba's history that a social movement created independent libraries as a tool to offer different educational venues than the officially sanctioned institutions. For example, as part of the general disillusion with the outcome of the independence process from Spain in 1898, Cuban anarchists agitated toward social revolution and emphasized anarchist education as a revolutionary tool to transform society. Kirwin R. Shaffer's analysis of Cuba's 1898–1925 anarchist movement shows how from 1898 until 1925, anarchists created day schools for children and libraries, as a way to counter not only religious educational institutions geared mostly to educate the rich, but also the public schools "which they believed taught a blind form of 'patriotic nationalism.' Anarchists believed that this patriotic education countered socialist working-class internationalism while stifling free, individual thought in children" (Shaffer 2003, 152). For instance, the anarchist-led Círculo de trabajadores (Workers Circle) created a library and periodicals reading room open to the public (161). They also created social studies centers and sociological libraries during the first fifteen years of the twentieth century. Cuban anarchism and the anarchists' alternative cultural institutions were badly weakened by President Gerardo Machado's repression of the Cuban workers' movement. Starting in 1924 the institutions created to promote the anarchist rationalist education were under systematic attack. Although there is no unified ideology behind the current independent libraries movement (as in the case of anarchism), it is also a result of a disillusionment with the outcome of the social changes, in this case brought about by the limits of and political exhaustion caused by the 1959 Revolution. The movement aims to provide the general public with alternatives to the carefully controlled type of patriotism and rigid education officially instituted for public instruction since 1959.

The Proyecto de Bibliotecas Independientes (Independent Library Project, PBI) was established on March 3, 1998, following the initiative of the Partido Solidaridad Democrática (the Democratic Solidarity Party), a dissident group not legally recognized by the Cuban government. Initially the libraries were created in people's houses with whatever books they had and without any norms to follow. Eventually, requirements were established by their organizers for their creation and functioning: have a minimum of 250 books, adequate sanitary conditions to receive library users, and a catalog with a registry of books loaned.[6] The "librarians" were expected to sign a form declaring that their work was not remunerated. The story of the development of the Project is fairly complex. It is an example of the difficulties of creating alternative organizations in Cuba, the convoluted relations with the United States, and the multifaceted interaction between Cubans working on the island and those in the United States.[7]

Berta Mexidor and Humberto Colas, a couple from Las Tunas, spearheaded the project. Berta was the first general director. But the couple lost their jobs as a result of their participation in the PBI, as well as the house in which they were living, and they immigrated to the United States in 2001. They became the representatives of the PBI outside of Cuba. They currently reside in Hialeah, Florida, the stronghold of the ever-growing and mostly conservative Cuban-American community. Gisela Sablón Delgado then became the general director of the project in Cuba. She is also the director of the Dulce María Loynaz library in Vedado, Havana. Gisela is the wife of one of the seventy-five dissidents incarcerated in the spring of 2003, when the Cuban government launched a crackdown on all existing dissident organizations for their purported ties to the U.S. government. Later, during a trip to the United States, Gisela learned of the mismanagement of funds granted by USAID to the independent libraries by Berta Mexidor and Humberto Colas in Hialeah (more on the role of USAID later). Upon her return to Havana in 2008, Gisela broke with Berta and restructured the PBI with a new board of directors. The complex and convoluted nature of this *proyecto* is even reflected in a controversy over its very origin. According to another dissident Cuban group, the first Biblioteca Independiente de Cuba was inaugurated in 1996 in La Habana by Dulce

Maria de Quesada with the support of the Colegio de Pedagogos Independientes de Cuba (see documents by Movimiento Cubano Unidad Democrática). So, there is disagreement amongst different dissident organizations as to who created the first independent library, which allows us to speak of a general independent libraries movement within which there are several organizations and divisions.

According to Castellanos's interview with Gisela Sablón, as of 2011 there were 156 independent libraries on the island, twenty of them in Havana, and the rest mostly in the provinces of Matanzas and Las Villas. There are around 2,576 readers' groups that receive books and materials from the libraries via an intermediary. This means that the readers do not need to go to the library to pick up the books. Around 2,000 of these groups are in Havana and Matanzas. Gisela also maintains that since the project began in 1998, around 2 million people have participated either by borrowing books, attending lectures and meetings, or participating in literary contests (see Dimas Castellanos, "*Bibliotecas independientes*"). Unfortunately, it is impossible to confirm any of these figures obtained through personal interviews with Gisela.

As with anything related to Cuba, emotions run high when this project is evaluated. A major point of contention is the funding. The libraries receive funds directly from four sources: (1) the U.S. Interests Section Office in Havana; (2) the United States Agency for International Development (USAID), which funnels money grants by the U.S. government with the implicit intention of undermining the Cuban system; (3) the U.S. government–funded broadcasts, TV, and Radio Martí, which also seek to disrupt the Cuban government); and (4) funds collected by Friends of Cuban Libraries. The latter is a New York–based organization founded in June 1999 by Robert Kent, a librarian from the New York Public Library, and Jorge Sanguinetty, an economist, a former Cuban government official, a contributor to Radio Marti, and a Miami businessman (see Neugebauer 2002, 3). There are accusations by both dissidents inside the island and academic critics like Neugebauer that funds provided by the aforementioned organizations have been misused by the recipients. For instance, in conversation with Castellanos in May 2008, Omaida Padrón Azcui, the director of the Reinaldo Bragado library since 2005 and general director of the PBI when Gisela was traveling abroad, insisted that Gisela Sablón had misused, for personal purposes, funds received for the libraries. This realization led Omaida to break with the PBI. For this reason, there are currently independent libraries not associated with the PBI but working in similar fashion, like the aforementioned library directed by Omaida Padrón, which I was able to visit in January 2013. This library is now part of an alternative to the PBI called Red de Bibliotecas Cívicas (Network of Civic Libraries), which has an Internet site created and maintained from Miami by the organization Nueva Esperanza.

Another point of contention is the fact that most directors of these libraries are also members of the different dissident groups, and most, if not all, have no formal training as librarians. This critique however is a bit ironic given that, on the one hand, the director of Cuba's official national library is also not a formally trained librarian, and on the other, that there is a long tradition of nonlibrarians directing libraries in Cuba (as examined before). Besides books mostly published in Cuba, the libraries carry publications donated by European and U.S. donors, and in particular, documents provided by the U.S. Interests Section Office with clear political goals in mind to disrupt the Cuban official system from the inside. Hence, critics contend that these libraries are not really interested in promoting a love for books but ultimately have a political agenda to undermine the Cuban government. Finally, several librarians have used their participation in the PBI as a way of obtaining visas as political refugees to travel abroad and permanently leave Cuba.

In spite of the controversies surrounding the origin and development of this movement, its very existence raises some interesting and indeed ironic issues: The movement's potentially subversive nature is in part due to the fact that the Cuban population is highly educated, a result of the Cuban government's policies that the independent libraries aim to criticize. One can claim that the need for the creation of book clubs, readers' groups, and the like, is a logical, indeed inevitable, outcome of fifty years of Cuba's school system promoting a love of reading, studying, and discussing books. In a country where transportation can be a nightmare and bureaucracy and inefficiency in state agencies a national plague, having neighborhood libraries without *infiernillo*[8] must be very appealing.

It is true, as Fidel Castro expressed in 1998, that there are no prohibited books in Cuba. But to read so-called problematic books one needs permission from an academic or other official institution to be granted access to the "Infiernillo" of the national library, where these books are kept inaccessible to the general public. On the other hand, books that are sold in Cuban bookstores are only those approved by the government since all bookstores are owned by the state. Similarly, books in the official libraries also serve a clear political purpose: Cuban government's control over what people read and what books can be sold are two of many tools in the ongoing effort to shape Cubans' political ideology and Cuba's political education. When traveling to Cuba, customs officials carefully review books that tourists or Cuban citizens are bringing into the island. In short, whatever the political impulses behind the existence of the current PBI, they do not minimize the thirst and need of the very educated population to read whatever it is they choose to read, free of government intervention. Perhaps the existence of the "not-so- independent libraries" will lead to the promotion of citizens' initiatives to read and discuss free of involvement of centrally censored institutions. This is a point absent in those ready to dismiss the current efforts of the independent libraries movement.

The Activist Academic Divide: To Condemn or to Support?

The controversy surrounding the existence of the Independent Library Project (PBI) also brings to the forefront the question for those of us in academia and in political activism outside of Cuba, particularly in the United States, of whether it is possible to offer a balanced analysis of this and other subjects in an area that is so politically charged? A quick search online reveals strong opinions amongst U.S. academics and activists either in favor of or against the existence of these libraries. Several on the Left are quick to dismiss the whole idea. They maintain that the movement is not credible because of the libraries' explicit political agenda; their ties with U.S. institutions whose goals are to disrupt the Cuban system; the fact that these libraries accept monetary and material support from foreign institutions, and in some cases, misuse these funds; the lack of professional training of the "librarians"; the quality and nature of the books and documents in them; and the fact that the project has not condemned the U.S. embargo. Ironically, the U.S. embargo makes it illegal for U.S. companies to sell U.S. books to Cuba in the first place. The Left thus maintains that all of this combined undermines the intellectual integrity of the movement.

On the other hand, the American Library Association (ALA) and the Federation of Library Associations and Institutions (IFLA) have all passed resolutions opposing the U.S. embargo and hostility against Cuba, "while calling on Cuba to respect human rights and intellectual freedom" (McDonald 2008, 100). But these organizations have not accepted the pressures of the group Friends of the Cuban Libraries, which has used blogs, e-mails, letters, and public speeches by important public figures (like Nat Hentoff, Sandy Berman, Madeleine Albright, Andrei Codrescu, and Anthony Lewis) to castigate the ALA for not recognizing the work of the independent library movement in Cuba and for not taking a strong stand against Cuba's censorship. In fact, ALA regrets these pressures and suspects "a hidden political agenda" in "the counterproductive activities of groups like the friends of Cuban libraries" (Mc Donald 2008, 102). In 1994 IFLA held its international conference in Havana. In 2001, a group led by then ALA's president John W. Berry participated in a conference on the island, toured the national library, and other public libraries as well as several independent libraries that are part of the PBI. Upon its return, the ALA has pushed for the U.S. government to improve access to information in Cuba, but even after several Cuban independent journalists and writers were imprisoned in Cuba in 2003, the ALA has not criticized the Cuban government directly for this repression.

Librarians like Rhonda Neugebauer and John Pateman who have visited the independent libraries and the state-sponsored libraries in Cuba, contrast the PBI with the official library system on the island. They point out that the nonpolitical stated goals of the Independent libraries are actually met by the Cuban official library system, which renders them unnecessary. Pateman reports: "The aims of the Independent Library Project are to: 1. Offer scientific, technical, cultural and general information; 2. Offer libraries in all municipalities and provinces; 3. Create inter library cooperation at home and abroad; 4. Create an open forum for discussion among readers; 5. Stimulate reading among youth and children; 6. Promote literary research and development. All of these aims are being met by the Cuban library system" (10). Some dissidents inside Cuba criticize the PBI for some of the same reasons as Neugebauer and Pateman, but rather than dismissing them, they call for this project to change in nature to become a legitimate part of the alternative civil society the activists on the island are trying to create (according to Dimas Castellanos in personal interview with the author in June 2011 in Havana, Cuba).

Most of these scholars' and activists' criticisms of the movement is the result of sustained and justified opposition to the United States's relentless policies toward Cuba historically based on the Monroe Doctrine, the Platt Amendment, the long history of neocolonial relations with Latin America, and a lingering Cold War mentality. But is it possible to separate the condemnation to the failed and hypocritical U.S. policies toward Cuba from the analysis of new institutions appearing on the island outside of the state system? If we do not separate and thus nuance our critiques, are we falling into the same polemical trap set up by both the U.S. and the Cuban governments? Does the fact that the independent libraries have managed to exist and spread imply failures in the Cuban policies related to reading? By dismissing outright any attempts at creating alternatives inside Cuba, are we (academics and activists in the United States) curtailing the very freedom to oppose that we enjoy in the United States? For instance, the current Cuban official branding of independent journalists like Yoani Sanchez and Orlando Luis Pardo as "cyber-terrorists" and "cyber-mercenaries" suggests that the existing attempts to work outside the official channels in areas related to education and journalism will be handled with increasing severity in the near future.[9] In the name of opposing the U.S. embargo, and its regime change policies, while saving the social gains brought about by the Cuban Revolution, are we to become accomplices in keeping Cuban society stagnant? The example of one of the outcomes of the existence of the independent library movement (PBI), the literary prize it has created and facilitated proves that opening new spaces can indeed benefit Cubans.

Opening Possibilities for Alternative Discourses: The Franz Kafka Novelas de Gaveta Literary Prize

The existence of the literary prize Novelas de Gaveta created in 2006 by the Bibliotecas Independientes de Cuba (PBI) in collaboration with the transition program of the foreign relations ministry in the Czech Republic, the Prohibited Books Czech library, and the humanitarian Czech organization Men in Emergency is probably one of the most positive outcomes of the existence of the Cuban independent library movement. However, it is ignored by those in the United States that are opposed to the movement. For instance, the prize is not mentioned in either Rhonda Neugebauer's or John Pateman's reports about this project. Since 2009, sponsors of the prize include the Czech publishing house Garamond, the National Czech Library, and the Jackson State University in the United States. The Czech Republic has been involved in this prize from its inception. This involvement might be related to the personal interests of Václav Havel, former president of Czechoslovakia and the Czech Republic from 1989 through 2003 and a dissident writer since the 1960s. Vaclav Havel formed the International Committee for Democracy in Cuba, "to draw the international community's attention to the human-rights situation in Cuba, to support that country's opposition and to encourage pro-democracy forces" (Havel 2006). According to the aforementioned Berta Mexidor (one of the founders of the PBI), the goal in creating this literary contest was to provide a venue for books that Cuban writers cannot publish on the island "because they don't belong to the official organizations devoted to literature" (Valverde 2008).

Amongst the international jurors that evaluated the entries of the first contest were the great Spanish writer Rosa Montero and the director of Radio Prague, Mirek Kruicka. The first prize was given in 2008 to Cuban writer Orlando Freire Santana for his novel *La sangre de la libertad*. In 2009 Orlando Luis Pardo Lazo received the prize for his novel *Boring Home*. Other winners include Ernesto Santana for *El Carnaval y los Muertos* in 2010, *Días de entrenamiento* by Ahmel Echevarría in 2011, and *Larga es la noche* by Frank Correa in 2012.[10] According to Czech organizer Dita Grübnerová, with the Czech sponsors, like Libri Prohibiti, the organizing committee launched a literary contest that is promoted through the independent libraries network in Cuba. The Cuban authors, with novels they were unable to publish in Cuba, thus stored in their drawers, send the books to the committee where they are evaluated by an international panel (Valverde 2011). The call for submissions only requires that the novels submitted are unpublished. There is no political or ideological preferred characteristic stated (InCUBAdora). The prize includes the publication of the novel, its free distribution in Cuba, and some monetary reward. However, as of yet, most winners have not received any money due to logistical complications. It is interesting to note that since the onset of the 1990s economic crisis, many Cuban writers, dissidents or not, publish their work outside of Cuba, as the national publishing options are quite limited. One difference here is that the books published outside of Cuba are not distributed on the island, but one goal of PBI is to distribute the published novels in of Cuba for free.

Judging by the 2009 winner of the contest, *Boring Home* (Garamond 2009), the award attracts excellent works. The author of this particular novel is a very interesting example of the alternatives that are appearing on the Cuban literary scene. Orlando Luis Pardo Lazo has no affiliation to any political party in Cuba. He produces probably the best photography in Cuba, and he is the photographer for the aforementioned award-winning blogger Yoani Sánchez (the creator of the blog Generation Y).[11] Pardo Lazo has a blog himself, http://vocescubanas.com/boringhomeutopics, mostly devoted to his photography, where he makes a point of clarifying that he does not receive any money for his work. The bloggers that produce "Desdecuba.com" fight to be truly independent from political affiliations and from the Cuban State. As a result, the Cuban *blogueros* are criticized by both the dissident parties and the Cuban government. As expressed by Cuban blogger Miriam Celaya,

> The Cuban Independent blogosphere is, as the name indicates, a phenomena not linked to either the Cuban government or the Cuban opposition. That is, it doesn't answer to or belong to anyone, it lacks a program because we are not a political group—or a group of any kind—, we don't have leaders; it is something completely free and individual. That doesn't mean

> that there aren't blogs written by dissidents that oppose the government, or that there aren't blogs that prefer to publish political opinions about political issues [like her blog]. Beyond all the differences, we do have some common interests. This leads the bloggers to exchange opinions, knowledge about digital technology, information, and other things. That is why sometimes we meet informally, without impositions or mutual obligations. This has created an environment of empathy and, amongst some of us, the feeling of belonging to a common phenomenon of these times: the spirit that is born out of the exchange of information, of the use of the technology of information and out of the citizenry's will to exercise the freedom of expression. We practice a new and peculiar way to confront the lack of liberties imposed by the government, using a space that, so far, for one reason or another, has been used very little by both the government and the organized opposition: the virtual space. (Celaya 2011, original in Spanish)

The manuscript *Boring Home* was selected to be published and presented at the International Book Fair of Havana in 2008. However, due to the opposition of Iroel Sánchez, then president of the Cuban Book Institute, at the last minute the text was banned from the fair for not being "politically correct." With the help of the blog *Generación Y*, the author orchestrated an alternative book reading of his text outside of the fair. *Generación Y* published this call to attend the alternative reading by Pardo Lazo:

> The radioactivity Orlando gives off stopped the presses, scared off the editors and keeps some acquaintances from greeting him in the street. His name disappeared from the list of writers promoted by the official institutions and was removed from the catalog of this Fair. However, the Lawton nutcase managed to print his book and now wants to release it. We, his friends—other excluded people—have decided to join him in the alternative launch of his writings on Monday, February 16th at three in the afternoon, outside the fortress of La Cabaña.
>
> Except for the threats, all this could have taken place with a little group sitting on the grass, talking about a published book. Since yesterday, an email is circulating on the intranet[12] of the Ministry of Culture, warning us of various reprisals for the alternative release of the stories. Intimidating calls, accusations of being employees of the Empire—how unoriginal they

> are!—and even veiled warnings about being beaten up. All this has raised the profile of the release of Boring Home beyond anything we were looking for, giving the greatest prominence to the presentation of a banned writer. We will be there, we will see if they let us leave."

His reading was attended by some public and a lot of police (the exact numbers are just a matter of legend by now). The author then submitted the book to the Novelas de Gaveta literary contest. The text is a collection of stories thematically linked by a negative utopian vision of Havana and the "Fatherland" with a masterful way of playing with language, including the use of many neologisms. As Yanira Angulo commented, Pardo Lazo "has given us a linguistic reworking of the dystopia account in Cuban society" (Angulo 2011, 6). In *Boring Home* Habana becomes Habanada (Havana-Nothing) and then loses syllables to become Hanada (which translated can mean "oh, nothing" or "there is nothing") and ends up being simply a silent, meaningless "H." The nation becomes "Ipatrianada, país sin hache, letra mordaz" (Pardo 2009, 9). The author's Cuba is "una larga y lúcida cámara de gas . . . sombras cubanescas que se quedaron sin tiempo . . . una librería de alta seguridad" (25), "una escuela eterna de sobremurientes que tarde o temprano nos va a graduar" (35). La Habana es "amnésica y anestesiada," "sin historia ni histología" (6), "una rutina de heroicidad" (8), el "exoesqueleto libre de América" (9), "un crucigrama sin clave" (16), "la unidad de medida para la velocidad de las mentiras" (66).[13] Roughly translated: "Nothing-and-fatherland, a country with no H, a caustic letter"(9); "a long and lucid gas chamber . . . timeless Cuban shadows . . . a high security bookstore" (25); "an eternal school of half-dead-survivors that sooner or later are going to graduate from life" (35); "La Habana is amnesic and anaesthetized, without history or histology"(6); "a routine of heroicity" (8); "the free exoskeleton of the Americas" (9); "a crossword puzzle without an answer key"(16); "the measuring unit for the speed of lies" (66).[14]

The collection offers the reflections of a wandering photographer, Orlando and his relationship with Ipatria. Ipatria is a diffuse being that changes identities: sometimes she is a Chilean exile living in the Alamar apartment, a famous concrete neighborhood east of Havana where, in the novel, the gardens produce *kimilsungia* flowers; at other times she is a "*sobremuriente del postdesarrollo*" ("a sur-*dier* of the after-development," [26]) who exists without substance in twentieth-, twenty-first-, and twenty-second-century Cuba. Ipatria is an inapprehensible symbol of the motherland that becomes apathetic, who has to be destroyed because

> No parecía entender el espíritu épico de la época. Quería oponerse y no sabía qué hacer. Ni por qué hacer. Había extraviado su intuición planetaria . . . Sin Ipatria, contra Ipatria. Era necesario por todos: no hay grupo humano que sobreviva a semejante estado de compasión . . . lo criminal hubiera sido dejarla sobremorir así, como una mediocre más en las madrugadas inciviles del apagón." (116)
>
> (She couldn't understand the epic spirit of the times. She wanted to oppose and she didn't know how. Or why. She had lost her planetary intuition . . . without Ipatria, against Ipatria. It was necessary for all of us: there isn't a single human group able to survive such state of compassion . . . It would have been criminal to allow her to *sur-die* like that, like another mediocre in the uncivil dawn of the blackout.)

Finally Ipatria becomes masculine; the text becomes a metafiction and Ipatria a writer that concludes the book by declaring, "Narres lo que narres te arrepentirás" ("Whatever you narrate, you will repent") (201).

This conclusion seems to summarize the so far tragic reality of Cuba's internal opposition, as exemplified by the Independent Library Project examined here and the difficulties to analyze, research, and narrate Cuba's realities. And yet, Cubans persist in writing their own history and telling their own stories while finding ways not only to survive but also to move forward and to find all possible and impossible interstices to create and to reinvent themselves. For activist/scholars in the United States, dismissing or embracing what Cubans decide to develop inside the island should not be based solely on arguments of the Left or the Right in the United States to move forward their own agenda. This will neither help us understand current Cubans realities nor create a path for effective scholarly activism in the United States or on the island. The old motto of "either with us or against us" clouds the possibility for a balanced analysis of the complexity of Cuban reality.

The task is to listen to as many different and contradictory voices as possible, particularly those who are expressing opinions that have been silenced for too many years. In many cases this will probably lead to having official representatives shutting their doors to avoid conversation or stepping down from a panel table to avoid direct engagement. But ultimately those same officials might later recognize the importance of constructive criticism and collaboration, or even the same evolving Cuban system will be in charge of eliminating extremists.[15] Engaging contradictions does not necessarily imply agreement with one side or the other but provides them with equal opportunities to be heard. As Craig Calhoun reminds us, "activist engagement connects social scientists to different people, problems and places in very particular ways. It is not just about universal truths –though these do mater- but about producing truth in particular contexts and making knowledge useful in particular projects. It is about the way the world looks from different particular perspectives" (2008, xxi). Whether we are studying gender issues, economic development, human rights, or libraries, the more the scholars/activists in the world listen respectfully and value the emerging Cuban ideological and cultural diversity, the more spaces for collective and individual creativity and expression will be open inside Cuba. Setting this example will also convey the message to Cubans (either in official government positions or members of independent groups) that dialogue and free exchange of ideas is the only way forward. Rather than stepping down from the podium to avoid interaction, as the women's studies Cuban delegation did to me in 1995, we should all share the podium and find ways for understanding and regeneration.

Notes

1. This chapter was eventually published as "Women, Family, and the Cuban Revolution," in *Cuban Communism*, ed. Irving L. Horowitz and Jaime Suchilicki (New Brunswick and London: Transaction, 2001).
2. The terms "Cuban" and "Cuban-American" are complex and difficult to define. (See the excellent analysis provided by Gustavo Perez Firmat in his *Life on the Hyphen: The Cuban-American Way*). In my case, I was born and raised in Cuba and have lived in the United States as a U.S. citizen for the past twenty years. As such, I am a Cuban-American given my current citizenship. But the experience of having lived in Cuba for thirty-two years sets me apart from those Cuban-Americans who were born in the United States of Cuban parents. In fact, Cuban officials on the island seem to be more inclined to dialogue with the latter than with those of us who experienced firsthand and for a long period of time life in Cuba after 1959.
3. I am the founder and president of the Tacoma-Cienfuegos Sister City committee, an organization devoted to educate and to build bridges of understanding and collaboration between the two cities. I graduated with a degree in philosophy from the University of Havana in 1982 and taught philosophy for nine years at a branch of the University of Havana until I was expelled. I hold a PhD in

romance languages and literature from the University of Washington and teach Spanish and literature at Green River College.

4. In January 2013 I finally took the risk and visited one of the main libraries in Havana.
5. Dimas Cecilio Castellanos, Jiguaní, Oriente, 1943. I am using his name here with his permission.
6. Some visitors to several libraries testify that the ones visited do not have the amount of books required (see Neugebauer 2002; Pateman 2011). In my recent visit it seems like the Reinaldo Bragado Library does have the required amount.
7. There are several blogs and internet sites created by representatives of different branches and offspring of the Project of Independent Libraries. See in the list of works cited the information about the blogs of Cubanet, Gisela Delgado, and Nueva Esperanza.
8. "Little Hells" is the popular name given to the room in the Biblioteca Nacional José Martí where the prohibited books are kept.
9. On March 22, 2011, *Granma*, the official newspaper of the Cuban Communist Party, published an article entitled "Cyber-war: Mercenaries on the Web." This was preceded by a series of news items on the Cuban TV program *Las razones de Cuba*, where the terms "cyber-mercenaries" and "cyber-terrorists" were used to talk about the independent Cuban bloggers. These terms represent grave accusations since the legal penal code in Cuba considers these as offenses against the Cuban state punishable with five to thirty years in jail (see http://www.diariodecuba.com/derechos-humanos/4007-blogosfera-alternativa-en-peligro).
10. To see the 2013 call for the contest visit http://in-cubadora.org/category/concursos-novelas-de-gavetas/.
11. For more information on Yoani Sánchez see her book *Havana Real* published in 2011 as well as articles by and about her (by Larry Rohter) in the *New York Times.*
12. Intranet in this context refers to the Cuban internal network. Most Cubans don't have direct access to the Internet, rather to the State-controlled intranet.
13. All citations from Boring Home are from the printed version published by Garamond.
14. All translations from the Spanish in this essay are by Marisela Fleites-Lear.
15. Such is the case of the Iroel Sánchez, the former president of the Cuban Book Institute who banned Orlando Luis Pardo Lazo's novel *Boring Cuba* from being published in Cuba. In 2009 he was removed from his position in the government by the Minister of

Culture Abel Prieto given Iroel's extremist positions (see in *Cuba-encuentro* the article "*Destituido Iroel Sánchez*").

References

Angulo Cano, Yanira. "Orlando Luis Pardo Lazo's Boring Home: A Brave New Dystopia." Accessed April 7, 2011, http://manguitoreview.blogspot.com/2010/02/orlando-luis-pardo-lazos-boring-home.html#comment-form.

Biblioteca Nacional de Cuba José Martí. 2007. "Historia de la Biblioteca Nacional." http://www.bnjm.cu/historia.htm. Accessed June 19, 2012.

Calhoun, Craig. 2008. "Foreword." In *Engaging Contradictions. Theory, Politics and Methods of Activist Scholarship*, ed. Charles Hale, xiii–xxvi. Berkeley: University of California Press.

Castellanos, Dimas. "Bibliotecas independientes." El Blog de Dimas. Accessed August 13, 2011, http://www.desdecuba.com/dimas.

Castro Ruz, Fidel. 1998. "Sostiene entrevista con periodistas en la VIII Feria Internacional del libro." *Granma*. 12 Febrero 1998: 1.

Celaya, Miriam. "La "privatización" del derecho a disentir." Abril 5, 2011 at 15:31. Accessed April 6, 2011, http://www.desdecuba.com/sin_evasion.

Cubaencuentro. 2009. "Destituido Iroel Sánchez." June 26. Accessed September 17, 2011. http://www.cubaencuentro.com/es/cultura/noticias/destituido-iroel-sanchez-189155.

Cubanet. 1998. "Proyecto de Bibliotecas Independientes en Cuba." March 25. Accessed May 19, 2013, http://www.cubanet.org/htdocs/bibliotecas/proyecto.htm.

Delgado, Gisela. 2009. "Voces de Cambio. Blog del Proyecto de Bibliotecas Independientes de Cuba." October 27. Accessed April 7, 2011. http://vocesdecambiobibliotecasindependientes.blogspot.com.

Generation Y. "Boring Home." Accessed September 01, 2011, http://www.desdecuba.com/generationy/?p=435.

Havel, Vaclav. 2006. "The discreet terror of Fidel Castro." *Havana Journal Online*. Accessed April 8, 2011, http://havanajournal.com/politics/entry/the-discreet-terror-of-fidel-castro-vaclav-havel.

Henken, Ted A., Miriam Celaya, and Dimas Castellanos, eds. 2013. *Cuba. Latin America in Focus Series*. Santa Barbara, California: ABC-CLIO publishers.

InCUBAdora. 2013. "Convocatoria: Concurso Franz Kafka de Novelas." January 10. Accessed May 19, 2013. http://in-cubadora.org/2013/01/10/convocatoria-concurso-franz-kafka-de-novelas.

Kent, Robert. "The Friends of Cuban Libraries." Accessed April 12, 2011. http://www.friendsofcubanlibraries.org.

McDonald, Peter. 2008. "ALA's Stand on Cuba's Independent Libraries." *American Libraries* (June/July): 100–102.

Movimiento Cubano Unidad Democrática (M.C.U.D.). N/D. "Documentos. Proyecto de bibliotecas independientes de Cuba." Accessed March 7, 2011, http://www.cubamcud.org/Documentos/Listado-Primerabiblioteca.htm.

Neugebauer, Rhonda L. 2002. "Payment For Services Rendered: U.S.-Funded Dissent and the Independent Libraries Project." University of California Riverside, November 8–9. Accessed March 5, 2011, www.cubalinda.com/English/Groups/RhondaNeugebauer.htm.

Nueva Esperanza. "Red de Bibliotecas Cívicas Reinaldo Bragado Bretaña." Web. Accessed April 15, 2013. http://reddebibliotecas-civicas.blogspot.com.

Pardo Lazo, Orlando Luis. 2009. *Boring Home*. La Habana: Ediciones Lawtonomar. Accessed March 09, 2011, http://penultimosdias.com/wpcontent/uploads/2009/02/Boring%20Home%20OLPL.pdf%3E.

———. 2009. *Boring Home*. Prague: Garamond.

Pateman, John. "Cuban Libraries Support Group Press Release June 28, 2000." Accessed March 7, 2011, http://libr.org/juice/issues/vol3/LJ_3.25.sup.html.

Pérez Firmat, Gustavo.1994. *Life on the Hyphen. The Cuban-American Way*. Austin, Texas: University of Texas Press.

Pérez-Matos, N., and Juan Carlos Fernández Molina. 2010. "The History of Library and Information Activities in Cuba: The Relationship with its Constitutional Periods." *Library & Information History* 26 (3): 213–224.

Rohter, Larry. 2011. "In Cuba, the Voice of a Blog Generation." *The New York Times* (7/05). http://www.nytimes.com/2011/07/06/books/yoani-sanchez-cubas-voice-of-a-blogging-generation.html.

Salim, Lamrani. "Cuba and the Myth of the 'Independent Libraries'." Online. Accessed March 7, 2011, http://www.zcommunications.org/cuba-and-the-myth-of-the-independent-libraries-by-lamrani-salim.

Sánchez, Yoani. 2011. *Havana Real: One Woman Fights to Tell the Truth about Cuba Today*. New York: Melville House.

———. 2012. "The Dream of Leaving Cuba." *The New York Times* (4/21) http://www.nytimes.com/2012/04/22/opinion/sunday/the-dream-of-leaving-cuba.html.

Shaffer, Kirwin. 2003. “Freedom Teaching: Anarchism and Education in Early Republican Cuba, 1898–1925.” *The Americas* 60 (2):151–183.

Silva Crespo, A., and Rivera Z. 2006. “Domingo Figarola Caneda: una personalidad de la cultura y la bibliotecología en Cuba.” *Acimed* 14, no. 2. http://bvs.sld.cu/revistas/aci/vol14_2_06/aci06206.htm . Accessed June 19, 2012.

Valverde, Freddy. 2008. “Escritor cubano galardonado con premio literario Novelas de Gaveta, Franz Kafka.” *Radiodifusión Checa* 7, Radio Praga. 28–04–2008 15:04. Accessed March 5, 2011, www.radio.cz/es/print/articulo/103525.

———. 2011. “El escritor cubano Ernesto Santana recibe el Premio Novelas de Gaveta, Franz Kafka.” *Radio Praga* 07–01–2011 14:14. Accessed April 8, 2011, http://www.radio.cz/es/rubrica/notas/el-escritor-cubano-ernesto-santana-recibe-el-premio-novelas-de-gaveta-franz-kafka.

PART 2

PERFORMED STORIES OF SOCIAL JUSTICE

INTRODUCTION TO PART 2

Performed Stories of Social Justice

JESSICA MONTEIRO MANFREDI

Performed stories have the ability to empower social justice movements in ways distinct from textual productions, as they utilize oral storytelling as one of their main tools. Oral storytelling transcends levels of literacy and as such appeals to wider audiences, becoming an effective way to communicate memories and demand social justice. The performed stories in this section of *Taking Risks,* serve as testimony to the power of oral and performed storytelling to subvert manipulative media and government portrayals of community members'/activists' experiences. Performed stories, as embodied here through video, community radio and TV stations, and theater productions, create immediate discourses that foster dialogue as a method to further activists' goals. This fertile exchange of ideas has spread the desire, among authors and activists alike, to establish channels to educate people beyond national borders. Engaging in these transbordered discourses through performed stories defies sociopolitical power structures and provides activists with legitimacy and recognition for their efforts.

As the chapters in this section reveal, performed stories are employed throughout the Americas as a tool to strengthen social justice movements, and Brazil, my home country, is no exception. While working on these introductions I was also closely watching the 2013 riots that swept across all of Brazil's major cities. I could not help but notice that, in my estimation, these protests have been largely successful in part due to the use of strategically performed stories. Common folks recorded several videos in which local and state police used violent tactics against peaceful protesters. The videos were then shared on popular social media websites to denounce the police's brutality and to create a space for dialogue surrounding the protests. Thanks to these efforts, more and more Brazilians and members of the international community were able to witness how the police were typically the ones to use violence. Activists then dismantled the mainstream media and government's false claims that the protesters were merely vandals and looters.[1] As a result, activists reclaimed ownership of their movement, a peoples' movement. This example speaks to the power of performed stories to engage in dialogues that deconstruct discourses created by power holders, in this case the Brazilian media and government.

The first chapter in this section speaks to the power of video and film as methods for resistance. Colombian *desplazada* activists use video testimonies in their fight to obtain recognition from Medellín's government that the activists are the main drivers behind that city's rebuilding process. By recording *desplazadas'* oral stories of resistance, and growing archives of video and films, Tamera Marko and her students and collaborators create spaces where dialogue can occur. The exchanges happen at three levels: when *desplazadas* tell their stories during interviews with students; when their stories are shared with *desplazadas'* families and people from other neighborhoods with similar experiences, and when their stories are distributed online, in film festivals, in U.S. classrooms, and beyond. Through the archives of performed storytelling in these video interviews, *desplazadas* create a dialogue in places far beyond their neighborhood. As such, they regain a sense of ownership for their work done to rebuild their city—despite the government's failure to acknowledge their labors. The *desplazadas* are ultimately achieving, step by step, their desire of seeing Medellín represented in Colombia and abroad as more than a hub of violence and drugs. Marko's and the *deplazadas'* goal is to ultimately challenge this widely accepted discourse by continuing to enrich archives with performed stories and systematically circulating the videos at a transnational level.

Robin Garcia's chapter then delves into the dynamics of community radio and television stations in Venezuela through the lenses of community media activists within the context of the Bolivarian revolution. Garcia reveals that historically, traditionally marginalized communities in Venezuela did not have the opportunity to engage in dialogue to create information and representations that reflected their communities' realities. Now, however, community radio and TV stations throughout Venezuela have encouraged these otherwise silenced voices to be heard by constructing a media platform where dialogue takes place. These media outlets create a very unique space in which, according to Garcia, "the documenter and the documented are the same." Often, a documenter is someone from the mainstream media or the government who may distort opinions and facts to advance one's own political agenda. However, in this case, the documenter is a community member performing stories that represent her own historical background, traditions, and political views. The result is the creation of "democratic archival productions" where the oppressed act as protagonists on TV screens and their voices echo through the radio. Venezuelan community media activists' efforts subvert U.S. narratives regarding Venezuela, creating networks of transnational solidarity via these performed media stories. Ultimately these processes challenge national and international political power imbalances, particularly with respect to community self-representation.

Last, Christina Marín's chapter tells us heartbreaking stories of femicide taking place on the border between Ciudad Juárez and the United States. Here, performed stories are embodied through three plays she directed in the United States using Theatre of the Oppressed as a framework. Marín demonstrates how the mass murder of women in Ciudad Juárez is both widespread and known, yet it remains largely invisible to the world due to the U.S. and Mexican governments' negligence and the absence of coverage in mainstream media. Through the use of ethnodrama, Marín gifts the audience with fictional stories based on research and testimonials from the affected families, including mothers who are organizing and fighting to bring justice to many open cases. Postperformance discussions are key features of Marín's work. They allow actors and the audience to engage in an in-depth dialogue about the murders. The plays thus educate the U.S. community about this transnational problem both through art and through conversational discourse, as many in the audience admit previously not knowing about the femicide that plagues Juárez. Above all, Marín teaches us how performed stories, as articulated through theater and enhanced by dialogue, can be utilized as activist tools to give voices to the hundreds murdered and unable to speak for themselves, to break the silence about femicide in Juárez, and to bring awareness of this issue across borders.

The chapters in this section illuminate how performance, largely construed, allows for dialogue in ways that written texts alone cannot. The authors/activists/performers demonstrate that verbally telling their stories, archiving them, legitimating them through media, and performing them through theater is politically significant on many levels. These "performances" foster collective empowerment as the storytellers become the framers of their own narratives. Subsequently they are politically significant as the performances ultimately talk back to the power holders who marginalize them. Finally, the performed stories are significant for the transnational solidarity they inspire. Thus, the story performers we meet in this section are further examples of activists defying local, national, and transnational power imbalances.

Notes

1. http://noticias.r7.com/sao-paulo/alckmin-chama-manifestantes-de-baderneiros-e-vandalos-12062013.

5

WE ALSO BUILT THE CITY OF MEDELLÍN

Deplazadas' Family Albums as Feminist Archival Activism

TAMERA MARKO

An Introductory Question

"Why are you here? What are you looking for?" I looked up from the desk in the Reading Room of the Photography and Newspaper Archive of the *Biblioteca pública piloto de Medellín para América Latina* to see the man who had asked me these questions. He was working through newspapers with a magnifying glass. It was December 2005. The city was still largely devoid of foreigners, and my husband's family insisted it was unsafe for me to walk around outside by myself. I had first come to Medellín the year before to meet my future in-laws. We spent three weeks poring over their family albums. It became clear that these were more than photos of a private family story; the albums were archives of local, state, and national history.

The albums told stories of immigration and resulting years of separation from loved ones in a (sometimes agonizingly failed) search for the American Dream. They told stories of rebuilding their homes burned by members of Colombia's two opposing political parties in their bloody fight for power since the 1850s. The photos told stories of La Violencia,[1] between 1948 and 1958, when the country erupted in war between guerrilla, military, and paramilitary groups. This violence prompted them to flee the countryside to the city of Medellín. They subsequently lived in the 1980s and 1990s narcotraffic epicenter when Medellín was known as the most violent city in the world.[2] In these albums, there are as many stories of bombs, death by assassination or stray bullet, negotiating with kidnappers, and Pablo Escobar legacies, as there are stories of baptisms, birthdays, Christmases, and vacations at the Colombian coast. Emerging from these photos were stories of a century of everyday life in a city and country (still) at war.

I looked up from the archive table and told him that I was researching stories about the then more than one hundred thousand *desplazados* who had settled in Medellín since the 1950s.[3] That is, the people who were forced to flee their homes in Colombia due to violence, often with nothing but the clothes on their backs, and their children in their arms. I was especially interested in stories about how *desplazados* had built more than fifteen sprawling neighborhoods in Medellín, largely without state support.[4] I wanted to understand the city government's (2003–2007) investment of 60 percent of its budget on "education," which included building state-of-the-art schools, libraries, gardens, and hospitals in the neighborhoods where *desplazados* lived as well as public transportation for all city residents to reach these new resources. My family's albums document the traumatic displacement of people who could resettle with their working-class and middle-class resources. I wondered about the family albums of displaced *campesinos*[5], who were forced to flee with little more than their farming expertise and the resources they could carry. How did these *campesinos* self-settle in the city? I did not tell the man asking me questions about my family connection. In Medellín, one does not offer personal details to strangers, especially if you are a foreigner, from the United States, researching human rights. I asked him why *he* was in this archive. He looked over the newspapers I had splayed out on the desk: photographs of bloody military incursions, dead bodies police found in the streets due to what the press attributed to gang or narcotraffic warfare, and residents mourning their children and picking through the rubble after a fire or tropical storm-induced landslide. Quietly, he told me that his job as a social worker was to prove the identity of displaced persons in Medellín so the government could issue them a new *cédula*. Without a *cédula*, or Colombian identity card, people cannot access government buildings or medical care, register for school, or apply for jobs.[6] His job was to confirm the transcript of a displaced person's story told to a government social worker with other documentation such as newspaper photographs or names of people and institutions listed in phone books from their hometowns to prove they are who they say they are. Then he asked me two final questions, which have served as my mantra and warning for this project: "What are you going to do with this information? *Gringuita*, who are you trying to help?"

There are three elements of this encounter I wish to unpack here. First, I was surprised by our exchange in the archive, not by the question, but by the tone with which he asked it. Growing up in the Tijuana/San Diego border region on the United States side, working as a U.S. human rights journalist in various countries, and then doing historical research in Brazil, I was accustomed to this question being launched at me and other U.S. researchers. It usually came in a tone ranging from shy curiosity to Yankee-go-home rage at white, "*gringa*" U.S. academics who come to their countries to mine their archives, publish in English without citing the country's native-language scholars' work, and use the research only to further their individual academic career. His use of the word "*gringuita*" was not meant as an insult, but to soften his question's tone. Second, I had once before found myself sitting at the same table with a researcher combing through newspapers with a magnifying glass. In an archive in Rio de Janeiro, a man dressed in military attire was not trying to help people rebuild their homes; he was looking for participants in antigovernment protests. His copies of these records could serve as grounds for police arrest or be saved in military files under the category of radical dissident. Third, I was struck with his assumption that my purpose was to "help." I was uncomfortable because it framed my research in terms of charity or social welfare. This was not my intention. My intention, however vague at that stage, was research as social justice. Why? Because I was there and have historical training, archival experience, and access to university resources. Furthermore, my status as a highly educated, U.S. born, native-English-speaking citizen grants me the mobility to cross the border between Colombia and the United States. But what about my research project was truly social justice? And for whom?

Haunted by this scarce circulation of *campesinas'* perspectives regarding their own displacement and subsequent self-settlement, I formulated a research question: what happens when the "official" and "popular" stories about your neighborhood do not match what you archive in your family album? In response, my partner Jota Samper[7] and I cofounded a historical memory archive in 2008. The archive consists of stories that *desplazadas* narrate from their family albums. These albums are often the only record of their life in the town they were forced to flee, how they built their neighborhood in Medellín and the last sixty years of everyday life there. People tell their stories in video, photograph, written word, and artistic performance. To build this archive we collaborate with U.S. and Colombian university students and faculty, City of Medellín officials and social workers, and hundreds of displaced people who built their homes in Medellín. Over the last five years this project has organically evolved into an ongoing alternative feminist archive of how women have built the city of Medellín. Called medellín, mi hogar/my home medellín[8] it includes twenty-three hundred hours of stories with 650 people. We have edited fifty stories into documentary videos of ten minutes or less.

Building this archive has taught me what in retrospect should have been obvious: there is a direct relationship between the risk each storyteller takes in telling her story and her relationship to the conflict in Colombia. This risk informs how and where her story circulates and at what cost. This chapter is about the building of this archive within the context of the unequal level of risk that faculty, students, social workers, and *desplazadas* make when collaborating in telling *desplazadas'* stories. It is also about how this risk inequity challenges the archive's mission of social justice research as activism. I hope that these stories, archived and distributed strategically, will provide an alternative narrative force that expands the archival and rhetorical landscape of women in Medellín beyond what Virginia Bouvier calls "the drug and violence prism through which people tend to view Colombia" (2009, 5). Our mission of social justice is two-fold. First, we seek to document women's first-person diverse experiences of displacement and self-settlement. Second, we seek to circulate a narrative force in which representations of *desplazadas* are not reduced to their displacement. We wish to insert *desplazadas'* perspectives into neighborhood, city, national, and global stories about who built the city of Medellín.

This chapter is divided into five sections. First, I walk us through the process of creating this archive. Second, I position how Jota and I intend this archive to contribute to knowledge production about displaced women in Colombia. Third, I discuss themes emerging from the stories housed in the archives. Fourth, I identify the storytellers' risks in telling their stories. I also discuss ways that the students, faculty, social workers, and *desplazadas* working on this archive have different motivations for telling the women's stories. Also different, sometimes radically so, are the risks we take in storytelling. I conclude with how different risks and motivations inspire and challenge the archive's mission of feminist and social justice research *and* activism.

Genealogy of *medellín mi hogar* / my home medellín, 2008–2012

In a tragic irony, *desplazadas* are the most "mobile" people in Medellín—having moved from their hometowns to another one foreign to them. *Desplazadas*, however, have the least mobility to circulate their stories. Between the 1990s and the early 2000s, Colombians were among the most denied visa applicants in the world. This is based on the fact that Colombians, for example, had to wait two years to get an appointment for a tourist visa to the United States and needed visas to travel to most countries in the world. Presently, Colombians still need visas to travel to over half of the world's countries. For the 2006 fiscal year, the U.S. state department lists its adjusted refusal rate for Colombians applying for B-Visas to the United States as 33.3 percent. A B-Visa is a temporary visa for tourism or business. These rates are listed according to nationality. These B-Visas are granted more easily to Colombians in recent years, as evidenced by the State Department's report for 2013 that names the B-Visa refusal rate for Colombians to travel to the United States at 10.4 percent (U.S. Department of State, 2006; 2013). In a competition of who gets to tell the past, present, and future story of Medellín, *desplazadas* have the least access to circulating their perspectives in citywide, national, and global arenas. So the *desplazadas* are displaced again, this time from their own stories of displacement. This I call *doble desplazamiento* (double displacement). In contrast, academics like Jota and I have privileged access to (1) university resources *and* (2) the City of Medellín's and Colombia's nationwide initiatives for displaced people *and* (3) community leaders who founded their neighborhoods in Medellín. Jota and I can cross international, geographical, cultural, and socioeconomic borders between these three groups. We initiated this archive in an attempt to mobilize local and transnational resources to disrupt *desplazadas' doble desplazamiento*.[9] This section details the genealogy of our archive.

In 2008, the City of Medellín's Secretaría de Bienestar Social[10] founded Medellín Solidaria in a painstaking process of official state-community encounters throughout Medellín. These encounters took place in neighborhoods that displaced people had self-settled over the previous fifty years, with little official state support. The process began with hundreds of social workers who, wearing blue vests with the Medellín Solidaria logo, began walking into neighborhoods that had been ignored by the city public transportation due to fear of entering the city's most violent streets. They walked into communities where for years narcotraffic and other armed leaders had blocked outsiders from entering without their permission. The community residents also had reason to fear and resent representatives from the city government, who over the past few decades had ordered military and police incursions into their neighborhoods and also looked the other way when armed groups burned down their houses. House to house, the social workers walked, asking if families wanted to speak with them about their rights as Colombian citizens and Medellín residents. Many people slammed doors in the social workers' faces. Some residents pulled guns. Some people invited the social workers into their homes and offered them *café con leche*. Over the course of a year, the social workers walked hundreds of miles. They risked their lives crossing *fronteras invisibles*, invisible borders, marking gang, guerrilla, and paramilitary turf. City government vans transported Medellín Solidaria participants to and from their homes to government buildings downtown. The social workers would point to the Mayor's Building and say, "This is *your* building." They showed community members how to process paperwork. The city government began fulfilling its promises to provide cement floors to cover dirt ones, access to potable water and other basic services, usually free of charge. News spread among residents that they might be able to trust this government program. These social workers could actually be a viable nonviolent move toward connecting displaced residents in Medellín with city resources.

This social welfare office cannot be easily critiqued in a scholarly activist box and tied up with a state-as-panopticon theoretical bow. In the context of Medellín, with ongoing violence and more displaced people arriving every day, being a state social worker means being a communications bridge between community members; the same state that had abandoned these members; and armed actors who are in direct contestation with the state and the military. Social workers also represent the front lines of communication between community residents and the last three mayorships in Medellín, the first in one hundred years to break from the two political parties whose war with each other had prompted La Violencia.

In 2008, a year before the Medellín Solidaria social workers began walking into displaced people's self-settled neighborhoods, Jota and I founded a study abroad civic engagement project with Duke University's DukeEngage pilot initiative. DukeEngage funds Duke undergraduate students to participate in one of forty-two civic engagement projects worldwide. Called DukeEngage Colombia, the project which Jota and I still direct brings U.S. university students to live and work in Medellín for eight weeks in the summer. This project's purpose is dedicated to human rights, not through social work but through social consciousness. We focus on ways students' lived experience in Medellín can help dismantle local and global stereotypes that reduce Colombia to nothing more than violence, drugs, and poverty.[11]

In 2008, we brought DukeEngage Colombia's first five U.S. students into self-settled neighborhoods under heightened safety conditions. Students ran free art and sports workshops with children and adults inside the *parques bibliotecas*, or library larks which the City of Medellín had just built in what had been the most isolated neighborhoods throughout Medellín. Like all government and many cultural centers in Medellín, these library parks are patrolled by armed security guards. Our students were among the first foreigners to give workshops in the parks, which had just opened their doors to 1,500 visitors a day. We quickly realized that our greatest privilege as U.S. students and faculty from an elite university in the United States was *our mobility, our time,* and *the way Medellín residents from various neighborhoods welcomed our presence there.* Medellín residents wanted to share their stories with us simply because we had come to their city *despite* the city's reputation for violence that for two decades had scared tourists and foreign residents away. Jota and I worked with the students to develop what we saw as our responsibility among community members: *to listen.* When these Duke students graduate, they will likely become people with power: doctors, journalists, public policy analysts, professors, lawyers, and scientists. A core intention of DukeEngage Colombia is that the students' experience in Medellín will instill an ongoing questioning of their responsibility to human rights and an awareness of how they move through the world impacts people's rights.

The following year's DukeEngage Colombia students worked with the library parks' staff in Medellín to make video documentaries about some of the city's new urban infrastructure and cultural programming. This time Jota, Medellín city and community leaders, and I gave the students more freedom to move around the city and neighborhoods. We worked with the historical memory project Sala Mi Barrio, located in the city's five library parks.[12] At each Park, we circulated by flyer and word of mouth an invitation for people to share any story they wanted. To our surprise, within three days, more than 1,000 people signed up. When we realized that more than 90 percent of the 250 people we interviewed were *campesina desplazadas* who had founded their neighborhood in Medellín, the idea for our alternative feminist archive was born.

After our archive's first DVD August 2009 debut to the people who were interviewed in the videos, the City of Medellín's Department of Social Welfare[13] invited us to make documentary videos with families who were collaborating with Medellín Solidaria. For the last three summers, DukeEngage Colombia has worked with Medellín Solidaria on the archive. Every summer, each of our eight students spends four days a week, waking up at dawn, walking with a Medellín Solidaria social worker on her route visiting families' homes. This collaboration with the social workers has moved our students out of the library parks and deep inside the neighborhoods and people's homes. This project has meant working with actors and institutions, which, at times, appear mutually antagonistic. Mobility in and out of the neighborhoods where the storytellers live also requires that Medellín Solidaria social workers vouch for the integrity of our university students and faculty so that people in power there allow us, and the stories we carry, to pass. Those with power include gang leaders, church leaders, NGO workers, activists, and police who have come to trust the social workers and the city government they represent. The students accompany the social workers via metro, bus, *metrocable* (gondola), and on foot up into neighborhoods fifteen hundred feet into the Andes Mountains. Other students travel by horse, taxi, and motorcycle forty minutes into Medellín's rural municipalities, where they then walk another hour on unpaved paths to people's homes. The families are supposed to be informed that the students are coming and are invited to tell any story they like. The family members receive the student and social worker in their home. There the student photographs and video records women and their families telling a story in their own words and images. We specifically ask how they built their home and neighborhood and their perspectives on the City of Medellín's recent sociourban interventions.

During the summer, Jota and I live in the same neighborhood where each Duke student is living with a Medellín homestay family. Students from the Universidad Nacional de Colombia in Medellín also guide the Duke students through their youth worlds of work, study, and social life in the city. This immerses the students in the intergenerational culture, colloquial Spanish, and various socioeconomic dimensions of the city's spaces and history. This all helps deepen the students' perspective when listening to the *desplazadas'* stories.

Eight Colombian university students in Medellín transcribe the original recording of a person telling her story. The stories range from fifteen minutes to two hours. The transcribers annotate the transcripts with possible meanings of colloquial terms and key words that mention an important event that warrants more context. These Colombian students and the social workers also critique the Duke students' or social workers' interview approach, suggesting ways they could be less controlling or more respectful to the storytellers. In addition, I run a weekly reflection session in my home in which each Duke student brings a written word, photograph, or video reflection about a common theme. We focus, for example, on culture shock and how they feel and think about their work with *desplazadas'* stories. We talk about ways that the conflict in Colombia is also connected with socioeconomic and political processes in the United States. Students express intense discomfort, fear, joy, love, pride, and anguish about their experiences and how to process them. They edit their reflections for our DukeEngage Colombia blog.[14]

Every week, each student summarizes the stories he or she recorded. From the 90–250 stories students record each summer, Jota and I select which two stories we will help each student edit for the DVD we produce that summer.[15] We choose these stories based on several criteria. Does the story help represent the cultural and ethnic diversity of displaced people in Colombia? We especially focus on editing stories that include perspectives on life before displacement, the displacement itself, the process of self-settlement, and interactions with the City of Medellín before and after its recent urban interventions. We also prioritize stories that explain negotiations with multiple armed groups. We carefully note stories that might place the storyteller's life at risk. For ten to thirty hours a week, Jota and I and other Colombian faculty members and students run workshops with the Duke students to edit the videos. We guide the students' work to put these stories into conversation with research in archives, human rights and government publications, media coverage, and academic literature. After three weeks of story recording and another three weeks of editing workshops, the students consult Jota, me, the transcribers, and homestay families to craft English subtitles for each video. Since 2010, film students from Emerson College have come to Medellín to help the Duke students with editing and to document our behind-the-scenes process. Jota and I edit the final versions of the videos.

The last week of our summer work, the students, Jota, and I debut a DVD of edited stories in a theater in Medellín. The social workers call or visit each family whose story we have edited for the DVD and invite them and their neighbors to the theater debut and offer their critique. Medellin Solidaria organizes round-trip transport for each storyteller and her family to travel from her house to the theater. In this theater, hundreds of storytellers—as protagonists, audience, critics, and respondents—are the largest presence in the room. The storytellers fill the two to four hundred theater seats. In a temporary inversion of power, the community members have more prestige and voice than the politicians, social workers, media, and university people also present.

After each video shows on screen, a student and an archive director receive critique from the storyteller who told her story. This face-to-face critique is nerve wracking for all of us. Here the *desplazadas*-neighborhood founders hold us responsible for the way we tell and circulate their stories. After the storyteller offers her critique, other members of the audience also share their opinions. Often this is the first time that community members have the chance to talk to people from other neighborhoods about their lives. In this moment, people share moral support, institutional resources, and questions about more details regarding the video story and exchange phone numbers to continue talking. If the storytellers want us to make changes to the videos, we do. When the storytellers approve the final version, we circulate their video stories online and in exhibitions, film festivals, and K–20 curriculum throughout the Americas. When we return to Medellín, we bring the storytellers photographs, video, and written comments and questions from the audiences where their video stories have traveled. The goal of this year-round production, archival, and circulation process? To be a small but steady feminist alternative force that expands the narrative landscape that represents displaced women in Colombia.

Producing Knowledge about Displaced Women in Colombia

This section outlines ways in which the archive *medellín mi hogar* seeks to produce feminist alternative knowledge about displaced women in Colombia. I begin by summarizing the dominant image of Colombia within which displaced women are represented. Hollywood movies, the media, and academic publications focus largely on stories about Colombia in terms of violence, narcotraffic, and poverty. This is similar for national (Colombian) and local (Medellín) production as well. In June 2012, a *telenovela* in Colombia was about Pablo Escobar. Another recent popular *telenovela* in Colombia featured sixty episodes of *Rosario Tijeras*, a television series about the real-life woman assassin of the same name. The most widely circulating national history of Colombia in English and also in Spanish translation is David Bushnell's *The Making of Modern Colombia: A Nation in Spite of Itself.* It was published in 1993, about two years after Medellín was labeled the most dangerous city in the world. Each of the previous three Latin American Studies Association conference program lists more than thirty-five presentations on Colombia. Nearly every one of these presentations focus on violence, be it guerrilla, paramilitary, military, domestic, narcotraffic, gang, assassin, globalization, and/or poverty.[16]

Women as key actors, and especially in feminist terms, are largely absent from national histories of Colombia. Scholarship about women in Colombia tends to position women within a national or local history of violence: as warriors or victims in the conflict. An exception to this is the groundbreaking *Colombia: Building Peace in a Time of War,* a multiauthored book of articles about international, national, state, and local peace initiatives, edited by Virginia Bouvier (2009). Bouvier maintains, and I concur, that the relative lack of coverage in English on Colombia, about anything other than violence is due to news stories being shaped by "policy hooks," which are "story angles that link events of the day to government policies or to an explicit relationship to the news consumer" (2009, 1).[17] Bouvier argues that "[s]ince most U.S. foreign aid thus far has been earmarked" for the war against drugs and leftist guerrilla movements, other agendas—regional stability; democracy, human rights, and the rule of law; socioeconomic development and humanitarian needs; and peace initiatives—make headlines only occasionally."[18] She highlights the fact that human rights practitioners "have generally focused their work on discerning the patterns of violence and abuse in the daily manifestations of Colombia's conflict" (7). In the conflict-resolution field, she cites an "ironic" and "inherent bias" against "actors who have eschewed violence in the pursuit of peace. Conflict analysis generally is performed with 'conflict actors' in mind" (7).

Scholarly literature about displaced women's peace movements tends to focus on high-profile national and regional women's movements or individual activists for peace and conflict resolution. Academic publications with a feminist approach regarding women in Medellín tend to be a broad overview or a regional study of women and displacement in Colombia.[19] Other histories of women focus on groups of women who work in factories,[20] NGOs, or community women's rights organizations.[21]

In Medellín there is a dizzying amount of careful and steadily growing historical and cultural production about women's rights. These projects produce a prolific number of multimedia publications created by and about women, including *desplazadas*.[22] In 2002, the Municipality of Medellín created the Metrowoman Undersecretariat,[23] or, "women from the city's *Metro*politan area." It was linked to the Department of Citizen Culture. In 2007, it created the Department of Women, whose mission is "to contribute to the equal rights and opportunities between women and men and the reduction of discriminatory practices that hinder the political, social, economic, and cultural development of women in the Municipality of Medellín."[24] Throughout this famously literary city, people share stories about women's experiences with violence and resilience. Women share these stories around kitchen tables, on blogs, and in exhibitions, posters, music, literature, and theater. Intertwined in these stories are women's efforts to grapple with contradictory and painful contexts of Roman Catholicism, *machismo*, narcotraffic, hunger, gangs, leaving their role in the conflict, and single motherhood. Women, of all classes, talk about societal pressures to have plastic surgery to conform their bodies to a narrow vision of physical beauty.[25] Young women who were born into displaced families in Medellín are producing their own cultural critique to counter sexual objectification of women and the social stigma against girls because they come from impoverished and violent neighborhoods.[26]

This literature emphasizes that women are courageous and effective actors in negotiating truces, kidnapped hostage release, and peace alliances between warring groups.

Woven throughout these publications and conversations are two intertwining tensions. The first tension regards women breaking their silence about their experience with the conflict in Colombia and domestic violence in their homes. The second tension focuses on gender norms that have five centuries of colonial roots in Colombia: women's place "at home" *or* "in the street." Women are pressured to "be good" by staying home or negotiate the negative consequences of operating outside of it. Our archive's stories complicate this dichotomy of "house versus street." This is because being displaced means both building your home in the street and protesting in the unprotected space of the street[27] to protect your home. *Desplazadas* also publish critiques challenging the ideal that city life is better than a rural one.[28] Many displaced women's stories frame negotiation of cross-class, house/street struggles as fundamental to their identity and dignity as *campesina desplazadas* and neighborhood founders.

A side effect of the literature's focus on the injustice and trauma of women's displacement is that it gives an impression of women as having a precarious and temporary position in Medellín communities. Everyday rhetoric reinforces this impression. Land that people occupy without purchase in Medellín is commonly called *una invasión*. Most of the women and children in our archive speak of the neighborhoods they built as "invasions."[29] There is little scholarly work on how women have built—*post* displacement—their homes and neighborhoods. Also largely absent from work on *dis*placement are women's perspectives on their *place* in the city of Medellín as not just refuge, but home.

There is another powerful source of knowledge production about displaced people in Colombia: the City of Medellín's international and national public relations campaign about what it calls "the transformation of Medellín." This campaign is tricky to disentangle into a dichotomy of "good" or "bad" state power structures versus an impoverished community. On one hand, it is crucial to know about a city government that invests 60 percent over ten years of its city budget on "education," that includes building three hundred points of infrastructure throughout the poorest and most violent and isolated city neighborhoods. It is these projects like Medellín Solidaria and the city-funded award-winning buildings, public spaces, and transportation between them that allow us to do this storytelling project. Medellín's metrocable, built in 2006, moves between the city's valley and Medellín's poorest neighborhoods located thirteen hundred feet up in the mountains. This is the journey many residents make between work and home to feed their family that week or day. The trip used to take 2.5 hours each way. With the metrocable, the same trip now takes 10 minutes. A ticket includes access to the metro, which runs from one end of the city to the other.

On the other hand, the city's campaign about the transformation of Medellin often positions itself in terms of "heroic rescue" of the communities. Slick public relations campaigns on Youtube entice tourists to come to Colombia with the slogan Colombia: The Only Danger Is Wanting to Stay. The Medellín campaign is problematic not just because of its myth of "rescue," but also because it makes invisible the labor, artistry, and expertise of thousands of community members who built dozens of neighborhoods five decades before state support. Currently, architects, urban planners and an interdisciplinary team of scientists and social scientists are crafting a new master plan for the next twenty years of the City of Medellín. The women neighborhood founders' stories are crucial to understanding the impacts of Medellín's massive city interventions in self-settled communities. The women's stories also provide crucial insight to city planners in other countries. This is because Medellín's city transformation is ongoing and being emulated in other Latin American cities.[30] Many of these women are approaching their late seventies and beyond. This puts the stories of these neighborhoods—and women's roles in founding them—at risk of being lost. The archive seeks to place women neighborhood founders' diverse perspectives into conversation with the City of Medellín's public relations campaign and the global dominant knowledge production about Colombia. The next section identifies some themes emerging from the archive's stories and specific audiences storytellers wish to reach.

Archiving Foundational Narratives: Emerging Themes

Before recording a woman's story for the archive, the student or faculty member doing the interview asks who the storyteller would like to hear her story and why. The leading answer? Women say they want government leaders and everyday residents of Medellín and beyond to know who originally founded their neighborhood and how and what they still need. They also want to share their perspectives on the City of Medellín's recent urban initiatives in their neighborhoods. Farconely Torres Usuga, co-founder and resident of the neighborhood El Triunfo narrates her story while seated at her kitchen table, which is covered in freshly pressed white linen. Sun streams through this room painted a robin-egg blue and filled with lush green plants. Throughout the interview, her children pass through a flowery golden curtain that offers privacy from the rest of the house. Pointing to photos in her family album, she says:

> [T]he neighborhood was started by an elderly man, a friend of ours. We were tired of paying for rent because if we paid the rent, we could not feed the baby . . . he invited us to come with him to the top of this hill where he had gotten a piece of land for him. . . . So we started collecting sticks and materials and began building our new homes . . . [T]he owners denounced us [meaning the police came]. First, they knocked down our houses, then, the second time, they burned them down with the flag and everything.[31] I sat to the side of the burning flag, watching my house and everything I had burning, and I began to cry. Because I knew they were never going to leave us alone. Later when more people had settled, we were already twelve families and we decided to get everyone together . . . and we all got on a bus and went down [downtown] to the government building to protest.[32]

Farconely says the women attended the protest with "their pillows perfectly in place" to appear heavily pregnant and had given the kids banana water to cause diarrhea. "We were demonstrating our need," she says, adding, "We stood all of us with our kids outside the building pooping and peeing all over the place. And so finally, they said yes, we could stay in our houses . . . [The mayor's office] gave us a paper that said they would stop knocking down our houses and burning them." When the protesters realized there were no signatures on the paper, they turned the bus around and returned to the city government building until the city officials signed it. Farconely says, "and when we got home, everyone started singing 'We have triumphed!' . . . so we decided that since we had triumphed, we would call the neighborhood The Triumph (El Triunfo)."

Farconely's story is one example in which women reveal ways they have organized unarmed protest against the city government to gain official legal protection of their right to remain in their homes and the neighborhoods they built in Medellín. Farconely's interview as participation in our archive more than half a decade after the City of Medellín's interventions in the city's self-settled neighborhoods reveals this community founder's willingness to work with the new state initiatives, but in the context of *also* remembering her history of tense state-neighborhood relationships.

Dozens of stories women choose to house in our archive focus on how women now work with Medellín Solidaria or other entities from a state and city government that in the past had burned down their house or looked the other way when it burned. Marta Nelly Villada Bedoya said when she was first displaced, she relocated with her family in Pereira where she built a *ranchito*. "I had been living there for fifteen days when 'Control Físico' came and knocked it down and burned it." As Marta Nelly speaks, she holds up newspaper clippings she saved, showing her and her family sitting outside in the dirt next to her burned home. "They burned my roof, all the walls. Everything. I just took out my beds, my storage closet, and my clothes. And since I had a newborn baby, I laid her in the crib outside in broad daylight." The newspaper report says she was one of the "forty families living in an 'invasion' settlement [who] woke up yesterday to the sound of machines destroying their homes."[33] Another newspaper clipping she saved stated, "Early yesterday, government employees from Control Físico, Public Works, and more than two hundred policemen began evacuating families out of the invasion settlement."[34] A day later, a different government commission arrived with humanitarian aid.[35] A few years later, Marta Nelly began working with Medellín Solidaria to register her children in school and have access to health care. She says that her work with Medellín Solidaria "has awakened me. Does that make sense? . . . I have more spirit."

Farconely's and Marta Nelly's stories reveal the complex relationships between civil society *desplazados* and representatives of city government entities and nonstate armed groups. Many women express this tension of not choosing to be part of the conflict, but nevertheless are caught in between. Many women say they are tired of violence and revenge, even in the name of justice for *campesinos*. Many women just want to raise their children to have a future without violence. These women try to avoid direct alliance with conflict actors and instead work day by day to live *una vida simple* (a simple life). The women also have years of expertise with living among the same people who have hurt them and/or their loved ones in the conflict and so have developed emotional and psychological capacities for resilience. This resilience is not necessarily forgiveness. It is, rather, the capacity to live simultaneously with grief and joy, anger and hope, and what the women have inspired me to call *la vida cotidiana como fuerza de paz* (everyday life as peace force). Surviving displacement and building their neighborhoods among ongoing violence has developed among many *desplazadas* what Paul Loeb in *Soul of a Citizen* says is necessary to engage in public participation without burning out: "radical patience."[36] This patience helps explain why despite human rights violations by some state entities, *desplazadas* are still willing to collaborate with other state entities.

Luz Amparo Duque Garcés, thirty-eight, has lived in Blanquizal in the Municipality of Medellín for nine years with her five children. She wanted to tell her story as a public service announcement about her neighborhood's community garden. While touring the garden with twelve-foot-tall trees lush with sweet-smelling fruit and flowers, Luz explains that tired of living in what had been a trash dump, the community members "brought the trees and fruits that grew on the street, and we began planting them. Mango, lime, orange, lulo . . . the banana tree." Luz wants to inspire people from outside the neighborhood to stop illegally dumping trash in the garden. This trash includes medical waste and contaminates the community well.

Marta Libia Velez Yepes is a community leader and founder of her neigborhood, San José de La Cima, in Manrique. She has six children and five grandchildren and for three decades has been married to her husband, whom she tells us with a gleeful smile she met while dancing at a party in the street. One of her children was killed. When we asked how, she shrugs her shoulders, and her face stamps with pain as she says, "*Violencia*."[37] Marta narrates how when she arrived thirty years ago in this neighborhood there were not yet any of the drainage channels, which she and her neighbors built. "There was absolutely nowhere to walk," she says. "And the houses would flood from the water that came down the mountain. Everything would get ruined." Every eight days she and her neighbors sold *empanadas* to raise money for supplies. "I would go house to house, and the wives would tell me, 'Look, he doesn't want to wake up.' And so [with the wive's permission], I would enter the house and pull them [the men] outside and say, 'Do you want to keep living in the mud?' That's how I would get them to come outside and help."

Looking at what she affectionately calls "her stairs" out her livingroom window in the house she and her family built, she adds with a grandmotherly tone, "The person who throws trash out here has to reckon with me."

Contrary to a focus on their displacement, which frames *desplazadas* as being far from their home, many women express a deep sense of belonging to the neighborhoods they have built in Medellín. In Guayabal el Bolo, Sherezade Filomena Isaza Restrepo's family profoundly illustrates this belonging. Sherezade, twenty-seven, begins telling her story while standing in the alleyway between dozens of homes her family members have built by hand and where they still live. The homes are tightly packed next to and atop of each other. Sherezade stands next to her mother, who throughout the interview helps hold her son Wilson, who is almost three. He yawns regularly into the camera. Sherezade points to a house that she says "has existed since my mother was born." Her mother, who still lives in the house, is fifty-one years old. "The entire family lives here." Her mother adds that this means one hundred family members, "which is why we are so united." Then daughter and mother begin speaking at the same time, "During Christmas, we have great parties with the whole family. Celebrations until six in the morning, dancing, and we have a spectacular time!"

When asked about their experiences with the City of Medellín's last decade of urban interventions, women collaborating in our archive will most often both praise and criticize them. They especially praise the scholarships to attend university, Medellín Solidaria services, and the *metrocable* for making transportation up and down the mountains affordable and safe. They sharply critique community resources lost when the government moves them off the land they had originally made home. Maria Consuelo Soto Gomez moved with her family to Moravia, which had been the city's landfill between 1973 and 1983, in 1980 when her family chose to sell their farm. With the little money the sale brought, they purchased a small plot of land near the city of Medellín's landfill. "We had to work really hard on the farm," she says. "We did all the manual labor," another reason why some people, seeking a way out of crushing rural poverty, chose to move to cities. Guerrilla and paramilitary control of the roads between her rural town and the city increased *campesinos'* struggle with poverty, because the armed actors' presence hindered access to Medellín, where they needed to sell their produce, purchase supplies, and attend schools. She says that when she first came to Moravia, "It was very green. It had trees, plantains, yuccas, onions, and was full of donkeys. I remember it was like the countryside. The water was brought in by a hose. There were only one or two light bulbs." El Morro (the Hill), as residents called it, was generated from piles of trash. More than ten thousand people came to live on the Morro, which covered 18.7 acres of land. María says,

> On the Morro, you saw everyone every day with their baskets, with their sacks, and with their hoes and their shovels, rummaging there in the trash. . . . It was the life, because most people found new things; I can say from experience that [we found] curtains, little packages of things; new shoes, everything new. It was a success because no one recycled. Many people lived off that, and it was very good. To me it seemed

> like a beautiful hill, like a market. But then, we were removed because they said we couldn't live there anymore. The people were sad, because many of them lived off what they found.

Maria Consuelo says what she misses most about living on the Morro was the community solidarity there: "The people were united, and there was a cooperative for women. First my mother began working there and then we joined her. We broke down cardboard and organized toothpaste tubes [for sale as recycled items or homemade building materials], sometimes working until one or two in the morning." From her family album, she shows a picture of dozens of children and women working on the Morro and continues, "We did whatever it took to survive, and to tell you the truth we were living better than we did in the countryside. . . . And previously no one [city officials] looked at this neighborhood, because it was scary to go into the mountains of trash." Maria speaks of her love for her house in Moravia off the Morro. She especially likes her home's finished walls and flooring, running water, and what she terms legal electricity. She adds, "Thank God, because honestly, having a house doesn't make you rich, but not having a house makes you poor." She says she is happy because if she gets sick nobody can ask her to leave it.

The women also gently critique the way in which the city's social assistance sometimes is delivered by middle- and upper-class people, with their attendant norms and biases against those from lower-income rural backgrounds. Community leaders often tell us quietly that they do not like being treated like "poor people without culture" or "*bobos*," people who do not know anything. They are usually referring to moments when program staff (consciously or not) express racism, sexism, or classism in the form of cultural codes of *buena gente* (literally, "good people"). In the name of what they call "good people conduct," staff officials mandate that people must conform to these codes to participate in social assistance programs.[38] Children, at the Parque Biblioteca España, for example, are turned away if they show up to use the computers while wearing their *pijamas*. The directors of the *parques* say that this is because they have to set a standard that the libraries are "a serious place" for "good people." The community members who balk at this communicate a message similar to that of one child we interviewed: "I didn't know that pajamas prevented me from being able to read."

This section articulates two intertwining themes. Women want to share stories about how they built their neighborhoods and why. Women also have a complex perspective on what is working well and what is not regarding the City of Medellín's recent interventions in their communities. The next section reflects on the risks *campesina desplazada* storytellers take to tell their stories.

Risks: (In)Justice of Story Mobility in Conflict Zones

In my analysis, there is a direct correlation between the risk a storyteller takes in telling her story and the relationship she has to the conflict in Colombia. The archive's core mission is social justice through including *desplazadas'* stories in the dominant local and global archival landscape that represents women in Colombia. Therefore, the risk a woman takes in telling her story should *also* be central to the story. Among all of our archive's collaborating participants, the *desplazadas* have the most intimate and violent relationship to the conflict in Colombia, take the most risk in telling their stories about it, and receive the least rewards for doing so. They risk damaging their amicable relationship with city government officials or their reputation in their community or family.[39] Sometimes this makes women regret details they revealed in their stories and ask us to burn the footage. We do.

Sometimes, storytellers and those documenting and circulating their stories wrestle with a tension between risking a woman's story truth and risking the storyteller's life. This happens when a woman knows her story might threaten her life, but she chooses to tell it anyway. Following is one such story. The storyteller's name is Sobeida Tinoco. She was born in the rural town Cudinamarca in Bogotá, and she is a descendant of one of Colombia's oldest indigenous tribes, which Spanish *conquistadores* nearly five hundred years ago named the Muisca de Indios. Throughout her childhood, she moved with her family to different towns in Colombia in search of work. When she was fifteen years old, she moved to Urabá, where she met her husband, and they had three children. Sobeida says, "Urabá was a very good region. I worked in the banana zone. I had to deflower the bananas . . . be the chief, fertilize, do everything on the farm." She tells this story while sitting in her home where she now lives with her children in Medellín. As she speaks, sounds and scents of meat frying for lunch waft from her kitchen. Sobeida explains how she became displaced from Urabá in 1995. "There were *paras* [paramilitaries] there, and after the *paras* came the army, followed by the guerrillas. So one was stuck in the middle of this conflict between three armed gangs."

She continues, "I went to protest in the marches, because they [members of all three groups] came into the field and didn't let us work. They were fighting for territories and also for [power over] organizations. The guerrillas arrived at my house. I couldn't tell them, 'No,

I won't do this favor for you.' I had to give them a tax [food and other supplies in return for sparing her life]. Finally, came the day when they [the paramilitaries] arrived at my house at six in the morning."

This raid was one of the dozens of massacres in Urubá between the 1980s and the early 2000s. These massacres in the banana zone killed hundreds and displaced thousands. The paramilitaries had come accusing Sobeida and other *campesinos* of collaborating with the guerrillas. Sobeida explains, "They burned my house down. . . . They closed the town, and they took what they could. Supposedly I had 14 heads of cattle. I had 105 chickens. I ran away towards the hills with the girls [her daughters]." Sobeida and her daughters went to the house of neighbors she knew. "I rested there because I was shaking with fear. I saw ahead that there were bullets flying. They were throwing bombs at me." Her son had been working in the farmhouse at the time of the attack. He fled and was reunited with Sobeida the following day. Her husband had been working in the fields. Neighbors told her he had fled with another farmer. Sobeida cries as she says that over the last fifteen years, even though neighbors told her that he had been killed, she feels she is waiting for him to return. Sobeida says. "If I had buried him, I would be able to say, 'There he is.' But no, every day I have always been waiting. I said, 'No, he will show up at any moment.' No, he never showed up. Never."

The day after the attack in Urubá, Sobeida fled with her three children. They moved from town to town, running from the paramilitary members who Sobeida could, and still can, identify by nickname and face. These men, Sobeida says, "were well known," in the towns where they lived because "they had left the guerrillas and joined the *paras*." In 1998 two of the paramilitary members who had been following her kidnapped her nine-year-old daughter. During the four months her daughter was missing, she posted a picture of her daughter on the television station Teleantioquia, which helped families find loved ones who had disappeared. Finally, Sobeida sought help from the International Red Cross. A U.S. nun working there finally located and returned Sobeida's daughter to her. The paramilitary had hidden the little girl in a convent in Medellín. After this, Sobeida remained on the run for three more years. In 2001, six years after she fled Urubá, Sobeida decided to declare her displacement to the government to receive housing subsidies and other assistance. In Colombia, *desplazados* have rights to national and state resources. Each time a *desplazado* like Sobeida applies for assistance, she is required to "declare," or tell her story of displacement, to government officials and social workers. They, in turn, do research to verify her story, so they can prove she is who she says she is. As I learned from the social worker I mention at the beginning of this chapter, this research can take months. Sobeida went through this declaration process three times before a judge granted her rights as an officially displaced person. During this process, she also moved with her three children to Medellín. They moved into a broken-down *ranchito* handmade from found wooden planks on a plot of land that belonged to her uncle's wife. The plot, like many in the Medellín neighborhoods *desplazados* have founded on unoccupied steep Andes mountain terrain, was located down a ravine. Sobeida says that at first, living in the ravine was "horrible" because the *ranchito* was precariously situated in "the steep hole." Her daughters slept on the *ranchito's* only bed, and she slept on the dirt floor next to them. Once she was officially declared displaced, the Medellín mayor's office sent three dump trucks to haul away dirt to clear more space on the plot and demolish the *ranchito,* so she could build a more stable home. Seven years later, she began working with the City of Medellín's Department of Social Welfare Office's program called Familias en Acción (Families in Action). This program provided her with 1.5 million pesos ($825 U.S.) to renovate her home. Another agency in Bogotá, Acción Social, also informed Sobeida of her additional rights to government resources because of her indigenous ethnicity. The same year, she received 4 million pesos ($2,200 U.S.) from an international aid agency in Bogotá. In 2010, Familias en Acción introduced Sobeida to Medellín Solidaria. Social workers met with Sobeida in her home to further clarify her rights as a Colombian citizen and Medellín resident. Medellín Solidaria helped Sobeida reclaim her *cédula,* her national identity card. Bit by bit, with assistance from family members, neighbors, NGOs and government agencies, she and her daughters built their home, which now has gleaming tile floors, electricity, running water, a kitchen with appliances, and family pictures adorning the walls.

Sobeida describes how she sustained her three children during these years. "I woke up at two in the morning, took a shower, and at three in the morning I went on foot to the airport Olaya Herrera. I worked for a woman, but I was the one who woke up early. She arrived at six in the morning." Sobeida says that when she left her house, "I would walk down the street, and the men from the neighborhood would tell me not to go because there was going to be a shootout, so I had to wait. . . . Many times, I would make my way down [the hill to the bus] in the middle of dead bodies because they had killed people!"

Sobeida also sold dishes at the traffic lights in front of the San Vicente hospital. "I sold limes, mangos. I sold whatever I could, but it took all day." Each day, Sobeida earned twelve thousand pesos. After paying for her transportation to and from work, she ended up with eight thousand pesos ($4.48 U.S.). "With that I bought the daily necessities for my daughters. By the time I got back from work, they had cooked our food, washed our clothes; they have worked hard . . . but I never let them come with me to sell limes; never. I made them study, so they could become someone in life. During the afternoon, I came back with a little meat on the bone, a little plantain, and a little rice. My daughters never went without food." Sobeida then describes what her neighborhood was like after the sun went down. "There were always gunshots at this time of day. There were moments when bullets were flying everywhere. You had to run and lay down on your stomach on the floor because they were fighting each other. After work you had to take a bus and . . . go straight back to your house or you went straight to where you were going and nowhere else."

At the time of the interview in August 2012, Sobeida says with a smile, "Now it has been more than a year since this neighborhood has been good! Better than good! We walk through every part of the neighborhood. Now one can go up to the *metrocable* (gondola) without fear of anything." Two of her daughters have now graduated from the university and are working. Now, Sobeida is working to buy a house closer to public transportation because it takes her two hours a day to commute to work, not including her walk up and down the 184 steps to her house in the ravine. She also wants to open a neighborhood shop that would be easily accessible for her and her neighbors. To accomplish this, she has been working with Acción Social in Bogotá who at the time of the interview was evaluating her request for a grant.

The week before the archive's August 2012 DVD debut, a social worker went to Sobeida's home to explain that the city government would provide transportation to and from the theater where the video version of her story and those of other families would show. Sobeida told the social worker she had changed her mind and did not want her story shown in the debut. She wanted the video to be edited, so her face was covered, and so she was not identified by name. Jota Samper, the archive's codirector and Medellín native, called Sobeida to ask what had happened. Sobeida informed him that she had gone "to declare" details of her displacement in Bogotá for the grant, which she received. She had to again name names of those who had burned down her house and kidnapped her daughter. Sobeida says that after she had gone to Bogotá this time, she heard someone was murdered in her neighborhood. This murder could have been a totally unrelated event. Scared, however, that this murder could somehow be related to her "naming names," Sobeida said she no longer felt safe enough to circulate her story. Jota asked her if she would like to come to the debut for a private showing of her video. She agreed. That morning she called to say that she could not come because she did not feel well. Without Sobeida's permission, we would not distribute the DVDs with her story on it. We debuted the other stories with the storytellers present but made arrangements to destroy all five hundred DVDs and reburn another master DVD without Sobeida's story.

Alexa Barrett, the student who had interviewed Sobeida, and Jota still wanted to fulfill their promise to show Sobeida the final version. They also wanted to give Sobeida a copy of the entire uncut interview and accompanying photographs as well as a DVD with the fourteen other edited stories. Story documenters do this for every one of the 650 people interviewed for the archive. Jota called Sobeida and asked if he and Alexa could show her the edited version of her story in the privacy of her home. Sobeida agreed. At dawn the next day, Jota and Alexa traveled to Sobeida's home. Alexa says, "When we walked into her home, Sobeida gave me a big hug and was so happy to see us."[40] She first watched the video story of a woman whose husband had also been murdered by paramilitaries, forcing her to flee her beloved rural town with her son.[41] This woman lives with her now grown son in another neighborhood she helped found in Medellín. Sobeida murmured, "Oh, I know someone who would really be interested in seeing this." She said she felt connected to the woman because of their similar experiences as *campesinas* and *desplazadas* and urban neighborhood founders. Then she watched the video of her own story. In the end, Sobeida said she wanted to circulate the video story as is. She emphasized how much it meant to her that Jota and Alexa made the effort to come show the story to her in her home. She also asked to be invited to future public showings of her story.

Sobeida's story reveals three reasons why the risks women make in telling their stories are both a core inspiration for this archive's mission of social justice and a challenge to fulfilling that mission. First, Sobeida's story exemplifies some of the most extreme risks that women take in telling their stories: physical violence. Second, her story highlights the double displacement I mention earlier. That is, people become displaced from their own stories of displacement because *campesinas desplazadas* have the least access to resources necessary to insert their stories into the dominant representations of Colombia. Sometimes the reasons for this limited access are not just socioeconomic. They also include risk to the storyteller's life. Furthermore, for *desplazadas* like Sobeida, the risks her storytelling poses to her life and that of her family are ongoing. The third inspiration and challenge to this archive's social justice mission is that the storyteller's risk to her life, reputation, and relationships with politicians and multiple armed actors, is unavoidably inherent to the archive's production and circulation process. Many of the storytellers in the archive openly discuss armed actors who burned down their homes or murdered their loved ones. Generally, the women do not frame this violence in terms of support of these armed actors' actions. Furthermore, it is usually implied and sometimes explicit that the women can identify these actors by face and name. This unsupportive stance and ability to name names could inspire armed actors or those who support them to commit more violence against the women storytellers.

The extreme, ongoing, and inherent nature of these storytellers' risks inspired Jota and me to critically reflect on the other dimension of the storytelling process that challenges this archive's mission of feminist social justice: motivation. The challenge is that each archive participant has a different motivation for documenting the women's stories. So, we first ask each storyteller who *she* wants to hear her story and why. But if the archive's social justice mission is to document the stories *and* to circulate them, we must then ask a crucial question. How might archive participants' differing motivations influence the stories' circulation?

Concluding Thoughts on Circulation

The circulation challenge and responsibility are shared in Ruth Behar's classic text *Translated Woman: Crossing the Border with Esperanza's Story:* "No one is quite sure anymore of how to reconcile feminist politics of social transformation and international sisterhood with a research practice in which relatively privileged academic women seek out, record, and publish the edited voices of relatively underprivileged women from somewhere else in the name of a feminism to be borne across the border" (1993, 297). Though it has been nearly twenty years since Behar's words started touching transnational feminist scholar-activists, we find ourselves confronting newer versions of older questions, and ideally, coming up with answers. This final section examines people's different motivations for participating in this archive, ways these differences challenge the stories' circulation as social justice, and one way we are beginning to address this challenge.

As cofounding director of this archive, I ask each participant "*Why are you here? What are you going to do with this information? Who are you trying to help?*" These are the same questions the social worker asked me seven years ago on my first day of fumbling research about *desplazadas* in Colombia. Each storyteller, student, professor, social worker, and government official we collaborate with on this archive, according to her or his own professional and community alliances and lived experiences, has distinct and sometimes contradictory motivations for participating in this archive.

The previous section outlined who the storytellers want to hear their stories and why. The women must tell their stories to government agencies to receive assistance as *desplazados*. But with all the risk involved, why do women choose to tell their stories for this archive? The storytellers often say they feel they can trust the students because they do not fear these U.S. youth are affiliated with warring groups in Colombia. The storytellers grant the students interviews precisely *because* the students are young, naïve,[42] with regard to what it means to live in a country in conflict, and foreign to Colombia. This naïveté, in turn, the *desplazadas* interpret as giving the students a kind of innocence and neutrality with regard to the conflict in Colombia. In their stories, they often slow down to explain what they mean by certain terms and events in the same way an expert teacher would patiently speak to a novice student. The storyteller's motivation comes from a position of self-perceived authority and power. The storytellers see the students' presence in their homes as an opportunity to teach not just the youth in their own neighborhood, but youth in the world at large. They know that the student has the mobility the *desplazadas* do not have. The U.S. students can travel throughout Medellín and across international borders and thus can carry the *desplazada's* story with them. Many storytellers say they want to tell people in Colombia that poor people also strive for peace.[43] Storytellers tell U.S. audiences that "Colombia should not be judged only by its violent side because nowadays violence is on a worldwide level."[44] The storytellers also ask that people from all over the world who come into their neighborhood should treat the community residents with respect and they will be respected in return"[45]

Storytellers also know that U.S. university members have the status necessary to share the *desplazadas'* perspectives with government officials, especially regarding the recent City of Medellín's interventions. In other words, Jota and I, and sometimes our U.S. university students, meet personally with officials in the Medellín mayor's office, including the directors of assistance programs for *desplazados*, the private secretary to the mayor, the city's first lady and, on occasion, even the mayor and the governor. A theme among the stories in this archive contradicts a one-dimensional image of the state as savior or evil invader of their neighborhoods. Instead, the women's stories complicate the state's public rhetoric of rescue with another interpretation: they view what the city government terms "the transformation of Medellín" as one of the most recent (and in many cases welcome) state interventions in a series of ongoing community collaborations these neighborhood founders have been directing for decades. These stories also highlight a fierce feminist dimension to their roles as neighborhood founders. *Desplazadas* strategically wield the power that Colombian culture grants to mothers to mobilize state leaders and male neighbors to build and protect their communities. Sobeida, like most of the *desplazadas* who tell their stories in this archive, frames her life story and the assistance she has received from multiple organizations in terms of her own initiative and agency. She says, "I have this home because of the help that I fight for." The women often position their role as storytellers in this archive within this practice of individual and community agency.

The social workers have their own motivations and risks for participating in this archive. The social workers occasionally do risk physical violence and sometimes their lives by working in neighborhoods where bullets can suddenly fly. Social workers fear that the camera presence might foster distrust among community members who think they are documenting crime. Some social workers see this archive project as an indirect way to tell their own experience with displacement. Other social workers genuinely want the storyteller's stories to be part of the larger story about Colombia and women in this country. Some city government officials want this archive to serve as national and international publicity for the City of Medellín's "transformation of Medellín" in general and of Medellín Solidaria in particular. On a rare occasion, this desire for publicity results in social workers interrupting storytellers, saying, "No, don't talk about that. We want to hear only about the *positive* things."

Some students, before embarking on training for this archive project, had never heard of Medellín or the concept *desplazamiento*. They come because they want to learn about it. In their DukeEngage application essays, during our weekly reflection sessions in Medellín, and on the DukeEngage Colombia blog, students express various reasons for coming to Medellín to work on the archive. Among the top reasons they cite are to add "civic engagement" to their resume; to live in a culture different from their own; to develop skills in their discipline; to learn Spanish; or to connect with the Colombian part of their *colombiana-estadounidense*[46] roots. U.S. and Colombian faculty members participate to study the conflict as an academic and sometimes politically motivated human rights endeavor.

Ultimately, I have come to believe that the biggest challenge to our archive's ability to complete its circulation mission of feminist social justice is rooted in the very fact that each person in the archive has a different relationship to the conflict in Colombia. Each person, thus, takes very different risks in telling stories about it. For the *desplazadas,* the risk they make in telling their story cannot be divorced from their motivation for telling it. Usually, those who are *receiving* the stories from the storytellers do not have to risk their lives to do so. Thus, running through the marrow of our archive is what I call "motivational dissonance" between a person's relationship to the conflict, her risk in telling stories about it, and her motivations for ultimately doing so anyway. The main mission of *medellín mi hogar* is for the women's stories to reach diverse audiences. For this to happen, at least some archive participants have to be as active at circulating the stories as they had been at documenting them. The challenge to this circulation is not the risks the *desplazadas'* make in telling their stories. The challenge is rather the *lack* of risk that other participants in the archive must make to tell the *desplazadas'* stories. In other words, story documenters in this archive do not need to tell the stories as a matter of life or death. Therefore, it is relatively easier for the story documenters to not worry about circulating the *desplazadas'* stories and move on to other pursuits. This then leads us back to motivation for participating in the archive. Where, how, and why archive participants circulate the woman's stories will be impacted by their motivation for engaging in the storytelling archive.

I do believe, however, that part of the storytellers' mission in sharing their stories with the students is, in a small but significant way, being accomplished. This mission is for people to listen to and care about the *campesinas desplazadas'* perspectives. DukeEngage Colombia student Julie Zuckerbrod wrote about her participation in the archive:

> I've come to realize something very special about this project . . . We did not fly into Medellín with a collective expertise that we planned on imparting to our community partners. . . . We didn't decide that a group of people was missing something and try to give it to them. What we did was open our ears, open our hearts, and open our minds. We asked the community to tell us what we needed to know, what they wanted to tell us. Winston Churchill once said, "courage is what it takes to stand up and speak; courage is also what it takes to sit down and listen."[47]

In this chapter, I have described the genealogy of how various groups have come together in the United States and Colombia to build this archive. I have identified how Jota and I, the archive directors, in conjunction with the *desplazadas*, intend the stories to contribute to knowledge production about Colombia. As noted, we seek to expand the archival and rhetorical landscape of Colombia beyond drugs, violence, and poverty. We also seek to expand the archival and rhetorical landscape of women in Colombia beyond sexualized commodities and victims and/or catalysts of violence and narcotraffic. We do this by documenting and circulating the perspectives and experiences of Medellín's *campesinas desplazadas* as urban neighborhood founders and collaborators in the City of Medellín's last decade of urban and social interventions in neighborhoods that for five decades had largely been isolated from official state resources.

My focus on the archive's next phase is circulation. Alexa Barrett, the Duke student who interviewed Sobeida, eloquently describes the kind of soul-searching question that I believe is necessary for this archive to move from documentation of thousands of hours of stories to meaningful circulation of them. Alexa writes after her first interview with Sobeida: "I had unexpectedly come across an incredible story of Colombia's history and a personal account that moved me but what were my motives for telling her story? As filmmakers, we want to tell an exciting story, one that will catch people's interest . . . How was I benefiting her by making this film?"[48]

Presently Jota and I are working with storytellers, students, faculty, and social workers who want to circulate the archive's stories. I ask each person to identify her privileged access to sites of knowledge production: neighborhoods, cities, the media, human rights groups, film festivals, universities. We seek to locate inflection points among these sites where dominant knowledge production about Colombia circulates. Throughout the past three years, the time and energy of people working on this archive has been absorbed with documenting the stories. The stories housed in the archive have been circulating to hundreds of people worldwide. But this has happened in a rather haphazard and spontaneous manner that depends largely on people finding our website or teachers and film festival directors requesting a showing. Our plan is to now strategically circulate the stories to audiences in diverse inflection point sites throughout the Americas and online. This archive, I hope, can intervene in these sites by including the perspectives of women who have lived—and who are still living—through conflict in Colombia. This circulation intervention could render a more inclusive and thus more accurate image of women's roles in the last sixty years of conflict and resilience in Colombia.

Notes

I wish to thank the many people in Colombia and the United States, who over the last five years have generously given their time to this project. This article is dedicated to the 650 women and their families who shared their stories for this archive. First, I thank my mentor and friend Christine Hundefeldt for all she has taught and continues to teach me. I also thank Eric Mlyn for taking the chance to include our DukeEngage Colombia project among the first DukeEngage pilot programs when most universities in the United States would not officially endorse bringing students to Colombia. I wish I could individually name here the many people from Duke University, Emerson College, the Alcaldia de Medellín, the Secretaria de Bienestar Social, Programa Medellín Solidaria, Agencia de Cooperación e Inversión de Medellín y el Área Metropolitana, the Universidad Nacional de Colombia in Medellín, SosPaisa, AULA Internacional, and the families in Carlos E. Restrepo. I thank Ryan Catalani, who came to Medellín and helped Duke students video edit and created a documentary about this archive as well as a website that houses all of *medellín mi hogar's* edited videos. I especially thank those who generously critiqued my writing about this project: Jota Samper, John Trimbur, Anupama Taranath, Suzanne Hinton, Clara Elena Mojíca Vélez, Estephanie Vásquez Gutiérrez, Alexander Silva Carmona, Natalia Isabel Pérez Villegas, Fabian Adolfo Beethoven Zuleta Ruiz, Hugo, Diana George, and Diane Shoos. I especially thank Julie Shayne for her painstaking and multiple critiques on this article. I also thank my family, whose love and labor, domestic and otherwise, made this project possible.

1. The 1948–1958 period in Colombia, known as La Violencia, was sparked by the assassination of Jorge Eliécer Gaitán, a populist Liberal Party leader. The *Partido Conservador* (Conservative Party) had just been elected into national office, evicting the Liberal Party that had been in office for the last sixteen years. See Bushnell (1993).
2. In 1992, Medellín was known as the most dangerous city in the world, due to the number of homicides per month there.
3. According to data from the Personería, la Unidad de Atención a los Desplazados (perteneciente al Municipio de Medellín), y Acción Social, antigua Red de Solidaridad Social, 21,596 displaced people registered themselves as displaced in 2000; 20,469 in 2002; and 7,536 in 2005. As of August 31, 2011, there were 216,288 people registered as displaced in Medellín, living in 52,769 homes. This represents 8 percent of the city's population of 2.7 million people, not counting the metropolitan area. This makes Medellín home to the second largest population of internally displaced people in Colombia, a country with the largest number of displaced people in the world. See Unidad de Atención a la Población Desplazada 2011.
4. In a complex legal argument that technically justified what some

criticize as the city government's socioeconomic abandonment of displaced people for six decades, the *desplazados* were squatting on land in Medellín, and thus by law the city government could not officially provide them with city resources. Instead of evicting people who many assumed were a temporary consequence of war, the state just looked the other way. See Samper "Granting of Land Tenure" 2012.

5. The term *campesino* refers to people who live and work as subsistence farmers in the countryside. Women who are such farmers are called *campesinas*.
6. Many displaced people flee their homes with what they can carry on their backs, often leaving their official papers behind. Or people live in a small rural town where everyone knows everyone else and so do not need a *cédula*. This means that once they arrive in Medellín, they need to apply for a *cédula*.
7. Jota Samper has worked as an architect for the last sixteen years and has done projects in informal settlements in seven countries. He has a master's degree in urban planning from the Department of Urban Studies and Planning at MIT, where he is now a PhD candidate. For his professional biography and articles informed by this archive, see his blog, http://informalsettlements.blogspot.com/p/medellin.html.
8. See our edited video stories on mobility17.com.
9. For a detailed critical discussion of four ways this archive's collaborators experiment with disrupting *doble desplazamiento,* see my article "Disrupting *Doble Desplazamiento* in Conflict Zones: Alternative Feminist Stories Cross the Colombian-U.S. Border," *Reflections: Public Rhetoric, Civic Writing and Service Learning* 12.1 (Fall 2012): 29–53.17.
10. The City of Medellín's Department of Social Welfare.
11. DukeEngage is a civic engagement program with the motto Change yourself, change your world. DukeEngage has funded two thousand students to participate in more than forty-two projects worldwide. See http://dukeengage.duke.edu/ and our students' Colombia program blog http://dukeengageinmedellín.blogspot.com. For a discussion of a pedagogical theory and practice emerging from the work my students and I do on this archive, see my forthcoming article "Proyecto Boston Medellín: Toward A Twenty-First-Century Feminist Pedagogscape," *Proyecto Boston Medellín 2011 & 2012* (Medellín, Colombia: Universidad Nacional de Colombia).
12. *Sala mi barrio* translates as "my neighborhood livingroom," which references the intimate home spaces where family members and friends spend hours, often daily, chatting about their lives.

For more about sala mi barrio and the Parques Bibliotecas, see http://www.reddebibliotecas.org.co/sistemabibliotecas/Paginas/parque_biblioteca_espana.aspx.

13. In Spanish this state entity is called Secretaria de Bienestar Social de la Alcaldia de Medellín.
14. See http://dukeengageinmedellin.blogspot.com>
15. The rest of the story video, photographs, and transcripts Jota and I save in our files and throughout the academic year continue to edit. We are now in discussions with Duke University about housing the entire archive there.
16. For another national history of Colombia published in English see Safford and Palacios (2002).
17. She continues: "In the United States, policymakers have promoted three sometimes overlapping paradigms that have shaped U.S. relations with Colombia": (1) counterinsurgency concerns that since the 1950s "governed U.S. foreign policy toward Latin America"; (2) the U.S. war on drugs that "dominated U.S. policy directives in the Andean producer countries; and (3) the U.S. government war on terror which, since the 9/11 attacks on the World Trade Center and the Pentagon Building, "has driven U.S. foreign-policy concerns around the globe." Within this frame, Bouvier also cites Plan Colombia. Launched in 2000, this multibillion-dollar plan was to strengthen the Colombian state's, especially its military and police, fight against leftwing groups and narcotraffic leaders and to protect oil pipelines. Plan Colombia made Colombia one of the leading recipients of U.S. aid, "surpassed at the time only by Egypt and Israel." Bouvier 5–6.
18. Bouvier 5–6.
19. See for example, Bouvier (2009); Rojas (2009); Roldán (2009); Alzate (2008); Unidad de Atención a la Población Desplazada (2011); Iáñez Domínguez and Pareja Amador (2011); and Murdock (2008).
20. See Farnsworth-Alvear (2000).
21. See, for example, Murdock (2008).
22. See, for example, Vamos Mujer; "Asociación Nacional de Usuarios Campesinos"; "Corporación para la vida: Mujeres Que Crean"; de Medellín; and "Centro de Desarrollo Cultural de Moravia."
23. Subsecretaria de Metromujer.
24. "En el año 2002 se creó la Subsecretaría de Metromujer, adscrita a la Secretaría de Cultura Ciudadana y luego, mediante el Acuerdo Municipal 01 de 2007 se crea la Secretaría de las Mujeres, la cual trabaja por contribuir con la igualdad de derechos y oportunidades entre hombres y mujeres de la ciudad de Medellín y

sus corregimientos, promoviendo la participación y el empoderamiento de las mujeres en los escenarios políticos, culturales, sociales, económicos, entre otros." See Municipio de Medellín (2012).

25. An equally popular theme is a media-perpetuated conception of feminine beauty that is as narrow as it is voluptuous. Complicating matters is that this "beauty" is achievable with extensive plastic surgery, which is easily attainable in Medellín if someone can pay for it. Hundreds of women every year in Medellín go under the plastic surgery knife. Many impoverished young women see this as their best way to marry into money and out of poverty.
26. See rap musician Soria Shorai's song "More Than an Image," which she released in 2008 on open-access subterraneos.net and posted her video for it on YouTube in 2009. The song encourages women to rip up fashion magazines, not sell themselves to men, and instead develop their mind and heart. In her song lyrics Shorai sings about "the destitute barefoot mother" who the media "clouds over" while lying "at their own convenience of course, yeah, only speaking of celebrity and expensive clothes." This mother is the woman who arrives to Medellín as a *desplazada* and builds a wooden plank house like the one in the music video where Shorai sings (Municipio de Medellín). For the full lyrics in Spanish and a book written by and about youth rappers from Medellín's poor neighborhoods, see Programa Planeación Local y Presupesto Participativo 2008. In this book rappers and graffiti artists position their work in the context of U.S. hip-hop as antiracist social justice movements.
27. Here I consider "the street" to include other public spaces outside the home, including the Internet.
28. María Elena Giraldo González's story "Little Red Riding Hood in Search of the Wolf," describes a young girls' decision to leave her grandmother's house in her rural pueblo in search of a better life in the city of Medellín.

Dejó el vestido dominguero sobre la cama, vistió jean rojo, encendió la mota roja por supuesto y llegó hasta el apartamento del lobo, quien esperaba impaciente.	*I left my Sunday dress on my bed, got dressed in red jeans, started up my motorcycle, which is red of course, and arrived to the wolf's apartment, who waited impatiently.*

This is one of nine story contests published by Medellín's Metro Company with the slogan One city, one METRO, 15 years of stories, and 100 words to tell one. This story was selected from among one thousand submissions for publication in the 2010 story contest called "A Story for Your City in 100 Words." Judges for this contest have received more than six thousand stories with similarly gendered and feminist themes from women and men who live in the city's most impoverished neighborhoods. Each book, which publishes a pocketsize paperback selection of the story submissions, is distributed for free in the metro stations' Bibliometro offices, which are open to anyone.

29. In one of the archive's videos, Marlin Fianco Aguime seeks to conceptually expand a vision of community founders that includes agency, creativity, and strategy. As *Promotora Cultural de Desarrollo de Centro Cultural de Moravia*, she explains: "I don't like to use the word 'invaders'; it is better to use the term *'colonizadores'* because in history when you talk about colonizers, you say that they *founded* a church, *built* the houses etc." See Samper, Marko, and Murphy.
30. The Favela Bairro project and the Morar Carioca project in Rio de Janeiro, the largest urban upgrading project in the world, are modeled after the urban intervention projects in Medellín. See Samper "The Granting of Land Tenure" 2012.
31. At this time in Medellín, there was an unspoken understanding between the state armed forces and the communities (a loophole in the constitution) in which any homes with a Colombian flag raised would not get torn down when the army or police was sent to "clear out" the settlements.
32. All translations from Spanish into English are by the author, unless otherwise noted.
33. "Zona de Despeje," *Diario del Otun,* 23 de enero, 2004.
34. "El pulmón en la calle," *La Tarde*, 23 de enero, 2004.
35. "Colaboración con los desplazados," *El Diario del Otun*, 25 de enero, 2004.
36. See Loeb 2011, 313–316.
37. Marta did not want to elaborate on her son's death further in her story.
38. Literature about displaced or impoverished women in Colombia also consistently reveals at least three dimensions of cross-class tensions. One tension is regarding cross-class feminist alliances and the interrelated requirements by NGOs and international funders to "professionalize," which might include enforcing literacy requirements and corresponding bureaucratic paperwork. A second tension is related to middle- and upper-class notions of "morality," "seriousness," and intelligence conflated with women's modes of dress and physical and racialized forms of "beauty." Finally, there are rural-urban tensions: the contradiction between

fleeing the country and its "backward ways," for the idealized "modern" city, only to arrive in Medellín and struggle to survive.

39. At one woman's request we made two versions of a video story about her love for her children. One version which circulates on the official website reveals that she sold her body at night to earn money for food, and another version obscured this work. She wanted her young children to attend the video debut but not learn that about their mother yet. See Marko, Samper, and de Armas "Un Techo que Brindarles / A Roof Over Their Head."
40. The students who participated in this archive via DukeEngage Colombia 2012 have read multiple drafts of this article. They have read the drafts and approved the inclusion of these quotes. All of this summer's eight DukeEngage Colombia students, Jota, and I discussed the two students' blog post excerpts quoted here as part of our weekly reflection workshop. The students were enthusiastic about these quotes being included in the article, even suggesting other blog posts they have written that might be meaningful as well.
41. See Zuckerbrod, Samper, and Marko "Ladera, vida y dignidad."
42. The students and I discussed this description of why the *desplazadas* feel they can trust talking to the students in part because these women perceive the students as "naïve." The students all agreed this was an accurate and respectful term. Part of the reason this term "naïve" worked for the students is because the *desplazadas* themselves use this term in Spanish to describe the students: *ingénue*.
43. See Marko, Samper, and Perez.
44. Ibid.
45. See ibid.
46. This translates as "Colombian-United States roots." Instead of the term "Americans," Colombians often prefer to refer to people from the United States as *estadounidenses*. They prefer this because, as they say, Colombians *are* American from the Americas.
47. See Zuckerbrod "The Last Word."
48. See Barrett "The Last Word."

References

Alzate, Mónica M. 2008. "The Sexual and Reproductive Rights of Internally Displaced Women: The Embodiment of Colombia's Crisis." *Disasters* 32 (1): 131–148.

"Asociación Nacional de Usuarios Campesinos." Web. July 19, 2012. http://anuc.co/.

Barrett, Alexa. 2012. "The Last Word." *dukeengageinmedellin* August. http://dukeengageinmedellin.blogspot.com/2012/08/the-last-word.html.

Bouvier, Virginia Marie. 2009. *Colombia : Building Peace in a Time of War*. Washington, DC: United States Institute of Peace.

Bushnell, David. 1993. *The Making of Modern Colombia: A Nation in Spite of Itself*. Berkeley: University of California Press.

"Centro de Desarrollo Cultural de Moravia." *Centro de Desarrollo Cultural de Moravia*. Web. July 20, 2012. http://www.comfenalcoantioquia.com/Cultura/CentroDesarrolloCulturalMoravia/tabid/488/language/en-US/Default.aspx.

"Corporación para la vida: Mujeres Que Crean." *Corporación para la vida: Mujeres Que Crean*. (Organization.) http://www.mujeresquecrean.org.

Farnsworth-Alvear, Ann. 2000. *Dulcinea in the Factory: Myths, Morals, Men, and Women in Colombia's Industrial Experiment, 1905–1960*. Durham, NC: Duke University Press.

Iáñez Domínguez, Antonio, and Antonio J Pareja Amador. 2011. *Mujeres y Desplazamiento Forzado: Estrategias De Vida De Jefas De Hogar En Medellín*. Sevilla: Aconcagua Libros.

Loeb, Paul Rogat. 2011. *Soul of a Citizen: Living with Conviction in Challenging Times*. Second edition. New York: St. Martin's Press.

Marko, Tamera, Jota Samper, and Carolina de Armas. 2011. *Un Techo que Brindarles / A Roof over Their Heads*. Vol. 2. 2 vols. Medellín, Colombia. video. medellín mi hogar / my home medellín. http://youtu.be/lSPxR19CMVk.

Marko, Tamera, Jota Samper, and Cesar Perez. 2012. *Mi gente me enseña . . . y me siguen enseñando*. Vol. 3. 3 vols. Medellín, Colombia. Film. medellín mi hogar / my home medellín. mobility17.com.

de Medellín, Alcaldia. "Museu Casa de la Memoria." *Museu Casa de la Memoria*. Web. July 19, 2012. http://www.museocasadelamemoria.org/site.

Municipio de Medellín. "Equidad de Género: Secretaría de las mujeres." Web. Aug. 10, 2012. http://www.medellin.gov.co/irj/portal/ciudadanos?NavigationTarget=navurl://507e69fb7031f77c2119e504afe51924.

Murdock, Donna F. 2008. *When Women Have Wings: Feminism and Development in Medellín, Colombia*. Ann Arbor: University of Michigan Press.

Programa Planeación Local y Presupesto Participativo. 2008. *Somos Hip Hop: Una experiencia de resistencia cultural en Medellín*. Medellín: Alcaldia de Medellín.

Rojas, Catalina. 2009. "Women and Peace Building in Colombia:

Resistance to War, Creativity for Peace." in *Colombia: Making Peace in a Time of War,* 207–224. Washington, DC: United States Institute of Peace.

Roldán, Mary J. 2009. "'Cambio de armas': Negotiating Alternatives to Violence in the Oriente Antioqueño." In *Colombia: Making Peace in a Time of War,* 277–294. Washington, DC: United States Institute for Peace.

Safford, Frank, and Marco Palacios. 2002. *Colombia: Fragmented Land, Divided Society.* New York: Oxford University Press.

Samper, Jota. 2012. "Granting of Land Tenure in Medellín, Colombia's Informal Settlements: Is Legalization the Best Alternative in a Landscape of Violence?" *Informal Settlements Research ISR.* Web. June 10. http://informalsettlements.blogspot.com.

Samper, Jota, Tamera Marko, and Kendall K. Murphy. 2011. *Los colonizadores.* Vol. 2. 3 vols. Medellín, Colombia. Film. medellín mi hogar / my home medellín.

Unidad de Atención a la Población Desplazada, Secretaria de Bienestar Social. 2011. Unidad de Análisis y Evaluación de Política Pública: Análisis descriptivo asentamiento y movilidad de población desplazada en Medellín. Medellín.

U.S. Department of State. 2006. "Adjusted Refusal Rate—B-Visas Only By Nationality: Fiscal Year 2006."

U.S. Department of State. 2013. "Adjusted Refusal Rate—B-Visas Only By Nationality: Fiscal Year 2013."

Vamos Mujer. "Vamos Mujer." *Vamos Mujer.* Web. June 25, 2012. http://www.vamosmujer.org.co/site/index.php.

Zuckerbrod, Julie. 2012. "The Last Word." *dukeengageinmedellin.* Web. Aug. 25 . http://dukeengageinmedellin.blogspot.com/2012/08/the-last-word.html.

Zuckerbrod, Julie, Jota Samper, and Tamera Marko. 2012. *Ladera, vida y dignidad.* Vol. 3. 3 vols. Medellín, Colombia. Film. medellín mi hogar / my home medellín.

6

WHO OWNS THE ARCHIVE?

Community Media in Venezuela under Hugo Chavez

ROBIN GARCIA

> The radio is not an end in itself. The radio should be an action of the principles that guide, should reflect the world we decide to build. If not, it does not work. The radio is for the processes of transformation we undertake in our communities. Yes. Our communities are our own. Not mine or this or that. There is no point in one radio. There must be many, working together from the struggles of now and forever.
>
> —Asociación Nacional De Medios Comunitarios, Libres y Alternativos (ANMCLA) ANMCLA newspaper, June 2009

The 1998 election of President Hugo Chavez shattered elite versions of Venezuelan history. During Chavez's second term, local media controlled by collectives of grassroots activists enlivened the shifting notions of democracy within what is known as the Bolivarian Revolution.[1] After the 1998 election of Chavez, initiatives such as land reform and government nationalization of the oil industry were met with opposition from the country's elite, which climaxed in the 2002 attempted coup against Chavez. Corporate media backed the coup by taking over state-sponsored media stations to air soap operas and cartoons while Chavez was being kidnapped. In response, grassroots media took on the responsibility of mobilizing Chavez supporters to bring him back to power. Two days after Chavez was reinstated as president on April 13, 2002, the government recognized the importance of democratized media and began to legalize and financially support community media stations.

Community media within the context of Venezuela, and for the purposes of this chapter, is media that is created and controlled by the community. For the cases that I discuss, it has engaged those traditionally excluded from the mainstream and reflects the emerging relationships between civil society and the state, which are increasingly democratic and participatory. While community media in Venezuela is state funded, I argue it has been able to maintain degrees of autonomy in determining its own programming and organization structure within the confines of a few state-stipulated regulations. Under the contemporary government,[2] and regulated through Venezuela's National Commission of Telecommunications (CONATEL), media outlets, in contrast with private news networks must dedicate 70 percent of their programming to local issues. In addition, the stations may only produce 15 percent of all programming, while community members must use the remaining air space. Each station is also required to provide training to community members ensuring that media literacy is developed among community participants. Most important, the directors of community media networks cannot be officials or members of the military or work in private media networks. In many cases, media collectives only obtain a small amount of funding from the state, which generally includes media equipment and program space. These groups often end up depending on the community for support. For example, in the case of Radio Crepuscular, which I discuss below, the community's communal council, who staffs and financially supports the radio, runs the station. In addition, community media networks are not limited to Chavez supporters. In fact, a large number of anti-Chavez groups have also benefitted from the democratization of media in the country. These groups have developed their own media stations and discuss local and national politics from their perspective. With the democratization of the media, both the left and right wing have been able to experience a wider range of political participation and expression.

Not even three years after the attempted coup against Chavez in 2002, community media increased by more than 100 percent, and most important, stations have emerged in communities historically pushed to the periphery of Venezuelan politics. The community media model has become a tool for political change, which encourages social engagement with local and national politics through community-based programming that brings traditionally marginalized voices into dialogue with the revolutionary process. This chapter explores these community-based media collectives through feminist scholar M. Jacqui Alexander's notion of the "pedagogy of the sacred," which sees the body and performance as a central site where ritual, memory, tradition, and history are archived. That is, as colonialism has replaced indigenous forms of knowledge production with elite representations, embodiment has become central to remembering and reclaiming political and spiritual agency (Alexander 2005). In the case of Venezuela, dominant narratives of nation, progress, and citizenship are being rearticulated at both local and national levels through the community media movement. Community radio and TV are created as intentional conduits of peoples' embodied experiences, which are rich archives of personal and collective histories. This chapter looks at how media collectives are producing local definitions of socialism, where grassroots producers become key protagonists in the rewriting of history. As we shall see, local histories are articulated through the media, as it becomes an important site of collective remembering and storytelling.

Additionally, this chapter explores the Venezuelan community media movement as representing a dynamic tool where the documented and the documenter are one in the same. Or, the same people who are making the news are also the ones watching it. This case study also acts as a tool to discuss the possibilities of conducting activist research, which can be an important arena for inciting, supporting, and illuminating social action in hopes to create a larger movement toward international solidarity, dynamic conversation, and social engagement. By looking at these complexities and possibilities while telling the story of Venezuelan community media, this chapter supports Alexander's notion of the "pedagogy of the sacred," which calls for a reconstitution and redistribution of who owns the historical archive.

Theory and Archives

The prominent deconstructionist theorist Jaques Derrida has illuminated the historical relationship between archives and power structures. Derrida suggests that the archive has traditionally been an imperial site, which emerged out of the construction of European enlightenment and empire-building projects. Derrida notes that "there is no political power without control of the archive" (Derrida 1996, 4). This idea shines light on the intimacy between imperialism and the construction and preservation of historical knowledge. Therefore, radical change beyond the context of an individual or small community can happen when the producers of the historical archive are no longer imperial powers but rather are communities and nations where the means of production and representation are democratized. As we shall see, a move toward the democratization of historically marginalized stories of the past, present, and future is underway in Venezuela.

Since the 1980s, performance theorists have challenged the traditional construction of the archive by locating historical knowledge within the body and acted out through performance. Scholars such as Rebecca Schneider have argued "performance remains" but acts differently than the traditional archive, which is dependent on the material remains of the past and considered authentic and original (Schneider 2001). Oral history, for example is characterized by what she terms "ritual repetition," which enables historical knowledge to be produced through repetition. In other words, oral historical practices are always dynamic, which challenges the creation of a static archive. This framework is useful to the case of Venezuela where community media is unresting the traditional archive from the hands of the elite, and reconstructing history as dynamic, unfolding, embodied, ritualistic, and active. Like Alexander, Schneider is concerned with decentering traditional epistemologies of knowledge construction as they both advocate for a rewriting of history away from the conventional forms of archive production.

Performance theorist Diana Taylor in her text *The Archive and the Repertoire* has similarly argued for a methodology that reunites the colonially imposed split between narrative/text and orality/embodied experience while situating grassroots protagonists as the central agents in the production of knowledge and history (Taylor 2003). For Taylor, the *Repertoire*, which she defines as embodied knowledge/practices, for example, sports, ritual, and spoken language, is in constant dialogue with the *Archive*, enduring materials such as texts, bones, and buildings (19). It is in the interaction of the two that memory is sustained. Traditional disciplines have been reluctant to explore the interconnection of both the *Archive* and *Repertoire* and have traditionally privileged the *Archive* over the *Repertoire*. However, Taylor calls for a radical revision and promotes a model for scholarship that integrates the disciplines of Latin American studies with performance studies while challenging the historical split between the *Archive* and the *Repertoire* (28). Other performance studies theorists such as Barbara Kirshenblatt-Gimblett and José Esteban Muñoz have also looked at these questions within the realm of tourism studies and queer theory. With the work of these theorists, performance studies has challenged traditional forms of knowledge production by advocating for the idea that there are alternative sites of knowledge making which manifest in forms beyond the written and preserved. As a result, oral/historical stories are one of many avenues used by communities not usually included in traditional archive production to pass on culture, history, and politics.

Community media in Venezuela draws on the realm of oral/historical storytelling to collapse the colonially imposed split between embodied knowledge/practice and text. Drawing from grassroots oral/historical memory, community media practitioners discuss contemporary news, create spaces for artistic interpretations of the political moment, host shows on women's and children's health, and most important, use the radios and TVs to mobilize around different community needs. In the case of Venezuela, collapsing the split can be seen as igniting social action where there is no distinction between text/discourse and performance. Thus, embodied histories are becoming the reference points for a community-based political analysis of the present moment. Rather than relying on official local and national discourses, communities rely on those already formed within their collective experiences. These memories are being used to shape new official and unofficial, local, and national narratives of Venezuelan history.

Since part of the work of this chapter is to look at how documented and documenter become one and the same, I similarly situate myself within that matrix where the lines between the two actions are collapsed. Over the course of the last three years these boundaries began to increasingly blur as academic, political, and personal projects pushed me to engage in simultaneous research and political work. Initially, I became interested in researching Venezuelan social movements in 2008 when I participated in a student delegation sponsored by the Bolivarian Circle of New York. The trip exposed students to the local and national political changes happening in the country where we met with community leaders and activists, visited several worker cooperatives and free universities, and met with government officials. I left deeply moved by many of the social initiatives. However, I was most inspired by the role that community media was playing to challenge state politics as well as push the process of change forward from the bottom up.

During the research process, my methodology began to reflect how the Bolivarian Revolution was being revealed to me. For example, during a trip to Venezuela in 2008, the friends with whom I was staying in the Caracas neighborhood of El Valle became deeply committed to assisting me with my research. They began to see the important role it could play in dispelling the myths promoted by the U.S. and Venezuelan corporate media about Venezuela. As a result, they helped me set up interviews and encouraged their friends and neighbors to join the project, as it were. Because of this, I was able to access the voices and stories of activists who might not have been interested in talking to me otherwise. My research became a collective project, and my questions evolved alongside the community-based discussions I had during the interviews. In this sense, my methodology became unique to the communities I worked with in Venezuela. While writing my master's thesis on the subject, I became increasingly aware of how important collective memory is to the political changes underway as collective organizations are literally rewriting the past through different creative and political mediums.

My analysis of the Bolivarian Revolution stems from fieldwork I carried out between 2008 and 2011. I conducted and translated interviews with sixty different members of community radio and TV stations in the pro-Chavez communities of Caracas and the states of Yaracuy and Lara, and I participated in prorevolutionary political events. My analysis also includes reflections on the observations I made during several visits to Venezuela where I spent most of my time in the Caracas barrio of El Valle, a prorevolutionary neighborhood, as well as in the capital of the state of Lara, Barquisimeto, where I worked as a summer intern for School of the Americas Watch. During the internship I investigated U.S. intervention in Latin America as manifest in the School of the Americas (SOA), a military training center located in Fort Benning, Georgia. In 2001, the School of the Americas was renamed the Western Hemisphere Institute for Security Cooperation (WHINSEC). This occurred when the Republican-controlled House of Representatives defeated a bill intended to close the school. Instead of closing, the school merely changed its name. Throughout the late twentieth century and even into the present, the SOA has been intimately involved in supporting right-wing governments, squashing guerrilla forces, and training Latin American militaries to overthrow leftist Latin American governments.[3] The SOA's most recent action was the overthrow of Honduran president Manuel Zelaya.[4] In addition to the School of the Americas Watch's (SOAW) political campaign, the program connected with different community organizations and initiatives to enhance interns' perspectives of the revolutionary process. Because of the nature of my own interests and academic research, I chose to work with Radio Crepuscular, a radio station housed in a local community center, the Centro de Poder Comunal (CPC). I chose this radio station because of its location and connection to several other grassroots community spaces such as Voces Urgentes, a free multimedia school, and the Aldea Don Pio Alvarado, a popular free art school for local youth.

After discussions on how we could be most useful to community producers at the radio, I, along with another SOA Watch intern and the community producers, decided to have a daily news segment about U.S.-based resistance to neoliberalism both within our own country and abroad. The community producers we were working with consistently said they knew nothing about the topic and saw it as a way to link arms with people in the United States fighting against the same system. We researched different political campaigns, contemporary forms of resistance, and invited representatives to call into the show and share the challenges and successes of their political work. For us, as students of revolutionary struggles in and outside of the United States, the program was an invaluable attempt to build solidarity and educate each other by using the democratized media outlets now being promoted by the government and community producers in Venezuela. We saw a great power in the utilization of previously inaccessible technology, to put disparate voices in dialogue with each other. In this light, this chapter is intended to act as an example of what can happen when communities seize the power of the archive, democratize its production, and break historical silences by promoting genuine forms of participatory democracy from the bottom up. This chapter additionally serves as an exploration of activist research, where the boundaries between participation and observation are blurred with the intention of creating lasting and long-term relations of solidarity built around transnational dialogue and action.

This blurring can be seen as the result of what feminist scholar bell hooks terms "looking back," where media networks are redefining civic and cultural life through the construction of multiple public spaces (hooks 2003, 220). hooks describes "looking back" as traditionally marginalized populations constructing their history as a countermemory and using it as a way to invert and shape the future. As grassroots media networks in Venezuela are in the process of "looking back," they are also talking back, as well as talking to, and ultimately creating a dialogical relationship with each other and the state. This "looking back" also signifies that the state is no longer taking center stage; rather, there is a distinct dialogue emerging between the state and the multiple enclaves of civil society. This exchange allows for creativity through media production that helps communities carve out room for the imagination, which is central to all forms of agency. Media collectives, then, theoretically engage in a creative assertion of themselves as historians and protagonists in the writing and rewriting of history (Appadurai 1996, 31).

Grassroots media in Venezuela is also competing against the tide of corporate media, which promotes the political agenda of elites. Under the contemporary government, state-sponsored media simultaneously promotes the agenda of the Bolivarian Revolution and the multiple and collective narratives coming out of grassroots media programming. The relationship between the state and the community media movement allows grassroots structures to maintain their political autonomy as the state provides equipment and funding to media stations that agree to use the radios or TVs for community development and education. The multiple public spheres of community media are creating a vibrancy that complicates and works against top-down, individualistic models of the Nation by advocating for unique relationships to the nationalist and institutionalized revolution operating at the level of the state.

With Alexander's "pedagogy of the sacred" in conjunction with Schnieder's argument for alternative archive production we can see the importance of the community media movement in pushing for community empowerment. In addition, Taylor's call for reuniting the colonially imposed split between the archive and the repertoire, and hooks' notion of looking back illuminates how this movement is at the forefront of challenging traditional interpretations of the past. Now community participants are drawing from their own lived and ancestral experiences to analyze present political formations. Most important, we see that the community media movement, as diverse and nuanced as it is, is creating alternative forums for political engagement; breaking historical silences; increasing levels of local political participation; and acting as a forum to explore the type of world local participants want to build through grassroots models that are shaped by the context from which they emerge.

Three Case Studies on Community Media

In the following sections I explore three case studies of Venezuelan community media: Comunare Rojo TV, a woman's media collective in the state of Yaracuy; Radio Crepuscular and Voces Urgentes at the Centro de Poder Comunal (CPC) in Barquisimeto, Lara; and Radio Verdura, a youth radio based out of an urban art collective in Caracas. As we shall see, all collectives are challenging state bureaucracies in diverse and nuanced ways as they create forums for community dialogue and political action.

One interpretation of Venezuelan politics suggests that radical leftist movements in the country began with the emergence of Hugo Chavez as a political leader (Fernandes 2010). Another interpretation, however, maintains that community-based media collectives draw on pre-Chavez and indigenous strategies that come from a long genealogy of resistance rooted in a history of guerrilla-, civilian-, student-, and military-based struggles (Fernandes 2010, 20). Scholar Sujatha Fernandes suggests that many contemporary urban movements also emerged from militant cadre-based groupings with roots in the guerrilla struggles of the 1960s, as well as political collectives that operated through assemblies, mass actions, and cultural groups based in music, song, and dance struggling against racism and urban displacement (20). These same movements spurred cultural activism in urban communities in the 1980s. In fact, the political history, out of which Chavez emerged, can be traced to the 1970s when foreign debt was on the rise and a decline in oil revenues sharpened the economic divide. Tensions burst open in 1989 with the Caracazo, a popular rebellion originating in communities neighboring Caracas that seeped into the capital as a response to hiked up petroleum prices and bus fares. During this time, militant student movements played a significant role in the antineoliberal rebellion (Kiraz 2007). The gap between the rich and the poor grew in the 1990s and paved the road for popular social movements and Chavez's upcoming political platform against neoliberalism. Notably, under the current government, social movements more than ever engage in collective action and protest, while rearticulating the past from their point of view. The state has thus carved out room to reflect and listen to the concerns of the grassroots by constructing local and national models of collective organization such as the *consejos comunales* (community councils), the *comuna* (the larger organizing body of the community councils), and the national assembly.

As extensions of these larger social movements operating at local and national levels, many community-based media collectives are creating a space for the political participation of traditionally marginalized voices such as women, indigenous, and Afro-Venezuelan groups. For example Jhoanna Jardines, radio producer at Radio Crepuscular noted, "[N]ow with the radio, not only do women and youth find programming that reflects their experience, they are also the ones producing it" (Jardines 2009). These collectives use production and distribution methods which resemble the organizing strategies of the movements that they come from as they respond to individual and community needs. Operating as vehicles for broader organizing initiatives, media collectives are locations for community-based articulations of local and national politics.

As we shall see, the survival of these groups is deeply tied to local contests over urban public space and the reclamation of privatized areas, which produce new meanings of the public sphere and advocate for community-based dialogue and debate (Fernandes 2010, 20). For example, at Voces Urgentes in Barquisimeto, the local community was experiencing a problem with the sewage system. Contaminated water was leaking into the concrete areas where local youth played. To document the issue and publicize the problem, the collective filmed the contaminated water and then interviewed local members about the issue. In between segments, different facts about the community were highlighted to call attention to the sanitary needs of the community. During my research over the last three years I also observed community-based media groups often utilizing the same socialist discourse as the state, while maintaining dialogue and actions critical of many of the state's stances. Voces Urgentes, for example created a series of video montages which they intersperse between their programs which advertise state-sponsored social services such as the free education and health care programs alongside images of peoples' heroes such as Che Guevara and Simon Bolivar. However, the programming offers critiques on many state policies as it feels it is the responsibility of the community to evaluate the process in order to push it forward. While, in the words of bell hooks, "looking back" at their own popular history, these collectives utilize the imagery of the state in order to convey a critique and analysis of the process. At the same time, through collective remembering, these media programs assume nationalist positions while promoting a Venezuelan anticolonial identity that integrates state-sponsored stories with embodied memories. As a result, the networks are characterized by their ability to maintain degrees of political autonomy from the state, which allows them to retain their relationship with community organizing at the base.

A majority of the community members I spoke with noted that their own activist origins stemmed from the 1990s student protests against repressive government policies and inflation (Rojas 2009). For example, Gerardo Rojas, media producer at Voces Urgentes explains that "in the 1990s we began to organize out of political necessity. We developed grassroots networks of communication which helped us reach a lot of people and dialogue across regions" (ibid.). These same people are now contesting private space and redefining the use of public space through their activism. The importance of public space as a catalyst in the formation of social movement webs becomes central to how many of the media collectives organize themselves (ibid.). As we shall see, in these confrontations, state and civil society negotiations often stem from varying interpretations and readings of Venezuela's proposed participatory democracy which grounds itself in a nationalist, anti-imperialist, and prosovereignty discourse.

Comunare Rojo TV

Comunare Rojo TV, an all women's TV station in the rural state of Yaracuy emerged in 2003 from local *campesinos* organizing around the right for the struggles between landowners and *campesinos* to be heard. After the attempted coup against Chavez in 2002 *campesinos* faced political repression as they attempted to pressure elites to enact several laws passed by the government to redistribute idle lands. For example, in 2001 a law was passed which entitled *campesinos* to build agricultural cooperatives by taking over unused lands. The produce from these cooperatives would be sold back to the government and distributed through the country's subsidized food markets or *mercales*, ensuring jobs to local farmers.[5] As a response, landowners would hire vigilantes to violently push the collectives off the land creating a series of bloody battles. It was not until stations like Comunare Rojo TV came into existence that these stories were publically aired and archived. Thus, Comunare Rojo TV emerged out of the process to combat corporate media's representations of these disputes and to bring into public view the social struggles of *campesinos* in the region. Weyli Duran, the community founder of the TV station notes: "The station was born out of the necessity to create a mechanism for the voice of the people to recuperate their democracy" (Duran 2009). As a result, the station operates as a vehicle for people to express their voices and opinions. According to Weyli, the people are participating in all levels of the revolutionary process by retelling the history of their ancestors and connecting them to their present day organizing. In this way, the medium of the camera becomes the filter for the women to enact Alexander's "pedagogy of the sacred" and articulate their social experiences through documented imagery, inserting historically silenced stories into the public sphere. As noted by Weyli, the same people working with the camera create programs and images usually repressed in dominant TV, which only show superficial and sexist images. Now the women of the community are creating images that revolve around their own customs. By using the television as a forum to tell their own histories the people in the municipality have, in the words of one activist "woken up to their roots and can now be heard" (2009). By recuperating the sound, music, and images that belong to their own culture, they envision the TV as a vehicle for the political transformation of the community.

Because of the station's direct involvement in the community they have been able to recruit a number of young women as TV producers who had never before had experience with media production. Lisette, a local high school student, for example, noted that Weyli used to go to her community and provide free media workshops. She participated in the workshop and then decided to get involved with the station. In the process she has learned not only how to produce media but also about local community politics. Her media education has made her an active community participant with the responsibility to represent the pulse of community politics on air. Weyli noted that while many members in the municipality still watch commercial television, Comunare Rojo TV has created an alternative reference point for audiences to engage in discussions, which distinguish local indigenous representations from imported and commercial news. Because of this, community members have developed their own skills as critics who understand the importance of seeing themselves as protagonists on screen.

Like Radio Crepuscular and Voces Urgentes at the CPC, Comunare Rojo TV uses media strategies, which stem from their community. Through call-ins to the station and visiting the communities when media producers get word of different issues arising, the station plugs into and represents the political and cultural expressions and experiences of the community. For Weyli and other members, the station builds on the historical activism and memory of *campesino* struggles in the area. The importance of this media and its power to document history are also reflected in Weyli's comment that in such a rural state the importance of creating community media to help facilitate dialogue around local concerns and issues is incredibly important: "Look at this, we are in a far place and we are dialoging, all people are organizing. Community media is part of this process because the media loves the community and it loves its country and the people have been working slowly and firmly to defend the process and to defend the right of the people to communicate and express themselves" (2009).

Comunare Rojo TV is distinct in its role as a space of articulation for political dialogue and action where community members are central to the station's organizational structure. The members of the station see themselves as the primary documentarians of the community's past, present, and future. The station utilizes oral/historical and embodied memories to analyze contemporary politics and frame the importance of social action. At Comunare Rojo TV, Taylor's *Archive* and the *Repertoire* become one in the same just as the documented and documenters become reflected in each other. The colonially imposed split between the two is collapsed as the station builds on the community's own collective knowledge. In the case of Comunare Rojo TV, the station is taking this call for radical revision a step further in the sense that they are centering women as the main archivers, interpreters, and protagonists of history and contemporary politics. The emphasis on women-generated representations is creating critical dialogue in the community where historical gender roles are coming under scrutiny. Thus, while the collective history of Yaracuy is archived within the community's memory, it is curated by the women, who are mostly young girls in the municipality.

While the women at the station do not necessarily self-identify as feminists, the methodology they use to produce media and break historical silences around gender issues and *campesino* struggles suggests that they are developing a theoretical analysis of the relationship between women, history, land, memory, and media, that is uniquely their own. In fact, according to Weyli, Comunare Rojo did not originally begin as an all women station but ended up as one because many young boys in the area were busy with paid work. The girls, on the other hand, had more flexibility in their day. Over time, the station began to identify itself as an all women station. Now, many shows are dedicated to women's health, education, child rearing, and empowerment. As women are the producers and curators of community knowledge, the relationship between women, men, and politics is changing.

The Battle of the Centro Poder Comunal

The Centro Poder Comunal (Center of Community Power, CPC) is located in Barquisimeto, the capital in the state of Lara, which has a similar history of *campesino* organizing and activism where organizers pull on local histories to create their media programming. The CPC is a community center which houses a free dental clinic, a community radio, Radio Crepuscular, a free video production school, Voces Urgentes, and a free school for popular art, Don Pio Alvarado. The CPC draws on local indigenous strategies of resistance in their community organizing efforts and media production methods. As Hector Salas, locally based popular educator notes, "the way we organize comes out of our history. Our ancestors resisted the Spanish, and our guerrilla movements resisted the dictatorships. The memories we have of them influence our politics and how we produce media" (Salas 2009). Local activists have used media technology to bring local and national attention to the political struggles of their local communities as well as produce different outlets for local forms of knowledge production. Important cross-regional activist networks like those facilitated by the Alternative Media Network of Venezuela (ANMCLA) have been created as a result of democratized media practices. With the power to produce media based on their own history and political realities, the media collectives at the CPC have been able to ward off a state bureaucracy whose interests have come into conflict with the local communities' visions of participatory democracy. Using media technology as a means to articulate community visions and organize, Radio Crepuscular and Voces Urgentes have been essential in heightening the level of civic engagement of local Barquisimeto residents, especially during political actions, which require cross-regional acts of solidarity.

Members of the networks at the CPC have been on the front lines of some of the most symbolic battles to push the process of change forward from the bottom up. For example, the battle over the CPC, which I discuss below, comes out of a long history of indigenous and *campesino* organizing in the state of Lara. Scholar Timothy P. Wickham-Crowley notes that in Venezuela, the state of Lara had a rebellious past and produced a major antigovernment revolt in the 1920s led by General Jose Gabaldon, father of later guerrilla chief Argimiro Gabaldon. During that time, these movements thrived, on pre-existing loyalties, organization, and a social base of kinship and/or patron-client relations that crossed class lines. Residents of Lara, for example, had given the Communist Party more than 50 percent of the vote in 1958 and the FALN guerrillas were in fact brought into being by the Communist Party in that state (Wickham-Crowley 2001, 154–56). Because of its mountainous geography, Lara was also an important base of the Venezuelan Tupamaro guerrilla movement, which emerged out of the tradition of Marxist guerrillas who took up arms to challenge military dictatorships throughout the 1960s.[6] All of these social and environmental factors have greatly influenced how community media activists see the importance of media in producing their own narratives of the past and organizing around the political process. In fact, many practitioners noted that the guerrilla organizing of their ancestors has influenced their media strategies. Like the guerrillas, the different radios and TVs in the regions organize through an unseen network, as the voices of programmers travel from one region to the next inciting dialogue and action.

During my first visit to the CPC in 2009 I witnessed how this history influenced contemporary contestations over public space. When I arrived the members of the community of the Carucenia, the barrio which surrounds the CPC, were squatting in its buildings to claim the space because deputies of the local government wanted to take the center away from the community. The CPC was built in 2001 by the Lara state government as a local neighborhood office but was taken under community control in 2007 by community activists who were unhappy with the misuse of the space, and its inaccessibility during the 2002 attempted coup against President Chavez. During the coup, the CPC was completely abandoned. According to Ricardo David Diaz Castillo, community radio producer at Radio Crepuscular,

> Before the coup, *El Comandante* Chavez inaugurated the center, and it was named the *Citizen Participation Center*. In the beginning, Chavez inaugurated it hoping that it would be a center for direct community participation where the same community would be in charge of the center. On his weekly program of *Aló Presidente*, Chavez stated that the radio should

> be used as a tool for the process, taking it to the communities, and that the same communities should take over the space. But during and after the coup it was not like that. The radio and the center were closed because they were in the hands of the governor. He was truly blind in the same way that the private media was, where no one knew anything, and nobody knew what was happening in the country. But the people organized and demanded the president's return. After his return Chavez went on *Aló Presidente* and stated: "this community radio has supported us this whole time and it is in your hands comrades." But that same community was bothered because we knew that wasn't the case. So we said to him, "Comandante, they are fooling you! This radio is not in the hands of the people; it's in the governor's hands! The space is professionalized, with 4 or 5 people getting a salary and defending the governor's interests, not the interests of the people." Soon after, Chavez confronted those in charge at the CPC and we presented a proposal for the self-management of the radio, which stated that the same community that produced and operated programs would be responsible for the transmission and equipment. The president liked the idea. He saw that our duty in that moment was to take the radio space. That was the first movement forward in this center. There were still issues of the governor of Lara paying those who worked in the center, and the institution was trying to maintain and expand its power here. The only space that was truly participatory at that time was the radio and not the entire center because the governor had closed it. (Diaz 2009)

In short, in January of 2007, Carucenia activists took over the CPC because the government was still denying the members of the Carucenia, the barrio where the CPC is located, its public use. Carucenia community members locked themselves in the CPC for two weeks until the governor agreed to negotiations (Korezek 2009). During the time activists aired news about their struggle on Radio Crepuscular and Voces Urgentes and used the stations to bring national attention to the battle. According to Katarina Korezek, community producer at Voces Urgentes,

> When the promoters from the governor's office arrived and announced that they had been sent to take over the CPC, an immediate assembly was called which *Voces Urgentes* filmed. The video was placed with a press note on *Aporrea* and the *ANMCLA* web page the same day which brought national

> attention and forced the governor to apologize for the action. Local TV stations were also called and gave announcements against the actions of the governor's office. The radio was used to create a space for debate between the representatives from the governor's office and the community. (Diaz 2009)

The ability of Voces Urgentes and Radio Crepuscular to document and publicize what was happening at the CPC is a result of the networks created through the use of this democratized media. According to the activists I interviewed, those involved with the 2007 takeover and the 2009 sit-in, the local government developed a fear of the community power being cultivated in the Carucenia through the CPC. The local government was additionally threatened by the rapidly growing electoral power resulting from community organizing. Juan de Villegas, the barrio where the CPC is located, became an important area for the governor to win over due to its large population. He wanted to consolidate all of his power at the CPC because it has its own radio (Radio Crepuscular), television (Voces Urgentes), and communication school and the Don Pio Alvarado center for folk art (Diaz 2009).

The history of land-based, student, and urban struggles in the state of Lara echoed through the organizing around community media. For example, Gerardo Rojas of Voces Urgentes highlighted how historical memories of resistance to Spanish colonialism are now reflected in these contemporary challenges to top-down power structures (such as the one employed by the local Barquisimeto government). Most significantly, all of the community activists I spoke with at the CPC noted that their activism predated the Bolivarian Revolution, as suggested above, while many activists at the CPC trace their current media work to their participation in the student movements of the 1990s. This collective consciousness of the past frames the contemporary culture of grassroots organizing as well as media use and strategy. Through visual documentation, the community archive of these social struggles is negotiated with contemporary politics, thus bridging the historical divide between Taylor's *Archive* and *Repertoire* (2003). In other words, while social struggles become embodied articulations of resistance, which take reference from historical forms of protest, community media preserves and at the same time brings to life the experience of the members of the CPC. Through community media, history is brought into the public realm and represented as both embodied and active. Here, the *Archive* bleeds into the *Repertoire,* thus collapsing the colonially imposed split between the two as community media produces an alternative representation of local social struggles.

Similarly, as the viewers and listeners of media at the CPC actively inform the news produced on air and vice versa, the split between the *Archive* and *Repetoire* is similarly dissolved, thus creating news that stems from the community's historical memory. For example, Jardines notes, "we draw from the stories of our community when we talk about our political situation. We look to the youth, the elders, and our experience here on this land to inform how we make news" (Jardines 2009). In addition, media producers trace their radical past to the contemporary moment. For example, Rojas notes that before the emergence of Chavez, the need to use the means of communication as an arm of organizing propelled the building of Archoto Biblioteca Comunitaria (Archoto Community Library). "Archoto was a leader from the Wayuu indigenous tribe that in the year 1600 commanded 100,000 men who struggled against European invaders for 60 years" (Jardines 2009). When it was opened, the library turned into a meeting place for the student movement, priests of the liberation theology movement, and women's groups. It housed cultural and political activities and ran a film club.[7] Rojas suggests:

> We weren't satisfied with one space so we did multiple activities in the community. We would show four productions a week with a projector or by carrying around a TV. However, the films didn't say anything about our community. From there, we started photographing, we picked up video cameras, and then we started putting the radio together. One thing was leading to the other. Communication became an instrument to strengthen community work. We were not going to get into communication and leave the community work. Rather, it became a tool along with our cultural activities and social work. (ANMCLA 2009)

Building locally specific forms of participatory democracy has been enabled by using the means of communication as a tool for community work. Additionally, Rojas explained the importance of communication in community work by noting that the producers at Voces Urgentes follow a pedagogy of liberatory education where they take what they know and multiply it by teaching others, making information more accessible. Rojas notes,

> What's important to us is not just what we're doing but how we're doing it. We are not going to promote a pedagogy of participatory democracy where I decide everything because I am

> the one who is most familiar with an issue. Instead, we prefer collective error with an individual truth because in collective error everyone learns from the mistakes. Generally what we see in a lot of the workshops we do is that when someone asks someone else about communication, the first thing they imagine is a microphone, a camera, equipment, and technology. This image generates the idea that this is what communication looks like. But for true communication to exist, we need each other, two people. It's impossible to be in communication individually. Communication is actually rooted in the word and idea of community. (ANMCLA 2009)

Working from the idea that community and communication come from the same root, Voces Urgentes produces media where "the people" appear on screen as protagonists.

In the case of the CPC, contestations to top-down models of democracy came in direct tension with the local Lara government. The community around the CPC was able to resist government intervention by calling on its own embodied historical memory of resistance and reconfiguring it against the backdrop of a changing political climate. The archive of radical movements in Lara exists within the collective memories of its residents as they analyze contemporary state centrist politics, especially when governmental notions of democracy differ from ones rooted in their own collective history.

All of the community producers at Radio Crepuscular and Voces Urgentes noted that they see community media as a critical instrument of the revolution within the nationally promoted Bolivarian Revolution; however, they do not follow a uniform notion of political engagement or audiovisual production. As Diaz suggests, "we use this media to communicate our political views, to articulate our concerns, to analyze our struggles, and to push the revolution forward" (2009). Although they formed their production methods by drawing on the diverse histories of resistance in Venezuela, each approached organizing and his or her relationship to the state differently. In Barquisimeto community media stations, anarchists, and democratic socialists can be found working together while each station has its own political, ideological, and cultural style, which is unique to its neighborhood. Where some stations find it necessary to work with the state by obeying state-sponsored laws, others either use those laws as guidelines or disregard them, thus promoting political autonomy through their critiques of the process. In the cases discussed above, activists at the CPC battled for autonomy from their local government, while at the same time utilizing state-sponsored discourses to frame their struggle. In this way, community media at the CPC has carved out its own form of knowledge production and strategic sensibility to push its community-based vision forward.

Radio Verdura

While the media networks at Comunare Rojo TV, Voces Urgentes, and Radio Crepuscular draw on local *campesino* and guerrilla history and activism to shape their media production methods, Radio Verdura, located in Caracas, utilizes the urban environment to produce radio. Radio Verdura is a mobile radio housed in a truck that circles the streets of Caracas once a day playing revolutionary hip hop while discussing revolutionary politics through a loudspeaker. This radio sees itself as a critical forum for urban youth in Caracas to explore local issues through artistic collaboration and activism. Its members suggest that their role within the Bolivarian process of change was to maintain a noninstitutionalized stance as they pass through the streets leaving behind only the memory of their presence. They see these guerrilla radio tactics as supporting the revolutionary process in the most intimate way. By connecting to urban life and passing through both pro-and anti-Chavez communities, the station accelerates the level of dialogue around contemporary politics by inserting the revolution into oppositional spheres. Radio Verdura's decentralized structure did not appear to be in tension with its relationship to the state, as we found earlier in the case of the CPC. In fact, during 2008, the Chavista mayor of Caracas funded the station just before the new opposition mayor was elected.

Radio Verdura is part of the Tiuna El Fuerte collective, an urban youth group which provides free art and hip-hop classes to the community of El Valle. The station's political framework, like others discussed, draws on national narratives, which promote traditionally invisible peoples' heroes as key protagonists in Venezuelan history. Similarly, Radio Verdura makes this recapturing of underrepresented heroes their own as they call on ones not traditionally highlighted in national representations. Like in the case of the CPC, Radio Verdura utilizes, and at the same time pushes against, these representations while articulating its own political position. For example, as the collective integrates less known historical protagonists such as Tiuna, an indigenous chief who fought against Spanish colonization, they simultaneously weave their own community-based stories into their historical narrative. As such, the collective sees itself as adding layers to the discussion of its own past.

Building on the urban revolutionary youth culture of Caracas, Radio Verdura adds educational and political flare to its programming, which combines elements of hip hop and urban DJ culture with nationally promoted revolutionary slogans, often interwoven with Chavez's own voice. The truck in which the radio is housed becomes the vehicle for the collective's political and cultural expression in the bustling pace of Caracas. In fact, the name of the station, Radio Verdura, also suggests that the station sees itself as providing musical, political, and cultural alimentation for those transiting the city. Pulling from their own experiences as working-class urban youth, the collective creates shows that are connected to the specific community needs through political dialogue and creative expression. The oral/historical memory of the surrounding community is framed through and articulated by the transmission of this youth perspective of the political process. The boundaries of formal structures of dialogue and action are pushed as the collective sporadically and intuitively intervenes in public space with their creative expressions and critical commentary often inciting extreme audience responses. Within Chavista communities other youth gather, follow the truck, and when it pauses at different intersections become involved in the discussion. They seize the microphone, yelling or standing on the corner discussing their views and perspectives as others dance alongside the truck. Radio Verdura temporarily creates community within the confines of the traffic on the street. It has carved out a political niche for urban youth culture and performance within the Bolivarian political process by drawing on urban art and unarmed guerrilla organizing tactics, which ultimately add nuance and layers to the political landscape of Chavista politics in Caracas. As a result, the political education of youth within the collective emerges from this hip-hop-centered urban youth pedagogy, which is unique to the experience of radical urban youth in the city. Radio Verdura collapses the colonially imposed split as it, like the cases discussed earlier, enacts Alexander's "pedagogy of the sacred" where youth embody a rich tradition of resistance, while "looking back" at government-promoted discourses, appropriating that which resonates with their experiences and then inserting their presence into Caracas with creative forms of expression. They simultaneously produce an analysis of the political process they are experiencing with a creativity that opens the door to an array of radical possibilities.

Reflections on Research

From the countryside to the city, grassroots communities are engaging in new and creative ways of producing information about their history and using it to frame contemporary organizing and discussions around local issues. This historical revisionism is marked by a diversity of experiences which draw on different interpretations of local and national history making for a nuanced and complex field of community media production and programming that challenges traditional forms of archive and media production. What remains consistent is the utilization of once inaccessible technology to bring communities together around political and educational agendas, rewrite elite sponsored histories by foregrounding traditionally silenced peoples' heroes, and use media as a means to organize by producing alternative archives of the past, present, and future. Although community media was largely responsible for bringing Chavez back into power after the 2002 attempted coup, these collectives remain loyal to the political change of the revolution rather than individual politicians. They stand out as critical voices and offer critiques of the political process.

Community media has helped facilitate new forms of democracy. As discussed above, before the emergence of Hugo Chavez, Venezuelan notions of democracy were overwhelmingly defined by the elite. Contestations to elite political dominance were quelled through the establishment of a liberal two-party political system that closely mirrored the United States. The representation of Venezuela as a "model democracy," emerged from the political grip over the economy these sectors exercised and through the promotion of this representation in the U.S social imagination. Now, the Venezuelan nation is in a transition, which is occurring through a re-vision of elite forms of history, an engagement in alternative representational practices, and a redistribution of some of the nation's wealth in the form of social programs that make once inaccessible social services available and, more often than not, free. In this light, degrees of direct and indirect state intervention through battles over public and private space become negotiated by community media, which challenge the glorification of capitalism and the individual with their own production strategies. This project of multiple public spheres proposes new methods to engage civil society and the state, where archive production is increasingly held in the hands of those traditionally excluded from discursive, symbolic, and material realities.

As the community media movement is producing a counter- and embodied narrative of Venezuelan history, politics, and identity, this chapter similarly attempts to carry that vision into spheres beyond the scope of the revolutionary process. In other words, my hope is that this chapter supports the mission of community-based media collectives by helping incite critical dialogue among communities outside of the political process in Venezuela. The methodologies used to conduct this research and curate these grassroots voices became increasingly popular, as discussed above, when community members began to see this research project as a transnational exercise of solidarity. This chapter is largely a result of the collective research experience we shared. Over the last three years I worked to build networks of solidarity with movements in Venezuela and allies in the United States. As noted earlier, working as an intern for School of the Americas Watch during the summer of 2009 in Barquisimeto Lara was a significant experience where the lines between activism and research were blurred. The coup in Honduras took place while I was an intern conducting research about U.S. intervention in Latin America vis-à-vis the School of the Americas. While I was working in the afternoons at the community radio stations we interns took the information we had gathered at SOA Watch and publicized it. As mentioned earlier, along with several community activists we held open forums on the coup in Honduras. These forums led to a daily news segment on the local radio about U.S. intervention and U.S.-based social movements where we invited representatives from different communities to call in to discuss their current campaigns, successes, and challenges. The program audience would also call in to ask questions and give their opinions about what was presented on air.

Community media collectives in Venezuela provide powerful examples of Alexander's "Pedagogy of the Sacred" and Taylor's notion of collapsing the split between the *Archive* and the *Repertoire* through hooks' notion of "looking back." As these groups are becoming dynamic archives of collective memory, history, and contemporary politics, I hope that this chapter reflects the creativity of that process. The relationships and networks that are fundamental to the project of transnational solidarity with grassroots communities in Venezuela and the U.S. are dynamic and unfolding as the politics of our countries are also always in flux. While media technology becomes increasingly accessible to grassroots communities, there is increased potential for democratizing archive production and therefore changing the landscape of political power locally, nationally, and internationally. Now communities who have been traditionally excluded may begin to produce information and representations based on their own historical realities.

The relationships built during my time in Venezuela were charged with a deep understanding of the need to promote transnational grassroots networks of information, solidarity, and action. My intention is to provide a small window into some of the ways communities are engaging their past, to write their future into existence on terms that resonate with their political visions of democracy. It also acts as a reflection on the sacred dialogue that can emerge when the boundaries between documented and documenter dissolve. That is not to eclipse the fact that all the protagonists involved in this chapter, myself included, maintain different relationships to power, privilege, and resources. In acknowledgment of those relationships the work of this chapter extends beyond the scope of the written word and acts as another sacred site of embodiment.

Epilogue

Since writing this book chapter, the political landscape of Venezuela has changed. With the passing of Hugo Chavez in March 2013, community media producers have become more committed than ever to the Bolivarian process. As noted throughout, the process of change did not begin with Chavez and will not end with him either. Social movements are working tirelessly to consolidate their organizing efforts and refine their vision of a more just society, while at the same time being forced to ward off a violent opposition that undermines the political gains of the last thirteen years. In regards to the passing of Chavez, many activists noted that while they mourn the death of such a charismatic leader, they see an opportunity to further "Chavismo" and truly transform Venezuela from the bottom up. As noted by Jhoana Jardines, "Chavez has passed, and we will truly miss him, but he lives on in us. I am Chavez, my mother is Chavez, my father is Chavez, and my whole community is Chavez. He is in us, we are all leaders, and now we are stronger than ever" (Jardines 2013). While the Bolivarian Revolution is at a political intersection, what is certain is that the communities discussed in this chapter will continue to work toward their own unique vision of a society where wealth is redistributed and where peoples' voices are privileged over elite politics and power structures.

Notes

I would like to thank the activists I met in Venezuela whose powerful stories inspired this chapter. Although there was not room to fit in all the voices of those I interviewed, what I learned from working with them has surfaced in how I organized this project. I am also grateful to the Cultural Studies Department at Claremont Graduate University for research support. In particular I would like to thank Dr. Eve Oishi, Dr. Cindy Forster, and Dr. Miguel Tinker Salas for their critical academic guidance and mentorship.

1. "Bolivarian Revolution" is a term commonly used to describe the political process underway in Venezuela. For more information

on the Bolivarian Revolution, see Richard Gott, (2011). Also visit www.venezuelanalysis.com.

2. This chapter was written while Hugo Chavez was still alive. Thus, "contemporary government" or "contemporary period" refers to Hugo Chavez's final presidential term.
3. For more information on the School of the Americas, see Thomas Wright (2007).
4. For more information on the 2009 coup in Honduras visit www.soaw.org.
5. The term "*mercal*" emerged out of the Venezuelan social missions where government sponsored food stores serve local communities with basic goods. *Mercales* differ from traditional *mercados* because they operate as subsidized food marts which embody the legacy of collective ownership of the social missions.
6. Fox, Michael (2006). See also Carlos Martinez and Michael Fox (2010, 17).
7. ANMCLA newspaper, June 2009.

References

Alexander, M. Jacqui. 2005. *Pedagogies of Crossing: Meditations on Feminism, Sexual Politics, Memory and the Sacred*. Durham, NC: Duke University Press.

ANMCLA newspaper. 2009. June.

Appadurai, Arjun. 1996. *Modernity at Large; Cultural Dimensions of Globalization*. Minneapolis: University of Minnesota Press.

Derrida, Jaques. 1996. *Archive Fever: A Freudian Impression*. Chicago: University of Chicago Press.

Diaz Castillo, Ricardo David. Summer 2009. Interview with author.

Di Eugenio Saravia, Jessica. Winter 2008. Interview with author.

Duran, Pedro. Summer 2009. Interview with author.

Duran, Weyli. Winter 2009. Interview with author.

Fernandes, Sujatha. 2005. "Growing Movement of Community Radio in Venezuela" Znet; The Spirit of Resistance Lives. http://www.zmag.org/znet/viewArticle/4743. Accessed December 2009.

———. 2008. "Social Policy in Chavez's Venezuela: A Radical Alternative or More of the Same?" *Revista Magazine, Harvard Review of Latin America* 8, 1 (41): 40–42.

———. 2009. "The barrios and Chavez" https://lists.resist.ca/pipermail/project-x/2007-April/015425.html. Accessed December 2009.

———. 2010. *Who Can Stop the Drums? Urban Social Movements in Chávez's Venezuela*. Durham, NC: Duke University Press.

Fernandez, Henry. Winter 2008. Interview with author.

Fox, Michael. 2006. 'CECOSESOLA: Four Decades of Independent Struggle for a Venezuelan Cooperative.' http://www.venezuelanalysis.com/analysis/1793. Accessed December 2009.

Ginsberg, Faye. 1991. "Indigenous Media: Faustian Contract or Global Village." *Cultural Anthropology* 6 (1): 92–112.

Gomez, Yarabid. Winter 2008. Interview with author.

Gott, Richard. 2011. *Hugo Chavez and the Bolivarian Revolution*. London: Verso Books.

Guevara, Ernesto. 1965. "Socialism and Man in Cuba." In *Socialism and Man in Cuba,* ed., Che Guevara and Fidel Castro, 7–29. Atlanta: Pathfinder.

hooks, bell. 2003. "The Oppositional Gaze: Black Female Spectators." In *Feminist Postcolonial Theory, A Reader,* ed., Reina Lewis and Sara Mills, 207–221. New York. Routledge.

Janicke, Kiraz. 'Venezuela's Resurgent Revolutionary Student Movement' http://www.venezuelanalysis.com/analysis/2581. Accessed December 2009.

Jardines, Jhoanna. Summer 2009. Interview with author.

———. Spring 2013. Interview with author.

Jones, Bart. 2008. *Hugo! The Hugo Chavez Story from Mud Hut to Perpetual Revolution*. London. Bodley Head.

Korezek, Katarina. Summer 2009. Interview with author.

Lander, Edgardo. 2007. "Venezuela Social Conflict in a Global Context in Venezuela." In *Hugo Chavez and the Decline of an "Exceptional Democracy,"* ed., Miguel Tinker Salas and Steve Ellner, 16–32. Lanham, MD: Rowman & Littlefield.

Martin, Michael T. 1997. *New Latin American Cinema: Theory, Practice and Transcontinental Articulations*. Detroit, MI: Wayne State University Press.

Martinez, Carlos, Michael Fox, and Farell Jojo. 2010. *Venezuela Speaks! Voices from the Grassroots*. Oakland, CA. PM.

Rainier Key Gonzalez, Jhaim. Winter 2008. Interview with author.

Rodriguez, Noel. Summer 2009. Interview with author.

Rojas, Gerardo. Summer 2009. Interview with author.

Salas, Hector. Summer 2009. Interview with author.

Schneider, Rebecca. 2001. "Archives: Performance Remains." *Performance Research* 6 (2): 100–108.

Solanas, Fernando, and Octavio Getino. 1997. *Towards a Third Cinema in New Latin American Cinema: Theory, Practice and Transcontinental Articulations*. Detroit, MI: Wayne State University Press.

Taylor, Diana. 2003. *The Archive and the Repertoire, Performing Cultural Memory in the Americas*. Durham, NC: Duke University Press.

Tinker Salas, Miguel. 2007. "U.S Oil Companies in Venezuela." In *Venezuela: Hugo Chavez and the Decline of an "Exceptional Democracy,"* ed., Miguel Tinker Salas and Steve Ellner, 35–59. Lanham, MD: Rowman & Littlefield.

Wickham-Crowley, Timothy P. 2001. "Winners, Losers, and Also-Rans: Toward a Comparative Sociology of Latin American Guerrilla Movements." In *Power and Popular Protest; Latin American Social Movements,* ed. Susan Eckstein, 132–181. Berkeley: University of California Press.

Wright, Thomas. 2007. *State Terrorism in Latin America: Chile, Argentina, and International Human Rights*. Lanham, MD: Rowman & Littlefield.

7

ECHOES OF INJUSTICE

Performative Activism and the Femicide Plaguing Ciudad Juárez

CHRISTINA MARÍN

> We cannot support any act of killing; no killing can be justified. But not to kill is not enough. We must also learn ways to prevent others from killing. We cannot say, "I am not responsible. They did it. My hands are clean."
>
> —Thich Nhat Hanh, *For a Future to Be Possible: Buddhist Ethics for Everyday Life* (2007)

Answering Difficult Questions through Art and Scholarship

How do you tell the stories of hundreds of women who have been murdered? How do you give voice back to those who have been viciously silenced? How do you give dignity to the families who are left behind? . . . How do you not? I am a Latina artist and scholar. This makes me a border crosser between the art world and the academy. As an artist, I choose to direct works that are socially conscious and speak out against oppression and injustice. As a scholar, I hope to give voice to the victims of femicide who have been savagely raped and murdered. Through my research and art I attempt to plant seeds of social consciousness, weaving the message through academic writing and creative praxis. I have always believed that the ivory tower would be worthless without the conversion of theory into practice throughout the broader context of society. I agree with Jill Dolan when she argues that "progressive academics need to translate and promote the usefulness of their work to wider audiences, and that activists need to respect and engage the potential of knowledge generated in academic settings" (2001, 3). These two sides of my identity combine to make me the activist who will not accept things as they are.

In my work as a theatrical director I combine a human rights activist lens with a *transfronterista* feminist perspective and respond to the hegemonic structures in our society. Only by speaking through all of these voices can I write about my experiences with the stories of the women of Ciudad Juárez. I situate this chapter at the interdisciplinary nexus between theatre/performance-based activism and transnational feminist theory (see this book's introduction), posing several ethical questions embedded in international human rights debates examining the rights of women and of human beings in general. At the heart of this narrative lie the stories of women, some who have been brutally silenced and others who, in response to this violence, refuse to be. I begin with my own first encounter with these women's stories eight years ago, in order to contextualize for the reader how I came to direct the three plays I discuss in this chapter. Next, I offer a panoramic view of the femicide plaguing Ciudad Juárez and recognize that this gender-based terrorism is spreading to other cities. Finally, I use my experiences directing three plays addressing the topic to frame a discussion regarding performative activism as a tool that engages theatre as a performance medium to help people see the human lives behind these stories, rather than just the statistics.

Crossing Borders between the Academy and the Arts

During the course of my doctoral studies in theatre at Arizona State University, I took a seminar called Borderland Survival Texts: Race, Trauma, and Gender in the Global Age, taught in the Chicana/Chicano Studies Department by Dr. Arturo Aldama. We studied multimedia artistic texts, fiction, and academic essays dealing with the pressing implications of globalization. Almost ten years after the first bodies were discovered in abandoned lots in Ciudad Juárez, Mexico, I was introduced to the stories of these women through the haunting documentary *Señorita Extraviada*, by the feminist filmmaker Lourdes Portillo. Over the image of a young woman painting a black cross on a pink background on a telephone pole in the streets of Ciudad Juárez, Portillo narrates: "It is impossible to know the exact number, but in the last decade somewhere between two and four hundred young women have been killed. Only a few of these crimes have been solved. Why are the deaths of so many young women being ignored? And why are the murders still happening?" (2001).

Devastated by the atrocities described in the film, and searching for a theoretical contextualization for this wasteland known as the U.S.-Mexico border, I turned to Gloria Anzaldúa's metaphor of a "1,950 mile-long open wound" (1999, 24). In *Borderlands/La Frontera*, Anzladúa vividly sets the stage for the development of a *transfronterista* feminist lens through which to explore this open wound explaining that "before a scab forms it hemorrhages again, the lifeblood of two worlds merging to form a third country—a border culture. Borders are set up to define the places that are safe and unsafe, to distinguish *us* from *them*" (1999, 25). Describing both the physical and metaphorical signification of this geographic construction, she writes, "[A] border is a dividing line, a narrow strip along a steep edge. A borderland is a vague and undetermined place created by the emotional residue of an unnatural boundary. It is in a constant state of transition" (1999, 25). Her warning is clear: "Do not enter, trespassers will be raped, maimed, strangled, gassed, shot. The only 'legitimate' inhabitants are those in power, the whites and those who align themselves with whites. Tension grips the inhabitants of the borderlands like a virus. Ambivalence and unrest reside there and death is no stranger" (1999, 25–26).

For days the images portrayed by Portillo plagued every thought that crossed my mind. I began to realize that if my picture were placed side by side with the photograph of any of the hundreds of young women whose faces are plastered all over Ciudad Juárez, one would be hard pressed to differentiate between the *maquiladora* worker and the doctoral student. Why was my life worth more than theirs? How could so many women disappear, many of them turning up as corpses in abandoned lots? And why were the federal and local authorities so unresponsive to this atrocious violation of human rights? Portillo explains in her documentary that the laws of supply and demand operate in this border region; for every young woman who loses her life, there are at least a dozen more ready and willing to take her place in the production lines at the *maquiladora* (factory or sweat shop). The more I read about the borderland, the more I realized that these borders were being crossed more frequently as the age of globalization progressed, and I felt the need to stand up and testify for the victims of this phenomenon; I needed to bear witness. But I was in school; I had to write a dissertation and finish my PhD. I could not imagine doing both simultaneously.

Parallel to my studies, I had been working with a local bilingual theatre company for several years. I had stage managed, directed, and acted in several productions from living room comedies about infidelity and friendship to ethnodramas dealing with the contentious immigration issues involving border crossings from Mexico into the United States. When it finally came time for me to focus on the dissertation stage of my studies, the artistic and managing directors of the production company gave me their blessing to go out, do my fieldwork, and sit down at the computer to write. I began an arts-based qualitative case study with the bilingual youth theatre for social change group I had been directing for several years. We focused on using Theatre of the Oppressed techniques as qualitative research methods to explore the concept of Latina adolescent identity. In the back of my mind would always be the young women who had lost their lives in Ciudad Juárez and how they would never have the chance to participate in such a positive experience. The teenagers I worked with had either crossed the border themselves or were in the United States because their families chose to come here for better opportunities. Many of the young women in Ciudad Juárez were often caught up in the web of trying to make enough money to cross over into the United States. My thoughts were on both sides of the border as I continued to complete my fieldwork.

In November 2004, I received an unexpected phone call. The artistic director of the theatre company needed to consult with me. I saved my work on the computer and turned my attention to this conversation. He explained to me that a board member had presented the company with a script she wanted to direct; however, she had recently gotten married and found out she was going to have her first child. She believed in the play and felt the timing was right to bring light to these issues. A second director was approached but declined the offer. Although I had been given a reprieve from my work with the company to finish my degree, I was being asked to direct the play that would forever change the course of my life. Without any promises, I agreed to read the text, and the artistic director emailed me the play that evening.

"Las Mujeres de Juárez" (The Women of Juárez), written by Rúben Amavizca Murúa, gripped my heart and led me to a place where, as a socially conscious theatrical director, I could attempt to give voice and dignity back to the hundreds of young women who had been swallowed up by the border. I knew that directing this play would also have an impact on my dissertation work. As we struggled to conceptualize Latina adolescent identity in a border culture using theatre, the young women in the study helped me realize that the stories of their counterparts in Ciudad Juárez contributed to the emerging global identity of Latinas. They asked the same questions I had been struggling with. Why? Why are our lives worth writing a book about, but their lives are worth nothing? How can they be considered disposable? I worked on my dissertation during the day and began to rehearse the production of "Las Mujeres de Juárez" at night. I revisited the research I had started in Dr. Aldama's class, and the geopolitical artist/activist in me went to the drawing board. I encountered another *transfronterista* artistic activist who wrote music lyrics that would inspire me through the process of bringing the world of these women to the stage. According to Sarah Ramirez, "Mexican singer Lila Downs presents a clear example of transnational feminist politics and identity" (2002, ¶ 3).[1] Downs "expresses a . . . critical stance towards both the United States and Mexico. . . . attempts to voice issues of gender and ethnicity as they relate to national identity, transnational economies, and power . . . [H]er music critiques relations of power . . . and gendered ethnic niches in which women become exploitable pools of labor" (2002, ¶ 5).

As an artist looking through a *transfronterista* feminist lens, my goal was to portray the human side of this tragedy that has affected too many families and taken too many lives. I needed to depict the everyday routine of these people who live and die on the border between the United States and Mexico. Even deeper than that, I wanted to convey to the audience that these atrocities are not only occurring on our border, but wherever, in Anzaldúa's words, "the Third World grates against the first and bleeds" (1999, 25).

Through my director's lens, I envisioned the opening of the play as a multimedia prologue, not actually written in the script by the playwright. Set to Lila Downs' song, "La Niña," a video projection appears above the set. The whirling lights of a nightclub in Ciudad Juárez fill the screen, and the audience is transported into the nightlife of what has been referred to as "The Murder Capital of the World" (Kolb 2012, ¶ 19), a place where even the devil is afraid to live (Bowden 1996, 44). The camera pans the dance floor where lively couples sway to the *cumbia* rhythm. But as the scene progresses the women begin to disappear. Each of the men is left dancing alone, never reacting to the absence of his partner. Through this artistic metaphor, I hoped to portray how life goes on in Ciudad Juárez *a pesar de todo* (in spite of it all). Certainly the authorities have not bothered to give a second thought to these young women for almost twenty years.

I return to Ramirez's article because I feel her words capture Downs' lyrical message succinctly. "In *'La Niña'* Downs sings directly to Rosa Maria, a dark-haired girl with a sad face, who toils without end or escape in the *maquiladora* border factories. . . . Not only does this young girl realize that her job is taking its toll on her, she also realizes that all her efforts, dreams, and desires are becoming distant memories" (Ramirez 2002, ¶ 6). Lila brings to life the harsh world of these women through her lyrics, as Lourdes Portillo has through documentary film, and as I have attempted to on the stage. We actively bear witness through our art forms and denounce the impunity that plagues Ciudad Juárez. I believe theatre has the potential to serve a higher purpose on many fronts; through performance as an artistic product, as well as dramatic activities like the ones I employed with my youth theatre group in the dissertation study, it offers us an artistic activism through which to address political issues and human rights violations.

The three plays I discuss in this chapter have given me the opportunity to look beyond the statistics into the lives of both the victims and the survivors of this femicide. I turn now, with the help of several journalists and activist organizations, to offer a panoramic view of a city that seems to be imploding on itself.

Provoking Critical Reflection through Performance

According to Nancy Pineda-Madrid, "how we perceive the suffering of others can make an enormous difference in whether we see, or not, its origins in social structures of human making" (2011, chap. 1, ¶ 1). Since 1993, the wasteland between Ciudad Juárez, Chihuahua, and El Paso, Texas, has been plagued by a gender-based violence that has claimed the lives of hundreds of women and left families searching for hundreds more who are missing. A recent Fox News Latino report reveals:

> According to statistics provided by Casa Amiga, between 1993 and 2007—before Mexican President Felipe Calderón escalated the war against the cartels in Juarez—there were a total of 385 women reported murdered. From 2008 through 2011, there were 789 women officially reported murdered, a more than 100 percent increase despite a saturation of military and federal police in the city. Through June of this year, 60 women have been killed, reports show. (Kolb 2012, ¶ 10)

While this statistic is frightening, the grassroots activist group Justicia Para Nuestras Hijas (Justice for Our Daughters) maintains a list on their website that tallies over 120 women murdered in Ciudad Juárez and the city of Chihuahua through the first *week* of June 2012 (*Femicidios*). Theories abound regarding serial killers, police corruption and involvement, foreign predators, snuff films, and organ trafficking. No one has any concrete answers for the activists who continue to fight for justice in a city where justice has turned a blind eye. Due to the atrocities of this "phallic terrorism" (Donohoe 2004, ¶ 6) the region is in mourning and the desert bleeds. Once, after a performance of "Las Mujeres de Juárez" in Phoenix, Arizona, I was approached by an elderly priest who was traveling with some of his novitiates from Ciudad Juárez. He explained to me, with tears in his eyes, that what people from the outside do not understand about existence in Ciudad Juárez is that it is like living in hell on earth. And in 2005, a *New York Times* article revealed the alarming reality that "there are growing signs that the serial-style killings have spread to other cities, like Chihuahua, 200 miles along the border; Toluca, a suburb of Mexico City; the Gulf Coast capital of Veracruz; and Tuxtla Gutiérrez in the southern state of Chiapas" (Thompson 2005, ¶ 14).

There are endless issues that can be investigated concerning the ethics of how we represent human rights violations through theatrical performance. Questions regarding who has the right to tell these stories, who should be the target audience, what the limitations of live theatre are, and what an audience can psychologically process in terms of violence enacted on stage all come to mind. Respect must be paid to the families who have suffered these tragic losses. Through the theatre we create to portray their lives we must stand in solidarity; we must not confound the problems.

For the past eight years I have focused both my academic research and theatrical practice around how theatre can be used as a tool to educate people about human rights violations and social justice issues throughout the world. As an artist, I ponder; if theatre holds up a mirror to nature, then the reflection we examine must also reveal the difficult truths many people face on a daily basis in countries all across the globe. As an educator, I am intrigued by the question: can theatre help people grapple with these often controversial, often heart-wrenching topics, without overwhelming them? I believe that theatre offers us a way into some of the most difficult human rights topics by giving these atrocities a human narrative. I believe that when we reveal stories about human suffering through theatre, we have the potential to provide public testimony and engage in performative activism. We can work to change the reflection we see in the mirror and not accept it as a foregone conclusion.

I bear witness to the stories of the women in Ciudad Juárez through the artistic and creative praxis of theatre. Beginning in 2004, through Rubén Amavizca Murúa's ethnodrama "Las Mujeres de Juárez" (The Women of Juárez) mentioned earlier, Marisela Treviño Orta's allegorical account in "Braided Sorrow," and the testimonial drama compiled by Humberto Robles in "Mujeres de Arena: Tesimonios de Mujeres en Ciudad Juárez" (Women of Sand: Testimonies of Women in Ciudad Juárez), I have worked with designers and actors to illustrate a vivid image of what it means to succumb to life and death in Ciudad Juárez in the flower of youth. We do this with the utmost respect for the families for whom this phenomenon is a reality, and not just a theatrical production.

In the following section I discuss my experience directing Rubén Amavizca Murúa's play, "Las Mujeres de Juárez" (The Women of Juárez), to contextualize how this playwright captures the lived experience of numerous families who have lost loved ones in Ciudad Juárez through *ethno*drama or *docu*drama.

Staging Impunity: An Ethnodramatic Account of Life and Death in Ciudad Juárez

According to Johnny Saldaña, one of the most prolific contemporary scholars on arts-based qualitative research methods, "Ethno*theatre* employs the traditional craft and artistic techniques of theatre production to mount for an audience a live performance event of research participants' experiences and/or the researcher's interpretations of data" (2005, 1). Los Angeles–based playwright Rubén Amavizca Murúa employs personal interviews, news reports, and journalistic sources to piece together the fictional narrative that mirrors the disturbing realities of the citizens of Ciudad Juárez. "The goal [of ethnotheatre]," Saldaña explains "is to investigate a particular facet of the human condition for the purposes of adapting those observations and insights into a performance medium" (2005, 1). Amavizca Murúa is more than a playwright, he is an artistic activist committed to unearthing the voices silenced in this forsaken bordertown through theatre.

I had the opportunity to meet Rubén in California in 2005 while I was directing his play. He was traveling with Norma Andrade and her daughter Malu (Maria Luisa) Garcia Andrade, who were speaking out against the femicide on this side of the border, educating people who attended a talk at the University of Southern California. In our conversation he explained to me that these stories are not finished yet and that the women he was traveling with continue to inspire him through their strength and perseverance. I recall this conversation now because within the last two years Norma Andrade has been attacked twice in Mexico. In December 2011 she was shot twice outside her home in Ciudad Juárez, and more recently in February 2012 she suffered a knife wound to her face in Mexico City (Nobel, 2012). Andrade's daughter, Lilia Alejandra Garcia Andrade, was the victim of sexual assault and murder over ten years ago. Her body was found on February 21,

2001, after she had been missing for almost a week (Osborn, 2004). Norma Andrade and her daughter Malu Garcia Andrade are two of the cofounders of the activist group Nuestras Hijas de Regreso a Casa (May Our Daughters Return Home),[2] who continue to actively demand justice from the Mexican authorities.

As a director, I have often been drawn to plays that reveal the harsh realities that some people may find hard to confront. Saldaña reminds us that "the traditional western canon of dramatic literature consists primarily of literary and commercial works whose content is more generally fiction than fact" (2005, 3). He further explains that "ethnodrama differs by maintaining close allegiance to the lived experiences of real people while presenting their stories through an artistic medium—'creative nonfiction,' as some genres of qualitative inquiry have been labeled" (2005, 3).

I believe my connection to this play is rooted in the fact that when I first read it I was deeply engaged in my own qualitative research study and found the style of writing compelling. As I prepared to direct "Las Mujeres de Juárez" I conducted the dramaturgical research (a contextualization of the world of the play) through newspaper articles and other journalistic reports. I collected scores of resources for the actors to read in notebooks I brought to every rehearsal. I wanted us all to be prepared to speak with audience members after the performances through formal talkbacks and in more informal settings, such as the lobby of the theatre. Norman Denzin recalls the work of ethnodramatist and scholar Jim Mienczakowski who "[used] postperformance discussions with informants and audience members as a way of making the performance of ethnographic texts more responsive to the demands of praxis and social critique" (Denzin 2003, 29). It was important to me as a director and human rights activist that the performers not see this work as just another acting credit for their résumés. I also wanted to make sure that the audience recognized the performance they saw as one reflecting the harsh realities of the lived circumstances in Ciudad Juárez, not just a fictionalized account. I saw this production as a source of education, not only for audience members, but for every one of us as a member of the production company.

With every newspaper article I read and with every documentary I watched, I began to notice how similar all of the reports were. The profiles of the victims were similar; the numerous theories involving drug traffickers, gangs, police corruption, snuff films, and even organ trafficking were ubiquitous; and the patterns connected to the North American Free Trade Agreement (NAFTA) and the multinational corporations who operate factories along the U.S.-Mexico border were alarming. Corie Osborn's article "Femicide Made in Mexico" gives us an example of one such account:

> Since the passage of NAFTA in 1994, which allows for an economic open door policy between the U.S. and Mexico, Juarez has been filled with factories owned by various multinational corporations. Currently over 400 maquiladoras operate in Juarez and produce tens of billions of dollars in goods for export into the U.S. annually. Maquiladoras employ mostly young women, a group they believe to be docile and unlikely of unionizing or striking for more pay.
>
> Young women from around Mexico flock to the overpopulated border town just south of El Paso with the hopes of finding economic security in Juarez's many maquiladoras—U.S. owned assembly plants producing goods for export.
>
> Thousands of young women in Juarez commute to maquila jobs everyday before dawn to work twelve-hour shifts where they will be lucky to make anywhere from $4.50 to $6 a day. For these women, a lack of outdoor lighting in the shantytowns and maquilas increases danger for those who face a long, unlit walk to the nearest bus stop. Women who arrive even three minutes late for their shifts are turned away into the dark night; as in the case of 20-year-old Claudia Ivette who was later found in a ditch alongside the bodies of eight other women. The meager Juarez police force of 1,200 does little to protect women against the rampant violence and crime in Juarez. (2004, ¶ 6–8)

In the *DePaul Law Review* Elvia Arriola concludes that "in general, what can be said about the *maquiladora* system is that it is hardly a humane system of employment and hardly something the knowing United States citizen would want to support" (2001, 35). We need to ask ourselves if this system is one we would choose to work in ourselves, or if we believe that these young women choose to subject themselves to these conditions. We need to speak out against a system in which "women's bodies and their essential attributes are suitable for particular kinds of harsh, detailed, high-producing volumes of work, paid at low wages and on long work schedules" (Arriola 2001, 5).

Amavizca Murúa captures this harrowing landscape in a short scene between the two narrators who appear throughout the play. In the version I directed in 2004–2005, these narrators took on the guise of diverse characters who commented on the situation in Ciudad Juárez. This particular scene was delivered by two men dressed as *maquiladora* guards who were out behind the factory smoking a joint:

SCENE 19

Narrator 1: The victims work for multinational corporations that do not pay taxes in Mexico. 70% of Fortune 500 companies use *maquiladoras* (factories) and the number is increasing annually.

Narrator 2: There are more than three thousand companies employing over a million people, with an annual product volume of $40 billion.

Narrator 1: 98% of this product is American. 90% of the factories are situated along the northern border of Mexico and one third of these are in Ciudad Juárez.

Narrator 2: These multinational corporations offer absolutely no security for their employees, the majority of whom are women who often have to come and go in the middle of the night.

Narrator 1: These corporations that make millions of dollars in the city should subsidize public security measures and help the government and civic organizations to put an end to these murders once and for all. (2004, 25)[3]

This scene reveals how the play reflects the economic turmoil plaguing Ciudad Juárez. I used the two guards smoking a joint during this scene to portray the blatant disregard for the safety of the female workers in the factories that I read about over and over again through my research.

As an ethnodramatic text, "Las Mujeres de Juárez" draws the audience inside the life of the fictitious Martínez López family and reveals their everyday idiosyncrasies. However, this family is not based solely on the playwright's creative imagination; he draws from interviews and the personal accounts of many families who have suffered this unspeakable loss. He stands in solidarity, side by side with members of these families, and his play pays homage to their daughters, sisters, cousins, aunts, and friends.

The protagonist in this play is Maritza Martínez López, a young *maquiladora* worker who is also studying to be a nurse. She has a boyfriend, a younger sister, and two adoring parents. She keeps her every hope and dream in a diary she writes in throughout the play, and she is a hopeless romantic. She likes to sing and hopes to have children someday. She is your average teenager, only she lives in one of the most dangerous parts of the world. One day, as she waits for the bus, two men attack her. They rape and stab her and then leave her abandoned and bleeding to death. This gruesome depiction can by no means capture the final moments of the hundreds of young women who have lost their lives in similar situations, but Amavizca Murúa does his best to portray these atrocities respectfully and artistically.

When Maritza does not return home, her family mounts a search through the desert that surrounds their home, goes to the Red Cross, and goes to the police station to file a missing persons report, but the police officer tells them that they must wait two days before filing such a report. When she returns after two days the police officer insults the mother by insisting that her daughter must have gone off with her boyfriend. In taking notes for the report he implies that the clothing she was wearing was probably tight–fitting, that perhaps she drank or did drugs, and that she had undesirable friends and multiple boyfriends. Here, Amavizca Murúa reflects the harsh treatment received by many families when the authorities insist that the young women who fall victim to this femicide led double lives and were looking for danger. Recently *The Los Angeles Times* shed light on the perception of the officers expected to uphold the law, "Mexicans have long been wary of police at all levels. Officers are notorious not only for soliciting the little bribes known as *mordidas*, but for shaking down innocents, running kidnapping rings, and serving as security forces and death squads for the drug gangs. One 2010 poll found that only 8% of respondents felt strong confidence in the police" (Fausset 2012, ¶ 10). If this is the security force in place protecting the citizens of Mexico, it is no wonder they have little trust in the police.

Amavizca Murúa also reflects the real world in "Las Mujeres de Juárez" when, at the opening of the second act, the two narrator characters take on the roles of activists who assist the Martínez López family in their quest for justice. International activists join Mexican citizens through numerous groups including Nuestras Hijas de Regreso a Casa (May Our Daughters Return Home) mentioned earlier, Justicia Para Nuestras Hijas (Justice for Our Daughters), the Mexico Solidarity Network, and Casa Amiga Esther Chávez Cano (Friendly House Esther Chávez Cano) to protest the impunity that has become endemic along the U.S.-Mexico border.

From December 2004 through October 2006, I directed the same core cast of actors in performances sponsored by the Phoenix, Arizona,-based Latino theatre company Teatro Bravo. We opened in March 2005 at Phoenix College for an extended three-week run and then traveled to Reno, Nevada for two performances in April, sponsored by the University of Nevada at Reno Latino Research Center. Later that month we performed for hundreds of high school students through the Latino Institute at the Phoenix Civic Plaza. On May 10, the day Mothers' Day is celebrated annually in Mexico, we constructed an outdoor stage and performed "Las Mujeres de Juárez" in front of the Arizona State Capitol. Several of the cast members drove to Ciudad Juárez to bring several of the mothers/activists to see this performance of the play and share their experiences with us. The final performance sponsored by Teatro Bravo took place in Puerto Peñasco, Mexico, as a benefit for the Mexican Red Cross and to build a cafeteria for a local senior center. Our final performance with this production was sponsored by Amnesty International for the Western Regional Conference that took place in Tucson, Arizona, in October 2006. Throughout this run it was gratifying to be able to educate people about a topic too many U.S. Americans know little about. During the final scene of Amavizca Murúa's play the actors take the stage and recite the names of over two hundred women whose bodies have been identified in Ciudad Juárez. We bear witness to this femicide and stand in solidarity with the families who mourn these women. The closing lines of the play are spoken by the character of the mother:

> Madre: The only thing we ask for is justice. That the murders be solved and that there not be a single murder more. We want to live and work in peace. We want to be able to go out in the street without the fear that one of us will not return. We want you to join us and say, "Enough!" Is that too much to ask? (Amavizca Murúa 2004, 46)

Ruben Amavizca Murúa asks the question that is on the lips of too many mothers in Ciudad Juárez, "Is that too much to ask?"

"Las Mujeres de Juárez" was the first play I directed that addressed the topic of femicide. When I graduated and left Arizona to take a job at New York University, I found a second play that caught my director's eye. Marisela Treviño Orta's play "Braided Sorrow," which I take up in this next section, offers us a fictional, poetic depiction of Ciudad Juárez through the lives of the Cardenas family.

Allegorical Representation, Metaphor, and Mythology: Artistically Rendering a Lamentable Reality

The use of allegory offers us a theatrical and literary device to tell one story through another. A multiplicity of meanings enriches the work and offers the reader/audience a myriad of possible interpretations from the same stimulus. This device has the ability to underscore the literal with the figurative, transforming characters, actions, and even stage properties into signifiers that lie beyond the text. "The surface level of metaphor is the named, exterior comparison, while the conceptual level is a more fundamental and less obvious comparison upon which the surface metaphor is built" (Aigner–Varoz 2000, 48). Gloria Anzaldúa describes the metaphor emblazoned on the flag of Mexico, one that belies its hierarchical order and gender dynamic since the migration of the Aztecs:

> *Huitzilopochtli*, the God of War, guided them to a place (that later became Mexico City) where an eagle with a writhing serpent in its beak perched on a cactus. The eagle symbolizes the spirit (as the sun, the father); the serpent symbolizes the soul (as the earth, the mother). Together, they symbolize the struggle between the spiritual/celestial/male and the underworld/earth/feminine. The symbolic sacrifice of the serpent to the "higher" masculine powers indicates that the patriarchal order had already vanquished the feminine and matriarchal order in pre–Columbian America. (1999, 27)

With such a symbol flying high above the Mexican countryside it is not difficult to read into the male domination that leaves the families who have lost their loved ones in Ciudad Juárez with nowhere to turn. Through theatre, we have the potential to enter the world of Ciudad Juárez and bear witness to the atrocities being perpetuated, not only against the women, but on the survivors of these vicious crimes, their families.

San Francisco–based playwright Marisela Treviño Orta, has offered a poetic rendering of the dismal circumstances that exist in this forgotten corner of the world. Through her play "Braided Sorrow," she weaves together the real with the surreal and leads the audience on a fatal pilgrimage, one to which too many young women have fallen victim. This journey is one that many families in Ciudad Juárez are condemned to: searching for answers and finding none, seeking justice and encountering impunity, grasping at memories that slip through their fingers like wisps of smoke.

Treviño Orta's play employs the allegorical figure of La Llorona to give the audience a sense of how mysteriously abysmal life can be in Ciudad Juárez. In the preface to *Secrets in the Sand: The Young Women of Juárez*, a book of poetry written by Marjorie Agosín, Celeste Kostopulos–Cooperman describes this haunted landscape:

> Pink crosses painted on the telephone poles that rise from the dry earth serve as monuments to the dead. They are constant reminders of the silenced victims whose brutal deaths demand

> that justice be served. They also underscore the need for serious measures to be taken to provide for the safety and protection of the women and girls living in the city who are most vulnerable to the predators that continue to threaten their lives yet escape from local, state and federal authorities. (2006, 15)

In "Braided Sorrow," we enter this terrain through the lives of the Cardenas family, but their experience is endemic in Ciudad Juárez, leaving behind grieving mothers, fathers, sisters, brothers, and in many cases, orphans. Ginger Thompson captured a glimpse of this despair for *The New York Times* in 2002:

> It has been seven years since Irma Perez steamed a plate of her daughter's favorite vegetables and waited all night for her to come home from work. Weeks later, a bag of bones was the only answer she got back from the police to explain why her daughter was missing. They lifted a chalky skull out of the bag and asked: is this your daughter's face?
>
> The bodies of many women and girls had begun to surface in the desert that surrounds this city like an ocean. Ms. Perez soon joined with other mothers in a quest for justice. But years of dead-end detective work, of public pleas for government action, of watching more daughters disappear have taken a toll on her body and mind.
>
> "Why should she keep talking?" interrupted Ms. Perez's father, who declined to give his name. "She has told the story thousands of times. What has she gotten but pain? What progress has been made?"
>
> Ms. Perez bowed her head, as if accepting her father's bitterness. Then she sat up straight and shook her head. "I will never stop talking about Olga," she said. "I cannot stop until the violence stops." (Thompson 2002, 1)

I am reminded of the title of this book, *Taking Risks*, when I consider the embodied activist conjured by Marisela Treviño Orta in the figure of La Llorona. Like many of the women who mourn their loved ones, she is persistent, tenacious, and in a constant search for the truth. Treviño Orta describes this character as "the weeping woman, an apparition, a mourning mother who has lost her daughter and a woman murdered in the desert. She is displaced by time and loss" (2010, 2). Through this character, all of the people of Mexico who struggle against the rampant impunity in this situation find a voice.

Most of the families in Ciudad Juárez are left without answers. Diana Washington Valdez covered the murders in this region from 1999, when she was assigned by the *El Paso Times* to cover the border. "Her 2002 series 'Death Stalks the Border' won a Texas Associated Press Managing Editors award and was nominated for a Pulitzer Prize" (Braine 2006, ¶ 15). When eight more bodies were discovered in an inner-city lot, she interviewed one of the mothers: "'She was my only daughter, my dream girl. . . . They took that away from me,' Irma Monreal said before she broke down and cried. 'The police wouldn't even let me see her body. They told me it would be too much for me to handle. They only showed me her clothes'" (Washington Valdez 2002, 1).

In "Braided Sorrow," Alma Cardenas, a sixteen-year-old girl from San Luis Potosí, comes to Ciudad Juárez to help her brother, Carlos, make enough money to send back to their parents. This is not an uncommon practice in Mexico; many young people leave the small ranches or pueblos where their families live in the interior to get closer to the border in hopes of crossing over into the United States. But what they find is a border city replete with danger. Pheona Donohoe reports, "Juárez is unique as it is a third world factory city relying heavily on a transient workforce. This means many of the two million residents of Juárez have no immediate family or support networks. The shantytown living conditions offer little security in the case of emergency, with telephone access minimal and police protection questionable" (2004, ¶ 2). This is hardly the epitome of a safe haven for young women, many of whom work the graveyard shifts and leave from their homes or travel back to them in the dark, desolate hours of the night. And as a global community we must ask ourselves, are these conditions we would allow our own daughters to work under? Are we willing to stand in solidarity and demand justice for these women?

In Ciudad Juárez, Alma and Carlos live with their Tía Socorro and Carlos's wife, Yadria. The audience follows Alma as she begins her new life on the border, but they are not the only ones watching. There is La Llorona (the Weeping Woman), whom Alma meets at the bus station when she first arrives in Juárez, saves Alma at a time when she needs help, and only Alma can see. She appears as a constant reminder of the oppression that has plagued Mexico for centuries in one form or another. Interestingly, however, the fact that only Alma can see her[4] can also be viewed as a powerful metaphor for the marked invisibility of the hundreds of women whose bodies have been recovered in the abandoned lots in and around Ciudad Juárez, as well as the hundreds of young women who are still missing. La Llorona acts as a spectral representation on behalf of all of the mothers whose daughters have traveled, unprotected, so far from home, vigilantly keeping watch over them. She tells Alma, "I know all my daughters, even before they are named. But I can't save them all. I can't do this alone, I never could" (Treviño Orta, 2010, 54).[5]

The first time Alma encounters her, at the bus station just after arriving in Ciudad Juárez, we hear La Llorona echoing a distant history:

> LA LLORONA: (*Looking at the ground as if seeing water*) Have you ever seen the waters of Texcoco? (*Pronounced: Tesh coco*) Moonlight, the canals shimmered with it and when you dipped your hands beneath its surface you could feel it envelop your skin, its coolness race up your arms and spread over your body until you glowed, white stone in the rain . . . (Treviño Orta 2010, 10)

Through the memories of the character, La Llorona, the playwright conjures the first meeting between the Aztec leader, Moctezuma, and Cortés; a meeting of two worlds, a prophetic encounter near Lake Texcoco, described throughout literature and political histories as tense and awkward. A conquest hidden in ritual greetings, lost in a cross-cultural crossfire, La Llorona mysteriously alludes to the waters in which, legend has it, she drowned her children.

In an attempt to untangle the mythology surrounding the character of Doña Marina/Malintzín/Malinali Tenepat/La Malinche, in many cases a historical and literary figure "intertwined with a Mexican legend that predates the Conquest and that in colonial times became known as La Llorona (The Weeping Woman)," Matthew Restall describes her as "a symbol of betrayal; an opportunistic sexual siren; a feminist icon; an Aztec goddess in disguise; the mother of the first mestizo, and thus of the Mexican nation; the ultimate rape victim of the Conquest" (86). It is this final allusion that figures prominently into the portrayal of the character in "Braided Sorrow." A surrogate for each of the young women who has lost her life in Ciudad Juárez, she is a poetic manifestation of mourning and loss. Historically, La Malinche is remembered as

> a Nahua noblewoman from the eastern edge of Nahuatl-speaking central Mexico. As a child she was either stolen by slave traders or sold into slavery, and ended up among the Chontal Mayas whose small kingdom lay a little further east on the Gulf coast. In 1519 she was given by the Chontals along with 19 other native women to Cortés and his colleagues as part of a peace agreement, an inducement to the Spaniards to keep traveling west. Still a teenager, she was baptized Marina and assigned

> to one of the captains of the expedition, Alonso Hernández de Puertocarrero. (Restall 2003, 83–84)

This notion of woman as property is one that has not been ameliorated, especially in today's global market. In Ciudad Juárez, as in many cities in the global South that serve as laboratories of globalization, young women are not seen as autonomous individuals, but in a very Marxist sense, they are regarded as disembodied hands that perform labor. "Materialist feminism," according to Jill Dolan, "deconstructs the mythic subject Woman to look at women as a class oppressed by material conditions and social relations" (Dolan 1991, 10). Their value is measured by their productivity, much as La Malinche was of value for her particular ability to translate the indigenous languages, Nahuatl and Mayan, into the colonial Spanish. Echoing Gayle Rubin's emphasis of the disparate power dynamics, Dolan reminds us "that through a system of social relations, females are fashioned into generalized products that are exchanged on a political economy that benefits men" (Dolan 1991, 11). As the story of La Malinche, the interpreter, is woven together with the story of the Weeping Woman, we encounter a voiceless entity; "her historical identity is based upon what she said. Yet because she spoke the words of others, as their interpreter, she is also strangely silent" (Restall 2003, 86). This hauntingly echoed, strangulated silence overtakes Alma, the young *maquiladora* worker, who confesses painfully to her brother after being attacked by three men on her way home from work: "They grabbed me in . . . I, I couldn't scream. I tried, I tried, Carlos I swear I tried. But my voice, it wouldn't, it wouldn't (*Catching her breath*)" (Treviño Orta 2010, 44).[6] The silencing of women along the U.S.-Mexico border dates back further than the 1993 discovery of bodies in abandoned lots in Ciudad Juárez; the silencing is centuries old; similarly, this impunity has a long legacy.

We can examine the emblematic role taken up by La Llorona in Treviño Orta's play through a *transfronterista* feminist lens, developed by Gloria Anzaldúa. Sonia Saldívar-Hull suggests:

> In keeping with this new feminism, the New Mestiza dramatically reclaims the female cultural figures that were marked traitors to the community. . . . By rewriting the stories of Malinali, *la Llorona* and the *Virgen de Guadalupe*, Anzaldúa is strategically reclaiming a ground for more female historical presence. Her task here is to uncover the names and the powers of the female deities whose identities have been submerged in Mexican memory of these three Mexican mothers. (1999, 6)

Mark Fortier writes that "feminism attempts to create a woman reader who sees otherwise and brings a different and other perspective to bear on culture" (1997, 71). Treviño Orta employs the depiction of La Llorona as a historical legend, deeper than myth, and rooted in spiritual beliefs tied to motherhood, mourning, and betrayal. Anzaldúa proposes, "*En unas pocas centurias*, the future will belong to the *mestiza*. Because the future depends on the breaking down of paradigms, it depends on the straddling of two or more cultures. By creating a new mythos—that is, a change in the way we perceive reality, the way we see ourselves, and the way we behave—*la mestiza* creates a new consciousness" (1999, 102). The figure of La Llorona in "Braided Sorrow" takes on a transnational activist stance against the impunity that has plagued the border for almost twenty years. By reclaiming the rights of every mother to the elusive answers regarding her daughter's murder, and by demanding justice, this character embodies the *transfronterista* feminist.

Set against the backdrop of this brutal femicide, Treviño Orta casts La Llorona as an extended metaphor in her play to capture the sociopolitical trauma inflicted on a society whose daughters are being savagely murdered, all in the name of global profit. The allegorical mystery of La Llorona, a haunting figure seen and heard by many people all throughout Latin America and the North American Southwest, represents the enigmatic circumstances of a patriarchal society unable (or unwilling) to solve the crimes perpetuated against the young women who work in the *maquiladoras* in the border towns of Mexico's northern region. This imposed modern-day slavery has a history that, like the silence, has deep roots. Anzaldúa, speaking in the voice of Malintzín, professes:

> Not me sold out my people but they me. Because of the color of my skin they betrayed me. The dark-skinned woman has been silenced, gagged, caged, bound into servitude with marriage, bludgeoned for 300 years, sterilized and castrated in the twentieth century. For 300 years she has been a slave, a force of cheap labor, colonized by the Spaniard, the Anglo, by her own people (and in Mesoamerica her lot under the Indian patriarchs was not free of wounding). For 300 years she was invisible, she was not heard. Many times she wished to speak, to act, to protest, to challenge. The odds were heavily against her. (1999, 44–45)

And the odds are heavily against the young women of Ciudad Juárez.

The figure of La Llorona takes on numerous meanings in this script. She embodies the protective stance of the mothers in Mexico who would give anything to shield their daughters from harm. She reflects the mothers in mourning who have already lost their daughters, but who offer their endless support in service to those who are still looking for their girls. And in a metaphorical sense, she represents the bigger picture of the country herself, Mexico, a country that has buried too many of her young flowers along the bleeding border that runs for almost two thousand miles. I believe Treviño Orta captures the multiplicity of layers that politicians; local, state, federal, and transnational authorities; and even journalists too often fail to portray.

When I first read the text, the character of La Llorona conjured in me images of the mothers I had met: Norma Andrade, Patricia Cervantes, Paula Bonilla Flores, and Eva Arce. These women are *transfronterista* activists who still tell their daughters' stories in countries all around the world, demanding justice and inciting social action. In a scene frozen in time, La Llorona appears to Alma and implores her to carry out a task only she is capable of completing:

> LA LLORONA: I need you to be my messenger. Listen to what I'm about to tell you. In the outskirts of town, outside the police station in Anapra, withering in its shadow is a rosebush. Go there and bury your braid deep into the ground. Dig up my river. Dig up my river of blood.
> (*ALMA starts to walk to away. LA LLORONA stops her.*)
> ALMA: No. I can't go there. Anapra is far away, it's dangerous.
> LA LLORONA: Yes, it is far away. Yes, it is dangerous. But I will be watching over you. If you need me, all you have to do is call me and I will come.
> ALMA: No. No.
> LA LLORONA: You must. You must dig up my river and let the earth bleed its sorrow. Tell them that the river will bleed into the desert as long as my daughters are hunted. They must be held accountable, they must be forced to act. Tell them that the river will bleed until the murders stop, until my daughters are safe, until there is justice in Juarez. It has to be you, Alma. (Treviño Orta 2010, 57–58)

La Llorona figures into this script as mysteriously as she figures into the legends of Latin America, an evocative spirit who teaches, frightens, mesmerizes, tricks, and betrays. The allegory of a mother, condemned to spend eternity searching for the children she herself has drowned, lends a surreal effect to the complex aesthetic experience offered by Treviño Orta. When she appears in a crowded marketplace at a fruit stand, the two *comadres*, Socorro and Eulalia stand speechless, mesmerized, as she delivers a monologue recounting the day her daughter never returned home:

> LA LLORONA:
> It was a little boy
> a little boy who found her
> while playing out in *Lote Bravo*.
> They wouldn't let me identify her.
> They said they were sure it was her.
> Her factory name tag
> was found next to her body.
> *(LA LLORONA puts the pomegranate back on the table.)*
> All they gave me was her torn
> faded blue shirt,
> crumpled, thick with dust . . .
> *(As she exits)*
> Torn, faded, thick with dust . . . smelling like the desert.
> (The pomegranates begin to bleed juice. A dark stain spreads down the length of the tablecloth, the juice spills onto the floor. EULALIA takes hold of SOCORRO's arm.)
> EULALIA: *Madre de Dios*.
> *(Lights shift)*. (Treviño Orta 2010, 22)

In another scene, the stage directions read,

> *(To one side of the stage stands a pink telephone pole. The majority of the telephone pole is covered with Missing Posters, some old and tattered, some new. All the posters have the pictures of young women, all with long dark hair. Underneath their photos in bold type is the word "Desaparecida." There is one very large poster, the eyes of the girl stare straight ahead. The top of the pole that is above one's reach is speckled with black crosses)* (2010, 60).

In this haunting scene La Llorona looks at the poster of the girl whose eyes stare straight ahead:

> LA LLORONA:
> Do you see her? Blanca. Blanca Gómez.
> The night I came to you

> That night in the alley
> On the other side of the city
> She also needed me.
> But I came to you.
> I come to you again. (Treviño Orta 2010, 58)

As Alma contemplates what she cannot seem to comprehend La Llorona slowly exits saying:

> LA LLORONA:
> Look at your sisters.
> I carry them inside me
> All their pain
> Your sisters, Alma
> They beg you.
>
> Look! Look how they cry.
> (The eyes of the girls in the posters weep black ink, it runs down the pole. The haunting sound of water dripping. Mesmerized, ALMA reaches out and touches the tears, looks at her fingertips.)
>
> ALMA:
> No, no! You can't make me! You can't make me! (Treviño Orta 2010, 59)

These surreal stage directions enhance the feeling that this allegorical character enters the world of this play from somewhere beyond; she reaches up from a place below the waters of Texcoco where her children lie sleeping, or a place beneath the sands of the desert where her daughters lie waiting to be discovered. The poetry and the poetic imagery used in this play are a gift from Marisela Treviño Orta to audience members and readers alike. She offers a buffer and acts as a surreal tour guide through the cavernous depths of hell on earth, to reveal what has too long been buried beneath the desert sand . . . justice. Treviño Orta is a feminist activist who crafted this world through words and bears witness to the impunity in Ciudad Juárez through her art form, theatre.

From September 2007 through March 2008, I directed four different casts for staged readings of "Braided Sorrow." We presented the play as a conference session in Baltimore, Maryland, for the Pennsylvania Coalition Against Rape (PCAR) at the National Sexual Assault Conference in September. We followed this performance in November with a reading at the Palladium Residential Hall of New York University sponsored by the Explorations Program and La Herencia Latina student group. An audience member at this performance invited us to stage the reading at Molloy College in Rockville Centre, New York, the following February. The final performance I was involved with took place in March, during Women's HerStory Month, at New York University again, sponsored by the student-organized chapter of Amnesty International on campus. Again, following each of these performances the company of actors and I engaged the audiences in a talkback in an attempt to tie up any loose ends the spectators may have experienced through the play and answer any questions they might have. It has always been my experience that at least some people in the audience admit to never having heard of this phenomenon of femicide and they feel embarrassed that they are so ill-informed on the subject. I try to assure audience members that they should not feel guilty because the press and the media in both the United States and Mexico have managed to keep a tight lid on murders of women in Ciudad Juárez. Irma Casas, the director of Casa Amiga Esther Chávez Cano (Friendly House Esther Chávez Cano), a woman's rights advocacy and counseling center, expresses her belief that "there is a concerted effort by the [Mexican] government to avoid the topic of violence against women in the media. She claims there is an agreement that keeping accurate statistics is daunting because of poor record keeping, institutional interests, public relations, and silence of the victims" (Kolb 2012, ¶ 18). I often add that what I believe is important is not what people did not know about yesterday, but what they are willing to do after learning about this human rights issue through this performance. How are we going to educate ourselves more about this topic, and how can we inform more people about what is going on in Ciudad Juárez?

Without a Conclusion in Sight, I Continue This Work: Theatrical Testimony through "Mujeres de Arena" (Women of Sand)

For many years now I have prayed for an end to the atrocities of femicide in Ciudad Juárez, but the drug wars that have claimed the streets of Juárez and the border between the U.S. and Mexico have perpetuated a violence that no longer discriminates between gender and age. There seems to be no end in sight.

The most recent project I have been involved with began in 2008 when I was introduced to the play "Mujeres de Arena: Testimonios de Mujeres en Ciudad Juárez" (Women of Sand: Testimonials of Women in Ciudad Juárez). To date, I have directed fifteen diverse casts at different colleges, conference, and community venues throughout New York, New Jersey, Chicago, and Boston, and have recently received funding from Emerson College to further develop my work on this staged reading compiled by the Mexican playwright Humberto Robles. I felt drawn to this play from the moment I read it because it is so closely linked to Rubén Amavizca Murúa's script of "Las Mujeres de Juárez." Many of the lines appear verbatim in both plays, and that is a result of both playwrights conducting research with the same families. While Amavizca Murúa weaves all of the interviews and writings he researched into a fictional narrative that follows one family through their traumatic ordeal, Robles calls for ten presentational scenes in which the actors deliver the text without any formal production staging. "The idea for the play was the result of watching the mothers and relatives of the victims of femicide giving talks and conferences on the subject; they sit on a panel and begin to give their testimonies in order to educate, denounce, and give information about these crimes. This is what the play intends to reproduce" (Robles 2010, 1).[7] For the most part, the words tell the stories, the actors deliver these scenes from scripts behind music stands. But the power of this play grips the audience as much as the narrative fiction. "Women of Sand" is a living document connected to an active blog kept by the playwright.[8]

This blog is updated regularly, and the play script reflects the evolving story and the lengthening list of names. The testimonials are collected from both men and women who raise their voices to denounce the human rights violations that have devastated their world.

But reality in Ciudad Juárez is darker today than it ever has been. In *Ciudad Juárez/2008–2010: A Photographic Testimony of Our Pain*, Guillermo Cervantes recalls: "2008 changed our lives. During its first weeks executions began to take place. Alarmed, we wanted to believe these were just isolated events, underworld quarrels prone to end soon and everything would be just as it was before. However, the killings did not stop, and increasingly became more sadistic and violent. We would wake up just to find bodies hanging from our bridges as we drove to work or to take our children to school" (2010, 7). Since 2008, the citizens of Ciudad Juárez do not walk their streets alone. They are constantly accompanied by the Mexican army, the federal police, and several major drug cartels who all fight for the lucrative smuggling route through the border between Ciudad Juárez and El Paso, Texas. "Here drug gangs are the law—judge, jury and executioner—vehemently defending trade routes in what the U.S. Government Accountability Office estimates is a $23 billion a year industry" (Baxter 2009, ¶ 7). It can be difficult to reconcile the fact that El Paso "is consistently ranked as the second- to third-safest big city in the United States" (Staudt 2008, x). But the violence is bleeding over onto the U.S. side of the border, of that we can be sure: "There have been increased incidences of kidnapping. Refugees from war-torn Juarez have begun to cross the border, seeking shelter in the States. Hotel capacity is often near 100%, with Juarez citizens looking for one night of peace. El Paso's city council unanimously signed a solidarity agreement to support Juarez. The trouble in Mexico is beginning to be noticed in America" (Baxter 2009, ¶ 3). And so I will continue to stand in solidarity with the families who fight for justice. I will stage play after play, performance after performance, in order to educate others about the femicide in Ciudad Juárez.

For me, as a director, the theatrical stage is an arena where we must risk telling stories that people might not want to hear. It is onstage and through performance that I answer Professor Arriola's call to arms that we must "reveal the human drama that underlies this historic economic conflict and inter-dependency between Mexico and the United States" (2001, 760). In my work, I insist that we must tell the stories of "workers, of people entitled to the minimum human rights of food, shelter, clothing, education, and medical care" (Arriola 2001, 761). Arriola asserts that "[a] human rights perspective based on women's narratives is able to capture graphically the tremendous social conflict and pain that is [sic] also a byproduct of the wildly 'successful' NAFTA along with the expansion of the *maquiladora* program at the border" (2001, 761). It is my belief that by combining a human rights perspective with performance theory we approach a critical feminist lens through which an examination of the difficult truths many people face on a daily basis might be possible.

Over the last eight years, many people have asked me what Ciudad Juárez is really like. There was a time when I struggled with this question because, the truth is, I have never been there. In 2006, when I had the opportunity to speak with Norma Andrade, Patricia Cervantes, Paula Bonilla Flores, and Eva Arce, all mothers who have lost their daughters to the femicide in Ciudad Juárez, they each cautioned me: "Don't come to Juárez . . . then who would tell this story here on this side of the border. We can't lose any more daughters . . . We have already lost too many." I am compelled to support the women of Juárez in telling their stories, to synthesize their desperate pleas for justice through performance so that more and more people will join them and shout, "'Basta! Stop the impunity, not a single murder more!' Is that too much to ask?" (Robles 2010, 8). Theatre is the medium I choose to tell these stories through, because as an artist/scholar who is also an activist, I still can't distinguish my image from theirs.

Notes

1. The ¶ symbol references paragraph numbers in all online and electronic resources.
2. For more information about Nuestras Hijas de Regreso a Casa please visit http://http://www.mujeresdejuarez.org.
3. All page citations for "Las Mujeres de Juárez" are from the unpublished text provided by the playwright. All translations from the original Spanish playscript are mine.
4. Breaking from the convention that only Alma interacts with La Llorona, the two *comadres*, Tía Socorro and Eulalia see her as a woman in the marketplace buying fruit. Treviño Orta, act 1, scene 6, "A Mother in the Market," 19–22. Likewise, the men who attack Alma are also able to see this female figure as she recites haunting stanzas recounting the overthrow of the city of Tenochtitlán and distracting them so that Alma can escape their clutches. Treviño Orta, act 1, scene 10, "Narrow Escape," 36–40.
5. All page citations for "Braided Sorrow" are from the unpublished text revised in 2010 and provided by the playwright.
6. The DC Rape Crisis Center outlines some of the emotions and reactions experienced by rape victims, including guilt, fear, avoidance, anger, distrust, loss of control, numbness, and reexperiencing. For more information please visit http://www.dcrcc.org/support_counseling/adult_sexual_assault_survivors/C120/emotional_effects.
7. All page citations for "Women of Sand" are from the unpublished English translation of the Spanish script provided by the playwright. The last revision of this translation was completed in 2010.
8. http://mujeresdearenateatro.blogspot.com.

References

Aigner-Varoz, Erika. 2000. "Metaphors of a Mestiza Consciousness: Anzaldúa's Borderlands/La Frontera." *MELUS* 25, 2: 47–62.

Amavizca Murúa, Rubén. 2004. "Las Mujeres de Juárez" ("The Women of Juárez"). Spanish version of unpublished play used for production.

Anzaldúa, Gloria. 1999. *Borderlands/La Frontera: The New Mestiza*. 2nd ed. San Francisco: Aunt Lute.

Arriola, Elvia R. 2001. "Voices from the Barbed Wires of Despair: Women in the Maquiladoras, Latina Critical Legal Theory, and Gender at the U.S.-Mexico Border." *DePaul Law Review* 49: 729.

Baxter, Samuel C. 2009. "Mexico's Drug Cartel War: Who Is to Blame?" *The Real Truth,* 10 February 10. http://realtruth.org/articles/090203-005-americas.html.

Bowden, Charles. 1996. "While You Were Sleeping." *Harper's Magazine* 283, 1759: 45–52.

Braine, Theresa. 2006. "Texas Journalist Patrols Grisly Juarez Beat." *WOMENSENEWS* Sept. 1. http://www.43things.com/entries/view/1161904.

Cervantes, Guillermo. 2010. *Ciudad Juárez/2008–2010: A Photographic Testimony of Our Pain.* Guillermo Cervantes: CreateSpace Independent Publishing Platform.

Denzin, Norman K. 2003. *Performance Ethnography: Critical Pedagogy and the Politics of Culture.* Thousand Oaks, CA: Sage.

Dolan, Jill. 1991. *The Feminist Spectator as Critic.* Ann Arbor: University of Michigan Press.

———. 2001. *Geographies of Learning: Theory and Practice, Activism and Performance.* Middletown, CT: Wesleyan University Press.

Donohoe, Pheona. 2004. "Women of Juarez." *Lucky Magazine* 21: 30–31, 9. (reposted online) http://womenofjuarez.egenerica.com/?p=40#more-40.

Faussett, Richard. 2012. "Mexicans See a Losing Battle in the War on Crooked Police." *Los Angeles Times,* August 29. http://www.latimes.com/news/nationworld/world/la-fg-mexico-police-20120830,0,5553526,print.story.

Fortier, Mark. 1997. *Theory/Theatre: An Introduction.* London: Routledge.

Justicia Para Nuestras Hijas (Justice for Our Daughters). 2012. "Femicidios" July 25. http://www.justiciaparanuestrashijas.org.

Kolb, Joseph. 2012. "Violence against Women Worse Than Ever in Juarez, Experts Say." *Fox News Latino,* July 5. http://latino.foxnews.com/latino/news/2012/07/05/violence-against-women-worse-than-ever-in-juarez-experts-say/print.

Kostopulos-Cooperman, Celeste. 2006. "Preface." In *Secrets in the Sand: The Young Women of Juárez,* Marjorie Agosín, 13–21. Buffalo, NY: White Pine.

Nhat Hanh, Thich. 2007. For a Future to Be Possible: Buddhist Ethics for Everyday Life. Berkeley: Parallax.

Nobel Women's Initiative. 2012. "Norma Andrade Attacked Again." February 2. http://nobelwomensinitiative.org/2012/02/urgent-action-for-mexican-human-rights-activist.

Osborn, Corie. 2004. "Femicide Made in Mexico." *Off Our Backs,* March/April. http://www.kersplebedeb.com/mystuff/feminist/femicide_mexico.html.

Pineda-Madrid, Nancy. 2011. *Suffering and Salvation in Ciudad Juárez.* [Kindle]. Minneapolis: Fortress.

Portillo, Lourdes. 2001. *Señorita Extraviada* (Young Woman Missing). DVD. Directed by Lourdes Portillo. Los Angeles: Xochitl Productions, Women Make Movies.

Ramirez, Sarah. 2002. "'Aquí La Justicia Sale Sobrando' (Justice is Superfluous Here): Lila Downs and Transfronterista Music." *Bad Subjects* 61: The Aesthetics of Violence. http://bad.eserver.org/issues/2002/61/ramirez.html/view?searchterm=Lila%20Downs.

Restall, Matthew. 2003. *Seven Myths of the Spanish Conquest.* Oxford: Oxford University Press.

Robles, Humberto. 2010. "Women of Sand: Testimonials of Women in Ciudad Juárez." English translation of unpublished playscript, revised.

Saldaña, Johnny, ed. 2005. *Ethnodrama: An Anthology of Reality Theatre.* Walnut Creek, CA: AltaMira.

Saldívar-Hull, Sonia. 1999. "Introduction." In *Borderlands/La Frontera: The New Mestiza,* second edition by Gloria Anzaldúa, 1–15. San Francisco: Aunt Lute.

Staudt, Kathleen. 2008. *Violence and Activism at the Border: Gender, Fear, and Everyday Life in Ciudad Juárez.* Austin: University of Texas Press.

Thompson, Ginger. 2002. "Wave of Women's Killing Confounds Juárez." *New York Times* December 10, late ed. – final: 1.

———.2005. "In Mexico's Murders, Fury Is Aimed at Officials." *New York Times* September 26. http://www.nytimes.com/2005/09/26/international/americas/26juarez.html?_r=1&ei=5070&en=167b78798c7444dd&ex=1128398400&emc=eta1&pagewanted=print.

Treviño Orta, Marisela. 2010. "Braided Sorrow." Unpublished playscript, revised.

Washington Valdez, Diana. 2002. "Latest Discovery of Bodies Fuels Fears Anew in Juárez." *El Paso Times* June 23. http://www.elpasotimes.com/borderdeath/page1–3.html.

PART 3

ACTIVIST STORIES FROM THE GRASSROOTS

INTRODUCTION TO PART 3

Activist Stories from the Grassroots

JULIE SHAYNE

When it came time to organize the chapters for this book I thought they all easily found their counterparts. But why make one section explicitly about grassroots activism when really the whole book speaks to this topic? This section looks at grassroots activism through the eyes of the organizers and considers how internal and external factors shape the strategic decisions activists and their organizations make.

As we saw, the first part of *Taking Risks* is anchored in processes of activism and research as embodied by textual representations. In part 2, we saw how activism is performed in various communities through videos, radio, TV, and theater. We saw that the process of claiming and giving voice to marginalized, silenced, and even murdered communities is an activist endeavor, one which cross-cuts literacy and formal political training and tactics. Both sections taught us about stories and risk taking in ways that further illuminate the complexity of social justice efforts and our attempts as scholar-activists to research and document them. In this section we will see these complexities further demonstrated through activists from the grassroots.

Part 3 continues the dialogues on grassroots social justice efforts; however, rather than understanding texts and performance as activism, in the chapters to follow we will see activism as embodied by forming organizations, articulating demands, struggling over ideologies, and perhaps most important, developing what Chela Sandoval calls "oppositional consciousness." Late twentieth- and twenty-first-century Latin America is replete with examples of women-led and/or feminist grassroots activism—including guerrillas, union activists, Christian base communities, human rights organizations, LGBT activists, environmental justice organizations, movements for gender quotas, student groups, indigenous rights, and global economic justice movements.[1] This section engages in a selection of feminist/grassroots activism including sex workers organizing in Bahia, Brazil; advocates of Latina immigrant survivors of intimate partner violence (IPV); and rural feminists in Nicaragua.

In this section the stories move beyond texts and performances to become narratives of activism. That is, we hear about how the sex workers in Brazil and rural feminists in Nicaragua came into their grassroots activism and how they advance their causes. Bahian sex workers struggle to establish their own agendas, free from the unsolicited intervention of what Erica Williams calls "eradicationist" activists who often operate from a racist rescue narrative in which sex workers are viewed as victims incapable of making empowering choices for themselves. In a sense, Williams' work exposes the struggle Brazilian sex workers have of demanding both their labor rights and health protection from the State, as well as staving off the well-meaning but agency-compromising efforts of the eradicationists.

We then move north to Texas and interact with an arguably more complicated narrative of activist stories. As we know neoliberal ideologies and policies are the modus operandi of the global political economy. As a result, civil service organizations are becoming increasingly more pressured to do the business once considered the purview of the State. This trajectory has had compromising effects on grassroots activism. In the case of Roberta Villalón's Organization for Refugees of America (ORA) we meet what might be considered "postactivists," women who joined a nonprofit organization to support immigrant survivors or IPV, now working more like employees and less like politically engaged grassroots workers. As Villalón explains: "Originally, ORA was a politically radical, volunteer-based, grassroots group focused on advocacy, legal, and social change. However, it gradually transformed into a politically moderate, employee-based, nonprofit organization focused on providing legal services." This transformation, as we will see, has typically been at the expense of their "clients"—the immigrant survivors of domestic violence.

In Nicaragua we, in a sense, revisit the feminist activists of the early and postfirst Sandinista era. That is, Nicaraguan feminism, like all feminisms in the Americas, has evolved alongside, within, and around the Left. The narratives Shelly Grabe shares in her chapter capture this ongoing feminist evolution with a historical fortitude that early 1980s Nicaraguan feminism had yet to develop. As Grabe explains of one of the women we meet in her chapter, "Martha's story of triumph reflects how a counternarrative can disrupt the stranglehold of dominant narratives and thereby lead to more democratic processes that encourage social justice." Grabe's use of the oral history technique allows us to really meet the activists and understand the roots of their "oppositional consciousness." It seems fitting to close our stories of activism with the experiences of women who have accrued generations of feminist wisdom.

These three cases tell stories of grassroots activism as it evolves and arguably devolves in response to internal and external forces. In Brazil, women push back against the State and eradicationists, often either battling against or working with well-meaning organizations. In Texas, we hear stories of grassroots activism compromised, partly in response to external factors brought on by neoliberalism. In Nicaragua, the feminists are shaped by their personal and political histories of class consciousness and struggles. As in the two previous sections, we hear the voice of the activist researcher attempting to share these complicated and not particularly straightforward stories from the grassroots.

Notes

1. While I cannot provide a lengthy bibliography of suggested readings on all of the aforementioned movements, I point the reader to two useful overviews. First is a recent collection titled *Women's Activism in Latin America and the Caribbean: Engendering Social Justice, Democratizing Citizenship*, ed. Elizabeth Maier and Nathalie Lebon (New Brunswick, NJ: Rutgers University Press, 2010). This collection is filled with essays by some of the top scholars-activists in the field, both in and outside of Latin America and the Caribbean. Together the essays touch on nearly all of the aforementioned types of movement, and then some. Second, for an overview of LGBT activism in the region I point the reader to Omar G. Encarnación, 2011, "Latin America's Gay Rights Revolution," *Journal of Democracy* 22(2): 104–18. This article is a brief overview of recent efforts of queer activists in Latin America.

8

FEMINIST TENSIONS

Race, Sex Work, and Women's Activism in Bahia

ERICA LORRAINE WILLIAMS

Dilemmas of a "Diasporic Anthropologist": Research Inspired by Personal Experience

In February 2001, I was a senior at New York University studying abroad in Salvador. Walking through the tourist districts of Pelourinho, Barra, and the Centro in Salvador, Bahia, Brazil, one often comes across colorful postcards portraying young black women in miniscule bikinis on idyllic beaches and muscular black men playing *capoeira*, a mix of Afrobrazilian martial arts, dance, and music. One day I was on the beach with another African American woman in my program. We often opted to only speak Portuguese to each other in public, both to enhance our language skills and to take advantage of the fact that we could "blend in" as women of African descent. Soon, a group of Italian male tourists approached us and initiated a conversation in broken Portuguese. Within just a few short minutes, they were aggressively inviting us back to their hotel room. Shocked at what was happening, my friend and I slipped back into our native tongue. When the Italian men heard us speaking English, they suddenly backpedaled. Obviously embarrassed, they apologized profusely: "Oh, you're American? We're so sorry, we thought you were Brazilian!" I thought to myself: if we *were* Brazilian, would that have justified their assumption about our sexual availability?

My scholarly interest in the sexual economies of tourism in Salvador was sparked by this visceral experience of how my racialized and gendered body was perceived by white European male tourists. Cultural anthropologist Kia Lilly Caldwell reflects upon a similar experience in which a white man referred to her and an Afro-Brazilian woman as *mariposas*, a vernacular term for prostitute, while visiting an upscale hotel in Rio de Janeiro. Caldwell points out how "diasporic anthropologists" are often "subjected to many of the same racialized and gendered discourses and practices that we set out to examine in our research" (2007, xxii). Like Caldwell, I realized early on that my positionality as a woman of African descent was integral to my understanding of Brazilian racial and gender dynamics.

What happens when we take our positionalities, social locations, and subjectivities seriously in the context of ethnographic research? This chapter describes some of my experiences as both an "insider" and an "outsider" in the field in terms of how my body has been read and reflects on the implications that these experiences had on my research. These are issues that graduate training often does not prepare women of color and other marginalized subjects to deal with; yet they are "difficult dialogues"[1] that we must have in order to prepare students for the challenges, rewards, and risks of ethnographic research. I have found that the routine, everyday sexualization that women of color experience all over the world is exacerbated when doing research on a sexually charged subject and while moving throughout sexually charged spaces. The contentious nature of my research topic, coupled with my positionality as a young, unattached woman of color in the field, put me in spaces where my respectability and sexuality were constantly scrutinized. Thus, my racialized and gendered body was implicated in the context of my research in multiple and shifting ways—from being seen as a sexually available Brazilian woman by Italian tourists, to a sexually available *negringa* (foreign black woman) by *caça-gringas* (Bahian male hustlers)[2], and even to my political identities of being a sex worker rights advocate.

In addition to looking at how my identity affected my research, this chapter will explore some of the methodological challenges and tensions that I encountered in conducting this research. For example, I often found myself navigating between vast cultural worlds and various understandings of the meanings of feminism and feminist activism. I straddled divides between academic university-based feminists, women affiliated with nongovernmental organizations, and sex workers who mobilized to demand their rights and improved working conditions. Tensions around issues of race, gender, class, sexuality, age, and nationality surfaced not only among my research interlocutors, but also in ways that implicated my own identity. Furthermore, my involvement with the Association of Prostitutes[3] of Bahia (Aprosba), challenged my politics and assumptions about women's agency, empowerment, desire, and victimization. Although adult prostitution is legal and even recognized as an official occupation in Brazil, sex workers still suffer from violence, stigma, and discrimination. Aprosba was founded in 1997 by sex workers who wanted to mobilize for their rights, recognition, and the full benefits of citizenship. According to Fabiana, cofounder and lead organizer of Aprosba, "we want to show that prostitutes are also dignified people who exercise a profession like any other" (Francisco 2006). Aprosba has weekly meetings for members, safe-sex workshops, and group activities and distributes condoms and educational materials. The organization is a member of the Rede Brasileira de Prostitutas (Brazilian Network of Prostitutes), an organization established in 1987 by Gabriela Leite, and regularly partners with the Ministry of Health and Ministry of Culture on education projects on the prevention of HIV/AIDS and sexually transmitted infections (STIs).

Something unanticipated happened from my initial "exposure" to sex tourism in Salvador in 2001 to the culmination of my doctoral fieldwork in 2008. As a graduate student, my research began by focusing on how Afro-Brazilian women's bodies were eroticized and commodified—even used in postcards to lure potential heterosexual male tourists to the state of Bahia. Thus, it was very much concerned with historical legacies of transracial erotics and exploitation from slavery and colonialism, to the contemporary globalized mass tourism industry. However, hearing Aprosba members' stories of empowerment, police violence, romantic dreams, and complex desires challenged my assumptions about sex tourism. I heard stories of women who fell in love with foreign ship workers, who had traveled to visit their clients'/boyfriends' countries, who escaped police violence and abuse from domestic clients and boyfriends to the arms of a *gringo carinhoso* (caring, affectionate foreign man) who gave them access to their own city in a way that they had never had before. What was I to do with these stories? Was sex tourism a simple and clear-cut manifestation of geopolitical, racial, and gender inequality, sexual exploitation, and the excesses of consumption and mass tourism? How was I to make sense of these complicated stories of affect, desire, strategy, and risk that did not fit into conventional narratives of a phenomenon that has been considered the "dark side" of tourism?

Stereotypes of black hypersexuality have come to characterize foreign tourists' imaginaries of Brazil as a racial-sexual paradise, to the extent that any black (presumed) Brazilian woman would be seen as sexually available. As it has developed over the years, my research has come to analyze "sex tourism" from various perspectives. For example, I have conducted interviews with foreign tourists, tourism industry workers, sex workers who engage in ambiguous liaisons with foreigners, Afro-Brazilian men and women who must contend with foreigners' stereotypical assumptions about their licentiousness, and nongovernmental organization (NGO) staff involved in campaign efforts to eradicate sex tourism and trafficking. In the next section, I will provide an overview of the bodies of scholarship that my work engages—activist anthropology and black feminist anthropology.

Activist and Black Feminist Anthropology

My engagement with these issues draws inspiration from the interventions of black feminist and postmodernist approaches to anthropology, which began to highlight self-reflexivity as an important strategy for ethnographic writing. This shifted away from the notion of the anthropologist as a white, male colonialist figure, a detached observer and blank slate, who claimed neutrality, objectivity, and moral authority. The discipline of anthropology has its origins as a "child of imperialism" and "handmaiden of colonialism," yet over time it has increasingly been used as a tool to understand and respect cultural differences. As Lynn Bolles highlights in her essay on black feminist "foremothers" in anthropology, black women who studied anthropology between 1915 and the 1950s saw it as a "tool to locate the sources of inequality, and . . . as a place where one could participate in finding the 'cure'" (2001, 27). Debates on both the limitations and radical possibilities of anthropology have persisted for decades.

In the classic edited volume *Decolonizing Anthropology: Moving Further toward an Anthropology of Liberation* (Harrison 1991), several scholars articulate their ideas about both the radical possibilities and limitations of anthropology. For Edmund T. Gordon, an "anthropology of liberation" must actively serve the interests of the oppressed by helping people understand the nature of their own oppression so that they may conquer it (1991, 153–54). Philippe Bourgois, in his essay reflecting on his early fieldwork experiences in war-torn Central American countries in the late 1970s, comes to the realization not only that anthropology has an overwhelmingly apolitical orientation, but also that the North American epistemology of relativism and value-free science, in a sense, forbids engaged research (1991, 120).[4]

Over the years, activist research has grown in popularity in the field of anthropology, as can be seen with the publication of several notable anthologies (Hale 2008; Sanford and Angel-Ajani 2008; Sudbury and Okazawa-Rey 2009). In his oft-cited essay, "What Is Activist Research?," Charles Hale (2001) outlines some of the benefits and demands of activist research. For one, activist research helps scholars understand the root causes of inequality, oppression, and violence. In activist research, the formulation of our research objectives is driven by "our deepest ethical-political convictions" (Hale 2001, 14). Hale calls for activist researchers to come to their research questions and objectives through dialogue and collective work, which is essential because activist research in anthropology should serve the needs of the people involved and affected. For Hale, there is no contradiction between theory and practice—activist research is both theoretically driven and intended to be put to use. Furthermore, Hale claims that activist research should challenge the dichotomy between researcher/analyst and "native informant"/supplier of raw data by enabling the research informants to also participate in analysis of data and by embarking upon a validation process in which people involved evaluate the usefulness of the research to resolve a problem or guide transformation. Finally, Hale claims that research outcomes are improved when tensions, contradictions, and ethical dilemmas are identified and confronted directly. Drawing inspiration from the fields of activist and black feminist anthropology, this chapter reflects not only upon some of the methodological challenges of my research, but also upon some of the stories of my research participants, which also challenged my thinking in many ways.

Black feminist anthropology shares certain characteristics with activist anthropology in its attempt to do liberatory and empowering research (Rodriguez 2001). Irma McClaurin, editor of *Black Feminist Anthropology: Theory, Politics, Praxis, and Poetics,* asserts that black feminist anthropologists must fashion a research paradigm that decolonizes and transforms, seeks to "alleviate conditions of oppression through scholarship and activism," and directly confronts how our identities are implicated in the research process (2001b, 57). Autoethnography is a way of writing that brings together identity, scholarship, and knowledge production. McClaurin asserts that it is at once a stylistic form, a theoretical lens, and a methodological strategy that enables black women anthropologists to use their personal experience as a lens through which to describe and analyze ethnographic data (McClaurin 2001a, 18). With its combination of personal memories (autobiography) and cultural descriptions (ethnography), McClaurin claims that "autoethnography is a viable form through which black feminist anthropologists may theorize and textualize our situated positions and elevate our subjugated discourses to levels recognized by both margins and center of the discipline" (2001b, 56). Toward that end, in this chapter I weave together personal stories of the multiple ways in which my racialized and gendered body was read in the context of my fieldwork, with ethnographic stories of sex worker's lives in the touristscape of Salvador. The next section describes my initial forays into this research topic.

Feminist Encounters: Scholars, Prostitutes, and Conceptual Tensions

In August 2006, a few years after my first trip to Brazil as an exchange student, I returned as a doctoral student to begin my year of fieldwork. The time I spent living, studying, and conducting preliminary research in Bahia had taught me that Salvador was a place where stereotypical notions of black hypersexuality created a situation in which foreigners perceived any Bahian of African descent as sexually available. For this reason, I arrived in the field with the intention of writing against scholarship that confined sex tourism to "sex work." I initially wanted to distance my work from the assumption that sex tourism necessarily involved sex workers because I felt that the eroticization of Bahia in the international imaginary rendered black Bahian women as objects of desire, whether they were sex workers or not. However, an early fieldwork experience with white Brazilian feminist scholars compelled me to reconsider this approach.

During my fieldwork, I was granted status as a Visiting Researcher with the Núcleo de Estudos Interdisciplinares sobre a Mulher (Interdisciplinary Women's Studies Institute, NEIM) of the Federal University of Bahia. That same year, the institute had just launched its new masters' degree program in women, gender, and feminist studies—the first such program in all of Latin America. I was invited to participate in the courses and seminars and to present my research. In December 2006, I presented my research-in-progress to graduate students and faculty affiliated with the institute. However, when I mentioned that I would be working with the Association of Prostitutes of Bahia (Aprosba), several of the professors opined that this would not be useful for my research. The feminist scholars characterized members of Aprosba as poor, low-class, drug-addicted streetwalkers whom sex tourists would not seek out. I found these statements shocking and replete with elitism, unfair generalizations, and class biases. These statements suggested that sex tourism in Salvador has little or no overlap with the local commercial sex industry. But how could it be that sex tourists did not seek sex workers who work in the Historic Center

(Centro Histórico) (like Aprosba members), when Praça da Sé was both a major site of the local commercial sex industry *and* a major site of the tourist industry? The Centro Histórico is a major site of the tourist district in Salvador, and it includes Praça da Sé and Pelourinho, an area that was declared a UNESCO World Heritage Site.[5]

When I began to attend Aprosba meetings and talked with members, I found that not only did members of Aprosba recount innumerable experiences with "typical" sex tourists—European and North American male leisure tourists who arrived by plane—but they also narrated extensive experiences with *marinheiros* (ship workers) from around the world whose ships docked in the Comércio and Cidade Baixa (Lower City) ports of Salvador. Thus, in terms of my research approach, I shifted from not wanting to focus *exclusively* on sex workers, to feeling like I *should* shift my focus in order to prove that their lives were worthy of engaged, respectful, nonjudgmental, critical, scholarly inquiry.

I first encountered Fabiana,[6] the cofounder and lead organizer of Aprosba at a labor conference in Salvador in August 2005.[7] Fabiana was in the audience when Gabriela Leite, a well-known prostitutes' rights activist from Rio de Janeiro, spontaneously invited her to stand and speak to the group.[8] The first words that she uttered before the audience full of feminist academics was: "Eu não gosto de feministas e feministas não gostam de mim!" [I don't like feminists and feminists don't like me!]. Her bold words, spoken with a smile, nonetheless hinted at the longstanding tensions between feminists and sex workers. Scholarly studies on prostitution often depict sex workers either as exploited "sex slaves" who are commodified and *forced* to sell their bodies against their will or as cosmopolitan heroines who brazenly "*choose*" to utilize their sexuality as a means of advancement.

Eradicationist, or abolitionist,[9] feminist perspectives have defined the parameters of international discourse on prostitution for over a century (Doezema 1998). The eradicationist approach naturalizes prostitution as "wrong" and "immoral" and considers it to be exploitative by its very nature, even likening it to rape. For instance, Kathleen Barry, cofounder of the Coalition gainst Trafficking of Women (CATW), argues that the existence of a "prostitute who is unharmed by her experience is an ontological impossibility" (Doezema 2001). Eradicationist feminist perspectives moralize and lament the oppression of "subjugated prostitutes" yet offer few substantial alternatives for women who engage in sex work to make a living. They attack the exploitation of sex work yet do little or nothing to actually change the exploitative conditions in which many prostitutes labor. Worse still, their call for criminalization or eradication of prostitution can often result in "punitive regulatory regimes" that deny sex workers legal and political rights and render them more vulnerable to agents and traffickers (van der Veen 2000, 126, 130).

Aprosba is an extremely important organization given that it is run *by* and *for* prostitutes.[10] While there are other social and religious organizations that work with prostitutes in Salvador, they are often engaged in moralizing missions to "rescue, rehabilitate, improve, discipline, control, or police" sex workers (Altman 2001, 101).[11] Fabiana expressed her critique of these types of organizations when she said: "[T]hey only want to take us out of prostitution. Only we know ourselves. We are searching for a better quality of life." Here Fabiana asserts that prostitutes are the most qualified to advocate on their own behalf.

Leaders of Aprosba contend that legitimizing sex work would guarantee them important protections and improve their working conditions. For instance, Fabiana claimed that "as much money as you earn, you lose because of illegality." She pointed out that prostitutes who work at night and sleep during the day are exploited by various people: from taxi drivers who charge them exorbitant rates or demand free sex in exchange for providing transportation, to mobile clothes saleswomen who knock on their doors at convenient times to sell clothes that are more expensive than if they purchased them at the store. Similarly, Gabriela Leite, the Rio de Janeiro–based sex worker activist, described the harsh conditions that sex workers confront when she told the audience at the 2005 labor conference in Salvador that she was compelled to return to sex work in São Paulo four days after her second child was born. There was no maternity leave, no vacation, and she even had to pay a *diária* (daily rate) where she was living. While eradicationists would take this as evidence that prostitution should be abolished altogether, Gabriela Leite uses this to argue for better working conditions and rights for sex workers (Lerum 1998).[12]

In researching and writing about sex work, I draw inspiration from the sex worker rights approach, as well as Dennis Altman's warning to not embrace stereotypes of prostitutes as "necessarily marginalized and self-hating" (2001, 113). The sex worker rights approach rejects the assumption that sex work is something morally reprehensible from which women must be rescued. This approach also advocates for the decriminalization of prostitution, highlights the empowerment and benefits of women in the sex industry, emphasizes the entrepreneurial aspects of prostitution, and rearticulates sex work as "laboring activity" (van der Veen 2000). Some have also elaborated a more nuanced position between the eradicationist and sex worker rights extremes. For instance, Bandana Pattanaik, program coordinator of the Thailand-based Global Alliance against Trafficking in Women (GAATW), argues that careful listening and nonjudgmental attitudes toward sex workers will result in "narratives that neither glorify sex work as liberatory nor denigrate it as soul-destroying" (Pattanaik and Thorbek 2002, 222). Thus, it is possible to oppose the abuse, violence, and deceit that sex workers confront while not opposing sex work as an occupational choice. In the next section, I outline some of the methodological challenges of doing research on the sexual economies of tourism in Salvador, Brazil.

Entering the Field: Methodological Challenges

When I first approached Aprosba with my research interests, I was met with resistance. I interpret this resistance as having to do with what activist Joo-Hyun Kang calls "research fatigue," which occurs when grassroots organizations are continuously sought out by academics to be subjects of research projects, yet rarely see any benefits.[13] Fabiana, the president and cofounder of Aprosba, bluntly told me that they did not want researchers to use them as objects of study, without giving them anything in return. I was determined not to be that type of researcher. Fabiana asked me to submit a letter of intent on official letterhead from my institution outlining what kind of information I was seeking from Aprosba and for what purposes. In my letter, I expressed my interest in learning about the history and activities of Aprosba and interviewing leaders and members of the organization. I explained that I wanted to understand the relationship between sex workers and the tourism industry. Were foreign tourists a significant part of their clientele? How significant was the tourism industry in their daily lives? Was sex tourism strictly linked to prostitution, or did it also involve people who did not identify as sex workers? I added that if it were possible, I would like to participate in the life of the organization by attending meetings and events. Finally, in the spirit of striving for "reciprocity" in the research exchange, I offered to teach a free English as a second language (ESL) class for Aprosba members. Though by Charles Hale's standards of activist research, my project was not fully developed in collaboration with the organization, I did make sure to do some things that were directly beneficial to them. In addition to teaching the ESL class, I cofacilitated a workshop upon their request, I translated their website into English, and I assisted them in conducting a survey of violence against sex workers in Praça da Sé.

Fabiana was extremely enthusiastic about my proposal to teach a free English class to Aprosba members. Several of the active members of Aprosba emphasized the importance of knowing English in a tourist destination and encouraged others to take my ESL class. Marisa, a woman of African descent who would be considered *morena* by local color classifications, was one of the cofounders. Although she said she was an "exprostitute," or "retired from prostitution," she still regularly attended and participated in the activities of Aprosba.[14] Marisa encouraged the women of Aprosba to learn English in order to be able to demand their rights and earn more money from foreign clients.[15] Barbara, a bleached-blond young mother of a nine-month-old son who had migrated to Salvador from the rural Bahian town of Joazeiro, also enthusiastically encouraged the women present at the meeting to take advantage of the opportunity to learn English. She told the women: "It's summer. It's the season for us to go after *gringos*; we have to know how to ask for our money, to say how much we charge. Soon we'll need to be bilingual or trilingual." Marisa's and Barbara's statements emphasize the significant presence of the tourism industry, and thus, foreign clients, in the lives of sex workers in the tourist districts of Salvador. In an increasingly globalized city in which they encountered people from all over the world on a daily basis, Aprosba members recognized the necessity of developing foreign language skills as a tool to enhance their "marketability" and appeal for foreign clients.

As much as the leadership and members of Aprosba challenged me to think in new ways, as a black feminist anthropologist, I could not ignore the racial dynamics of the organization or the situation of sex workers in Salvador as a whole for that matter. The major leaders in Aprosba are white Brazilian women, yet the majority of the sex workers in the tourist districts are black women. This is in part due to the sheer numerical majority of people of African descent in Salvador—approximately 80 percent. Due to the racialized stigma which assumes that black and brown women in Bahia are either sex workers or at the very least sexually available, I worried that my "reading" of certain "couplings" as potential cases of sex tourism would ultimately reaffirm those stereotypes. I would often see couples on the street, in bars, cyber-cafes, and restaurants that consisted of an older foreign tourist and a younger, Bahian woman of African descent. How would I know which couples were potential cases of sex tourism? Furthermore, how does one study and write about black women's sexuality without "re-pathologizing an already stigmatized and marginalized population" (Miller-Young 2008, 119; Wekker 2006)? While the ambiguity that characterizes the sexual economies of transnational tourism in Bahia was precisely what I wanted to capture, at times it proved to be ethereal, intangible, and difficult to grasp. Consequently, I found that in terms of access, it was more convenient and efficient to focus on Aprosba, because it brought together a group of women who self-identified as sex workers.

As a black feminist anthropologist who critically interrogates questions of desire, anxieties, intimacy, agency, and sex in the context of the transnational tourism industry in Salvador, I often feel caught between sex-positive research that is often racialized as white and discussions of the ways in which black women's bodies have been subject to historical processes of hypersexualization, victimization, and exploitation (Miller-Young 2007). In grappling with this issue, I am reminded of Chandra Mohanty's classic and unfortunately still salient critique of the notion of "third world difference." Mohanty argues that "third world difference portrays third world women as sexually constrained, ignorant, poor, uneducated, tradition-bound, domestic, family-oriented, and victimized (1991, 56). Western women, on the other hand, represent themselves as educated, modern, having control over their bodies and sexualities, and enjoying the freedom to make their own decisions (Mohanty 1991, 56). However, I would add that, in this case, the Western/Third World divide is actually also a racial divide both within the national context of Brazil and within the African diaspora. In my work with Aprosba, I could not ignore the prevalence of white Brazilian women in the leadership roles, despite the overwhelming majority of black and brown women sex workers in the streets and plazas of the Historic Center of the city.

How do we reconcile sensationalist discourses of sexual tourism that situate any and all sexual relations between foreigners and locals as "sexual exploitation" and a violation of human rights, with black Brazilian women's articulations of agency, advantages, and cosmopolitan strategies of mobility in their pursuit of transnational liaisons and encounters with foreign men? The historical legacies of the sexualization of black women can be traced over time from the display and preservation of the body parts of Saartjie Baartman (the Hottentot Venus), to enslaved African women being treated as the master's sexual objects, to the Brazilian *mulata* being seen as the national erotic icon. Black feminists have usually responded to this legacy by distancing themselves from sexualized images and embracing a "culture of dissemblance" (Clark Hine 1989) and "politics of respectability" (Higginbotham 1993; Miller-Young 2007). As a black feminist anthropologist, this has forced me to grapple with the question: is centering black women's sexual agency in the context of sex work an "act of betrayal" to black feminisms? These are questions that are as of yet not completely resolved in my work. All I can do is stay true to the stories that were told to me, even when they may challenge everything I thought I knew. What does a black feminist anthropologist do when she enters the field expecting stories of subjucation, exoticization, objectification, and exploitation, but instead encounters stories of agency, empowerment, and resistance?

Sex tourism has profound implications for daily life and romantic relationships in Salvador. One day, I was sitting at an outdoor café in Pelourinho, and I saw two black Bahian women and two European men sitting at a neighboring table. When an elderly white Brazilian woman street vendor walked by selling necklaces, she suddenly stopped and stared at them incessantly. One of the men said in Portuguese: "Do you have a problem? You're looking at us as if you don't like what you see. This is my wife." He emphasized *wife*, as if he knew instinctively what assumptions the elderly woman was making about them. This scenario reveals the anxiety that the specter of sex tourism produces for those who must contend with other peoples' assumptions about the "validity" or "authenticity" of their relationships. Whether this man was telling the truth about the woman being his wife, I was unable to find out. The fact that I even questioned whether he was telling the truth speaks volumes about the powerful effects of the specter of sex tourism in Salvador. It creates anxiety and raises suspicions about any and all transnational, and most importantly, cross-racial, relationships. Also, in its ambiguity and fleeting nature, this ethnographic anecdote highlights some of the methodological challenge of conducting research on transient, mobile populations. Sally Ann Ness (2003) notes that studying tourism challenges the viability of long-term participant observation. In addition to the obvious fact that foreign tourists are dislocated and transient, I found that in some cases, sex workers were also transient. They commonly shuttled between different *pontos* (points where they solicit clients), and sometimes even different cities. Sometimes they missed appointments, suddenly disappeared (only to resurface amidst rumors of having killed a police officer), or became addicted to drugs.[16]

Why Ask, "Why Sex Work"?

Asale Angel-Ajani, a cultural anthropologist who conducted research among incarcerated black women in Italy, avoided revealing why her interlocutors were imprisoned when sharing her research with academics. She did this in an effort to refrain from further criminalizing African women in the face of academic colleagues' prurient fascination with sordid stories of black women's criminality. Angel-Ajani found that academic audiences often doubted the reliability of her informants due to presumptions that "crime still defines the criminal." Similarly, in my research, I made a conscious decision in interviews with sex workers not to inquire as to why they had entered into sex work. I felt that the presumption underlying this inquiry stems from a moral and judgmental frame of reference that maintains the preconceived notion that sex work was a "wrong" and "immoral" activity that one would only resort to under extreme circumstances. That was not the starting point I wanted to create with my research participants. Instead of asking why they become sex workers, I strove to find out about the lived realities of their experiences as sex workers. Reflecting on my uneasiness with asking "why," I think it was simultaneously a decision motivated by respect for sex workers' dignity and right to choose to engage in sexual labor, as well as a methodological decision. I felt that my ability to build a rapport with sex workers depended on their understanding that I was not judging them. These two motivations are not mutually exclusive.

In my interview with Bel, a twenty-four-year-old woman who had migrated to Salvador from the northeastern city of Recife, I did not have to broach the "why sex work" question. She raised it for me when she told me—unsolicited—the story of her entry into sex work. I met Bel on a Wednesday afternoon when Fabiana had taken me to a bar in the Centro Histórico where sex workers gathered to meet foreign *marinheiros* (seamen/ship workers). At the bar, I witnessed clandestine tour guides bringing the *marinheiros* to the bar directly from the docks. Prevalent in the Historic Center, these unofficial, unlicensed, illegal "tour guides" offered their services publicly to tourists on the streets. Bel, an attractive, slim woman with bleached blond hair, referred to sex tourism as "the best source of income for pretty women." She had worked almost exclusively with Asian seamen and even spoke some Tagalog and English. She told me that she did not necessarily have a preference for *gringos*. Rather, she preferred Asian *marinheiros* in particular because "they pay well and treat me well." Bel said that the worst thing about sex tourism was that "we fall in love and then the ships leave. I already entered into depression three times because of Filipinos. The ships leave, and I cry. They are very caring."

After we had discussed her experiences with foreign leisure tourists and seamen, I was just about to thank Bel for her time and end the interview when she said: "Oh, you're going to write a book about my life. I have a lot to tell!" I hunkered down and prepared myself to listen attentively to her story. In what follows, I will present the story she told me in detail and focus on the issues it raises for the study of ambiguities in the sexual economies of tourism in Salvador.

"Why did I end up in this life? It was destiny. I was always a good girl from a good family. My mother only let me go to school and mass . . ." Bel crafted her narrative to highlight her moral upbringing in the countryside of Recife. In the following quote, she discussed her romantic relationships and her desire to enter into the arena of sexual commerce.[17] Bel states: "I only had three boyfriends before starting to *piriguetar* . . . I found my second boyfriend on the Internet. I am an *interesseira assumida.* I was seventeen years old, and he was twenty-two. He had a car. I started dating him for *interesse* [ulterior motives]. He was awkward, he wasn't cute, and he only talked about work. We dated for six months. I passed the *vestibular* [college entrance exam] at that time. I went to school for the first six months without paying." Bel's narrative shifts from the imposed moral turpitude of her upbringing to her proclaimed *interesseira* attitudes in selecting her boyfriends. She dated a man to whom she was not attracted or particularly interested in because of the benefits of mobility and money. The fact that he paid for her monthly college fees during their relationship was an added benefit.

In what follows, she continues to discuss her relationships with men, her college experience, and financial struggles: "I chose Geography because it was the cheapest program of study that I liked. My friends bought books for school, and I would photocopy them. My debt from the Xerox went up to $R600 the first year, and I didn't pay the monthly payment for school. . . . My stepfather became unemployed, so I had to get a job. I earned $R180[18]—that was barely enough to contribute to the household." The precariousness of Bel's family's financial situation after her stepfather's job loss put her in a position where she could no longer be a carefree college student. Rather, she had to assume the responsibility of finding a job to contribute to the family expenses. She quickly realized that her options were limited and that the meager salary she earned for her hard work was far from desirable.

> I had ulterior motives [in dating the second boyfriend]. I wanted to lose my virginity to a nice guy so that I could begin to *piriguetar*. The first time [I had sex] I was drunk. I didn't feel anything. Afterwards, I felt blood drip down my leg . . . I cried. Now I was no longer a *moçinha* [respectable young lady]. I only did it two more times with that boyfriend, and I wanted to *entrar na brega* [begin to do sex work].
>
> I met another guy in college. I wanted to marry him because he fulfilled one of my dreams: he took me to the Chapada Diamantina. He worked for the *Receita Federal* (federal government treasury) in Recife, and we dated for six months. I really liked the third boyfriend, so much so that I broke up with him when I decided to *entrar na brega*.

It is interesting how Bel narrates her story through her romantic relationships with men. At the age of nineteen, Bel met a woman who worked as a prostitute with foreigners from the ships at the port in Recife. Bel was still in college, so she would go to the port on the weekends: "I was studying Geography, but I didn't want to. I wanted to be a psychologist . . . I did a year and a half of college. I even taught classes for first and fourth graders. I worked for a year in an office. I worked as an administrative assistant in another office. My boss wanted to have sex with me."

Bel's story reveals her desire to seek a higher education and also the financial difficulties that made that dream difficult to obtain. Eradicationist scholarship tends to situate sex workers as women who have limited educational and occupational experience and opportunities and who have "no other option" than to "sell their bodies" as a survival strategy. Certainly, the limited opportunities available to women based on their educational level, socioeconomic status, race, and color play a role in making sexual labor a viable option for women. However, one must also consider women's autonomy in choosing sexual labor over other forms of labor in which they would be exploited. Steven Gregory (2007) makes this point clearly in the context of women's labor in the Dominican Republic, where the low wages, exploitative working conditions, sexual harassment, and abuse women experienced working in export-processing zones (EPZs) made the autonomy and higher pay of sex work more appealing. While export-processing zones are not common in Bahia, a relevant corollary can be seen in domestic work, which is seen as an exploitative form of labor that is often the only option available for low-income women, particularly those of African descent (Williams 2013a).

Bel describes her first *programa* (commercial sexual exchange) as an experience where her naïveté was almost her downfall:

> My first *programa* was a bit crazy. A tall, handsome blond man asked how much I charged, and I said $R70–100, but the girl who brought me there told me that I could charge $R200 to gringos. He said, "No 150," I said, "180." He paid for the taxi, hotel and gave me $180 USD. I said, "I don't want this. This money is worthless!" The girl told me that money was worth a lot: "Take the money!" I went to the *câmbio* and exchanged the dollars for *reais*. I had never seen so much money in my life!

Here, Bel recounts her first experience of the financial benefits of doing *programas* with foreigners and earning U.S. dollars. However, the money seemed to slip through her fingers: "I was young and stupid. I spent money on lots of frivolous things—clothes, shoes, and cell phones—all nonsense. It wasn't until I got pregnant that I realized that this money wouldn't last forever . . . I've been with men, ship captains, who gave me R3000, but I don't know where that money is now." Bel migrated to Salvador because the port had a heavier influx of ships docking than Recife, and thus a greater number of potential clients. At the time of the interview, Bel had lived in Salvador for five years. She described the intricate workings of the sexual economies involving foreign seamen:

> This bar is specifically for *marinheiros*. Sometimes we accompany them to Rio. It's an exchange. I know people [sex workers] from Natal, Recife, and Maceió. They all go to different ports. November to March is the summer season, when the tourism ships come in, and we work during the day. During the other months, we only work at night. In the summer we gain more money than in the rest of the year. In the summer, we check online to see what time the ships will dock. We call each other. We go down to wait in the bar at 9 or 10 o'clock. Down at the dock, there are women who used to do *programas* but are now too old. They speak English, Filipino, and Greek very well. They bring the men. We give them a tip of $R5. They all come here—even Egyptians have been here!

Bel's statement offers insight into how the system operates and how sex workers' lives and livelihoods are affected by the influx of tourist ships. With a combination of technology, word of mouth, and the collaboration of retired prostitutes, women such as Bel are able to procure their foreign clients. Bel's narrative about her upbringing, romantic and sexual experiences, personal financial struggles, and her entry into the *brega* offers a compelling example of some of the factors and conditions that shape women's lives in the socioeconomic and cultural landscape of northeastern Brazilian port cities.

When Research Challenges Everything You Thought You Knew

"I believe there are valuable lessons to be learned if we opened our ears to experiences that might not fit what we think we know" (Asale Angel-Ajani 2004, 142). This quote from Asale Angel-Ajani, the cultural anthropologist who conducted research among incarcerated African women in Italy, speaks volumes about the need for researchers to be open to the stories our research participants want to tell—even, and I would say especially, those that challenge our previous assumptions and ways of thinking. Women in Salvador like Bel challenged many of the things I thought I knew about sex tourism before embarking on ethnographic fieldwork. This is significant in capturing the experience of learning and growth that results from ethnographic research. As Asale Angel-Ajani stated, "if we think we know it all before a word is uttered then what does that say about our ability to receive the details of another person's experience or testimony?" (142).

Bel recounted a "love story" about Pierre, a seamen/client from Madagascar to whom she referred as "the beautiful African." When she met this man, she was four months pregnant by a Filipino seaman. Throughout the course of their "relationship," Pierre bought things for her baby and gave her money. When his ship left the port of Salvador, he called and sent money regularly. After two years without seeing each other, he returned in 2006. Bel said when she saw him again, "Everything was beautiful. I went to Rio to be with him." Before his second departure, Pierre told her that she should get a passport because he wanted her to embark on the ship with him back to France:

> I got my passport and identity cards, but I didn't believe he was really going to take me. It was $1700 just for the fare on the ship, and he only earned $1500/month. I went to Rio, bringing my suitcase and all, but I didn't believe it. I embarked that same day on the *MSC Melody*. The room was the most luxurious house in my life. Everything was luxurious [*xiqui*]. I got off the ship in France, met his family. I spent seventeen days with him, and then I returned to Brazil. I ended up falling in love with him because I didn't have to have sex with him several times a day. I thought that if we were going to be together in the same place, I would have to have sex with him all the time, several times a day. Now he is in Africa and isn't able to send money to me. He says that he's going to stop working on the ships. He's worked on the ships for ten years. He says that he's coming here in April to marry me. I want to marry him. What he did for me, no man has ever done.

Bel's story reflects some of the ambiguities implicit in sexual/romantic encounters between foreign clients and local sex workers. *Marinheiros* from the Philippines, Greece, Egypt, Madagascar, India, Norway, and several other countries constitute an overlooked group in the transnational sexual economies of the port city of Salvador.[19] In fact, I was completely unaware of this phenomenon before speaking with these women. The presence of this category of foreign travelers in search of sex challenges the notion of "sex tourism" as the domain of white middle- and upper-class leisure tourists from Europe and North America whose gender, racial, class, and national privilege empowers them to fulfill their fantasies of adventure and arousal through vacationing in destinations of the global South.

Although some of the encounters between local women and foreign seamen were strictly *programas* (commercial sexual exchanges) in which money was exchanged directly for sexual services, other encounters resembled *namoros* (romances), in which the lines between and romantic relationship were blurred. The fact that Bel fell in love with the *marinheiro* from Madagascar, as well as a few men from the Philippines, suggests that there is more to the sexual economies of tourism in Salvador than sex, money, and illicit activity. Rather, "socially acceptable" behaviors and values, such as travel, romance, leisure, consumption, and sometimes marriage, are also a part of the package (Cabezas 2004).[20]

Bel's story also reveals a cosmopolitan scene in which there is an exchange among sex workers from different cities, as they travel to different ports to engage in sexual labor. Other informants expressed the notion of cosmopolitanism and mobility among sex workers. For instance, Fabiana once claimed that "all prostitutes are tourists" because of their tendency to travel to different places. She explained that in her experience as a prostitute who was "viciada em carona" (addicted to hitchhiking) she was able to "explore Brazil in trucks, and even earn money with the truck drivers." Similarly, Gilmara, a young black sex worker at a meeting told the group: "Prostitution has brought me many things. I had the opportunity to travel to other places. For me, it's been marvelous."

The women of Aprosba demanded their right to work as prostitutes and to be protected, rather than criminalized and vilified, under the law. They saw sex tourism as an opportunity to earn more money than with local clients. Furthermore, sex with foreign clients often allowed an opportunity to transform into what I call *ambiguous entanglements* with transnational connections and cosmopolitan experiences within their own city. I utilize the term *ambiguous entanglements* to encompass the broad range of ambiguous liaisons and relationships forged in the "ethnosexual frontier" of Salvador (Nagel 2003) in my book *Sex Tourism in Bahia: Ambiguous Entaglements* (2013).[21]

As I have discussed, my involvement with Aprosba made me rethink my assumptions about agency, pleasure, and victimization. In much the same way that Asale Angel-Ajani encountered challenges in presenting her research on incarcerated African women to academic audiences, I noticed feminist tensions between eradicationist and sex worker rights perspectives rearing their heads when I began to present the results of my research publicly. When I mentioned my research, people often conflated my work with "trafficking," something that I contend is distinct from sex tourism. Many expect the stories of my research participants to fall clearly into the category of victims. However, the stories that women shared with me were often more complicated than that and did not fit neatly into the paradigm that sensationalist news stories, for example, portray.

Insights from feminist ethnography are useful in problematizing the dichotomy between "victims" and "agents." Paulla Ebron criticizes feminist scholars who quickly point to "victims" rather than seeing complex negotiations and who only see "agency" as erasing oppression (Ebron 1997, 183, 188). Ruth Behar offers a critique of feminist anthropologists who, in their efforts to reject the common description of women as passive victims, established a model of life history narrative that unproblematically portrays women as "feminist heroines." Anne McClintock foregrounds her interest in agency in terms of the "host of difficult ways in which people's actions and desires are mediated through institutions of power: the family, the media, the law, armies, nationalist movements," and so on (1995, 15). In addition to the attention that feminist anthropologists have paid to the question of agency, recent scholarship in the area of transnational and postcolonial feminisms has been attentive to the relationship between capitalism and patriarchies (Mohanty 2002; Shohat 1998). Considering how notions of agency, capitalism, and patriarchies are mobilized in an ever-increasingly globalized world is crucial to the study of a transnational mode of production like sex tourism.

In addition to activist anthropology and black feminist anthropology, feminist ethnography offers useful tools for thinking through issues of power relations and the politics of authorship in research. Ruth Behar's reflections on the dilemmas of feminist ethnographic research are still relevant today: "No one is quite sure anymore of how to reconcile feminist politics of social transformation and international sisterhood with a research practice in which relatively privileged academic women seek out, record, and publish the edited voices of relatively underprivileged women from somewhere else in the name of a feminism to be borne across the border" (1993, 297). This brings up yet another tension or dilemma of attempting to do black feminist activist anthropological research. How does a researcher satisfy both the demands of one's collaborators while also satisfying the requirements of one's academic institution? Admittedly, since finishing my dissertation in November 2009 and starting a tenure-track job at a small, private liberal arts college, I have yet to fulfill one request that Aprosba made, which was to write something for the organization in Portuguese. Sending my dissertation or an article would not suffice, because they would not be able to understand it. However, with publication expectations for tenure review, the demands of teaching, and year-round service commitments, it is difficult, despite my best efforts and intentions, to find the time to write something in Portuguese or maintain a sustained engagment with the organization from my homebase in Atlanta. As a scholar who embraces the noble tenets of activist and black feminist anthropology, I am sure that this is something that I will have to grapple with and figure out how to accomplish over the course of my career.

Autoethnography: Revisiting Insider/Outsider Debates

During my interview with Bel, a large group of Filipinos walked in. Promptly, one of the women yelled, "Table!" and everyone rushed into action to attend to them. There was also a group of four South Asian men with whom Barbara was flirting. She kept asking them to buy her a beer. The men glanced several times in my direction, and Fabiana jokingly said to me, "You might be able to make some money here." This was one of many moments in which my own sexual subjectivity was implicated in the context of my research. Once, two young black women asked Marisa, one of the cofounders of Aprosba, "Does she do *programas* too?" Marisa responded, "No, she's the English teacher." Like my experience on the beach with the Italian tourists reading my racialized and gendered body in a particular way, my body and identity yet again played a role in how I was perceived in the course of my research. As Irma McClaurin notes, "Identity remains a contested and negotiated arena in which we struggle to fashion transformative strategies that allow us to 'name and describe our diverse experiences'" (2001b, 55). What struck me about these experiences was the contrast from the experience on the beach. In one space I was read as sexually available, and in another I was marked as different before even opening my mouth. As a sex-positive researcher who interacted with sex workers in a nonjudgmental, open-minded way, my sexuality and identity were always called into question.

In the course of my fieldwork, I learned that how I was perceived by various people shifted according to my location, what I was wearing (particularly swimwear), and even my hairstyle.[22] One particular experience involved how I was perceived by an Afro-Brazilian man who was a *caça-gringa* (male hustler) who seeks liaisons and/or relationships with foreign tourists. What follows is an excerpt from my fieldnotes July 2005:

> Last night after returning from the theater, I went to check email at the Internet café near my apartment in Barra. After that, I walked home and saw two black men and one black woman walking down the street, speaking English. I could tell that the men were Bahian. One of the men said in English to the others LOUDLY that he liked my hair (AFRO). I turned around and said "Thank You," and they seemed surprised that I spoke English. I walked and talked with them, and they invited me to accompany them to a bar. The black woman, it turned out, was from Cleveland, doing a five-week exchange program. She was dating one of the Bahian men. I was surprised at how well Francisco (the one who spoke to me) and her [the African American woman's] boyfriend spoke English. Francisco was twenty-three years old and dressed in an American hip-hop style. He was very flirty with me, but I was not interested. He pressed me for my number, so I gave it to him, reluctantly. If he calls, I might try to interview him.

My initial impression of Francisco was that he may be a *caça-gringa*. To my surprise, Wilson called me the very next morning, in an effort to make plans with me. I was at the bus stop, and I told him that I was very busy with my research. When I disclosed the topic of my research, his response was detached and disinterested. He said he knew of some guys who "do that." My intuition was confirmed when I seemed to run into Francisco everywhere in the tourist district, several times a week. I would see him in Pelourinho with a blond, foreign woman one day, and then in Barra with an African American woman the very next day. Every time I saw him, he would avoid eye contact with me or have an embarrassed look on his face, as if I had caught him with his hands in the proverbial cookie jar. About one month later, I ran into him at a *lanchonete* in Pelourinho where I was having a quick snack before my evening dance class. He sat down and had coffee with me and finally revealed the truth. Later that night, I wrote about our conversation in my fieldnotes journal: "He knew I was a gringa the very first night we met. He said he could 'smell gringas from far away.' That night, he said that he liked my hair in English loud enough so that I could hear him. He did this intentionally to elicit a response from me and prove to the others that he was right about identifying me as an American."[23] I was shocked that even something as simple as a compliment in English could be a part of his strategy to attract foreign women. No matter where I turned in Salvador, I seemed to be the object of someone's assumptions about my sexual availability based on my perceived nationality and my racialized and gendered body.

In recent literature, scholars have articulated complex and varied experiences of the impact of their racial identities on their research. For instance, in reflecting upon her research on race and gender in the Dominican Republic, Kimberly Simmons contends that our personal histories of otherness often provide a bridge that is not necessarily accessible to white anthropologists (2001, 97). Despite warnings from white colleagues that Dominicans did not discuss issues of race, Simmons was able to elicit information about race and color from her Dominican informants with ease. How do our "personal histories of otherness" intersect with or contradict our "politicized identities?" In my research, it was not only my racial identity that had a profound impact on my research, but also my gender, sexuality, age, and nationality as well. Asale Angel-Ajani recounted her first time going to the women's prison in Italy that would be her research site, where she was treated differently due to her racial identity as a black woman. Not only was she forced by guards to verify her U.S. citizenship, but the guards also called the Nigerian women prisoners her "compatriots" and said that she spoke Italian with an Arabic accent. While the guards could not quite place her in a discreet racial category, what they were sure of was that she was racially "other." Angel-Ajani reflects upon this experience: "[M]y race and apparent difference put me squarely in the corner of the detained African women in the eyes of the administration" (2004, 139).

However, it is clear that being an "insider" is by no means static or fixed. For instance, Michael Hanchard problematizes the notion that his blackness would provide automatic entry into Afro-Brazilians' homes and conversations, given that many Brazilians privileged nationality over race (2000, 170). What his blackness *did* provide was "a basis of experiential knowledge" that enabled him to grasp what was being offered as sources of information" (Hanchard 2000, 167). Not only do we experience alternating "insiderness" and "outsiderness" in our research, but our experiences of "insiderness" can often lead to detrimental effects, such as my experience on the beach with the Italian tourists. Sometimes our political commitments and investments contribute to "insider" status with our research participants. My politics of being sex-positive and a sex worker rights advocate made me somewhat of an insider with Aprosba, but the fact that I did not engage in *programas* made me an outsider.

Conclusion

In this chapter, I have tried to weave together reflections on the multiple feminist tensions I encountered in the field with the methodological challenges that I faced in the course of my research. Using an autoethnographic approach that draws from black feminist anthropology, I have highlighted how, for women of color in the field, "taking risks" is often not even a choice. Rather, risks are imposed on us due to our racialized and gendered bodies, particularly when dealing with an already sexualized field site and research topic. I have also attempted to make sense of some of the stories that were told to me that challenged my thinking. The lesson, or "moral of the story," is that while our graduate training, with its emphasis on research proposals, hypotheses, literature reviews, and so on may encourage us to think we already know everything there is to know about our research topic, the experience of being in the field may challenge us in unanticipated ways. Something as simple as being who we are, looking how we look, our politics, and our imagined communities may have an impact on our research in terms of how we are perceived, who will take us seriously, or how we may have visceral experiences that bring us that much closer to knowing/understanding/feeling what our research participants go through on a daily basis.

What does it mean for feminist scholars to "take risks" in our scholarly/activist research endeavors? In my broader project, I map out the diverse and, at times, conflicting understandings of sex tourism. As a cultural anthropologist, the goal in my research is not to judge people's behaviors, desires, and sexual practices, but rather to attempt to understand the cultural worlds in which they are constructing their experiences, their pleasures, and their anxieties. Yet, at times, my willingness to be open to hearing and retelling stories that challenge common assumptions about "sex tourism" has felt risky, particularly as an emerging scholar. If scholars are invested in distancing contemporary anthropology further away from its colonialist past, we must continue to draw upon activist and black feminist anthropology in order to forge a path for a more progressive discipline and a more equitable and just world, no matter what the risks may be.

Notes

I would like to thank the University of Illinois Press for allowing me to include a few pages from my book *Sex Tourism in Bahia: Ambiguous*

Entaglements. Copyright 2013 by the Board of Trustees of the University of Illinois.

1. Here "difficult dialogues" is in reference to the 2009 and 2010 theme of the National Women's Studies Association (NWSA) conferences. NWSA conference organizers utilize this term to explore how difficult dialogues across differences are urgently needed but frequently avoided, either consciously or unconsciously.
2. *Caça-gringas* (hunt foreign women), also known as *pega-turistas* (grab tourists) are known for using their Afro-Brazilian cultural expertise of *capoeira*, dance, and music to attract foreign tourists.
3. In my work, I use "prostitutes" and "sex workers" interchangeably. "Prostitutes" is the preferred term by the women of Aprosba and the larger prostitutes' rights movement in Brazil because it emphasizes that they are referring to women who sell sexual services. However, in academic circles, scholarship that supports sex workers' rights use the term "sex worker" to highlight the fact that sex work is a form of labor and that the workers' rights should be protected like those of any other worker. See Kempadoo and Doezema 1998.
4. Furthermore, Bourgois raises questions about the risk of publishing anthropological accounts of people's lives in times of war, when your words could unwittingly contribute toward more efficient oppression at the hands of counterinsurgency experts.
5. In "Geographies of Blackness: Sex Work and Exclusion in the Tourist Districts of Salvador, Brazil" (2013), I elaborate on the sites of Praça da Sé as a major point of prostitution and tourism.
6. This, and all other names of research informants, is a pseudonym. Interestingly, while "Fabiana" did not mind me using her real name in my dissertation and subsequent publications, I chose to use a pseudonym anyway due to requirements of the Institutional Review Board at Stanford University.
7. The conference was Transforming the Relationship between Work and Citizenship: Production, Reproduction, and Sexuality.
8. Gabriela Leite is the founder of Davida, a prostitutes' rights group in Rio de Janeiro, as well as the Rede Brasileira de Prostitutas (Brazilian Network of Prostitutes).
9. I prefer to use the term "eradicationist" over "abolitionist," because of the latter term's close association with the abolition of African slavery.
10. While Aprosba is the only organization run by and for sex workers in the state of Bahia, it is important to note that it is a part of a national network of prostitutes' rights organizations, the Rede Brasileira de Prostitutas (Brazilian Network of Prostitutes). For

more information, see the following link: http://www.redeprostitutas.org.br. One of the largest such organizations is Davida, which was founded by Gabriela Leite in Rio de Janeiro in 1992. For more information, see the following link: http://www.davida.org.br.

11. Here Altman is quoting from the statement of the Durbar Mahila Samanwaya Committee in India.
12. Fieldnotes, August 11, 2005. For more on tensions between feminists and sex workers, see Kari Lerum (1998).
13. This was from a lecture that Joo-Hyun Kang gave at the Future of Minority Studies Seminar, Queer Politics in Transnational Contexts, facilitated by M. Jacqui Alexander and Minnie Bruce Pratt at Cornell University in July 2009.
14. Marisa's identification as an "exprostitute" was controversial among the other members of Aprosba. She often did outreach in the same neighborhoods where she had previously "battled" as a prostitute. For some, her identifying as an "exprostituta" signified that she thought she was better than those who still were prostitutes. Fabiana pointed out that "no one says they're an ex-lawyer" (interview, May 15, 2007).
15. Aprosba meeting Dec 5, 2006.
16. Perola was an interviewee who disappeared amidst rumors of her having killed a police officer who was known to sexually assault prostitutes. Another informant, Barbara, was a single mother who was once an active participant in Aprosba until she fell in with the wrong crowd when she began working the *ponto* of the Patamares beach and became addicted to drugs.
17. A few notes on Portuguese colloquial terms and my translations are relevant here. An *interesseira* is a woman who dates someone to seek social mobility or material benefits, such as what would be called colloquially in U.S. popular culture, a "gold digger." By calling herself an "*interesseira assumida*," Bel is saying that she proudly proclaims and admits that she is an *interesseira*. *Piriguete* is a colloquial term used in Bahia to refer to promiscuous women. Thus, *piriguetar* means to "whore" or engage in sex work.
18. As of March 17, 2009, $R600 is the equivalent of $262.64, and $R180 is the equivalent of $78.79.
19. For instance, a recent book that focuses on maritime prostitution is Henry Trotter's (2008) *Sugar Girls and Seamen: A Journey into the World of Dockside Prostitution in South Africa*.
20. However, one must beware of assuming that marriage is the great equalizer in power relations, an expression of true, pure love (Giddens 1992).
21. *Sex Tourism in Bahia: Ambiguous Entaglements* features in-depth

ethnographic research on the sexual economies of tourism in this state touted as the "Black Mecca" of Brazil.

22. In terms of swimwear, I learned that a woman's bikini bottom was enough to identify her as Brazilian or a gringa (foreign tourist).
23. Excerpt from fieldnotes, July 25, 2005.

References

Altman, Dennis. 2001. *Global Sex*. Chicago: University of Chicago Press.

Angel-Ajani, Asale. 2004. "Expert Witness: Notes toward Revisiting the Politics of Listening." *Anthropology and Humanism* 29 (2): 133–144.

Behar, Ruth. 1993. *Translated Woman: Crossing the Border with Esperanza's Story*. Boston: Beacon.

Bolles, Lynn. 2001. "Seeking the Ancestors: Forging a Black Feminist Tradition in Anthropology." In *Black Feminist Anthropology:Theory, Politics, Praxis, and Poetics,* ed., Irma McClaurin, 25–43. New Brunswick, NJ: Rutgers University Press.

Bourgois, Philippe. 1991. "Confronting the Ethics of Ethnography: Lessons from Fieldwork in Central America." In *Decolonizing Anthropology: Moving Further toward an Anthropology of Liberation*, ed., Faye V. Harrison, 110–126. Washington, DC, Association of Black Anthropologists, American Anthropological Association.

Cabezas, Amalia. 2004. "Between Love and Money: Sex, Tourism, and Citizenship in Cuba and the Dominican Republic." *Signs: Journal of Women in Culture and Society* 29 (4):987–1015.

Caldwell, Kia Lilly. 2007. *Negras in Brazil: Re-Envisioning Black Women, Citizenship, and the Politics of Identity*. New Brunswick: Rutgers University Press.

Doezema, Jo. 1998. "Forced to Choose: Beyond the Voluntary v. Forced Prostitution Dichotomy." In *Global Sex Workers: Rights, Resistance, Redefinition*, ed., Kamala Kempadoo and Jo Doezema, 34–50. New York: Routledge.

———."2001. "Ouch! Western Feminists' Wounded Attachment to the Third World Prostitute." *Feminist Review* 67:16–38.

Ebron, Paulla. 1997. "Traffic in Men." In *Gendered Encounters: Challenging Cultural Boundaries and Social Hierarchies in Africa*, ed., Maria Grosz-Ngate and Omari H. Kokole, 223–244. New York: Routledge.

Francisco, Luiz. 2006. "Prostitutas vão administrar rádio FM em Salvador." (Prostitutes are going to administer an FM radio station in Salvador). March 8. Folha Online - Agência Folha. Electronic Document, http://www1.folha.uol.com.br/folha/cotidiano/ult95u119147.shtml. Accessed May 13, 2009.

Giddens, Anthony. 1992. *The Transformation of Intimacy: Sexuality, Love and Eroticism in Modern Societies*. Cambridge: Polity Press.

Gordon, Edmund. 1991. "Anthropology and Liberation." In *Decolonizing Anthropology: Moving Further toward an Anthropology of Liberation*, ed., Faye V. Harrison, 149–167. Washington, DC, Association of Black Anthropologists, American Anthropological Association.

Gregory, Steven. 2007. *The Devil behind the Mirror: Globalization and Politics in the Dominican Republic*. Berkeley: University of California Press.

Hale, Charles. 2001. "What Is Activist Research?" *Social Science Research Council Items and Issues* 2 (1–2): 13–15.

———, ed. 2008. *Engaging Contradictions: Theory, Politics, and Methods of Activist Scholarship*. Berkeley: University of California Press.

Hanchard, Michael. 2000. "Racism, Eroticism, and the Paradoxes of a U.S. Black Researcher in Brazil." In *Racing Research, Researching Race: Methodological Dilemmas in Critical Race Studies,* ed., Frances Winddance Twine and Johnathan Warren, 165–185. NY: New York University Press.

Harrison, Faye V., ed. 1991. *Decolonizing Anthropology: Moving Further toward an Anthropology of Liberation*. Washington, DC, Association of Black Anthropologists, American Anthropological Association.

Higginbotham, Evelyn Brooks. 1993. *Righteous Discontent: The Women's Movement in the Black Baptist Church, 1880–1920*. Cambridge, MA: Harvard University Press.

Hine, Darlene Clark. 1989. "Rape and the Inner Lives of Black Women in the Middle West: Preliminary Thoughts on the Culture of Dissemblance." *Signs* 14 (4): 912–20.

Lerum, Kari. 1998. "12-Step Feminism Makes Sex Workers Sick: How the State and the Recovery Movement Turn Radical Women into 'Useless Citizens.'" *Sexuality and Culture* 2: 7–36 (Special issue on Sex Work and Sex Workers).

McClaurin, Irma. 2001a. "Introduction: Forging a Theory, Politics, Praxis, and Poetics of Black Feminist Anthropology." In *Black Feminist Anthropology: Theory, Politics, Praxis, and Poetics,* ed., Irma McClaurin, 1–21. New Brunswick, NJ: Rutgers University Press.

———. 2001b. "Theorizing a Black Feminist Self in Anthropology:

Toward an Autoethnographic Approach." In *Black Feminist Anthropology: Theory, Politics, Praxis, and Poetics,* ed., Irma McClaurin, 49–76. New Brunswick, NJ: Rutgers University Press.

McClintock, Anne. 1995. *Imperial Leather: Race, Gender, and Sexuality in the Colonial Contest*. New York: Routledge.

Miller-Young, Mireille. 2008. "Review of *The Politics of Passion: Women's Sexual Culture in the Afro-Surinamese Diaspora by Gloria Wekker." Feminist Theory* 9 (1):119–120.

———. 2007."Hip Hop Honeys and Da Hustlaz: Black Sexualities in the New Hip Hop Pornography." *Meridians: feminism, race, transnationalism* 8, no. 1: 261–292.

Mohanty, Chandra Talpade. 1991. "Under Western Eyes: Feminist Scholarship and Colonial Discourses." In *Third World Women and the Politics of Feminism,* ed., Chandra Mohanty, Ann Russo, and Lourdes Torres, 51–80. Bloomington: Indiana University Press.

———. 2002. "Under Western Eyes' Revisited: Feminist Solidarity through Anticapitalist Struggles." *Signs: Journal of Women in Culture and Society* 28 (2): 499–535.

Ness, Sally Ann. 2003. *Where Asia Smiles: An Ethnography of Philippine Tourism*. Philadelphia: University of Pennsylvania Press.

Pattanaik, Bandana, and Susanne Thorbek. 2002. *Transnational Prostitution: Changing Patterns in a Global Context*. London: Zed Books.

Rodriguez, Cheryl. 2001. "A Homegirl Goes Home: Black Feminism and the Lure of Native Anthropology." In *Black Feminist Anthropology: Theory, Politics, Praxis, and Poetics,* ed. Irma McClaurin, 233–255. New Brunswick, NJ: Rutgers University Press.

Sanford, Victoria, and Asale Angel-Ajani, eds. 2008. *Engaged Observer: Anthropology, Advocacy and Activism*. New Brunswick, NJ: Rutgers University Press.

Shohat, Ella. 1998. *Talking Visions: Multicultural Feminism in a Transnational Age*. New York: Logo.

Simmons, Kimberly Eison. 2001. "A Passion for Sameness: Encountering a Black Feminist Self in Fieldwork in the Dominican Republic." In *Black Feminist Anthropology: Theory, Politics, Praxis, and Poetics,* ed. Irma McClaurin, 77–101. New Brunswick, NJ: Rutgers University Press.

Sudbury, Julia, and Margo Okazawa-Rey, eds. 2009. *Activist Scholarship: Antiracism, Feminism, and Social Change*. Boulder, CO: Paradigm.

Trotter, Henry. 2008. *Sugar Girls and Seamen: A Journey into the World of Dockside Prostitution in South Africa*. Johannesburg: Jacana.

Van der Veen, Marjolein. 2000. "Beyond Slavery and Capitalism: Producing Class Differences in the Sex Industry." In *Class and Its Others,* ed., J. K. Gibson-Graham, Stephen A. Resnick, and Richard D. Wolff, 121–141. Minneapolis: University of Minnesota Press.

Wekker, Gloria. 2006. *The Politics of Passion: Women's Sexual Culture in the Afro-Surinamese Diaspora*. New York: Columbia University Press.

Williams, Erica Lorraine. 2011. "Moral Panic and Racialized Sexuality: 'Sex Tourism,' 'Trafficking' and the Limits of Transnational Mobility in Bahia." In *Policing Pleasure: Global Reflections on Sex Work and Public Policy*, ed., Patty Kelly and Susan Dewey, 189–219. NY: New York University Press.

———. 2013a. "Geographies of Blackness, Sex Work, and Exclusion in the Tourist Districts of Salvador, Bahia, Brazil." *Gender, Place, Culture: A Feminist Journal of Geography*. Published online May 7.

———. 2013b. *Sex Tourism in Bahia: Ambiguous Entaglements*. Urbana: University of Illinois Press.

9

LATINA BATTERED IMMIGRANTS, CITIZENSHIP, AND INEQUALITIES

Reflections on Activist Research

ROBERTA VILLALÓN

Immigrant women are extremely vulnerable to interpersonal and structural violence. The intersection of their gender, sexuality, nationality, immigration status, race, ethnicity, and social class influences the way in which violence is inflicted and endured and affects the availability of resources for immigrant women to escape and overcome abusive relationships (Abraham 2000; Menjívar and Salcido 2002; Salcido and Adelman 2004). Feminists of color and advocates for battered immigrants' rights have been struggling for acknowledgment of the particular victimization of this group of intimate partner violence survivors. To some extent, their efforts have been fruitful: the Violence Against Women Act (VAWA), which is the main piece of legislation addressing gender violence for all survivors in the United States, includes regulations for special groups, such as battered immigrants. Rights include, the opportunity to access social services and legal protections conducive to breaking free from violent relationships, stabilizing their immigration status, and obtaining citizenship without the active sponsorship of the abusive spouse.[1] Moreover, law enforcement authorities and governmental and nongovernmental service providers have been trained on gender violence and immigration issues, and slowly, they have become more sensitive to cultural diversity, thus enhancing the way in which immigrant survivors are assisted.

Interestingly, however, as I developed activist research at a nonprofit legal organization in Texas, I found that battered immigrants encountered significant obstacles when they tried to end their abusive relationships and become U.S. citizens. Some of these obstacles were embedded in the formalities of the immigration provisions of VAWA. Other obstacles emerged informally at the nonprofit level. While both formal and informal obstacles affected all immigrant survivors of intimate partner violence, it was the most underprivileged immigrants who found the greatest hurdles along the way. In my fieldwork, I found that Latina immigrants who were women of color, native to Mexico, undocumented, in relationships with residents or other undocumented immigrants, LGBTQ, extremely poor, having complicated migration or criminal backgrounds, with few years of formal education, and/or unable to fit within the nonprofit organization's ideal client profile were significantly delayed or even prevented access to citizenship. These exclusionary dynamics not only countered the efforts of advocates for battered immigrants' rights, but also pointed to the pervasiveness of unequal "cultures of citizenship" (Rudrappa 2004, 11).

A feminist-of-color theoretical framework and the methodology of activist research[2] allowed me to reach these findings, findings which would have been kept opaque, if my research was done from above, and uncontested, if my research was done without involvement in the community. Activist research "can be thought of as an approach to doing research, one with a very specific aim—the creation of social change—and one that involves creating particular kinds of relationships among all of those involved in the research process" (Esterberg 2002, 136). Accordingly, as opposed to following a prescription on how to apply this methodology—which would produce "constraining" results (Hale 2008, 3)—activist researchers are led by fundamental principles with the goal "to produce an analysis that retains the integrity of political processes, specific events, diverse actors, and social context while revealing the broader processes at work that may not have been visible to the individual participants or even to the researcher at the time they were engaged in the struggle or when they conducted the research" (Naples 2003, 31).

Three main principles are (1) the "open and democratic" (Esterberg 2002, 136) relationship between researchers and participants; (2) the collaborative way in which knowledge is produced by researchers in dialogue with the traditionally called "research subjects," which indeed are the "knowledgeable, empowered participants" (Hale 2008, 4) with and about whom the research is being developed; and (3) the political implications and applications of developing the research project, which are usually related to provoking social change and bettering whatever oppressive circumstances are affecting the group of people involved in the study.

Inspired by this perspective, I developed an activist research project at a nonprofit organization in Texas that I call Organization for Refugees of America/Organización para Refugiados de América (ORA).[3] At ORA, I was able to learn about the actual experiences of Latina survivors seeking relief through the Violence Against Women Act (VAWA) as well as contribute to addressing their needs and those of the advocates working for them. In this chapter, I reflect on this particular methodological framework. I argue that while activist research is an invaluable tool in order to understand and challenge oppression, one must pay close attention to the manner in which the researcher develops her links to the community as well as to how the voices of all of those involved in the project are brought into the analysis. I look into the nuances of this kind of research projects and discuss the complexities of the liaisons between activist scholars and community. I discuss the differences between the ideal and real ways in which activist scholars and people in the community may develop relationships and consider how activist scholarship is expected to mobilize the researchers' and the community members' knowledge base, and thus, their interactions.

In order to analyze these aspects of activist research methodology I draw on a number of scholars. Specifically, Naples' (2003) discussion about developing a reflexive praxis; Hale's (2006; 2008) thoughts on the contradictions of politically engaged research and work on activist scholarship; Spivak's (1988) ideas on the incorporation of subaltern populations' voices into research; Mani's (1998) development of Spivak's work, particularly her point on acknowledging the relational manner in which these marginalized voices may be included; Menon and Bhasin's (1998) mode of centering the stories of those who had been excluded from mainstream narratives; and Gloria Anzaldúa's (2002) insights on standpoint, testimonies, and the worth of politicizing research to counter hegemonic structures of knowledge and power.

I build my discussion by including primary data that I collected on these issues since I began conducting activist research on violence against Latina immigrants. After providing background information on the nonprofit organization (ORA) where I did activist fieldwork, I share the story of Luisa, a Mexican immigrant survivor of intimate partner violence who sought protection at ORA. Her case condenses much of the complications of such process and allows the reader to more fully capture the contradictions of such reality. As I continue with the analysis, I include excerpts of field notes from participant observation, individual and group interviews, and workshops that I conducted with service providers for battered immigrants. All of these data illustrate the richness and difficulties of activist research and point to how this methodological tool can be better applied for developing scholarship and provoking social change.

Organization for Refugees of America and Activist Research

At the time of my research, the Organization for Refugees of America/Organización para Refugiados de América (ORA) was the only secular organization in central Texas that provided legal services to underserved immigrants.[4] Texas, a border state, has one of the largest numbers of documented and undocumented immigrants in the United States.[5] Texas also has a disproportionately high level of incidents of family violence.[6] ORA devoted four of its five legal programs to immigrant survivors of different kinds of abuse (domestic, sexual, extortion, false imprisonment, human trafficking, and political, racial, ethnic, religious, gender or ideological persecution). An overwhelming majority of ORA's clients were from Mexico and Central America, but ORA served immigrants from all over the world. ORA, with its ethnically diverse staff, presented itself as an inclusive organization, providing services to all immigrants, regardless of native language or ethnic, religious, or political background. In this way, ORA allowed me to explore the workings of culturally sensitive organizations, which feminist researchers both celebrated as safe havens for immigrants (Abraham 2000; Menjívar and Salcido 2002) and criticized as colonial and patriarchal (Menon and Bhasin 1998; Mindry 2001; Ong 2003; Rudrappa 2004).

Originally, ORA was a politically radical, volunteer-based, grassroots group focused on advocacy, legal, and social change. However, it gradually transformed into a politically moderate, employee-based, nonprofit organization focused on providing legal services. This organizational history helped me think about the effects of the institutionalization processes that most nonprofits have gone through in the last thirty years (Fox Piven and Cloward 1977; Perlmutter 1994; INCITE! Women of Color Against Violence 2007; Kivel 2007; Alvarez 1999). Since the 1980s, nonprofit organizations have become increasingly important in the provision of social services and implementation of community development programs as a result of policies intended to reduce the size of the state and its welfare capacities (Trudeau 2008). An essential piece of the "shadow state" (Wolch 1990), nonprofit organizations have grown in their function as institutions providing "the arena, the mechanisms, and the point of institutional access through which the offer of citizenship is extended and social integration can be accomplished" (Lake and Newman 2002, 110). In this context, nonprofit organizations devoted to immigration matters have been located at the crux of citizenship access, particularly when they serve poor immigrants who are in compromised situations due to precarious labor conditions and unstable immigration status—ORA being a case in point.

At the same time, gender violence–based legislation like the Violence Against Women Act (VAWA) has underscored the importance of the role of nonprofits as intermediary organizations between immigrant survivors of intimate partner violence and governmental immigration authorities. Indeed, battered immigrants have been strongly encouraged to obtain the formal assistance of advocates, social workers, counselors, and legal representatives in order to seek relief through VAWA (Family Violence Prevention Fund 2005; WomensLaw 2009). While these services can be obtained through the private sector, poor battered immigrants must rely on community and nonprofit organizations offering services at low or no cost. These organizations are typically the one (and usually last) resort for survivors seeking escape from lives of abuse and dependency. Thus, the "gatekeeper" role of nonprofit workers—with the capacity to facilitate or impede battered immigrants' access to citizenship—has become increasingly significant (Villalón 2010, 79).

While I developed activist research at ORA, I worked for two years as a part-time volunteer intern in its battered immigrant assistance program. The program provided legal services, free of charge, to low-income immigrants who were eligible to apply for citizenship under VAWA. As noted, through VAWA,[7] battered immigrants are given the opportunity to access social services and legal protections conducive to breaking free from violent relationships, stabilizing their immigration status, and obtaining citizenship without the active sponsorship of the abusive spouse. In order to do so, an immigrant survivor must prove that (1) she was married to or in a common law union with a U.S. citizen or a legal permanent resident in good faith; (2) they resided together as wife and husband; (3) she was subject to domestic violence and/or extreme cruelty during the marriage in the United States; and (4) she is a person of "good moral character" (that is, does not have a criminal record). Once the VAWA self-petition is approved by immigration authorities, the battered immigrant is granted deferred action on deportation procedures and is allowed to apply for an employment authorization (renewable yearly) while she waits for her legal permanent residency application to be processed and granted. After three years of continuous and lawful presence as a legal permanent resident in the United States, VAWA self-petitioners may be able to apply for citizenship.[8]

If the battered immigrant was married to an undocumented immigrant, or separated but not divorced from previous spouses while engaged in the abusive relationship, she can apply for a U visa instead of a VAWA self-petition. This visa offers temporary status for up to four years (meaning deferred action on deportation procedures) and authorization to work in the United States for one year with the option to renew the permit twice. In order to obtain a U visa, the battered immigrant has to collaborate with the police on the scrutiny of her abuser's deeds against her. The police have to certify to the United States Citizenship and Immigration Services (USCIS) that the battered immigrant was victimized and that she has been helpful with law enforcement in the crime investigation. If the police issue such certification, USCIS may grant the U visa for the immigrant victim. Once the immigrant has been continuously and lawfully living in the United States as a U visa holder for more than three years, she may apply for legal permanent residency. A U visa holder may be granted the latter if her U visa status was not revoked, and she did not "unreasonably refuse to provide assistance to an official or law enforcement agency investigating or prosecuting the person(s) who committed the crime that made her eligible for U visa status" (WomensLaw 2012).

At ORA, I did prescreening phone and in-person interviews, collected immigration and abuse histories and translated them from Spanish to English, prepared immigration forms and citizenship applications, and performed other tasks on an as-needed basis. My direct participation in these activities allowed me to collect data about a host of immigrant women's experiences: how they presented themselves; spoke and wrote about their experiences of migration and violence; expressed their demands and concerns about going through the citizenship application process; showed their feelings, fears, frustrations, and hopes; made sense of their situations; and reacted to the formal and informal requirements of the VAWA application process. Furthermore, my participation allowed me to observe the legal assistants, attorneys, and other ORA staff in their interactions with the immigrants (or "clients," as they were called by the organization's workers). For example, I noted the ways in which ORA staff expressed themselves; their oral and body language used with both clients and co-workers; their reactions to the histories of abuse, and their attitudes in their dealings with law enforcement officers and immigration authorities.

I also participated in meetings related to immigration and women's issues to which ORA staff members were invited on a regular basis (such as legal advocacy and violence against women conferences). In these meetings, I collected source data on how legal and social workers organized their activities and modified their services on the basis of changes in legislation and one another's working experiences. After my work day, I recorded my field observations in journal form, including not only immigrants' and staff members' stories, but also my own role, feelings, and thoughts (Esterberg 2002).

I complemented my participant observation by conducting personal interviews with attorneys, legal assistants, and other ORA staff. Through these interviews, I gathered primary data on how nonprofit workers comprehended and implemented immigration and citizenship norms and regulations. I asked them about their thoughts and feelings about their tasks and skills; their commitment to the state, immigration authorities, and funders; and their responsibilities to the local community and the immigrants. We talked about how they saw themselves in their interactions with all of these individuals and organizations. We discussed what they wanted to change about their jobs and/or about gender violence–based and immigration laws. While I did the interviews, I did not follow a rigid form, but instead adopted a more informal dialogue with the interviewees. This form not only allowed me to "emphasize the informant's world of meaning and utilize the informant's categories of understanding" rather than my own (Sjoberg and Nett 1997, 211), but also reinforced the open, democratic, dialogic, and reflective principles of activist research.

In following another fundamental aspect of activist research, I shared my findings in a collaborative fashion with ORA staff, other battered immigrant advocates, and the community of Latina immigrants and survivors of gender violence both during and after my field research. While I was developing the project, I frequently talked about my observations with ORA staff to check my accuracy as well as if my labor was conducive to addressing the needs of both the organization and the battered immigrants. After I completed a full-length write-up of my findings, I presented my analysis to ORA staff, first in writing, and later through a workshop as well as individual and group informal interviews.[9] All of these instances added a reflective layer from the perspective of ORA staff, which tested the validity of my analysis and was critical to furthering the understanding of the processes at play at the organization.

I also conducted workshops at battered immigrants' advocate trainings and meetings where participants (nonprofit and governmental immigrants' advocates) reflected upon the formal and informal barriers that stand in the way of battered immigrants' quest for citizenship. Workshop participants proposed means to avoid or dismantle these barriers as well. These events provided me with an opportunity for contextualizing my work at ORA by obtaining other advocates' perspectives on how they have helped (or not) immigrants in their organizations, what they expected from immigrants as they were obtaining services, and how they tried to overcome organizational and legal limitations. Moreover, these opportunities furthered the links between academia and community (another main goal of activist research) so that the findings did not linger uncontested by those who were intimately involved in these matters beyond scholarly circles.

As I developed the research, I adopted a "reflective practice," as theorized by feminist ethnographer Nancy Naples, through which I was able to incorporate my standpoint and also remain "sensitive to the perspectives of others" and critically aware of the "power dynamics" at play in the community where the research was taking place (2003, 41). For instance, even though my background gave me the opportunity to quickly gain access to and build trust with the immigrants and the nonprofit workers, my involvement at ORA posed some problems regarding my double role as researcher and worker. While I was performing ORA's job by respecting the organization's rules and interests, I also had a critical understanding of the activities and processes that were taking place during my working days. To cope with tensions resulting from my double role, I maintained a transparent attitude with the members of the agency and the clients and regularly wrote about my observations, thoughts, and feelings in a journal. I also paid close attention to how my personal characteristics shaped "ethnographic encounters" (Naples 2003, 41) "to reveal the inequalities and processes of domination that shape the 'field'" (Naples 2003, 38). I wondered how my occupation, nationality, immigration status, race, ethnicity, gender, sexual orientation, socioeconomic status, and age permeated my relationship with both battered immigrants and ORA staff.

On the one hand, the immigrants tended to be comfortable with me because of my position as a volunteer and researcher, my sympathy as a woman survivor of intimate partner violence, my youth, our shared status as Latina immigrants in the United States (which took precedence over my light skin color or seeming whiteness), and my open attitude about sexual preferences. Class differences were mostly manifested in two aspects: immigration status and education. My documented immigration status as a researcher and my ability to speak and write Spanish and English fluently differentiated me from the immigrants seeking services at ORA, who appeared comfortable with this gap since I was working with them to complete their citizenship application process before USCIS. Rather, I was often the one who became upset because of the imbalances resulting from their underprivileged position as opposed to ORA staff's or mine.

On the other hand, ORA staff tended to be comfortable around me and grateful for my volunteer work. They perceived me as similar to them in terms of class background, gender, openness in regard to sexual preferences, and age and different from them in terms of my nationality and occupation. Some of them took me as a foreign focal reference with whom they could either clarify or discuss cultural differences; others maintained some distance as they recalled my double role as a volunteer and researcher and occasionally thought of me as threatening their authority at the workplace. By maintaining a critical awareness of my position as an "outsider within" (Hill Collins 1986, S14), I was then able to reap the most fruits from such a position's advantages and to work through its disadvantages.

Overall, the further I moved forward into the project, the more I realized the revealing potential of activist methodology as a research tool. As I mentioned before, I am convinced that if I had not developed activist scholarship, I would not have been able to uncover the processes that affected Latina survivors of intimate partner violence in such depth and complexity. In my book based on this research, I included large portions of my field notes and a significant number of excerpts of interviews, so the experiences of all the immigrants with whom I worked at ORA and their interactions with the organization's staff remained at the front and center of my analysis (Villalón 2010).

In a similar spirit, in what follows, I share, at length, the story of Luisa; a Mexican immigrant survivor of intimate partner violence who approached ORA. Her story, far from being an exception, was representative of many of the battered immigrants I met in the course of my research, including Claudia, Julia, Laura, Martha, Rosa, Manuela, Ana, Susana, Clara, Silvana, Rosario, Mónica, Samuel, Yolanda, Patricia, Ramona, and Leticia, who found a similarly unfortunate fate in their search of justice.[10] By incorporating Luisa's story in full, I help the reader appreciate the complicated and intense texture of the processes that I was able to unveil through activist research.

The Case of Luisa

Luisa was a survivor of physical and psychological domestic violence perpetuated by her partner, Richard, a U.S. citizen, who was incarcerated after the last violent episode. Luisa approached ORA in search of legal help in regards to her immigration status because the police had informed her of her rights to apply for a U visa,[11] which would allow her to stay and work in the United States legally on the basis of the abuse she had endured. In our first meeting, the intake appointment, I followed the steps to gather as much information as possible in order to have the attorney review her case and decide whether Luisa could become a client of the organization or not.

The appointment was unusually long; it lasted almost three hours as opposed to a typical one-hour meeting. The first set of questions regarding biographical information was daunting for Luisa. She had difficulty remembering exact dates about her marriage and the births of her children. She could not recall precise information on her entry to the United States or the addresses of the various places where she had resided. Regarding her marital status, Luisa shamefully told me that she had not married Richard because she was "Casada, bien casada" ("Married, really married") back in Mexico. Then she explained to me that even though she was still married, she had lost touch with her husband since she migrated to the United States years ago. Luisa got involved with Richard as she had considered herself separated and lived with him for several years. Luisa had four children, all of whom had different fathers. Her children were still living in Mexico.

Regarding her history of migration, it took me more than an hour just to clarify when she had left Mexico and arrived in the United States. She told me that she had come in the early nineties and that she had never returned to Mexico, but as I went through the birth dates and places of her children, she told me that three of them were born in Mexico in the midnineties. While I thought she had gotten confused between the early nineties and the early 2000s, she insisted, "No Miss, 1990 . . . But, no, it was 1990 . . . 1990, I'm telling you!" It was after many explanations that she realized that we were currently in the 2000s and not the 1990s. Luisa laughed, embarrassed, when she realized it.

As we began to talk about her current and past addresses, she could not recall exact information and was certain about not possessing rental leases since her residences had been arranged informally, including her current one. After Richard was incarcerated, Luisa moved out and rented a room from a woman who did not even give her the key to the apartment: "I have to leave the apartment at the same time the other woman does, and then I have to wait outside until she comes back from work late at night." As I heard about her current living situation, I gave her information about shelters for battered women. Luisa showed interest in them; "Can you help me? I don't have a phone in the apartment." I let her use the phone at ORA (the closest public phone she had was miles away). As soon as the person in the shelter picked up the phone and replied in English, Luisa handed me the receiver, "I don't know what they are saying, Miss. Please . . ." As soon as I began talking about Luisa, the shelter apologized, "We don't have any vacancy at the moment."

Then, Luisa called another shelter where they spoke Spanish. After ten minutes or so of questions, they told her that they could not accept her because her children were not residing with her, and their shelter was "exclusively for mothers with children." Finally, she called a third shelter, which was further away from the city where Luisa lived. Nobody spoke Spanish, so Luisa asked me to talk with them in English. They had space available, "She can stay with us from today onwards. What time will she arrive?" I offered to give Luisa a ride that same afternoon, but she reminded me, "I don't know when I will be able to get in the apartment, late at night probably . . . I can't go to the shelter without my things, and they are all in there, in the apartment."

As we spoke, one of the ORA staff came to the office and told us that we had a message from one of the shelters saying that they could make an exception and take Luisa in (this was the shelter that only accepted mothers with children—after all, Luisa was a mother whose children were back in Mexico). Excited, Luisa said that she preferred this option because it was in town, and she could use public transportation to go to work. Then, I canceled the arrangements with the other shelter, thanked them, and apologized. We called the shelter for mothers and arranged for her to move in there the following morning. I would pick Luisa up by car the next day as she could not bring all of her belongings on the bus, on her own.

After these preparations, I explained to Luisa the next steps at ORA (her file would be reviewed by the attorney and then, in our next meeting, I was going to be able to let her know what her options were). Next, I helped her look at the bus map and schedule to see if she could take a bus from ORA to her place of residence. It was very hard for her to understand me, so I walked her almost all the way to the bus stop. She thanked me and continued to walk with a doubtful and fearful demeanor; "Bye, Luisa, see you tomorrow morning. Take care!" When I arrived back at ORA, Cathy, the lawyer, and Maggie and Jenna, the two legal assistants, expressed their surprise about the length of my meeting with Luisa: "Oh, Roberta . . . You are too nice."

The following morning I went to pick Luisa up, but I did not find her. I was worried; I thought something could have happened to to her, or maybe I had gotten a wrong address from her. I went to ORA, and after an hour or so of trying, reached her friend by telephone—"I'm sure that Luisa is working . . . Yes, I'll tell her about the shelter and the next appointment. No problem, Miss. Thank you." I called the shelter and explained what had happened, "Don't you worry. We will do our best to get in touch with her."

Before the next appointment, Luisa called me to let me know that she was not going to be able to make it because "a work opportunity that she could not miss had come up." We rescheduled our meeting, and when I asked her if she had gotten in touch with the shelter, she told me that she had. But, "I have to call them again to see how I will bring my things over—I can't bring my bag, the table, my bookcase, and the other things on the bus, as I told you." As much as I understood how important her belongings were for Luisa, I thought that she was not convinced that moving to the shelter was the right thing for her; perhaps she feared the loss of proximity to the one friend who had provided her with emotional, informational, and material support; perhaps she felt that living in a shelter was depriving her of her autonomy (as opposed to what shelter advocates aim for, that is, to provide a safe haven for survivors and help them regain their sense of self and independence) (Schechter 1982; Rudrappa 2004). Not possessing the keys to the apartment where she was living was not as disturbing for her as I had originally thought.

In our rescheduled appointment, I was excited to tell Luisa that ORA had approved her case—she qualified to apply for a U visa. I explained the steps to follow, particularly the requirement of collaborating with the police in the investigation of the crime committed against her, as well as the benefits of applying for this visa—deferred action on deportation procedures and employment authorization. Then I asked, "So, Luisa, do you want to go ahead with this?" Luisa, confused and fearful, replied, "Well, I don't know, miss. What do you think? Should I?"

Luisa's doubts probably emerged from listening to how lengthy and intricate the U visa application process was going to be. Moreover, she probably felt threatened by the fact that she was being asked to keep an open connection with the police. Immigrants, particularly those unauthorized, commonly feared the police because they had been known to profile them and collaborate with immigration authorities. At the same time, survivors of domestic violence tended to have mixed feelings about criminalizing abusers, especially if they had to contribute with the police investigation against them. After I explained the U visa application procedure in detail one more time, Luisa seemed to overcome her (fairly characteristic and reasonable) fears: she agreed to go through the process.

The supervisor of Luisa's case, Courtney, was ORA's expert on U visas. She told me to "go easy on the case, because until we get the certification from the police, we should not waste resources on it." I tried to make progress on other matters related to the case as much as possible in order to have everything ready for when the certification arrived. Luisa missed many appointments (because of temporary work opportunities and even threats from the abuser's relatives), so the pace was very slow in comparison to other cases on which I worked. Whenever we met, Luisa raised questions about her immigration application status: it was difficult for her to understand that despite all the paperwork done, there was no news about her case. She also expressed her fear of her abuser and his family's threats, particularly about being deported: "I'm so scared, Miss; what can I do? I thought all of these would help, but you tell me there's nothing yet." Luisa's confusion and concerns were legitimate, especially at a time when raids of undocumented workers were increasing and debates about restricting immigration laws flooded the media. While my explanations were not necessarily pleasing, at least she knew who to call and what not to say or do if she were apprehended by immigration officers.

I followed up on Luisa's case with Courtney at least once a month because I could not believe how long the police were taking to give her certification, especially because Richard was indeed incarcerated with charges of domestic violence against Luisa. Courtney was not surprised at the length of the wait: "I wait an average of four months to receive responses from the police." After seven and a half months from the intake appointment, I received an email from Courtney: "The police denied Luisa's certification. They claim she did not cooperate in the investigation. They called Luisa, but she did not return their phone call." When I asked Courtney if there was anything Luisa could do about it she explained to me that she could call the police and explain that she never got their message because she had moved several times. Luisa followed our instructions, and in her conversation with the police, she reiterated that she was willing to collaborate in the investigation of her abuser's crime against her.

After several weeks, I tried to get in touch with Courtney to check on Luisa's case, but I did not hear back from her. Three months later (that is, eleven months after the intake appointment with Luisa), I finally received an update from Courtney: the police had refused once again to certify Luisa, and consequently, ORA was not able to proceed with her U visa petition. Courtney disagreed with the police's double denial of Luisa's certification; clearly frustrated, she told me that it was "plain bullshit." I asked her if we could further complain. Hastily she replied, "I cannot take care of her case at the moment. I'm busy with other U visa applicants." As I left her office, Courtney said, "*Pobrecita*" (poor thing) and clarified that she would get in touch with her to let her know about her options to complete a victim's compensation petition. Upon receiving the news from Courtney, Luisa never came back to ORA.

Learning from Luisa's Case: Formal and Informal Barriers to Citizenship

Unfortunately, Luisa's case is typical of the fate of many battered immigrants who approached the nonprofit organization. Her case is also representative as it illustrates the revealing potential of activist methodology as a research tool as well as its promise to advance struggles to dismantle the particularly oppressive circumstances and needs of minority battered women. By developing activist scholarship from a feminist of color perspective in my years of research at ORA, I found that independently from their histories of abuse and legal entitlements under the Violence Against Women Act (VAWA), immigrant survivors confronted additional formal and informal barriers when they tried to break free from violence and dependency and become U.S. citizens.

Formally, battered immigrants are bound by the immigration provisions of VAWA, which by mirroring the broader family-based immigration law system, prioritize heterosexual, economically self-sufficient, married U.S. citizens as arbiters of citizenship for immigrant spouses. Therefore, even if battered immigrants can self-petition for citizenship through VAWA without the sponsorship of their abusive spouses, their ability to do so depends on (a) their marital status and sexual identity, (b) their abuser's nationality and immigration status, and their own country of origin, and (c) their socioeconomic capacities.

First, the marital status and sexual identity of abused immigrants determine the options available for them. VAWA provides full protection for married, heterosexual immigrants by allowing them to self-petition for citizenship as survivors of abusive intimate partners. However, VAWA partially protects battered immigrants who are not married or in a common law union with their abusive partners or who are separated but not divorced from a previous spouse while being involved with the perpetrators. This group of immigrant survivors may be able to obtain immigration relief through a U visa (like Luisa), which in comparison to VAWA self-petition for citizenship, is a less certain and more difficult process to traverse given the fact that immigrants must collaborate with the police in the investigation of the crime. Battered LGBTQ immigrants are the least protected of all: because their intimate relationships are not considered legal at the federal level, they cannot self-petition for citizenship through VAWA. They can only apply for a U visa as survivors of violent crimes like rape, sexual assault, abusive sexual contact, and sexual exploitation (but not domestic violence) committed against them in the United States. Besides the complications and disadvantages of U visas relative to the benefits of citizenship self-petitions, battered LGBTQ immigrants face the sociocultural barriers rooted in sexism and homophobia (Luibhéid 2002; Calvo 2004; National Resource Center on Domestic Violence 2007).

Second, the national origin and immigration status of the abuser determine the options available for battered spouses, no matter the intensity of the abuse. If abusers are U.S. citizens by birthright or naturalization, their victims can obtain legal permanent residency as soon as their VAWA applications are approved and apply for citizenship three years later. If abusers are legal permanent residents, their victims can also obtain legal permanent residency and apply for citizenship three years later. However, the waiting period to obtain residency varies depending on the nationality of the battered immigrant, ranging from less than a year to more than eight, according to the length of the backlog that the United States Citizenship and Immigration Services (USCIS) has in processing petitions from the applicant's country of origin. The longer a petitioner has to wait for her residency, the longer the path toward citizenship.

The noncitizen status of the abusers damages their victims not only in terms of the length of the process, but also in terms of its certainty. On the one hand, if the abusive resident is deported (that is, loses his status as legal permanent resident) due to an incident of domestic violence, the survivor has two years to file a VAWA self-petition, or her chances to gain legal status perish. On the other hand, if the abusive resident is deported due to other reasons before the VAWA application of the battered immigrant is approved by USCIS, all chances to gain legal status for the applicant end instantaneously. If abusers are neither United States citizens nor legal permanent residents (that is, if they are unauthorized immigrants), victims cannot self-petition for citizenship but rather apply for a U visa. As I explained before, U visas provide the longest and least certain path to stabilize the immigration status of survivors.

Third, the socioeconomic status of battered immigrants shapes the chances they have to access VAWA's benefits. On the one hand, the costs associated with the application process are high because of USCIS fees, the charges for supporting documentation, and legal representation. While this burden has been partially lifted by the assistance of pro-bono lawyers and nonprofit legal organizations like ORA, the costs that are not waived delay or impede the application process for the immigrants most in need. On the other hand, VAWA applications require immigrants to possess and provide documents, bills, payment receipts, and health reports and to trust official authorities, such as policemen, and government bureaucrats. These requirements weed out the neediest immigrants, who either lack the ability to collect personal documents and receipts to prove identity and common residency with the abusive spouse, may not ever have possessed such papers, or may not have been able to systematically file them or access them because of their controlling abusers. Simultaneously, police reports (or the collaboration with the criminal investigation in the case of U visas) and the inclusion of psychological evaluations are a threatening obstacle for the applicants, who not only fear the police but also find counseling too much of a foreign and demanding practice. As a result, the poorest immigrants continue to find the process unaffordable, complicated, and thus, unattainable.[12]

All together, the formal barriers that stand in the way of battered immigrants' access to citizenship replicate long-standing gender, sexual, racial, ethnic, and class hierarchies of the United States. So, as much as the immigration provisions in VAWA have made a positive impact on many survivors, inherited biases from the broader family-based immigration system limit the reach of the benefits. The state utilizes immigration laws to sustain its sovereignty (by regulating which individuals are welcome to join a given population), build nationhood (by setting citizenship ideals), and control productivity (by stimulating or preventing foreign laborers to legally join its working force) along gender, sexual, racial, ethnic, and class lines. In the United States, immigration laws have historically prioritized men over women, married over unmarried, heterosexual over LGBTQ, white over person of color, European over non-European immigrants, Christian over other religious identities, citizen over foreigner, and richer over poor (Haney López 1996; Glenn 2002; Hing 2004; Ngai 2004). Confined by these laws, the spirit of VAWA—to protect all survivors of intimate partner violence regardless of their gender, sexual orientation, race, ethnicity, class, or immigration status—is truncated by such overarching exclusionary ideals and institutions.

Besides these formal barriers inscribed into the law, additional ones informally emerge at the level of the nonprofit organization. As I developed activist research at ORA, I found that advocates created tacit parameters that guided their dealings with battered immigrants seeking services. They expected battered immigrants to present themselves and behave in particular ways in their frequent interactions with them and in their potential interactions with official authorities. As I paid close attention to ORA staff's practices, thoughts, feelings, and case management decisions, I found that immigrants who were compliant, tidy, constant, resolute, autonomous, responsible, deferent, considerate, discreet, redeemable, considerably recovered from the battering, and good parents (when applicable) were prioritized by nonprofit staff, regardless of their traumatic past and eligibility under VAWA. Immigrants who fit the "ideal client" profile not only were supposed to be easier to handle throughout the application process, but also were supposed to have simple, solid cases that immigration authorities would most likely approve. This attitude corresponded with organizational frameworks focused less on human rights advocacy and more on service provision with an emphasis on obtaining funding through satisfying funders' requirements, which usually awarded high volumes of approved VAWA applications.

These informal barriers, coupled with the formal ones, affected all immigrant survivors of intimate partner violence. However, my research showed that it was the least privileged immigrants who encountered the most hurdles along the way, regardless of their histories of abuse. Latina immigrants of color who were native to Mexico, undocumented, in violent relationships with residents or other undocumented immigrants, and/or LGBTQ found greater disadvantages. Furthermore, battered immigrants were significantly delayed or even prevented access to citizenship if they were extremely poor, had few, if any, years of formal education, had complicated migration or criminal backgrounds, and/or were unable to fit within the nonprofit organization's "ideal client" profile.

Reflections on Activist Research

The use of activist methodology allowed me to uncover the workings of the formal and informal obstacles that stand along the way of battered immigrants' access to justice. The potential of activist research as a revealing methodological tool, however, was furthered by its collaborative and applied character: I was also able to think about and elaborate suggestions on how to dismantle such exclusionary institutions and practices together with advocates and Latina survivors. The fact that these suggestions were created in collaboration with those who were part of the community with whom I was developing my research had two major, interrelated, consequences. First, the traditionally hierarchical, oppressive, or colonial dynamics of scholarship (derived from the scholar/expert versus research subject/object dichotomy) were significantly reduced. Second, the chances for the collaboratively created scholarship to be critically adopted by those who needed it the most (in this case, Latina battered immigrants and their advocates) significantly increased (Naples 2003; Esterberg 2002; Hale 2008).

At the same time, the practice of the collaborative and applied qualities of activist research was quite challenging: How would members of the organization and community react to findings that were controversial, critical, or negative? Would they open up and continue to allow for activist research to be developed in their setting, or would they shut down and cease to participate in the project? How would the working relationship between us change? How could the project and its findings survive beyond the potential emergence of tensions? In order to discuss how activist scholars might navigate these challenges, next I focus on my experience at ORA, particularly, on the various instances when I shared my analytical observations with ORA staff and how their responses, in turn, fed the research.

To begin with, ORA staff members were aware of my research purposes and my intention of actively collaborating with the organization's needs in order to better serve battered immigrants. All the while I was involved as an intern for the immigrant survivors of intimate partner violence program at ORA, I would informally bring up comments and observations with the goals of testing the resonance of my views and thinking about how to take action together with ORA staff. I found these informal exchanges to be very fruitful for the development of the research because they not only reaffirmed the usefulness of my active participation for the organization and the battered immigrants' community, but also served as indicators of what issues I should continue or begin to focus on research- and workwise.

A little more than halfway into my field research, I presented my preliminary findings to ORA staff with the double aim of sharing what I had been able to compile so far as well as obtaining their feedback on my observations: Did my preliminary findings make any sense to them? Would they share their thoughts on these observations? Were they interested in working on some of the issues that I (and they) had identified as problematic, yet solvable? Could they clarify some of the doubts I had? Researchwise, this was also a rich instance; particularly because it revealed working contradictions of the nonprofit organization as well as important limitations of activist research. First, ORA staff appreciated my labor and the analysis, and they also seemed to agree with my views. They expressed their willingness to let me continue with my research while I was "doing such great work as a volunteer at the organization."[13] In addition, they were open to the suggestions of trying to improve access to counseling for battered immigrants and exploring ways to provide childcare services or more child-friendly practices in the organization. But they were clear to point out that if anybody, I should be the one person taking care of it, since they were already overwhelmed with their caseloads.

After a couple of weeks of gathering information and developing some ideas on how to take care of both issues, I shared the information with ORA staff. It was then that I realized that I had misinterpreted their message. Their asking me to take care of it was more probably meant to be taken as a deterrent rather than as an encouragement: my proposals to facilitate counseling access and organize childcare services ended up finding an institutional void. In other words, the proposals were shunned, and I was then given a clear message not to "waste time pursuing such ideas."[14]

Despite frustrations, I took this "incident" as part of the data to be collected, data that would help me understand both the dynamics of the nonprofit organization and the nuances of activist researchers' proposals. On the one hand, I took note on how overburdened staff felt as well as the ways in which they drew specific boundaries on their tasks (like focusing on processing legal paperwork alone while outsourcing the labor, and responsibility, of psychological and family assistance for battered immigrants). On the other hand, I reflected on how ORA staff framed my double role at ORA as volunteer and researcher: while they were interested in my labor as an intern for the program for battered immigrants, they preferred to keep me at bay; some staff perceived too much involvement on my part as a threat to their jobs as well as an invasion of an outsider telling them what to do differently. Consequently, I thought about how to limit my volunteer work (since it was not my intention to take anybody's job away) and also how to better share my observations and ideas in a way that they would find productive as opposed to insidious.

Accordingly, when I completed a full-length final write-up of my findings, I tried to organize a meeting with ORA staff where I would once again test my views and obtain their feedback. Because of coordination difficulties, I was only able to share my analysis in writing. This means of communication generated very little reaction on their part. I sought to overcome this second "incident" since I did not want my final writing to neither include their views and reactions nor have at least the potential of being of any use to the organization. One year later, I was finally able to organize a workshop at the organization where I presented a report on my analysis and gathered ORA staff's thoughts. Because at the time of this workshop only three of the people who used to work while I was doing research at ORA were still there,[15] I also organized group and individual informal interviews with them. All of these exchanges were particularly fruitful for the final development of the research given that I was able to strengthen the analysis in a collaborative fashion, while adding a reflective layer from ORA staff's perspective, both of which were absolutely critical to contextualizing and furthering the understanding of the processes at play at this kind of nonprofit organization.

In the last workshop and interviews, I made sure to frame my analysis of ORA within the broader context of the immigration system and nonprofit organizations, while emphasizing the important role that ORA and its staff played in providing services to underserved immigrants as well as their key position as gatekeepers of citizenship. Key to these exchanges was my invitation for them to express their thoughts on my analysis as well as to brainstorm ideas on how to tackle those formal and/or informal barriers that they identified as being problematic.

Overall, ORA staff members were attentive and found my analysis accurate and sensible. They carefully listened and thoughtfully shared their comments and questions. First, they agreed with my depiction of their role as gatekeepers (or brokers) of citizenship between the state and the immigrants, a role that emphasized their enormous power and responsibility in being the ones who could either open or close immigrants' access to stabilizing their immigration status and becoming autonomous individuals in the United States. Then, as I explained the problematic formal barriers of VAWA's immigration provisions, they expressed their discontent, but, because these barriers were inscribed in the law as inherited from the broader immigration system, many advocates took the position that while unfortunate, these hierarchies were unavoidable. They also claimed that despite its biases, VAWA at least provided some battered immigrant women the opportunity to break free from abuse and become citizens; in other words, they believed that the disadvantages were counterbalanced by the advantages of VAWA's immigration provisions.

The section on informal barriers was the one that triggered most of the reaction on the part of ORA staff. Among their laughter and jokes, they spoke up and collectively confirmed that they "dreaded working with clients who cried a lot; clients who brought and could not control their kids in appointments; clients who called too much (many times per week, more than once a day), and clients who were too demanding (the ones with higher economic status)."[16] If the clients behaved this way, the staff members explained that they "didn't rush to make appointments with them."[17] The staff's consensus on this matter seemed to work as a relief on their concerns about the consequences of leaving these clients unattended—even if before they may have informally had shared their frustrations about what I identified as "problem clients," this seemed to be the first occasion when they saw it as a group or institutional issue. They also seemed to be able, for the first time, to share their preoccupations about the effects that this differential treatment would bring to the clients. ORA staff also expressed their disorientation on how they could dismantle the organization's informal barriers. Lucy, for instance, said, "I realize that these client preferences ended up reinforcing the barriers you are talking about (particularly social class). But, I'm not sure what we can do about it."[18]

In response to this, I shared my suggestion of setting time apart to discuss these matters at the organizational level, a suggestion that was received with enthusiasm. I also pointed to the importance to think about what was happening at ORA in the broader context of nonprofits: staff's role as gatekeepers, the formal and informal barriers were not unique to ORA, but common to many other nonprofit organizations providing services to battered immigrants. They were curious to read about what was going on in other institutions, so I offered references to articles, reports, and books written about and by other organizations that had identified similar patterns and were working on dealing with them. Additionally, I suggested that fostering network communication through trainings or conferences with similar groups could help as well. I signaled the relevance of keeping both a reflective and a political attitude with regard to their work given their power as gatekeepers of citizenship. The contextualization of my analysis of ORA's workings among other nonprofits calmed some of the anxiety resulting from hearing such a critical report.

However, the initial enthusiastic reception of the report/workshop was tamed in my individual and group interviews with staff members who used to work at ORA while I was doing field research. Cathy told me that my analysis "made sense but it was very difficult to address when working—abstractly was OK, but practically was impossible."[19] Similarly, Jenna believed that my analysis made sense, even if "it was hard to hear."[20] However, she did not think that change was necessary; "We do a very good thing."[21] Jenna and Cathy resisted my proposal to address the informal disparities at ORA. Cathy explained, "I don't think this would work. It wouldn't be welcomed. People would be like . . . 'What the fuck?!?' if I asked them to spend time talking about dropped cases while they have been working plenty on other cases that had been selected and approved."[22]

Courtney, who used to be ORA's U visa expert, reflected on the organization's role as a gatekeeper and its resistance to change. She argued that funding conditions and the growth of the demand of services has changed the nonprofit's attitude:

> If ORA didn't get any more clients, the story would be different. I remember that at the very beginning of the U visa program at ORA, I had very few clients. I had to do a lot of outreach to get enough clients. But later on, I had so many, that prioritizing or dropping clients didn't matter. There was a Nigerian woman, one of the first cases I had . . . I had so much time [on] my hands that I did everything I could until I got the certification from the police. Later on, the case of this woman

> would have been dropped once her certification was denied in the first place—I would have thought, I tried hard enough and there are so many other clients waiting.[23]

It was in the latter context that Courtney had dealt with Luisa's case. As we talked about her, I shared my frustration about how she had let Luisa's case sit in the file cabinet for several months and later decided not to insist on getting the police certification of Luisa's collaboration with the investigation. Courtney empathized, and added that "the fact that we were still helping many others made it hard to recognize these informal practices as problematic. There were also issues of self-preservation. For example, not getting too involved or sad with the clients' stories allowed me to distance myself from the immigrants and focus on doing business."[24] Finally, Courtney articulated her thoughts about the importance of contextualizing ORA's experiences,

> It is hard but necessary to hear criticism in order to be able to change. It helps to know that other nonprofits are going through similar things—it would be great to be more collaborative between nonprofits (here is difficult because nonprofits are competing for the same funding sources, but it would be nice to see more collaboration). I believe that thinking about how the organization is doing is very important. Retreats can help—at a retreat staff could focus on what is happening and develop ways to deal with whatever is thought of as wrong. Another way to provide better services is to get thorough, constructive feedback from the clients (as opposed to the feedback that ORA collects right now, which is useless because the survey that clients complete provides set answers), as well as keeping and evaluating records of the flow of immigrants through the organization (even if these may require resources, I think it would be worthy). . . . Also, I see that even if it's hard, and one may be tired from working so much, it is very important to keep politics alive.[25]

Courtney's reference to politics was indeed a poignant one since ORA had moved away from being a politically active grassroots group to becoming a quasiapolitical nonprofit organization. Cathy and Jenna acknowledged that the formal barriers inherited in VAWA were problematic; however, they expressed that it was not their responsibility to deal with that. While they would not resist other advocates' efforts to make immigration policies more inclusive, they were not interested in joining the struggle. They added that if ORA staff were requested to engage in political activism, this work would have to be calculated as part of their labor rather than left unpaid.[26] If ORA paid for these efforts, and there was enough time to still take care of the same number of cases, then ORA staff interested in politics could become actively involved. So far, the slight political activism that ORA staff had engaged in (like signing online petitions or joining community rallies) had gone unpaid, while their regular case work was put on hold. ORA staff felt that this trade-off was unfair both to their clients and to themselves.

In retrospect, the reactions of all ORA staff were indicative of the worth of going through the challenging phase of sharing findings with them, who were indeed fundamental collaborators of my activist research project. Given their responses, I was able not only to check the accuracy of my analysis, but also to modify, improve, and expand my analysis based on their responses, and more importantly, elaborate courses of action collectively. All the frustrations were counterbalanced by the richness of ORA staff's feedback, which was useful in identifying the interpersonal and institutional dynamics that may or may not allow for change to happen. As I reflected; wrote my book, articles, and book chapters; and prepared new workshops for and with immigrants and their advocates, I took all of the ORA staff's feedback into account and built on it critically. Specifically, as I observed that ORA staff members seemed to be reluctant to push for legal change to modify the formal barriers inherited from the larger immigration system or to engage in actions to dismantle the informal barriers emerging from their own inequitable practices, I wondered how my research could still contribute to furthering battered immigrants' access to justice.

I realized that one of the main ways to overcome interpersonal, organizational, and political barriers in activist research projects was by broadening the front of action. My activist research project did begin at ORA but did not end there or when I did the report/workshop or interviews with the staff. Activist research was a process that had to continue beyond the location and the time of the original fieldwork. Thus, besides sharing my work while emphasizing both the particular obstacles that battered immigrants cope with and the invaluable activist research methodologies within academic circles at professional meetings,[27] university talks, and college courses,[28] I made my research easily accessible on the Internet[29] and proactively offered to join meetings and do workshops to discuss these topics in the community.[30] Moreover, I got involved with battered immigrants' rights networks and women's rights organizations which had a membership inclusive of activists and advocates, such as Arte Sana, ALAS, Mujeres del Movimiento, and Women's Worlds, where I have regularly participated in online discussions and in-person meetings and learned from other participants.

Other concrete examples of how I expanded my activist research project beyond ORA are the workshops I conducted at Arte Sana's 2008 and 2010 National Conferences devoted to "help bridge the gaps in victim services by promoting the development of culturally competent programs and the active participation of the Latino community in anti-sexual violence work," with little to no "private or governmental financial support" (Arte Sana 2008, 22). In my workshops, I emphasized that the processes that I discovered while working as a volunteer at ORA are common to other nonprofit organizations subjected to similar legal and funding constraints and that the objective of thinking about these issues was to develop more inclusive policies and practices for battered immigrants. Workshop participants (nonprofit and governmental immigrants' advocates) were asked to form groups, reflect about the formal and informal barriers that stood in the way of battered immigrants' search for citizenship, and propose means that they had used or could use to avoid or dismantle them.

Most participants mentioned the constraints attached to grants and seemed to be doubtful about overcoming these, mostly because of a tremendous need for resources. A few argued for developing alternative sources of funding in order to be able to serve a broader spectrum of the immigrant population in tandem with the nonprofits' inclusive missions. Common propositions were collaborating with other nonprofits, educating the community, increasing the number of bilingual speaking advocates, and developing culturally sensitive services. While the strategy of pushing for policy changes was put in the context of founders' constraints, participants recognized its importance and noted the fear that immigrants felt in regards to deportation due to increasing anti-immigrant sentiments in the country. Finally, regarding informal practices at the nonprofit level, most advocates pointed to their struggles between allocation of scarce resources and faithfulness to their organizations' missions. They also emphasized the need to connect and cooperate with other organizations and valued the possibility of thinking of and developing strategies to handle these issues at in-house and network meetings, trainings, and conferences.

The diversity of the group of advocates that attended the workshop was exemplified by their main concerns: while victim services specialists from the police department felt constrained by bureaucratic red-tape that significantly slowed down the process to assist battered immigrants, recently hired advocates were surprised to find out that VAWA's immigration provisions reflected gender, sexual, racial, ethnic, and class discriminatory institutions typical of the broader immigration system. The range of responses, however, stressed the need to take a proactive, comparative, and collaborative approach on how to resist formal and informal barriers that stand in the way of battered immigrants' access to justice. As Laura Zárate, Arte Sana's founding executive director, stated in the conference's opening remarks: "We are very diverse. . . . We are a big family. . . . We are all experts. . . . We are all survivors,"[31] and in order to survive organizationally and struggle for the well-being of "newly arrived or third generation" immigrants, "we need to create ways to work together, include each other, refer each other, and support each other's efforts" (Arte Sana 2008, 1).

Concluding Remarks

Despite its challenges, there was not a moment when I doubted the richness and potential of activist research. Hence, to end I share a set of ideas that I believe researchers should keep in mind before, while, and after taking on this sort of methodological framework. First, in order to develop activist research, scholars ought to believe in the ideological reasons beneath this methodology, evaluate its particular relevance to the subject matter at hand, and be prepared to become politically committed to the work. In other words, if scholars are incredulous of the politics of activist research, they can instead make use of other qualitative tools that are not inherently politicized, like participant observation or interviews. Second, scholars should be truthful in their relationships with the members of the community and/or organization with whom they are developing the activist research project. An open attitude, transparency, and humility will allow scholars to gain and maintain access to the community, as well as to build a constructive, long-lasting, and ethical working relationship.

Third, activist researchers ought to be faithful in how to incorporate the views, opinions, and voices of the community members to the analysis: having talked with "them," or worked with "them" is not enough and does not automatically provoke a change in the understanding of otherness or the oppressive structures of power (Mani 1998; Menon and Bhasin 1998). This is particularly important given that one of the purposes of activist research is to counter hegemonic practices in research and beyond, a purpose that would be voided if researchers reinterpret, omit, or ignore community members' perspectives. Accordingly, activist researchers should be conscious of the possibility of disagreeing with the community, as well as finding resistance or indifference to ideas that they believed had emerged from their working relationship with the community. If such tensions occur, it is the responsibility of activist scholars to critically take care of frustrations and disputes while incorporating them as data to be later analyzed as part of the greater project. Therefore, researchers should not take conflict as a deterrent or a failure, but as an intrinsic part of activist methodologies. Scholars ought to be persistent, reflective, and critical, so their analyses will bear fruit despite the challenges that may emerge during the research project.

Fourth, and last, researchers should keep in mind that activist projects are relational processes of knowledge creation and that as such, they ought to be conceived as collective, complex, and long-term endeavors that are expected to become larger than their own protagonists and locations. This knowledge is destined to change the standpoint of researcher and community members, and consequently of their relationship. If such changes mean that their links come to an end, activist scholars should remember that good activist research projects continue to develop and have an impact beyond their original sites and members since in the end, the most important is to advance the political and practical issues at hand.

The careful and critical use of activist research is particularly useful when addressing controversial, complex, mobilized, politicized, and of course, unjust social issues. The worth of engaging in activist research in the Americas is indeed increasing, because of not only the dire circumstances in which most Latin American countries presently are but also the highly discriminatory and exploitative situations in which most Latin American immigrants find themselves in the world. Moreover, the transnational and activist participation of scholars becomes especially significant given the unequal distribution of resources (which of course affects the academic arena). If the ultimate aim of sociological studies is to contribute to processes of social change that will ameliorate living conditions for all in the Americas and beyond, the significance of the methodological framework of activist research is only on the rise.[32]

Notes

I would like to thank New York University Press for allowing me to use some excerpts from my book *Violence Against Latina Immigrants: Citizenship, Inequality, and Community* in this chapter (2010).

1. Regularly, an immigrant who marries a U.S. citizen or a legal permanent resident is allowed to apply for legal permanent residency on the basis of her/his union. The citizen or resident is the one person who has to sponsor—that is, file the application and

provide economic support for—the immigrant spouse in front of the United States Citizenship and Immigration Services (USCIS). When the citizens or residents are abusive partners, they tend to take advantage of their power to sponsor or not sponsor the immigrant spouse's USCIS application as a means of control.

2. Activist research is also referred to as action research, participatory action research, feminist action research, collaborative research, grounded theory, and the like (Hale 2008; Esterberg 2002). Because there is no one unique definition of activist scholarship, all of these kinds of activist research have significant similarities and also certain differences that should be neither overlooked nor minimized. For example, while feminist action researchers always pay attention to gender inequalities, collaborative researchers may develop their projects with no attention to gender matters.
3. All the names used here are pseudonyms. I also changed dates and locations for security and confidentiality purposes. All immigrants, ORA staff, and members of other organizations working on battered immigrants' issues provided me with their informed consent to participate in this research project and be referred to in publications of my authorship. My transparency in sharing the goals of my research project was grounded not only in the traditional ethical guidelines of the American Sociological Association and Institutional Review Boards, but also on the ideological principles fundamental to activist scholarship, including openness, democracy, and equality (on ethics and activist research, see for example Esterberg 2002, 148–49).
4. In order to be eligible for free services, immigrants had to have earnings below 125 percent of the officially defined poverty line (that is, annual earnings lower than 17,500 dollars for a household of two in 2008, according to the official guidelines of USCIS. Accessed at http://www.uscis.gov/portal/site/uscis/menuitem.5af9bb95919f35e66f614176543f6d1a/?vgnextoid=6a096c854523d010VgnVCM10000048f3d6a1RCRD&vgnextchannel=4f719c7755cb9010VgnVCM10000045f3d6a1RCRD, March 2009).
5. According to data released by the Office of Immigration Statistics of the United States Department of Homeland Security. See, for example, the reports of 2007 at http://www.dhs.gov/ximgtn/statistics.
6. Calculation based on data available at the Bureau of Justice Statistics of the United States Department of Justice (http://www.ojp.gov/bjs/intimate/ipv.htm#contents), the Texas Council of Family Violence (http://www.tcfv.org/pdf/dvam07/Year%202006%20Family%20Violence%20Statistics(HHSC).pdf), and the United States

Census Bureau (http://factfinder.census.gov/servlet/ThematicMapFramesetServlet?_bm=y&-geo_id=01000US&-tm_name=DEC_2000_SF1_U_M00092&-ds_name=DEC_2000_SF1_U&-_MapEvent=displayBy&-_dBy=040#?306,337).

7. VAWA was first enacted in 1994 and must be reauthorized every five years. The reauthorization process opens the opportunity to revise the act's regulations and budgets, which has had positive and negative effects. On the one hand, activists for women's and immigrants' rights have been able to push for improvements in the regulations and increments of funding. On the other hand, opposite groups have tried to reduce the extent of assistance offered for survivors of gender violence. A case in point is the last reauthorization round (2011–2012—as of this writing, currently underway) which found strong groups pushing to roll back benefits for LGBTQ, immigrant, and indigenous survivors (see Villalón, forthcoming).
8. There are several conditions and requirements that legal permanent residents have to meet in order to successfully apply for citizenship. Besides paying all application fees, residents have to show that they have been living continuously in the United States, have been economically self-sufficient and autonomous, and have not committed any crimes, among other things. For more information on this, visit http://www.uscis.gov/portal/site/uscis/menuitem.eb1d4c2a3e5b9ac89243c6a7543f6d1a/?vgnextoid=d84d68112 64a3210VgnVCM100000b92ca60aRCRD&vgnextchannel=d84d6811264a3210VgnVCM100000b92ca60aRCRD.
9. For these individual and group interviews, the nonprofit workers who were members of ORA while I was doing my fieldwork were given notes on my analysis in writing. In the interviews, I went through the main findings and clarified any questions they had. We talked freely about their reactions while I took notes.
10. You may read about all of these immigrants in my book, Villalón (2010).
11. As noted earlier, one of the achievements of the battered women's movement was to educate police and other key civilians (like health practitioners and teachers) of the rights that victims of gender violence have under the Violence Against Women Act (VAWA). Police officers, and particularly, victim services units' staff, are trained to become aware of the rights that gender violence survivors have and the organizations where they can be assisted.
12. For a full explanation of these formal barriers, see Villalón (2010, chapter 3).
13. Group interview with Cathy, Jenna, Magie, Courtney, and Marina,

Central Texas, mid-2000s (exact date not revealed for confidentiality purposes).

14. For more details see Villalón 2010, 112–17.
15. Staff rotation at nonprofits is very high indeed and very common (advocates refer to this phenomenon as "the revolving door of nonprofits"). See Villalón 2010, 132–34.
16. Field notes from report/workshop to all ORA staff, central Texas, July 11, 2008.
17. Field notes from report/workshop to all ORA staff, central Texas, July 11, 2008.
18. Field notes from report/workshop to all ORA staff, central Texas, July 11, 2008.
19. Personal interview with Cathy, central Texas, July 1, 2008.
20. Group interview with Cathy, Jenna, and Maggie, central Texas, July 11, 2008.
21. Group interview with Cathy, Jenna, and Maggie, central Texas, July 11, 2008.
22. Group interview with Cathy, Jenna, and Maggie, central Texas, July 11, 2008.
23. Personal interview with Courtney, central Texas, July 24, 2008.
24. Personal interview with Courtney, central Texas, July 24, 2008.
25. Personal interview with Courtney, central Texas, July 24, 2008.
26. This position reflects the change of grassroots social change organizations to nonprofit social service organizations. As Hawk explains when she is recalling her years of activism in the American Indian Movement (AIM) in the 1960s and 1970s and in Women of All Red Nations (WARN) in the late 1970s, "When we first started organizing, we were rookies. We did not know how to organize but learned as we went along. Today, when young people ask me about my days in AIM and what they could do now, their first question is: 'Where will we get the money?' Often they are surprised by my response. But back then, we did not focus on fundraising. (Nor did we see activism as something we would get paid to do.) We organized first, and then figured out how to make it happen" (Hawk 2007, 102).
27. Examples of these are presentations at conferences organized by the American Sociological Association, the International Sociological Association, the Latin American Studies Association, Sociologists for Women in Society, and the Association of Black Sociologists.
28. As an assistant professor at St. John's University, I created and taught courses like Family Violence, Immigration and Inequality, and Human Trafficking, all of which are directly related to the topic

of my activist research. I also included these issues when I taught Sociology of Gender, Gender in a Global Context, Sociology of the Family, and Research Methodologies.

29. You may visit my webpage (https://sites.google.com/site/robertavillalonphd/) and join me on Facebook (http://www.facebook.com/pages/Violence-Against-Latina-Immigrants/135417359821439).
30. An example of this is my participation at the Free Adult Literacy Program organized by the Committee of Latin American and Caribbean Studies at St. John's University (http://www.stjohns.edu/academics/centers/clacs/adult_literacy_program.stj).
31. Zárate, August 18, 2008, opening remarks of the Arte Sana National Conference "*Nuestras Voces*/Our Voices: Collaboration and Transformation *en la Comunidad.*"
32. Villalón 2011.

References

Abraham, Margaret. 2000. *Speaking the Unspeakable: Marital Violence among South Asian Immigrants in the United States*. New Brunswick, NJ: Rutgers University Press.

Alvarez, Sonia. 1999. Advocating Feminism: The Latin American Feminist NGO 'Boom.' *International Feminist Journal of Politics* 1 (2): 181–209.

Anzaldúa, Gloria. 2002. "(Un)natural bridges, (Un)safe spaces." In *this bridge we call home: radical visions for transformation,* ed. Gloria Anzaldúa and AnaLouise Keating, 1–5. New York: Routledge.

Arte Sana. 2008. *Nuestras Voces/Our Voices: Collaboration and Transformation en la Comunidad*. Arte Sana Nacional Conference, August 18 and 19.

Calvo, Janet. 2004. "A Decade of Spouse-Based Immigration Laws: Coverture's Diminishment, but Not Its Demise." *Northern Illinois University Law Review* 24: 153–209.

Esterberg, Kristen. 2002. *Qualitative Methods in Social Research*. New York: McGraw-Hill.

Family Violence Prevention Fund. 2005. "You Have a Right to Be Free from Violence in Your Home: Questions and Answers for Immigrant and Refugee Women." San Francisco: Family Violence Prevention Fund.

Fox Piven, Frances, and Richard Cloward. 1977. *Poor People's Movements: Why They Succeed, How They Fail*. New York: Vintage Books.

Glenn, Evelyn Nakano. 2002. *Unequal Freedom: How Race and Gender Shaped American Citizenship and Labor*. Cambridge: Harvard University Press.

Hale, Charles. 2006. "Activist Research v. Cultural Critique: Indigenous Land Rights and the Contradictions of Politically Engaged Anthropology." *Cultural Anthropology* 21 (1): 96–120.

———, ed. 2008. *Engaging Contradictions: Theory, Politics, and Methods of Activist Scholarship*. Los Angeles: University of California Press.

Haney López, Ian. 1996. *White by Law: The Legal Construction of Race*. New York: New York University Press.

Hawk, Madonna Thunder. 2007. "Native Organizing Before the Non-Profit Industrial Complex." In *The Revolution Will Not Be Funded: Beyond the Non-Profit Industrial Complex,* ed. INCITE! Women of Color Against Violence, 101–106. Cambridge, MA: South End.

Hazen, Andrea, and Fernando Soriano. 2007. "Experiences with Intimate Partner Violence among Latina Women." *Violence Against Women* 13 (6): 562–582.

Hill Collins, Patricia. 1986. "Learning from the Outsider Within: The Sociological Significance of Black Feminist Thought." *Social Problems* 33 (6): S14–S32.

Hing, Bill Ong. 2004. *Defining America through Immigration Policy*. Philadelphia, PA: Temple University Press.

INCITE! Women of Color Against Violence, ed. 2007. *The Revolution Will Not Be Funded: Beyond the Non-profit Industrial Complex*. Cambridge, MA: South End.

Kivel, Paul. 2007. "Social Service or Social Change?" In *The Revolution Will Not Be Funded: Beyond the Non-Profit Industrial Complex,* ed. INCITE! Women of Color Against Violence, 129–150. Cambridge, MA: South End.

Lake, Robert, and Kathe Newman. 2002. "Differential Citizenship in the Shadow State." *GeoJournal* 58: 109–120.

Luibhéid, Eithne. 2002. *Entry Denied: Controlling Sexuality at the Border*. Minneapolis: University of Minnesota Press.

Mani, Lata. 1998. *Contentious Traditions: The Debate on Sati in Colonial India*. Berkeley: University of California Press.

Menjívar, Cecilia, and Olivia Salcido. 2002. "Immigrant Women and Domestic Violence: Common Experiences in Different Countries." *Gender & Society* 16 (6): 898–920.

Menon, Ritu, and Kamla Bhasin.1998. *Borders and Boundaries: Women in India's Partition*. New Brunswick, NJ: Rutgers University Press.

Mindry, Deborah. 2001. "Nongovernmental Organizations, 'Grassroots,' and the Politics of Virtue." *Signs: Journal of Women in Culture and Society* 26: 1187–1211.

Naples, Nancy. 2003. *Feminism and Method: Ethnography, Discourse Analysis, and Activist Research*. New York: Routledge.

National Resource Center on Domestic Violence. 2007. *LGBT Communities and Domestic Violence: Information and Resources Overview*. Harrisburg: National Resource Center on Domestic Violence.

Network to End Violence Against Immigrant Women. 2005. 10th National Network Conference. *Conference Participant Training Manual*. Irvine, California. November 9, 10, and 11.

Ngai, Mae. 2004. *Impossible Subjects: Illegal Aliens and the Making of Modern America*. Princeton, NJ: Princeton University Press.

Ong, Aihwa. 2003. *Buddha Is Hiding: Refugees, Citizenship, the New America*. Berkeley: University of California Press.

Perlmutter, Felice. 1994. *Women and Social Change: Nonprofit and Social Policy*. Washington, DC: National Association of Social Workers.

Rudrappa, Sharmila. 2004. *Ethnic Routes to Becoming American: Indian Immigrants and the Cultures of Citizenship*. New Brunswick, NJ: Rutgers University Press.

Salcido, Olivia, and Madelaine Adelman. 2004. "He Has Me Tied with the Blessed and Dammed Papers": Undocumented-Immigrant Battered Women in Phoenix, Arizona." *Human Organization* 63(2):162– 172.

Schechter, Susan. 1982. *Women and Male Violence: The Visions and Struggles of the Battered Women's Movement*. Cambridge, MA: South End.

Sjoberg, Gideon, and Roger Nett. 1997. *A Methodology for Social Research: With a New Introductory Essay*. Prospect Heights, IL: Waveland.

Spivak, Gayatri. 1988. "Can the Subaltern Speak?" In *Marxism and the Interpretation of Culture*, ed. Cary Nelson and Lawrence Grossberged, 271–313. Urbana: University of Illinois Press.

Trudeau, Daniel. 2008. "Toward a Relational View of the Shadow State." *Political Geography* 27: 669–690.

Villalón, Roberta. 2010. *Violence Against Latina Immigrants: Citizenship, Inequality, and Community*. NY: New York University Press.

———. 2011. "Feminist Activist Research and Strategies from within the Battered Immigrant Women's Movement." *Interface: A Journal for and about Social Movements* 3(2): 246–270.

———. Forthcoming. "Economics, Politics and the Demise of Battered Immigrants' Rights." *Journal of Civil Rights and Economic Development* 27, no. 3.

Wolch, Jennifer. 1990. *The Shadow State: Government and the Voluntary Sector in Transition*. New York: Foundation Center.

WomensLaw. 2009. *VAWA Laws for Abuse Victims*. Accessible at http://www.womenslaw.org/laws_state_type.php?id=10270&state_code=US&open_id=10837.

———. 2012. U Visa Laws for Crime Victims. Accessible at http://www.womenslaw.org/laws_state_type.php?id=10271&state_code=US&open_id=10846#content-14747.

10

RURAL FEMINISM AND REVOLUTION IN NICARAGUA

Voices of the Compañeras

SHELLY GRABE

> And I think, now, the women, knowing that they are their own property holders, they are starting to feel that they decide how to run their farm, they make the decisions over their bodies, or any other decisions.
>
> —Juana Delia Rojas, board member of Xochitl Acalt, a rural women's center

The Women's Autonomous Movement in Nicaragua

The Movimiento Autónomo de Mujeres (Autonomous Women's Movement) in Nicaragua emerged, like many other Latin American social movements in the 1970s and 1980s in the context of dictatorial regimes, as a marginalized and restricted movement (Alvarez 1990; Shayne 2004). It is now characterized as expansive and diverse, with feminist agendas being found in multiple sectors (e.g., government, labor, health, agriculture). The objective of this chapter is to better understand how gender has been negotiated within the agricultural sector of the *movimiento* and how these negotiations have been related to processes surrounding neoliberalization. Foremost feminist scholars have highlighted that although rural women have always been more oppressed than their counterparts, organization among rural women in Latin America has generally been low (Deere and León 1987; Stephen

1997). Nicaragua is an exception to this rule. In Nicaragua, a combination of oppressive conditions and new channels for participation, led to the rise of a mobilized rural feminism, a feminism theorized and practiced by rural women that takes into account the distinct needs of rural women.

During its more than forty-year control in Nicaragua, the Somoza[1] dictatorship had what was considered the most heavily U.S.-trained military establishment in Latin America, and Somoza's family owned more than 20 percent of Nicaraguan land and businesses (Walker 1985). The Movimiento Autónomo de Mujeres was, in part, birthed out of the Sandinista Revolution[2] when many women joined the massive national uprising in the 1970s in an effort to overthrow the Somoza dictatorship (Kampwirth 2004). Women's participation in the Revolution was considered greater than nearly any other revolution during the time: women made up approximately 30 percent of the FSLN's combat forces, and after the overthrow several women were appointed to senior positions in the newly established ministries (Kampwirth 1996; Molyneux 1985). Despite the fact that women were involved in nearly every aspect of the insurrection and played a crucial role in weathering the Reagan-imposed trade embargo and the U.S.-backed contra war in the 1980s, feminist concerns of patriarchy and male privilege were largely marginalized during the Revolution (Kampwirth 2004; Molyneux 1985). As a result, women gradually began to move beyond adherence to party directives (made by the male-dominated leadership of the FSLN) and to formulate their own agendas based on the needs and interests of women (Criquillón 1995; Randall 1994).

A country grown tired of war and U.S. programs of economic strangulation voted out the Sandinistas in the elections held in 1990. Although the Sandinistas fell short of eradicating gender inequality, the new U.S.-backed Chamorro administration actively promoted neoliberal policies that resulted in dramatic cutbacks to public services, which disproportionately impacted women. The economic reforms and structural adjustments aimed at privileging foreign investment and the international economy reflected an era characterized explicitly by new policies driven largely by the International Monetary Fund and the World Bank. The gender consequences of this shift throughout the world were enormous. For example, it has been widely documented that as a consequence of the structural adjustment programs there has been an increase in women's unpaid labor in the home and a feminization of low-paid service labor (see for example, Desai 2002).

Nevertheless, in Nicaragua, ten years of revolutionary government left a legacy of political mobilization and a network of organized women. Both would play a role in shaping the birth of a women's social movement that coordinated efforts in various sectors to address the challenges stemming from global economic restructuring. By 1992 Nicaragua had the largest, most pluralistic, and most autonomous feminist movement in Central America (Kampwirth 1996).[3] This plurality can be explained, in part, because a large number of women from all social classes had joined the Revolution. Given that the mobilization and cooperation of women from the upper and middle classes, university students, and landless peasants were a crucial part of the efforts that eventually overthrew the Somoza regime, the women's movement emerged out of a "multiclass revolutionary coalition" (Kampwirth 2002). Moreover, because the structural adjustments that accompanied the new administration in 1990 created consequences that cut across sectors and classes (for example, threats to health care, land reform, etc.), cross-class and urban-rural alliances remained critical to the viability of an autonomous women's movement. These alliances are reflected in a slogan the Movimiento began using to characterize themselves in 1992: Diverse but United (Randall 1994).

The agricultural emphasis in the Movimiento Autónomo de Mujeres began during the Revolution when a number of steps were taken to remove institutional obstacles that traditionally prevented women from gaining access to land and other natural resources. For example, the Agrarian Reform Laws of the 1980s recognized equal rights for both genders and made it possible for women to become direct beneficiaries of land allocation. In 1987, Nicaragua adopted a new national constitution that explicitly granted women and men equal rights in land ownership. Moreover, the Asociación de Trabajadores del Campo (Association of Rural Workers; ATC), the principal FSLN labor organization for farmers founded in 1978, was considered at the cutting edge of feminist organizing within the workplace. Over the course of the 1980s the membership of the ATC became increasingly female, as many men left their agricultural positions to join the contra war, and a women's secretariat within the ATC was formed in 1986 (Kampwirth 1996). The new secretariat's goal was to raise agricultural workers' consciousness through workshops on judicial, union, and gender rights. Despite these advances, data from the rural titling office indicate that between 1979 and 1989 women accounted for only 8–10 percent of beneficiaries under the agrarian reform. The small gains made during the 1980s were further eroded under the neoliberal agrarian legislation of the 1990s. By the early 1990s the former state-oriented model of agrarian reform had been discredited in favor of counterreforms that focused on privatization, or the individualization of land rights, that was thought to be more conducive to profit-maximizing the export-oriented agriculture sector (Deere and León 2001).

The gender consequences of this shift were reflected in the feminization of agricultural labor coupled with the gap between women's and men's property rights (Deere 2009). However, until the publication of Deere and León's (2001) book *Empowering Women: Land and Property Rights in Latin America,* virtually no attention had been given to the gendered implications of neoliberal reform in agriculture.

The change in focus from a revolutionary state that took into account agricultural workers' rights and livelihoods to a market-based model of counterreform raises the questions: what has happened in terms of rural women's land rights under neoliberalism and how, in the context of these changes, is gender being negotiated. Despite much that has been written about the cultural obstacles women experience, there has been little empirical data collected to flesh out the mechanisms by which women's participation operates in the agricultural sector. This chapter is, in part, about the way the agricultural sector within the women's social movement in Nicaragua was birthed out of a political climate antagonistic to progressive collective voices. It seeks to chronicle how the efforts and experiences of social movement actors function when the political climate and strategies of the powerful political actors are hostile. Two women tell their stories of triumph in this chapter. Although both women were involved in the Revolution, they each articulated an eventual need to move beyond the FSLN party. In their stories they demonstrate how their resistance led to a feminist praxis that allowed them to transform existing social structures in order to create spaces for rural women to mobilize and have their rights recognized.

Bridging Activism and Academic Research: My Story

As researchers, we inevitably bring our own stories to bear on the research process (White and Dotson 2010). From the outset I realized that my interest in the women's social movement in Nicaragua was partly about my own experience and interests as a woman from a working-class background. It was also driven by my desire to focus on women's communities as sources of feminist protest and as sites where women negotiate counternarratives that challenge dominant power structures. My initial exposure to feminism occurred through locating feminist texts in used bookstores and reading authors such as Nawal El Saldawi and bell hooks, whose critical perspectives pointed me in unforeseen directions that challenged my silence. Their perspectives encouraged me to use my position to give voice to those who had been severely marginalized, especially those marginalized by the involvement of my own government. I went from turning pages in the shelter of the bookstore, to rapidly moving those conversations into my life and work. I had already finished graduate school, and, as a research psychologist, my shifting lens was repeatedly labeled "radical" within academia. With the label came the suggestion that my new interests bordered on irreverent. As a result, I increasingly found my home and my people in the activist community, and like other women participating in social movement research, it seemed as though the work I was to become involved in chose me, rather than me choosing it (Shayne 2009; Taylor 1998).

A year after receiving my PhD in psychology I became involved in local community organizing surrounding women's rights. I co-organized events with another community member who was the director of an organization that was part of a social movement that aimed to end the U.S. military intervention in Nicaragua in the 1980s. Despite the fact that Nicaragua had experienced over a century of U.S. intervention and interference, I knew embarrassingly little about it. The director of the organization, Carlos Arenas, invited me to accompany him on a social delegation to Nicaragua that was to be focused on women's empowerment. Although I was strongly committed to women's issues and involved in local community activism, the trip seemed a bit far afield from my focus as a psychologist, and I suspected, given my lack of knowledge, that it was perhaps even inappropriate that I be part of the delegation. Carlos convinced me otherwise.

During my first trip to Nicaragua in 2005 we visited several key women's rural organizations that were working to empower women. One of the organizations, Xochitl Acalt, facilitated rural women's access to land as a means to alter structural gender inequities in a manner that would transform women's subordination. Both the leaders and the members of the organization took countless risks to boldly and brazenly challenge gender norms, with seemingly incredible effectiveness. Despite the fact that our conversations with each other included "solidarity" language, I had yet to contribute anything substantive to the dialogue. However, as a social scientist, I could not help but inquire whether research might play a role in their efforts toward social justice. A determinedly emphatic response indicated that, yes, being able to empirically demonstrate the efficacy of the programs being administered could afford their efforts more credibility with people in positions of power.

I returned to the States to inform a senior (feminist) colleague that I aimed to pursue collaborative research with a feminist organization in Nicaragua that was engaging in radical and, I believed, demonstrable change. She looked bewildered and asked, "Have you some forgotten

Peace Corps dream?" The question was followed with some suggestion that I take care lest I burn my academic bridges. To be fair, we were located in a mainstream, quantitative, R1 environment where using the f word (i.e., feminism) positioned one in an "alternative voices" box. However, I remained certain I could uphold the standards of my discipline and develop a sound research partnership with the leaders of the Nicaraguan organization. I began writing grants and pursued funding to run a quasiexperimental study examining the effects of land ownership on women's empowerment and receipt of violence.[4] In planning the research, I was candid with my collaborators at Xochitl Acalt that I knew little of Latin American politics, I was not trained as an international field researcher, and that I could not speak Spanish. Within academia, these disclaimers would often be read as incompetence. However, my collaborators noted astutely that *they* were, of course, the experts in these areas of knowledge. We thus began a longer-term collaboration and have since collected and disseminated data, with support from the National Science Foundation, demonstrating that landowning not only empowers women, but reduces their receipt of psychological and physical violence (Grabe 2010; 2012; Grabe and Arenas 2009; Grose and Grabe, forthcoming).

Over time I became increasingly committed to solidarity and traveled with Witness for Peace to learn more about U.S. interventions in Latin American foreign policy, spent a summer in Central America taking language classes, and visited other parts of revolutionary Latin America to increase my breadth of knowledge. Although a common and justified concern with transnational work is that Western feminists are deploying a universal Western feminism, I entered into these relationships with no formal training in feminism and rather, became a student of activists who have devoted their lives to social change. In doing so, I learned a women of color, decolonial, rural feminism that largely influences most of the work I do today. I did also, of course, scurry to familiarize myself with relevant literatures informed by sociology, economics, and feminist studies (e.g., Agarwal 1994; Connell 1987; Kabeer 1999; Naples and Desai 2002).

Years later, after having secured a position as an assistant professor at the University of California Santa Cruz (UCSC) where scholar-activist collaborations are well supported, I returned to Nicaragua to conduct a project documenting the life stories of several key feminist leaders in the Movimiento Autónomo de Mujeres. Although my collaboration with Xochitl Acalt was a community-driven feminist project that aimed to use research toward liberatory processes, I was also motivated to document the voices behind the broader movimiento autónomo—a multisector, coordinated mobilization of women that had weathered the unremitting power differentials characterized by patriarchy and capitalism. Although work of a similar nature surrounding the role of women in the Revolution and the birth of the women's movement had already been conducted by Margaret Randall (1981; 1994), many years had passed, each creating an ever more marginalizing situation for women due, in part, to the political conservatives in power. I knew documenting the experience of social movement actors in this context would demand a methodology different than the large-scale survey designs and quantitative analyses that I had mastered and were more widely respected within my discipline. In this case, feminist thinking and practice would require eliminating the boundaries of division that privilege dominant forms of knowledge building, boundaries that mark who can be a knower and what can be known (Hesse-Biber 2007). In short, it was clear to me that the women needed to tell their own stories.

Accessing the Stories

The oral history method, which allows women to describe their experiences on their own terms, was used to elicit the women's stories. In this case, women were invited to be narrators, to tell stories about biographical particulars that were meaningful to them. In the pursuit of knowledge aimed at creating social justice, women's own voices have the potential to document how women are enacting transformation, rather than having the researcher abstractly define or quantify it. Mohanty (2003) has argued that understanding struggles of justice must involve illuminating "Third World women's" engagement with feminism and resistance to oppressive regimes in relation to states and histories of imperialism. To best understand these processes of resistance and oppression, the current study privileges an activist standpoint, which can be conceived as a transformative exploration of activists' experiences of resistance to oppression (Maddison and Shaw 2007). *Testimonio*, in particular, may be used to refer to a type of oral history or life story that is an explicitly political narrative that describes and resists oppression (Chase 2003). *Testimonio* has been widely used with Latin American activists involved in revolutionary movements (Golden 1991; Maloof 1999; Menchú 1984; Stephen 1997; Randall 1981; 1994; Tula and Stephen 1994). Privileging an activist standpoint through *testimonio* can bring into focus a greater range of activity, the invisible and often undocumented activity that takes place within social movements, yet without which no publicly visible movement would exist (Maddison and Shaw 2007).

Because an underlying goal of activist research is a reconfiguration of knowledge production that shifts power and control into the hands of the oppressed or marginalized (Fals-Borda 1985; Sandoval 2000), I relied heavily on Carlos Arenas and his years of solidarity with the Movimiento Autónomo to construct a list of interviewees. Carlos, in collaboration with the elected representative of the Movimiento Autónomo, Juanita Jiménez, arranged interviews with eighteen key women leaders in Nicaragua. This secured me interviews with women to whom I most certainly would not otherwise have had access and without whom the story of women's resistance in Nicaragua could not adequately be told. These women reflected various positions and sectors and included former guerrilla commanders during the Revolution, congresswomen, the director of the national human rights center, grassroots organizers, journalists, and professors. I set up a small team that included an extraordinary driver and assistant, a videographer, and a U.S. translator who actively participates in solidarity work with rural feminists in Nicaragua.

To facilitate rapport and ease, the interviews were scheduled in a location of the woman's choosing. Sometimes this was her home; sometimes it was her office. All of the interviews were preceded by a conversation that explained how the woman's story might be used, and each was given a list of the other interviewees. The larger project aims to reproduce the stories as text in a manner similar to the method used by Margaret Randall (1981; 1994) and to archive a video recording and transcript of the interview with the Global Feminisms Project[5] at the University of Michigan. All of the women agreed enthusiastically to have their stories reproduced.

The interviews, which occurred through simultaneous translation, lasted approximately an hour and were audio and video recorded. A loosely structured set of questions guided each interview, intended simply to facilitate the progression of the woman's story. The objective was to allow each woman to elaborate on her experience, which was particularly important with this sample, in part because the women were more accustomed to being spokespersons for the larger social movement and had vastly less experience talking about their personal histories.

Of the eighteen women interviewed, three were participants in the agricultural sector. Because of space limitations, only two of their three life stories will be reproduced here. The third woman, Anita del Socorro Chavez Tursio, offered a powerful *testimonio* of her experience as a beneficiary, and later board member, of the Xochitl Acalt women's center. The other two, Martha Heriberta Valle and Diana Martínez, were both active participants in the Revolution, and each later came to mobilize rural women with a focus on land access and production. As will be seen in each woman's story, the interviewees elicited specific social identities and contexts in which gender issues were intertwined with their relationships to land and rural production. Despite being from vastly different social class backgrounds, both women demonstrate a resistance to gender inequalities that manifests in their agency. In their life stories, we can examine how the women developed an oppositional consciousness—or a rhetoric of resistance—that they employed when countering patriarchal and capitalist struggles surrounding land (Sandoval 2000). As Chela Sandoval highlights in her analysis of U.S. Third World women's activism, oppositional consciousness can be viewed as a methodology of the oppressed and a technology for social transformation. As we will read in these women's stories, an oppositional consciousness surfaces early for both of these women, and each of them uses it to negotiate injustices in gender and agriculture, thereby historically influencing the struggle for women's land rights. In the interest of space each interview was reduced by nearly a third of its original length.

The Risk-Takers

Martha Heriberta Valle

Martha is the founder and current president of Federación Agropecuaria de Cooperativas de Mujeres Productoras del Campo de Nicaragua (Agricultural Cooperative Federation of Rural Women Producers of Nicaragua, FEMUPROCAN), a women-run agricultural cooperative that helps women in poor rural regions organize to grow and sell crops sustainably. Her office, where the interview was conducted, is located in Managua off of a busy and loud street. Martha and her longtime coworker and vice-president of FEMUPROCAN, Matilde Rocha, greeted us together. Martha and Matilde were familiar with research processes because they had been previously interviewed by economist Carmen Diana Deere regarding the role of their organization in rural social movements. I explained that the current project was distinct in that it focused on individual life history, rather than on their organization. Immediately they both smiled and pointed at the other indicating she was the one who should be interviewed for the oral history. Even without knowing they had worked together for over twenty years, the level of respect and warmth between the two women was evident. After a brief discussion it was agreed that Martha would be interviewed for the oral history project, and Matilde would be interviewed to gain a better understanding of the role of the FEMUPROCAN in the broader movement.

Despite her humility, Martha has been involved in the cooperative land movement since its start in the 1980s, helped found the Sandinista-affiliated Unión Nacional de Agricultores y Ganaderos (National Union of Farmers and Cattlemen; UNAG), and is also the current president of del Consejo Nacional de Cooperativas (the National Council of Cooperatives). Martha's early experiences of marginalization and illiteracy, having come from a large peasant family in the central region of Nicaragua, led to her participation in the Revolution and to her sustained commitment to justice for rural women. She tells a story of personal triumph and dedication to change here:

SG: Martha, I know you're probably more used to talking about your organization, but I'd actually like to start the interview today talking about you and asking you some questions about your own history.

M: There are times when talking about yourself is difficult, but I'm going to give it all I've got . . . I was born in a community where there weren't schools, and my parents had fourteen children. Of them, I was the first daughter. We didn't have potable water; we didn't have electric lights; we would use oil lamps for light. Eh the whole family worked; there were 31 of us in the house. My two parents were illiterate, and the whole family was illiterate. . . . In *La Montaña* we had to go eight hours on mule with the *café* production to sell in to the department of Matagalpa. In this world, men and women both worked. This is how we were able to be efficient producers of something. But we never had shoes.

SG: How old were you when you started working in the fields with your family?

M: At age eight I was the tortilla maker, and I went to the orchard to plant with an oxen *yunta*. We did this together as a family. It gave us the great virtue of being efficient and at the same time broke with the traditional structure. What are the traditional structures in the country? That the girls don't work. But my father said that all of us had to work, so all of us could have goods. I—this virtue that God gave me and that my father taught is the one that gave me the strength to fight from the time I was very young until today. . . . With the triumph of the Revolution, the first thing I did was study in adult education classes. And there I completed sixth grade, I began secondary school,[6] and I completed an agronomy technical certificate, already having three children.

SG: How old were you when you did that?

M: I started at age twenty-seven.[7] That's why I believe that humans aren't defeated when we have this desire to grow and to serve. . . . If there is something that I have always valued it's that my father didn't differentiate—despite not knowing the term feminism—the different gender roles. We did it out of a real necessity, and he was proud because all us girls produced results equal to those of the boys. When I was thirteen, my father told me—I had asked him for a horse that was very pretty, a beastly horse—and he told me, "I'll give it to you if you break him." So I tell him, "He'll throw me off." "No," he tells me, "If you—look, I'll pull him—if you see that he's going to throw you, take this tamer, this bridle, and put it on, restrain him, because you aren't going to let yourself be hit by anybody." And this stuck with me; it stayed recorded in me because it was during my adolescence, and I think this gave me a lot of strength . . . When I was—I got married when I was sixteen, but I also started getting involved in the movements at the farming level. And we began to work for the communities.

SG: What kind of strategies were you using at the time to organize people in rural areas?

M: Well, in the first place, someone has to motivate you, come—peers come to you, and they tell you that things aren't going well; you're feeling them too. In that moment, it wasn't just anyone who risked doing that. This was a death sentence then, right. But the reality is that we saw that the country worked with an attitude as if we were animals; they went by, and if they knew that there was a *guerrilla*[8] there, then they would sweep the area, the area would be bombed. You have to start by collaborating and you begin entering into the process. I liked it because it was a struggle, and more than the motto that we had, it was only workers and peasants that made it to the end, right.

But the dream that I had was that one day the country would have light, would have water. But also, those challenges come from—once when I was an adolescent, when I was an adolescent I got on a bus with my grandmother. I was already about fourteen, almost a young lady, right, but

I was carrying a sack with the hens' eggs, the milk curds, to sell in the city, right. But I got on the bus, and when I got on there was a woman with nice glasses, and she looked at me, and she covered her nose, and I began to cry. Because dirty peasants had gotten on, right, and so then she did that, and I just cried. I grabbed my grandmother, but I told her, "I promise you, I promise you that I am going to fight so that one day I can be in power and transform." I didn't say transform because peasants don't say transform, but I said this: "One day I will change this, so they don't look at us like animals."

So then, battles don't come so easily, but they come within these feelings, right. So then what it is to only create values of hard work, of a vision, where are you going to focus? We didn't say vision, we only said this, "We want to live well, have food, that we have enough food, never to worry about shoes." I put on shoes [for the first time] when I was fourteen years old. When the Revolution happened, I began to study, I finished sixth grade, I finished secondary school, and I began to study for a technical degree in agronomy. I already had children. I completed it at age thirty-six, right. A two- or three-year degree . . . This gave me strength, and I was able to participate in the first movement that happened here in Nicaragua in the decade of seventy-nine,[9] the peasant movement. I'm part of it at the—at the regional level.

SG: Can you tell us a little bit about what you were doing right after the Revolution?

M: I started at the ATC [Asociación de Trabajadores del Campo (Association of Rural Workers)], it was the organization that worked, worked underground, and I started with the triumph, that's where we began to organize. . . . The ATC worked with the revolutionary movement of the Sandinista Front. It started because when the workers organized, their rights were violated. And it was—the ATC was from the workers in the unions. The first meeting was December 14 of 1979. In eighty-one we created the peasant organization that is called the Unión Nacional de Agricultores y Ganaderos.[10] . . . So then I became the first provincial president of this *campesina*[11] movement. They elected me. I don't know why.

SG: As a woman.

M: Yes, but this woman had won, like I said—what my father left me, he didn't leave me an inheritance. He left me strength, this vision that we also could, right. . . . He told me that he was teaching me so that a man or my husband wouldn't hit me. You have to be strong. And he told me a very important slogan. He told me: The poor and women cross the same paths. But when we see them, he tells me, among those who have money and those that don't, at the end everyone ends up in the same bag, but the women suffer more, he tells me. You have to defend yourself because you're my daughter, and I adore you; you are going to defend yourself . . .

SG: Were you treated differently as a woman working for this organization?

M: Yes, of course. The elements of work contradict those of the culture. But when I saw this—there was a colleague with a lot of passion and knowledge about production; he was elected (as president of the organization). Well, they say he won, but well the truth is that I had two more votes than him, but the agreement was, you go. I want the vice presidency because I want to work on a topic that I haven't worked on, and that was to work with *campesina* women because in the 27,000 people we had, we had 819 women. And these women only participated—but not actively—it was like "oh we need to have women" so they would bring women. And sometimes they didn't even know why they were there. They [co-workers] would say to me: "So? We have women here, there are women and men here in the organization." Yes but the women don't make decisions, they don't plan, and they sure aren't the presidents of the cooperative. They are the wives of the members. And when they bring them, that's when we have women. Then that is where we have to make our fight.

. . . So while I was there, I come and I plant the idea that it's necessary to organize women in collectives. They tell me, "You're crazy; that's divisive." I tell them, but this isn't a big deal—it's so that they identify [with the organization] and learn to be coordinators, presidents, secretaries, and it's very important. So then they say, "Well, you'll have to take it to UNAG's national conference." We proposed—it was four, eight women who brought this up, right. These women proposed that was necessary that the organization's planning and statutes state that women should also participate in the cooperative movement. I never will forget the paragraph that says—the participation—it said "participation of *campesina* women in UNAG"—that was it, the rest was a document like this, but that's all it said. . . . So then they come and say to me, one of them says, "C'mon let her do that." The vice president doesn't have a role so then I am going to make a role with the women.

So I had my first meeting in a co-op, and I talk with the president of the co-op, and I tell him, I want to have a meeting with the women because we want to organize them. Then he told me, "First you organize us, now you came to organize the women, and you come saying that we have the same right." We're talking about 1982. Then he comes, and he says, "How is it that women have the same rights? A woman doesn't have the right to pass out drunk in the street." "They'll grab her, tipsy, drunk with liquor." So I tell him, "You don't even have the right to pass out drunk in the street either because"—look, I used a vulgar word, but it's because they respected me, and I told him, "If you pass out, and some ass goes by and rapes you and is that a right? That's not a right. And it's also not a right for a woman to pass out in the street. Rights are different. "Rights," I told him, "are that the woman works equally or that you work equally with her or that she works equally to you, and you work together for the legacy of the *finca*[12] that you have." I had to use techniques they would understand. I tell him, "For example, if you die tomorrow, and this woman doesn't know how to work in the *finca*, what does she have to do? Look for another man? Do you want another man to ride your horse? [laughter] That's it, "Would you like someone to ride your horse?" "Of course not," they tell me, but I was giving it a double meaning. [laughter] "Well that's what we want, that now you and your wife both manage. She can decide when she'll enter into a relationship, but she's not going to decide to do it because she's ignorant of how to manage the *finca*." So these were the methods that I started using because in the country you couldn't openly have a confrontation. So a member of the executive board stood up and said, "Let her do it." But this meant let her do it without resources—without resources.

So I began to visit a women's collective in Matagalpa. . . . So, I'm talking about 1983, and I put a brigade that was called—the first group was María Castilblanco, a *campesina* that was killed by the Guardia [National Guard], while pregnant. Two groups, or three—people like you came to visit us from Holland, from Switzerland, from Spain, from everywhere. So we asked for their collaboration, not money. . . . Then I tell the *compañeras*[13] that were in the city, "Get the media." They got the media, and the local media come out with big headlines: "The María Castilblanco Women's Brigade refuses to leave until the National Farmers' Union approves the line for women's work." The National Committee for the Sandinista Front immediately says they are going to go see those women. And that's where they promise to have a line and section for women. . . .

SG: What is the vision now? What strategies are you using now?

M: Well, first we have to value the context. . . . At the beginning we initially had to make a federation within the organization. We asked the National Farmers' Union why they had allowed the men to make a men's federation, but then why didn't they want our women's movement—that had almost twelve thousand women—to make an incorporated women's federation. They told us that this was divisive. . . . Then they cut off all of our resources, they cut off the projects from our section, they cut off our vehicles, they cut off everything and they left us—they left the women that supported us unemployed, Matilde, Morena, Bertha, all of them, they all end up unemployed. And they took our access to vehicles. They took everything. So we ended up with nothing. So then, I aim for something different; I aim to launch myself into politics. While the others continue the struggle, and I launch myself, and I win at the national level, I win second place of all the deputies in this country. And within the Assembly, right. I win with a percentage of—almost half a million votes. This makes me, that my salary is injected into this federation so that women can go on with that, and we negotiate . . . With what I made in the Assembly, we rented a house, I bought a car, I bought an air conditioning unit, a computer, and I put it in. I'm saying it clearly because sometimes people don't know it because we don't say it. And finally, a little help for the *compañeras* to mobilize. I invested it all in that. I'm a deputy that left [the Assembly] with the same shoes, but I was able to became a deputy . . .

What I do want to make clear is that when we are women with goals, women are more persistent. We are capable. And I think, they say that men don't respect us. How is that? When you are taking power, you are respected, and this is important.

SG: Can you tell me a little bit about your definition of feminism in your work?

M: Look, I think that the processes, the processes—it's that there is some confusion here. Here, when people hear about feminism, they think you're a lesbian, that you're—well they say everything, bisexual, that you're this, that you're that. I interpret feminism as my fight, as an ideology in defense of women, with the different expression that everyone has decided to make theirs.

SG: In your opinion, are there any international policies or international economic policies that impact women in Nicaragua?

M: I think that talking—talking about gender politics, what has happened is that the focus that it had in one decade, the focus it had in another decade, what has changed is the language at the political, economic, and family level. . . . There is still a lot to fight for. And we still lack the application of so many laws that we have that aren't being applied in real life. And global policies are still bound to the media. Here when they talk about women, they talk about the environment—of going to plant a tree. The programs are for vegetable gardening, you understand. They're not of much significance. We must have programs of greater significance or scope, since we women are the ones that drive the world economy. And you ask me why. Because you say that the economy is driven by a corporation, a bank corporation. But that's not how it is, the ones who make the products, all of us little people, that when we come together, we become a corporation . . . There are many women that are secretaries, but they aren't the directors of universities, in the United States, for example, or in other countries. There's only a few of them, you need tweezers to find them, ask Carmen Diana[14] about it.

SG: Can you tell me a little bit about the relationship between scholarship like Carmen Diana's and the activist work you're doing?

M: Look, Carmen Diana has always had a focus on the women's struggle for land acquisition, for women to become empowered, and that is something that I really admire. She's a great woman. . . . She came to share with us here in the country. And we have shared with her because a professional also has to get feedback from the product in order to be a good professional, and it's the informative part. And we give feedback for those concepts that they are focusing on in the world. And there are also a lot of very smart women here, and I think the Revolution gave us a lot of space. It gave us space that we take advantage of, but not very much. Here even though we had the Revolution, hardly 13 percent of people obtained land. Right, we didn't accomplish everything. We have to keep fighting, yes . . .

Martha's narrative details the way in which her oppositional consciousness—or the awareness that drove her resistance—becomes enacted within the constraints of powerful social and political relations. The development of her oppositional consciousness is evident when she discusses her personal experiences of poverty and illiteracy. Her recollection of being discriminated against by an affluent woman and the strong messages of equity that she received from her father help illustrate how she became impassioned for justice. Martha's interest in and awareness of the gendered nature of land evolved steadily and becomes apparent through her experience of marginalization within FSLN-affiliated organizations. She details a climate of antagonism for women's interests and how she begins to adopt an explicitly feminist agenda that advocates for the importance of women's access to and control over resources.

Martha's awareness of the structural limitations facing women is demonstrated in her commitment to integrating women into agriculture beyond their role as day laborers, but rather as people who come to the table to make decisions. Her resistance demonstrates the belief that equality cannot be achieved without women's participation. She took countless risks to participate, as a woman, in positions and offices that could be influential in establishing gender equity. In these positions she would confront her male coworkers and insist on the recognition and support of women's rights and cooperatives that valued women as legitimate producers.

Moreover, Martha's discussion of neoliberalism reflects the understanding that power constrains the lives of women around the world and that women need to be in influential positions, where they are involved in decision making and have meaningful access to resources and power. Her reflections on globalization also highlight that many analyses miss the gendered nature of most large-scale economic policies, and she indirectly calls on the international community to engage in action that has a sincere potential for transformative change. Martha's story of triumph reflects how a counternarrative can disrupt the stranglehold of dominant narratives and thereby lead to more democratic processes that encourage social justice.

Diana Martínez

Diana's story similarly reflects how understanding a differential form of consciousness can generate a new form of knowledge and oppositional activity. Coming from a very different social location than Martha, Diana was raised in an upper-middle-class family and attended the private schools of the elite ruling class. However, from a young age she demonstrated an awareness of inequities and a commitment to justice. Like Martha, she was involved in the Revolution, has a history of organizing in rural communities, and developed a sustained focus on the political empowerment of rural women. Like other rural feminists involved with the ATC, in 1995 Diana eventually broke away from the oppressive male leadership and began her own organization to support rural women. She is currently the president of la Fundación Entre Mujeres (Foundation Between Women, FEM), a female-led cooperative of women organized from rural communities to grow and sell fair trade coffee while simultaneously supporting and promoting women's rights. The cooperative is located three hours east of Managua in the department of Estelí where much of the land is devoted to tobacco production and largely controlled by male producers. We met Diana in FEM's office in Estelí for the interview. Before we began I shared with her publications from the collaborative research conducted with Xochitl Acalt, a women's center with which she is greatly familiar. She asked astute questions and expressed interest in collaborative research with rural producers organized with FEM. Given her interest in research, she also demonstrated great enthusiasm for the current project before we began.

SG: Diana, I know you're probably more accustomed to talking about the history of your organization, but I'd like to ask you to start by telling me some of your personal history.

D: Well I was born in 1958 . . . I am the second daughter of an upper-middle-class family. In the first years of my life I studied at the school Purity of Mary. It was a school run by nuns in Managua. . . . And then my family decided to come to Estelí because my father was a banker. In Estelí I enrolled in another nun's school named Our Lady of the Rosary. People from the dominant class (the elite) of Nicaragua studied there. In secondary school, for example, my classmates were the daughters of the Cubans that had settled there after the fall of Batista. There were many people there linked to Somozism.[15] It was a school that serviced the dominant class, one that very few people had access to. And I, well, ever since I was young I think I had noticed a sense of the inequality that existed. For example the way the female workers that were employed in my home were treated. As well as some of the sexual abuses committed against them by my father. And at the time that was the most normal thing in the world.

SG: How old were you when you, when you are remembering this?

D: I was eight at the time. Yes, I also would go to my grandfather's farm in Matagalpa. They had a large coffee farm. And at the age of eight or nine, I would notice the huge gap there was between the workers and the families that lived in the main house . . . I developed a friendship with the female cooks. They lived in very, very bad houses . . . At around thirteen or fourteen years of age I organized my first domestic workers literacy group. It was a group of five women, and we had a little book, a type of book that is known as a *coquito*, and it was used to teach reading. Their bosses, their owners of the house, would let them have these classes with me because I was, uh, me.

SG: What did your parents think of you doing this?

D: Well they had always thought I was a little strange you see. When I was fifteen I had stopped going to mass with them. I had become involved in a revolutionist Christian movement. Here there was a priest who was a great figure in the Revolution; his name was Father Julio César López, he was Colombian . . . I would frequently go with him and lecture about the need to renounce the dictatorship. . . . When I was in middle school things got intense because that is when the FSLN really came to prominence. In the year seventy-six I was already very involved with the FSLN. Then my parents decided that I should leave Nicaragua, and they took me to go live with my sister in Guatemala. There, in 1977, I finished secondary school in another all girls' school in Guatemala called the School of the Sacred Heart for Young Women. I was really hurt by that decision, the imposition that my parents had put on me, because all of my friends were going into hiding, and there was a very strong consciousness among many of the youth that opposed the dictatorship and were ready to die for the cause of liberating Nicaragua from Somoza.

Then my parents decided that the following year I should study at Rafael Landívar University, which is like a Jesuit school in Guatemala. I was only there for about three months because I then decided for myself to go to the University of San Carlos, which is the national university. I studied political science and sociology. I changed at that school; in reality I became an atheist and Marxist. In January of seventy-nine, I left the university to come back. I flew to Costa Rica so that I could work in an underground hospital in Liberia, where there were forces from the Southern Front until I returned to Nicaragua. . . . A new school in sociology had opened at UCA [*Universidad Centroamericana,* University of Central America], and so I decided to continue my second year of sociology in Managua. And at that moment I had the idea that honestly only the hard workers and field hands would make it to the end. To quote Sandino, "Only after you focus your strength will you attain victory."

From that point on I truly wanted to become a worker. I involved myself in a factory that belonged to Somoza. They called it the textile factory, and I was a driver for a very large machine. In those years I wanted to erase from me the remnants of the petit bourgeois that remained in me and become a worker. . . . contradictory I know. In the end of 1984, I managed to combine my work at the textile with my university work. But it was very difficult because I had to meld two very different worlds . . .

In my fifth year of sociology, I became a research assistant in a very important study called "Women in the Exports in Nicaragua" by Ana Castillo from the Center for Research in Agricultural Reform. . . . It was the first feminist study in Nicaragua from the ATC. . . . Using the results from the study, I attempted to create a political proposal to organize the women agricultural workers in the ATC. And I stayed working there during the final years of the Revolution in conjunction with Women's Secretariat of the ATC. The ATC represents one of the biggest historical outcomes for rural worlds, for the poorest people of Nicaragua, because the capitalist system and the dictatorship unleashed immense abuses to farm workers. Many people that had farms also had workers in states of absolute exploitation and vulnerability and denial of rights . . . Only the Sandinista Revolution and the ATC could change these situations for the field workers by organizing agricultural unions for groups of producers.

SG: Were there other women involved in the ATC?

D: Oh yes, there were some; there were many women that had shared experience, the horror of having been kicked out of the ATC. Many of the women that had positions that were in favor of women had a falling out with the male directors. Because after . . . well at first they were open to our demands, but then uh, well when issues about equality and power came up the directors would abandon us. You see this happens in all of the corners of the world, and the ATC was no exception. It was a mixed [men and women combined] organization; you see we had all given our all for the Revolution and for the ATC, but those who were our beloved comrades during the war would not compromise on our demands in regards to gender and women. And then the best thing for them to do was expel us from the organization; you see there were various fallings out during the nineties and in the years before the nineties and then they continued of course. And me, well I was kicked out from the ATC in 1993, when I was the director of the women's health program named Pine Flower. It was a clinic that attended to all of the workers from the tobacco fields. And then there was uh, bit of a scandal; they did great harm to me to tell the truth. They accused me of a lot of things that were simply not true; they did it to simply get me out of the ATC . . .

SG: Why do you think they kicked you out?

D: Because, in my opinion, we were the women who had the moral authority to confront and demand from the leaders that they make compromises that would favor women . . . I had acquired a few contacts with organizations in Austria, and those organizations would send letters to the National

ATC and protest over my firing. And that came with a great political cost to the national board, to the ATC. But it was very painful you see; it was one of the biggest crises in my life . . . And from that came the idea to create a foundation between women. The lesson that I learned was that in mixed organizations it was not possible to work towards a real agenda that was in favor of gender equality. I had to construct legitimate organizations, transparent organizations, and create them with the women that it would affect in the process. And without autonomy we would not be able to do anything either; autonomy from the state, from partisanship, from the mixed organizations, and from the directors. Only women could do something on the behalf of women. Therefore I had to create la FEM.

SG: In what year was that?

D: La FEM was founded in 1995. . . . And that the culture of the nineties, ninety-five worsened the conditions, the lives of the people of Nicaragua due to privatization. And because of the structural changes in place brought by Violeta Barrios's[16] government.

SG: Can you explain those structural changes; what was it like during the Sandinistas, and how did Chamorro change those policies?

D: Yes, well clearly we had a great revolutionary state where we had free education, free healthcare, scholarships, social programs, programs for production. A great state that assisted cooperatives, there was childcare available in rural areas, there were collective agreements between the workers and the institutions or between the companies they represented. There were rights that never had existed. But when I saw the changes Violeta was making, the state began to collapse; it was weakened completely, and it left the population in peril. For example healthcare was privatized, education was privatized; we began to feel as if we no longer had a roof over our heads. And uh they began to return land that belonged to Somocistas, and new people would come and claim their land, and other capitalists would emerge to look and take advantage of the privatization of Nicaragua. Then obviously the people from the fields always are left behind; they were ignored even more, and under these circumstances the need to create an alternative form of resistance led to the birth of la FEM.

. . . We decided that this organization would not have professional women, or women from the upper classes as leaders, but rather the women from the communities would be the board of directors. And thus la FEM was born out of the women from the fields. Only I am not from the fields, but I already told them about my past and that in my heart I feel that I am from the fields myself . . . And one of our priorities was to buy land for women. Thinking that without the land we could not make structural changes on the status of subordination. Because we transform subordination, it is essential to be aware of gender. Both are complementary, with no consciousness of gender; the land is useless given to the women, because men make the decisions on the land. But there is no purpose to gender awareness if the women do not have land and the resources necessary to be productive. So we began linking the purchase of land with feminist thinking, becoming aware of how women have been constructed, to deconstruct the model that was the obstacle to leaving the kitchen, and work in the field, to leave the care for home, and to dedicate ourselves to visible work and recognition outside the home. . . . And we have also developed other strategies at the same time to educate adults, health care programs on proper self-care, educate them about parts of the body part of themselves, control of their sex lives, they control their reproduction, and also, uh, now after fifteen years, uh, the possibility that some women can recognize that they have alternate sexual preferences. In the rural world it is rare that women are out as lesbians for example, and this is a huge thing . . .

We have maintained stable strategies that stem from a conversation about the theoretical concepts that are, uh, in the best interests of women, for example the fight against violence, the creation of self-managed organizations. For example, economic power. The creations of cooperatives and having our coffee be a part of the fair trade market . . . These aren't short-term changes; they are long and process driven, profound changes that cannot occur over night . . . For example, the theme of sexual diversity is a very salient and important issue in the community. Fifteen years ago you never would have thought about those things. . . . And la FEM feels very comfortable in this space because we can enrich ourselves by learning from the lives of what the women of African descent network from the Caribbean coast. And all these new groups like Pink Flag give a face to the new feminism, the different, uh, a rural feminism, we could not imagine before. One that is different from the feminism of the very, very middle class, high, urban, ally to the upper class, right? That is what had been considered feminism, but this feminism that we defend, that we created, we believe that it is possible is a feminism embodied in the actual processes of life of women . . .

SG: Can you define feminism for me? The way that you mean it?

D: All right, for me feminism is a proposed policy. It is an alternative means for change that is in favor of equality for women. And it is a proposal as well, a concept in relation to the inequality of genders, we cannot believe there to be a feminist that is against abortion, one that is not against sexual violence, one that is against sexual and reproductive rights and liberty for women . . .

SG: You mention during the Revolution that the state was responsible for healthcare. Can you tell me in recent years, what is the role of women's organizations in meeting women's health needs?

D: The government maintains a concept eh, very androcentric concept over the health of women. The priority is the parental rights for women, newborn care, pregnancy. The government wants at all costs to be recognized by the Millennium Goals and take the high rate of maternal death that the country has and make it drop, and they put a lot effort into that. But they limit women from being seen from the state's perspective as an integral subject, where not only the reproductive health counts. Contradictorily, they have made a suspension in the penal code criminalizing medical abortion. Since 2006, the feminist movement has been leading a fight for reinstitution of medical abortion in Nicaragua - one of the things that most threatens the lives and health of women . . . Therefore health conditions are not favorable and there is no chance that things will improve any time soon. So, much of our agenda is based on our fundamental belief in the reinstitution of medical abortion, but we as feminists not only want to be able to perform medical abortion, but elective abortion

> as well . . . The country also has, well, the issue of violence to tell the truth. There is a large amount of abused women and violence of all kinds is also a public health problem. And we have an increase in AIDS and HIV cases, and women, groups and groups of women, housewives, who are infected, and no clear policies for prevention, no policies that see us as women, a subject that uh, leading to our lives and our health, because the state has a conception of ourselves as women beggars and, not as subjects of rights.

Diana's story reflects how early encounters with injustice enabled her to create solidarities based not on preconceived identities, but on circumstances that were constraining the lives of laborers and women who worked for her family. The experience she gained, both as a student and as a textile worker, further sharpened her oppositional, feminist consciousness. Like Martha, Diana also experienced political hostility with FSLN-affiliated organizations when confronting the existence of gender inequity. In both cases, there are clear tactics of marginalization discussed, whereby the women responded with resistance. Similar to Martha, in the end Diana's strategies involve creating an organization that is autonomous to any party-affiliation that allows for the mobilization of progressive collective voices committed to the rights of women. The transformative potential of la FEM that Diana describes focuses on increasing the rate of women's share of paid economic activity as rural producers, rather than employing women in low-wage service work. In addition, the evolution of Diana's oppositional consciousness includes a critique of other social inequities (e.g., sexual orientation) and the importance of broadening the women's movement to incorporate the numerous intersections of oppression experienced by women. Finally, Diana's resistance strategies embody solidarity and an affirmation of the grassroots as a site from which claims on women's political organizing should be staked.

Rural Feminism and Oppositional Consciousness

Martha and Diana's stories underscore Sandoval's (2000) notion that oppositional consciousness is not a lost utopian ideal. Rather, with a differential form of consciousness, and the alliance-building strategies it demands, revolutionary resistance is possible. Both women demonstrate the diverse ways that women respond to political hostility and marginalization and how their activism can pose challenges to dominant narratives. For example, Martha's creative manner of interjecting rights discourse into *campesino* organizing, and strategically positioning herself to organize rural women, reflect strategies that led to changes in participatory processes and greater social equality for rural women. Similarly, Diana's perseverance and commitment to facilitate a space for rural women, in the face of unremitting obstacles, reflects the power of solidarity at the same time it underscores the imperative to have local women be the drivers of their own transformation.

Despite being from very different class backgrounds and being located in different parts of the country, both women were involved in actions that challenged gender forms of structural inequality by facilitating women's access to land as a means of restructuring gendered power relations. The narratives suggest that among rural feminists there is a breaking away from the conventional notion of the male head-of-household as the principal landowner and rural producer. In this manner, land and productive means were discussed not only in material terms, but access to land and production was presented as a new basis for the construction of women and the gender relations they experienced. This is reflected in the analogy Martha uses with a male co-worker to explain women's rights. In the analogy she moves clearly beyond women's ownership of land as an important indicator of economic efficiency and demonstrates instead recognition for the importance of rural women's rights and pursuits of autonomy. The rural feminism represented in these women's stories reflects how gender and land are central elements to a new social, political, and gendered identity that can facilitate social justice.

The women's *testimonios* flesh out the behind the scenes mechanisms by which women become marginalized within the agricultural sector, but more importantly connect obstacles to the creation of political subjects and agents who seek change. In each case the women's stories demonstrate how breaking dominant narratives provides a space for the 'other's' perspective to be privileged, thereby reflecting a counter narrative that more accurately reflects a just world. In enacting an oppositional consciousness, Martha and Diana provide access to a different way of conceptualizing not just oppositional activity in general, but the importance of a rural feminist consciousness. Understanding differential forms of consciousness and social movements through an activist standpoint can generate a new form of knowledge. One meeting ground for activists and researchers is the mutual awareness that the production and dissemination of information gathered is imperative for transformative social change (Melucci 1992). Indeed, as a beneficiary of this knowledge, the doubting senior colleague I referenced earlier is now one of the staunchest supporters of this line of work. But, more importantly, disseminating knowledge informed by a rural feminist consciousness is critical to the struggles of women within communities, who are often invisible to researchers, who face discrimination and marginalization all over the world.

Notes

1. Anastacio Somoza García took power as the director of the National Guard in 1933 and president in 1936. He was succeeded by his sons, and the Somoza dynasty ruled Nicaragua until the triumph of the Sandinista Revolution in 1979.
2. The Frente Sandinista de Liberación Nacional (Sandinista National Liberation Front, FSLN) was a guerrilla movement founded in 1961 that overthrew the dictatorship in 1979. Converting itself into a political party after the overthrow, the FSLN won the first institutionalized election in 1984 (Walker 1985).
3. The autonomous women's movement in Nicaragua is comprised of 150 organizations in various sectors. The leaders of each organization meet semiregularly to ensure coordination. The movement has a manual of by-laws, agreed upon strategies, operates on consensus decision-making, and has had an elected representative since the 1990s. In 2007 members of the movement voted to create an organization that would serve as the umbrella for the whole movement and named it Movimiento Autónomo de Mujeres. The coordinated efforts of the movement have placed it in the national public agenda earning it recognition as a main political actor in the country.
4. I intentionally use the word "receipt" when describing violence against women over other widely used terms such as "incidence." Terms such as incidence, more commonly used in public health, suggest passivity, as if violence is a disease with epidemiological rates that are not connected to a power structure. The word "receipt" highlights the interpersonal nature of the act, or at the very least, that something has been done to the woman.
5. The Global Feminisms Project (GFP) is a collection of individual life stories of women activists and scholars archived through the Institute of Research on Women and Gender at the University of Michigan. The incentive for collecting life histories of Nicaraguan activists came from a conversation with the GFP project coordinator, Abigail Stewart. This project could not have been completed without the generous methodological and financial support provided by the GFP. The GFP also transcribed, translated, and archived eleven of the interviews. They can be viewed and read,

along with interviews with women from China, India, Poland, and the United States, at http://www.umich.edu/~glblfem.

6. Comparable to high school in the United States.
7. Martha enrolled in her adult literacy classes and began reading for the first time at age twenty-seven. She completed advanced classes over the course of ten years.
8. The term is used to refer to a member of the Revolution, often an armed combatant.
9. The Sandinistas triumphed July 19, 1979.
10. Unión Nacional de Agricultores y Ganaderos (National Farmers and Ranchers Union, UNAG).
11. Female peasants, farm workers.
12. A plot of rural or agricultural land, often a large farm or ranch.
13. Companions, comrades in struggle.
14. She is referring to Carmen Diana Deere, coauthor of *Empowering Women: Land and Property Rights in Latin America* (2001). Deere is a Distinguished Professor of Latin American Studies and Food & Resource Economics at the University of Florida.
15. Somozism refers to the ideological and political structure and system organized by the former dictator, Somoza.
16. Violeta Barrios Torres de Chamorro was the elected president in 1990 who unseated the FSLN. Her administration implemented structural adjustment programs driven by neoliberal lenders.

References

Agarwal, Bina. 1994. *Field of One's Own: Property Rights in South Asia*. UK: Cambridge University Press.

Alvarez, Sonia. E. 1990. *Engendering Democracy in Brazil: Women's Movements In Transition Politics*. Princeton, NJ: Princeton University Press.

Criquillón, Anna. 1995. "The Nicaragua Women's Movement: Feminist Reflections from Within." In *The New Politics of Survival: Grassroots Movements in Central America*, ed. Minor Sinclair, 209–237. New York: Monthly Review.

Connell, Raewyn. W. 1987. *Gender and Power: Society, the Person, and Sexual Politics*. Palo Alto, CA: Stanford University Press.

Deere, Carmen Diana. 2009. "The Feminization of Agriculture? The Impact of Economic Restructuring in Rural Latin America." In *The Gendered Impacts of Liberalization: Towards "Embedded Liberalism"?,* ed. Razavi Sharha, 99–130. New York: Routledge Press.

Deere, Carmen Diana, and León, Magdalena. 1987. *Rural Women And*

State Policy: Feminist Perspectives on Latin American Agricultural Development. (Series in Political Economy and Economic Development in Latin America.) Boulder, CO: Westview.

———. 2001. *Empowering Women: Land and Property Rights in Latin America*. Pittsburg: University of Pittsburgh Press.

Desai, Manisha. 2002. "Transnational Solidarity: Women's Agency, Structural Adjustment, and Globalization." In *Women's Activism and Globalization: Linking Local Struggles and Transnational Politics,* ed. Nancy Naples and Manisha Desai. New York: Routledge.

Fals Borda, Orlando. 1985. *Knowledge and People's Power: Lessons with Peasants in Nicaragua, Mexico and Colombia*. New Delhi, India: Indian Social Institute.

Golden, Renny. 1991. *The Hour of the Poor, the Hour of Women: Salvadoran Women Speak*. New York: Crossroad .

Grabe, Shelly. 2010. "Promoting Gender Equality: The Role of Ideology, Power and Control in the Link between Land Ownership and Violence in Nicaragua." *Analyses of Social Issues and Public Policy* 10: 146–170.

———. 2012. "An Empirical Examination of Women's Empowerment and Transformative Change in the Context of International Development." *American Journal of Community Psychology* 49: 1–13.

Grabe, Shelly, and Carlos Arenas. 2009. "Promoting Gender Equality Through Development: Land Ownership and Domestic Violence in Nicaragua." *Gendered Perspectives on International Development, Working Paper no. 295,* East Lansing, MI: Gender, Development, and Globalization Program, Michigan State University.

Grose, Rose, and Shelly Grabe. Forthcoming. "The Explanatory Role of Relationship Power and Control in Domestic Violence against Women in Nicaragua: A Feminist Psychology Analysis." *Violence against Women.*

Hesse-Biber, Sharlene. N. 2007. "Feminist Research: Exploring the Interconnections of Epistemology, Methodology, and Method." In *Handbook of Feminist Research: Theory and Praxis,* 2nd edition, ed., Sharlene Hesse-Biber, 1–28. UK: Sage.

Kabeer, Naila. 1999. "Resources, Agency, Achievements: Reflections on the Measurement of Women's Empowerment." *Development and Change* 30: 435–464.

Kampwirth, Karen. 1996. "Confronting Adversity with Experience: The Emergence of Feminism in Nicaragua." *Social Politics: International Studies in Gender, State & Society* 3 (2–3): 111–135.

———. 2004. *Feminism and the Legacy of Revolution: Nicaragua, El Salvador, Chiapas*. Athens: Ohio University Press.

Maddison, Sarah, and Frances S. Shaw. 2007. "Feminist Perspectives on Social Movement Research." In *Handbook of Feminist Research: Theory and Praxis,* 2nd edition, ed. Sharlene Hesse-Biber, 391–408. UK: Sage.

Maloof, Judy. 1999. *Voices of Resistance: Testimonies of Cuban and Chilean Women.* Lexington: University Press of Kentucky.

Melucci, Alberto. 1992. "Liberation or Meaning? Social Movements, Culture and Democracy." *Development and Change* 23 (3), 43–77.

Menchú, Rigoberta. 1984. I. *Rigoberta Menchú: An Indian Woman in Guatemala.* London: Verso.

Mohanty, Chandra. T. 2003. "'Under Western Eyes'" Revisited: Feminist Solidarity through Anticapitalist Struggles." *Signs: Journal of Women in Culture and Society* 28: 499–535.

Molyneux, Maxine. 1985. "Mobilization without Emancipation? Women's Interests, the State, and Revolution in Nicaragua." *Feminist Studies* 11: 227–254.

Naples, Nancy A., and Manisha Desai. 2002. *Women's Activism and Globalization: Linking Local Struggles and Transnational Politics.* New York: Routledge.

Randall, Margaret. 1981. *Sandino's Daughters: Testimonies of Nicaraguan Women in Struggle.* London: Zed.

———. 1994. *Sandino's Daughters Revisited: Feminism in Nicaragua.* New Brunswick, NJ: Rutgers University Press.

Sandoval, Chela. 2000. *Methodology of the Oppressed.* Minneapolis: University of Minnesota Press.

Shayne, Julie. D. 2004. *The Revolution Question: Feminisms in El Salvador, Chile, and Cuba.* New Brunswick, NJ: Rutgers University Press.

———. 2009. *They Used to Call Us Witches: Chilean Exiles, Culture, and Feminism.* Lanham, MD: Lexington Books.

Stephen, Lynn. 1997. *Women and Social Movements in Latin America: Power from Below.* Austin: University of Texas Press.

Taylor, Verta. 1998. "Feminist Methodology in Social Movements Research." *Qualitative Sociology* 21: 357–379.

Tula, María Teresa, and Lynn Stephen. 1994. *Hear My Testimony: María Teresa Tula, Human Rights Activist of El Salvador.* Boston, MA: South End.

Walker, Thomas. W. 1985. *Nicaragua: The First Five Years.* Westport, CT: Praeger.

White, Aaronette M., and William Dotson. 2010. "It Takes a Village to Raise a Researcher: Narrative Interviewing As Intervention, Reconciliation, and Growth." *Journal of Black Psychology* 36: 75–97.

CONCLUSION

Interdisciplinarity and Privilege

JULIE SHAYNE AND KRISTY LEISSLE

> For me, the Revolution sought to end mistreatment, not to democratize it.
>
> —Gioconda Belli (2003, 190)

We close this collection with a brief discussion of interdisciplinary spaces as the logical home to scholar activism and the privileges and responsibilities of activist scholars to advance social justice agendas. We see the chapters in this volume as both a reflection of and a contribution to the still-thin but increasing validation of interdisciplinarity across the academy. Indeed, collaboration between scholars and activists of diverse methodologies often helped our contributors to push the pursuit of knowledge and praxis further than any one individual might have felt authorized to do on her own.

Interdisciplinarity

Fourteen scholar-activist-artists contributed to this volume, and we hold degrees in the following disciplines or interdisciplines: American studies; cultural and social anthropology; cultural studies; education; English; global studies; Latin American history; philosophy; psychology and quantitative statistical methods; romance languages and literature; sociology; theater, and women's studies. Additionally, we teach or study in African studies; anthropology; cultural studies;

interdisciplinary arts and sciences; literature; psychology; Spanish; theater education, and writing. In total, we represent about eighteen academic departments or programs. So how did a theater director, novelist, and psychologist end up in the same collection? How about a sociologist and language scholar? We find ourselves side by side in these pages because of our passion for justice in the Americas and our commitment to learning and teaching about social movements. Our commonality lies in a shared political conviction, not the methodological training used to study "it."

In our experiences, activist scholarship is most warmly received in interdisciplinary spaces, where certain institutional challenges may be more readily overcome. One barrier to conducting social justice scholarship, for example, lies in assessing it. How do professors charged with making decisions about tenure and promotion "count" a video archive of thousands of hours of testimonies? Why was Shelly Grabe assumed to have a "forgotten Peace Corps dream" when she shared her desire to research rural feminist activism in Nicaragua? Why was Julie Shayne told that documenting a social movement was *just* listening to stories? In these cases, our home disciplines were not able to make the leap to assessing our research beyond the quantifiable boxes of the social sciences. As a result, the contributors to this volume often feel somewhat out of place within certain disciplinary structures. Indeed, one of our colleagues,[1] also in the School of Interdisciplinary Arts and Sciences, affectionately refers to our faculty, himself included, as "misfits." There is nothing disparaging about the label; rather, he is making a matter-of-fact statement that, though no one ever abandons her academic training (nor do we want to), we have found ourselves moving beyond the confines of disciplines that tend to be less open to thinking about scholarship and research in new ways. This is not to suggest that all interdisciplinary programs are inherently open to activist scholarship. But in our experience, interdisciplinary programs have been more flexible than traditional departments, and with that flexibility comes a potentially more welcoming attitude to scholar activism.[2]

As we know, social justice scholarship is in part about praxis: theory, reflection, and action. We believe interdisciplinary spaces demand reflection, or they cannot survive and thrive, thus, another reason they tend to be more hospitable to activist scholarship. David Meyer maintains that "[t]he concept of praxis, that is, action with reflection, not in much favor in the academy, can provide a model for thinking about the utility of scholarship" (2005, 194). In our estimation, praxis actually is in *growing* favor in the academy, even though this growth is occurring in limited (though not limit*ing*) spaces. In departments like Latin

American studies or gender, women, and sexuality studies, which are by design interdisciplinary, reflection is key. For example, looking back upon four decades of scholarship in what began as women's studies, we see that praxis and self-reflexivity pushed gender analytics to forge new genealogical branches—black feminist thought, transnational feminist analysis, queer studies—some of which inform this collection.

As we explained in the introduction, this collection is a product of an interdisciplinary conference and part of an interdisciplinary series conceptualized around praxis. Though reflection may not as yet have "infiltrated" the wider academy, this volume suggests that interdisciplinary spaces are nevertheless opening sites for collaborative, activist, praxis-based scholarship.

Privilege and Responsibility

We opened this chapter with a quote from Nicaraguan revolutionary feminist Gioconda Belli's memoir, *The Country Under My Skin* (2003). The quote comes from an exchange Belli had with her then-husband, while she waited, suffering, in a public hospital to learn whether their newborn child would survive. Belli's family had the money to move her and her son to a private hospital that could provide the medical attention that all women and children deserve. In the end, she opted to use those resources to save her life and that of her son. Her husband, like Belli, was a Sandinista fighting to topple the Somoza dictatorship. He argued she was being self-centered and "un-revolutionary" by acting on her class privilege. Of the whole exchange, she says, "[F]or me, the Revolution sought to end mistreatment, not to democratize it" (2003, 190). We do not invoke the quote to imply that we are all revolutionaries. Rather, it frames our understanding of activist scholarship as a way to mobilize privilege, rather than be paralyzed by guilt.

As social justice scholars and educators, we are all familiar with the guilt that can consume our students upon learning about injustice and violence—be it physical, economic, or social. (See for example, Marín's chapter, this volume.) But guilt is not a productive sentiment; often, it merely perpetuates apathy and inaction. As academics we have privileges and thus responsibility. In some cases, our privilege is the ability to travel (somewhat) safely across borders, while in others it means having the time to write articles and books, make documentary films, or direct plays to advance social justice (to say nothing of the privileged education that taught us how to write, film, or direct). Certainly "having time" is a bit of a misnomer, when ultimately we might also have spent that time with our families or engaging in leisure activities, even sleeping. Limits aside, we have all found the time to produce activist scholarship, and that is indeed a luxury.[3]

We are not the first collection of scholar activists who see our cultural capital as a responsibility and resource to be shared. For example, M. Brinton Lykes and Amelia Mallona use the term "research activists" to describe themselves, which applies equally to those in this collection. They argue that before its documentation even begins, we must use our privilege during the research process: "Those of use with access to university privilege and power are forging some relationships of 'just enough trust' through which we continually strive to deepen our understanding of the root causes of social illness and collectively engage in problem-posing alongside communities historically marginalized from power and resources" (2008, 117). Lykes and Mallona remind research activists that to understand and thus challenge the structural violence to which the majority world is subjected, we must partner with the marginalized with whom we claim solidarity.

Jennifer Bickham Mendez speaks to what we might call the "postresearch phase." Based on her academic and political work with laborers in free trade zones, she maintains that one possible role for academics is to "put their cultural capital to work for social movements as translators who 'package' oppositional narratives or lived realities so that they resonate with policy makers" (2008, 143–44). As much as scholars may resist using jargon and academic language, a paper written for an academic audience is truly different than one written for what Mahala Lettvin (this volume) refers to as the "real world." Similarly, activists and their supporters use a political language that can be alienating to nonactivists. As scholar activists, we can potentially speak both languages and thus translate activist claims to policy makers with the power to implement change.

The contributors to this volume speak to the aforementioned and other ways to mobilize our cultural capital in support of social movements. For example, Carmen Rodríguez discusses the power of writing for shantytown dwellers, who wish to become literate with limited means to do so. Our privileged access to education is a starting point, the first resource we have the ability to share. Mahala Lettvin and Julie Shayne speak of the power of memory, museums, and historical archives in capturing the truths of stakeholders often excluded from articulating a nation's story. Marisela Fleites-Lear reminds us that scholar activists can support social movements by showcasing their dignity through literary accomplishments. We must not forget that the marginalized often remain so because those who hold power perpetuate a narrative of the Other, less deserving of respect. Showcasing literary accomplishments forcefully contradicts that narrative. Tamera Marko, Christina Marín, and Robin Garcia remind us of the power of opening theaters and radio/television airwaves to activists, so they can share their stories of struggle and triumph. Erica Williams offers an example of how scholar activists who work with "taboo" populations can, as Bickham Mendez suggests, work as "translators" to well-meaning but misguided NGOs or policy makers.[4] Roberta Villalón's chapter reminds us that social justice scholars can offer support in maneuvering through the legal system. Finally, Shelly Grabe speaks of using her research to support women and feminist activists who need evidence that their strategies are effective.

In addition to these "services" social justice scholars can offer social movements, educating our students is key to this agenda. Mahala Lettvin eloquently reminds us of the mobilizing power of being a recipient of activist scholarship and teaching. Whether you call yourself a social justice scholar, student, activist, writer, or reader, we hope this volume inspires you to learn even more of the stories of social justice activists across the Americas.[5]

Our Closing Musings

Kristy Leissle

When Julie invited me to contribute to the introduction and conclusion to this volume, I knew a moment of confusion. Julie's work deals mainly with Latin America, and while my own research has lately engaged with Mesoamerican histories, my area of expertise is West Africa. And then I reread Julie's message. She was asking me to contribute as a scholar of feminist methodologies, not an area specialist. Now, much later, I recognize the significance of that moment, when I had to consciously recalibrate as a feminist academic. I hold a master's and a doctoral degree in women's studies. Since I defended my dissertation in 2008, however, I have spent just two academic quarters teaching in my field; I soon moved to lectureships in global studies at the University of Washington Bothell and in African studies at the University of Washington Seattle. Of course, feminist theory and methods inform everything I teach and write. What drew me to women's studies as a graduate student was the profundity of gender as a tool for analyzing conditions of social (in)justice, but my daily consciousness of that scholarly background had receded in a surprisingly short time.

In her chapter in *Women's Studies On Its Own* (Wiegman 2002), Robyn Warhol claims that as director of women's studies at the

University of Vermont, she would rather not pursue tenure lines for her department. Rather, she prefers to "infiltrate" a whole host of departments with scholars who draw upon feminist theory and methods within their disciplinary frameworks. I wondered: Have I become the scholar that Warhol had in mind? Am I valuable to gender, women, and sexuality (GWS) studies because I have "infiltrated" the also interdisciplinary and newish field of global studies, as well as African studies, with my feminist thoughts?

Perhaps I have. But infiltration comes with its own risk: for me, that was the subtle erosion of my conscious position as a feminist scholar. Because I have been absorbed into another interdiscipline, I do not actively invoke feminist studies as often as I once did in my teaching and writing. This weakens the positive discourse surrounding GWS studies—itself a form of (in)activism, as feminist theory and methods almost never receive their due credit for shifting the terms of academic discourse and orienting young minds to the pursuit of social justice. My contribution to this volume is the first time since I defended my dissertation that I claim women's studies as my area of expertise, and has been a compelling reminder not to make it the last.

Julie Shayne

I write this from my home office just north of Seattle, Washington. Six years ago if I was sitting down to cowrite the conclusion to this book I would be writing in my luxurious, private campus office, an entire wall lined with floor-to-ceiling bookshelves, two desks to myself, as much filing cabinet space as I needed, and an RA *and* a TA somewhere in the vicinity. Now I write this from home with two interrupting kids running in and out of my office, little campus space to fall back on, and that which I do have is shared.[6] However, my writing time is now punctuated by the soothing sound of the Washington State Ferry crossing the Puget Sound, sunshine and lush green trees, and yes, the rain and occasional snow. Lack of institutional support aside, this setup is far more beneficial to my family and my quality of life than a big, well stocked, and unshared campus office was. Indeed, this arrangement allows for lovely family walks in our neighborhood where we take in all of the sights and sounds.[7] As I explain in this book's afterword, I walked away from one seemingly luxurious version of academic life and fortunately found myself here.

Recently, it occurred to me that I tried to start a book project like this while at my former institution. I remember brainstorming it in my lovely campus office. My potential coeditor, one of the most senior and well-regarded professors on campus, and I were envisioning a book framed around activists as intellectuals. As I shared my enthusiasm for the project with one of my mentors in the department, she immediately told me not to pursue the project as it was too "applied."[8] As an assistant professor racing the tenure clock I did not even consider challenging her recommendation. As I explain in the introduction, *Taking Risks* is my passion project. It has been since I was a women's studies undergraduate student at San Francisco State University in the early 1990's, after reading Margaret Randall's books for the first time. I have always felt that activists are theorists, and academics who theorize without turning to activists have little credibility in advancing our theories. I am thrilled this project has finally come to fruition and hope very much it inspires others to pursue their activist, academic, and personal goals in a way that none is compromised for the other.

Notes

1. Here we are speaking of our colleague David Goldstein.
2. Charles Hale shares the same sentiment in his introduction to *Engaging Contradictions*: "Not one of the authors in this collection feels completely at home in his or her discipline or in the university setting where he or she works. Many have found a more hospitable environment in interdisciplinary programs" (2008, 14).
3. See Maula (2006) for a provocative essay about lacking the time to write.
4. See also Kari Lerum, Kiesha McCurtis, Penelope Saunders, and Stéphanie Wahab (2012), for another interesting case study about scholar activists supporting the human rights of sex workers.
5. We do not want to end with advice but do point the reader to a wonderful essay by Laura Pulido titled "FAQs: Frequently (Un) Asked Questions about Being a Scholar Activist" (2008, 341–65).
6. In the final six months of this project I acquired funds from the University of Washington Bothell, from the Office of Research to fund undergraduate student Jessica Monteiro Manfredi to write the section introductions and the School of Interdisciplinary Arts and Sciences to fund Mahala Lettvin to assemble the index for this collection.
7. I would like to thank my six-year-old son, Aaron, for making sure that I made special mention of our neighborhood walks.
8. As we know, "applied" is often code for "atheoretical," thus unscholarly. See also Massey (2008, 324).

References

Belli, Gioconda. 2003. *The Country Under My Skin: A Memoir of Love and War*. New York: Anchor Books.

Bickham Mendez, Jennifer. 2008. "Globalizing Scholar Activism: Opportunities and Dilemmas through a Feminist Lens." In *Engaging Contradictions: Theory, Politics, and Methods of Activist Scholarship*, ed. Charles Hale, 136–163. Berkeley: University of California Press.

Hale, Charles R. 2008. "Introduction." In *Engaging Contradictions: Theory, Politics, and Methods of Activist Scholarship*, ed. Charles Hale, 1–28. Berkeley: University of California Press.

Lerum, Kari, Kiesha McCurtis, Penelope Saunders, and Stéphanie Wahab. 2012. "Using Human Rights to hold the US Accountable for its Anti-Sex-Trafficking Agenda." *Anti-Trafficking Review* 1 (June): 81–103.

Lykes, M. Brinton, and Amelia Mallona. 2008. "Towards Transformational Liberation: Participatory and Action Research and Praxis." In *The Sage Handbook of Action Research: Participative Inquiry and Practice,* second edition, ed. Peter Reason and Hilary Bradbury, 107–120. Los Angeles: Sage.

Massey, Doreen. 2008. "When Theory Meets Politics." In *Practising Public Scholarship: Experiences and Possibilities Beyond the Academy*, ed. Katharyne Mitchell, 142–147. Malden, MA: Wiley-Blackwell.

Maula, Erme C. 2006. "Why I Don't Write." In *Why We Write: The Politics and Practice of Writing for Social Change,* ed. Jim Downs, 159–169. New York: Routledge.

Meyer, David. S. 2005. "Scholarship That Might Matter." In *Rhyming Hope and History: Activists, Academics, and Social Movement Scholarship*, ed., David Croteau, William Hoynes, and Charlotte Ryan, 191–205. Minneapolis: University of Minnesota Press.

Pulido, Laura. 2008. "FAQs: Frequently (Un)Asked Questions about Being a Scholar Activist." In *Engaging Contradictions: Theory, Politics, and Methods of Activist Scholarship*, ed. Charles Hale, 341–365. Berkeley: University of California Press.

Warhol, Robyn R. 2002. "Nice Work, If You Can Get It—And If You Can't? Building Women's Studies without Tenure Lines." In *Women's Studies on Its Own*, ed. Robyn Wiegman, 224–232. Durham, NC: Duke University Press.

Wiegman, Robyn, ed. 2002. *Women's Studies on Its Own: A Next Wave Reader in Institutional Change*. Durham, NC: Duke University Press Books.

AFTERWORD

Mother's Day

JULIE SHAYNE

In 2000 my husband and I left the West Coast for my excellent job in the Southeast. Neither of us wanted to leave but my career took priority. Every year on Mother's Day my mom and stepdad would travel from the Northwest to the Southeast so we could spend five rushed days together. And every year I went to my university's honors graduation. I was always quite thrilled to see my brilliant women's studies students graduate and wish their mothers happy Mother's Day, but it never stopped angering me that I could not be with my own mother and daughter. On Mother's Day 2006 all that changed; I resigned from my job, and my husband, two children, and I moved to the Northwest. I had no job waiting for me, just some good contacts and faith that my decision would work out.

As a native Californian I never imagined myself living in the South. As it turned out, the only job offer I got out of grad school was at one of the three southern universities to which I had applied. My now husband picked up his life from the San Francisco Bay Area and followed me to the other end of the political and cultural world. We always thought it would be temporary. We thought I'd get tenure and then I would just find that perfect job on the West Coast. I applied to a few jobs, and we fantasized about leaving. In the meantime, we got married, bought a house, had a daughter, made many friends, and visited the West Coast every chance we got.

My daughter was born two years after I started my job, and I was granted maternity leave and the option to stop the tenure clock. I did stop it but not without much consideration. Many senior faculty, typically moms, advised me not to stop it as reviewers expect one year extra of work. Others assured me that was not the case; you remind them you have a kid, and everyone understands ebbs and flows in productivity. In retrospect, I am pretty sure the moms were correct. For example, the first thing that goes when one has a new baby is conference presentations. When I got my postpartum review I was told I needed to present more papers at conferences. Observations like this made me feel extra pressured to prove myself at my pretenure review. So I finished my first book. This meant I spent the first fourteen months of my daughter's life writing a book. I was so obsessed that her first word was "book." As soon as my leave ended I was working fourteen-hour days, seven days a week. My husband did everything for my daughter except for nursing: he fed her, took her to daycare, bathed her, and so on. The days I worked on campus I left the house before she even woke up. I tried very hard to pick her up from daycare because it was one of the highpoints of the day even if I had to immediately hand her to my husband once we got home. I am grateful I have a husband and she a father who supported me in my efforts though it killed me when I would hear them giggle through the walls, and I was stuck at my computer. But I had to pass the review if I wanted to go up for tenure, so I just kept working. I had to get tenure to get a job on the West Coast. I missed my daughter like crazy, and we were living in the same house. I did, however, pass my review and received kudos for having published a book so early in my career.

After flirting with jobs on the West Coast it started to become clear that this was not going to happen. I would not find a job as great as mine in the area in which we wanted to live, and I wasn't willing to compromise my career. My husband was miserable. I felt guilty, and I missed my family as well. Every time my mother had to say goodbye to my daughter at the airport I cried. It killed me to watch my daughter and mother have to remake their relationship over and over and yet again have to say goodbye. It never got easier, only harder. We talked often about me just quitting my job and trying to teach at a community college. But how could I just throw away all of my hard work? What would people think? Why did I even bother going to graduate school if I am not even going to have a real job? My husband and I would go back and forth, and I would get close to saying, "Ok, I quit," but then the thought of ruining my career scared me back onto the tenure track, not to mention the message from my colleagues and mentors that deprioritizing my career isn't even an option.

On Mother's Day 2005 I found out I was pregnant again. Like all Mother's Days, I had been at the honors graduation while my family waited at home for me. We found out that evening, which proved a pretty spectacular Mother's Day gift. I went on sabbatical and maternity leave for a year, at which point we got ourselves back to the West Coast for what we thought was a temporary and rejuvenating stay. While pregnant I worked furiously on my second book right up until the day before my son was born. After his birth, long before I was getting any real sleep, I resumed writing. I was writing my maternity leave away, getting increasingly frustrated and depressed that rather than spend those precious early months with my son, I was worrying about tenure. I loved both my job and writing, but I also loved being a mother and knew that my son was the last baby I would have, and those early months are an amazing time. The stress from work, the frustration of not getting to spend time with my son, the postpartum hormones, and sleep deprivation merged to create a mild case of postpartum depression.

Mother's Day was approaching. It was going to be a special one because my mother and I could be together with our husbands and my two children, and it required no more than a six-minute drive. But it was also going to be the last Mother's Day we would have like that because just a few months later my family and I were heading back to my great job, in a place we did not want to live, with our families nowhere in sight. But what choice did we have? I did not go through graduate school for nothing, right?

Then it occurred to me: Why would quitting an excellent job mean graduate school was a waste? When I decided to be a professor did I mean only at an elite university? Did I intend to live someplace I did not want to live, just for a job? It is, after all, just a job, right? No, it is much more. As many of us know, being a feminist academic feels like more than just a job. We see ourselves charting new intellectual territory: writing women into history, discovering new ways to learn and teach, filling the universities with women faculty and thus role models for girls, and creating a reality where GE requirements include women's studies, western civ, and English composition. How could I abandon that agenda? How could I contribute to accomplishing these goals if I did not have a prestigious position? What message would I send women students, and worse yet my own kids, if I just up and quit and put motherhood first? What sort of intellectual and emotional cataclysm takes place in feminist academics that makes us feel guilty, feel like a failure if we let our families take priority over our careers? These questions had spiraled in my head since the moment my daughter was born. I remember telling one of my grad school mentors that I couldn't stand having my daughter so far from my mother, and I wanted to quit, and he convinced me that was not an option. Similarly, I remember telling a senior colleague, also a mother, that we were miserable away from the West Coast and our families, and I wanted to quit; she said, "You can learn to be happy anywhere." She might be right, but why should we have to?

Just before Mother's Day 2006 I called my dean and both of my chairs and told them I was leaving my job. All three were incredibly kind and supportive. Academics understand being separated from their families, living somewhere they never imagined they would. Many academics do not even live fulltime in the same cities or states as their spouses. Academics are mentored to put our jobs first. We are taught that temporary or community college positions are not real jobs. I decided not to follow these guidelines any more. I cannot put my career first, nor can I stop working entirely. I love feeling like I am a part of something important for girls and women. I love teaching. I love watching youngish women learn things they would not have learned if women's studies did not exist. I love that my daughter pretends to write books and thinks everyone is her mommy's student. I love that she knows I am a professor. I have not given up on my career, but as one colleague (a mother) said, I have just taken it in a new direction.

I wrote "Mother's Day" in October 2006 after sharing my decision with both of my chairs and one of my deans. I close our collection with this chapter because it was this professional risk that provided me the intellectual space to pursue the project that resulted in this book. I am uncomfortable using the word "risk" to describe my move, especially in a volume that discusses risks replete with violence and alienation. But academia has defined my decision as a risk, so I use the term here. I include this chapter to contribute to our typically private conversations about family, quality of life, and career.

CONTRIBUTORS

Marisela Fleites-Lear graduated from the University of Havana in 1982 with a degree in philosophy. She worked as a professor of philosophy at a branch of the University of Havana until 1990. Marisela did part of her doctoral work at the University of Karl Marx in Leipzig, until the fall of the Berlin Wall, and then continued in Havana. Fleites-Lear came to the United States in 1992 after marrying her American husband in Cuba. She earned a PhD in romance languages and literature from the University of Washington, Seattle, in 2006. She is currently the head of the Spanish department at Green River Community College and publishes on themes related to the intersection of gender, politics, and literature.

Robin Garcia is an educator, organizer, media activist, and advocate for the arts. She is currently a doctoral candidate in cultural studies at Claremont Graduate University. Robin is active in Venezuela solidarity work and has conducted fieldwork in the country in preparation for her dissertation on the cultural activism emerging out of Venezuela's changing political climate. Garcia's research interests include media studies, performance studies, postcolonial studies, Latin American social movements, and feminist/queer theory.

Shelly Grabe is an assistant professor of psychology at the University of California at Santa Cruz. Her research uses a multimethod approach from within feminist liberation psychology to focus on the structural and individual components of women's rights violations and social justice in the context of globalization. Shelly is currently working on three transnational projects exploring (1) the role of land ownership in empowerment processes and gender-based violence in Nicaragua; (2) land ownership, civic participation, and violence against women in Tanzania; and (3) the role of the grassroots social movement in promoting justice for women in Nicaragua.

Kristy Leissle earned her PhD in women's studies at the University of Washington Seattle in 2008. She also holds degrees from Oxford University and Boston College. She is a lecturer in the School of Interdisciplinary Arts and Sciences at the University of Washington Bothell, and in African studies at the Jackson School of International Studies, UW Seattle. Kristy's research focuses on the global cocoa-chocolate trade. She is director of education for the Northwest Chocolate Festival and lectures widely on topics related to social justice in the chocolate trade. Her current research explores the renaissance of artisanal chocolate in the United States.

Mahala Lettvin graduated from the University of Washington Bothell in 2012 with a BA in American studies. She is a graduate student in the Masters of Cultural Studies Program also at UWB. Mahala was awarded a Mary Gates Scholarship in 2012 for her research examining the memory processes of Chilean exiles. Additionally, Mahala serves as a member of the *UWB Policy Journal* editorial board. Outside of the university, Mahala has worked as a paralegal for a criminal defense attorney for over twelve years. She hopes to find a way to use her passion for research to continue defending those marginalized by the U.S. criminal justice system.

Jessica Monteiro Manfredi will earn her BA from the University of Washington Bothell in 2014 with a double major in global studies and law, economics, and public policy. Jessica has served as a Civic Fellow and is a member of the *UWB Policy Journal* editorial board. Inspired to fight the social injustices she witnessed in her native Brazil and beyond, Jessica hopes to attend graduate school to produce knowledge that can act as a catalyst for change in people's lives and communities. Ultimately, she aspires to be a college professor and become a mentor to the next generation of leaders of women of color.

Christina Marín teaches Theatre of the Oppressed, Drama Education, Theatre Performance and Community, and Human Rights in Theatre in the Theatre Education Program at Emerson College in Boston, MA. She is an international practitioner of Theatre of the Oppressed and a professional theatre director who focuses on plays addressing human rights violations, especially along the U.S.-Mexico border. Christina earned a PhD in theatre at Arizona State University in 2005.

Tamera Marko specializes in multilingual, multimedia community literacy and historical memory projects in the Americas. As a historian and compositionist, she produces transnational multimedia publications, academic scholarship, and pedagogy. Tamera founded three transnational community projects in the Americas, including an alternative feminist community archive of *desplazadas* (displaced women) in Medellín, Colombia, and a writing project with Latin American maintenance workers at Emerson College. Before coming to academia, Marko worked as a journalist covering human rights in Africa, Asia, Latin America, and the United States. She is the director of the First Year Writing Program at Emerson College and the director of Duke-Engage Colombia at Duke University, where she is a faculty affiliate. Tamera earned her PhD in Latin American history at the University of California at San Diego in 2001.

Nora Patrich was born in Florida, a city in the Province of Buenos Aires, Argentina. She was a student of architecture at the University of Buenos Aires and studied art in the studio of the famous Argentine painter Martinez Howard. In her youth, Patrich became highly motivated by the principles of the Spartacus movement, an important art movement in Argentina. During her forced exile from Argentina, she lived in Israel, Spain, Cuba, and Mexico, where she attended the School of Art and Design. Patrich's work is widely exhibited and forms part of the permanent collection of different museums and selected institutions around the world, such as the Vancouver Art Gallery, the Simon Fraser University (Canada), the Museum of Modern Art (Buenos Aires, Argentina), and the Museum of the National Palace of Guatemala. Since 1982, Patrich has made her home in Vancouver, Canada. She currently divides her time between her studios in Vancouver and Buenos Aires.

Margaret Randall is a feminist poet, writer, photographer, and social activist. She has published more than one hundred books. Some classic and new titles include *Cuban Women Now* (Women's Press, 1974); *Sandino's Daughters* (New Star Books, 1981); *Sandino's Daughters Revisited* (Rutgers, 1995); *To Change the World: My Years in Cuba* (Rutgers, 2009); *Che on My Mind* (Duke University Press, 2013); and *More Than Things* (University of Nebraska Press, 2013).

Carmen Rodríguez Bilingual writer Carmen Rodríguez left Chile following the 1973 military coup and made her home in Vancouver, Canada. She is the award-winning author of *Guerra Prolongada/Protracted War* (Women's Press, 1992), a volume of poetry; *De cuerpo entero/and a body to remember with* (Arsenal PulpPress, 1997), a collection of short stories; and *Retribution* (Women's Press, 2011), a novel. Carmen earned a BA in English and a teaching certificate from the University of Chile in 1970 and an MEd at Simon Fraser University in 1990. Most recently, Rodríguez taught Latin American Literature, Cultural Studies, and Creative Writing at Simon Fraser University and the University of British Columbia.

Julie Shayne earned her PhD in sociology at the University of California at Santa Barbara in 2000. She is a lecturer in the School of Interdisciplinary Arts and Sciences at the University of Washington Bothell and an affiliate associate professor of gender, women and sexuality studies and Latin American and Caribbean studies at University of Washington Seattle. Julie is the author of *The Revolution Question: Feminisms in El Salvador, Chile, and Cuba* (Rutgers, 2004), and *They Used to Call Us Witches: Chilean Exiles, Culture, and Feminism* (Lexington Books, 2009).

Roberta Villalón is an associate professor of sociology at Saint John's University, New York City. Originally from Argentina, she has devoted her professional career to study and struggle against all shapes and forms of power abuse, from governmental corruption to intimate partner violence. Roberta earned her PhD in sociology at the University of Texas Austin in 2007. Her background in political science and international relations, together with her expertise in Latin America and Latin American immigrants, has shaped her sociological perspective distinctively. Villalón is author of *Violence Against Latina Immigrants: Citizenship, Inequality and Community* (NYU Press, 2010) and editor of "The Politics of Collective Memory-Making" forthcoming in *Latin American Perspectives*.

Erica Lorraine Williams is an assistant professor of anthropology at Spelman College in Atlanta, Georgia. She earned her PhD in cultural and social anthropology at Stanford University in 2010. Erica's research interests include race, gender, sexuality, tourism, Brazil, the African diaspora, and the anthropology of globalization. Williams is author of *Sex Tourism in Bahia: Ambiguous Entanglements* (University of Illinois Press, 2013), which won the National Women's Studies Association/University of Illinois Press First Book Prize in 2011.

INDEX